# Mastering Qt 5

Master application development by writing succinct, robust, and reusable code with Qt 5

**Guillaume Lazar**
**Robin Penea**

BIRMINGHAM - MUMBAI

# Mastering Qt 5

First published: December 2016

Production reference: 1121216

Published by Packt Publishing Ltd.
Livery Place
35 Livery Street
Birmingham
B3 2PB, UK.

ISBN 978-1-78646-712-6

www.packtpub.com

# Credits

**Authors**

Guillaume Lazar
Robin Penea

**Reviewer**

Ray Rischpater

**Commissioning Editor**

Kunal Parikh

**Acquisition Editor**

Sonali Vernekar

**Content Development Editor**

Rohit Kumar Singh

**Technical Editor**

Vivek Pala

**Copy Editor**

Safis Editing

**Project Coordinator**

Izzat Contractor

**Proofreader**

Safis Editing

**Indexer**

Rekha Nair

**Production Coordinator**

Aparna Bhagat

# About the Authors

**Guillaume Lazar** is a software engineer living near Paris in France. He has worked for different companies, from startups to multinationals, for the last 7 years. He took the opportunity to observe and learn from many team organizations and technologies.

He eventually founded his own software development company, NeuronalMotion, at the age of 27 with his friend Robin Penea in 2014. Information about it and its open source projects can be found on the comapny's website, `www.neuronalmotion.com`.

NeuronalMotion represents to Guillaume "a different way of working." The current hierarchical organization that applies to most companies seems obsolete to him. With his own company, he wants to try something different, where each employee will be autonomous.

Although he defines himself as a Qt framework lover, he likes to mix different technologies and platforms. He also spends time on game development, machine learning, and electronics, because "things" become "alive."

*Creating examples and writing chapters for this book was a serious challenge this year. Some sections were fundamentally changed to match Qt evolution. I would not have been able to achieve this task alone. I wish to thank Robin Penea, my friend and the coauthor of this book. He gave his all to create with me a robust Qt book with modern C++. Our review team, Rohit Kumar Singh, Ray Rischpater, Quentin Canu, Chistophe Dongieux, and Hugo Loi, have done excellent work: they corrected us and raised some important issues. I also want to thank Packt for the good follow up during the writing process. Finally, I thank my family and, particularly, Sophie, my girlfriend, for her support.*

**Robin Penea** is a software engineer living in France. He has worked for several companies over the last 7 years, on many different technologies (ranging from server application development to embedded programming).

He founded NeuronalMotion with Guillaume Lazar in 2014 to implement his vision of entrepreneurship and project development. He aims to achieve a self-organized company. More information is available at www.neuronalmotion.com.

Besides developing with Qt, he likes to tinker with the Android AOSP framework, learn new programming language paradigms, and discover how to interweave technology and real life.

*This book would not have existed without Guillaume Lazar, my friend and the coauthor of the book. He was truly dedicated to designing and crafting the best possible book. I wish to thank our reviewers, Rohit Kumar Singh, Ray Rischpater, Quentin Canu, Christophe Dongieux, and Hugo Loi. Their input was invaluable and definitely raised the quality of the book. Packt played a sensible role, listening to our requests and changes, guiding us through the writing, and monitoring our mental states during this year with benevolence. I also wish to thank my father, Calin, for believing in me. A last word for Flore, my girlfriend, who kept my motivation up and supported me.*

# About the Reviewer

**Ray Rischpater** is a software engineer and author with over 20 years of industry experience and sixteen books to his credit. Beginning with software development for mobile platforms, he's done work in several areas, including mobile, web services, building tools for mapping and geospatial engineering, and applying machine learning to geospatial processing problems.

During this time, he's participated in the development of Internet technologies and custom applications for Newton, Magic Cap, Palm OS, Java ME, Qualcomm BREW, Apple iOS, and Google Android, as well as several proprietary platforms. Over the last six years, his focus has shifted from mobile applications and services to building tools, software processes, and machine learning models to facilitate mapping the real world. Presently, he's employed as a software engineering manager at Uber, doing work on mapping and machine learning.

When not writing for or about software development, he enjoys making music, hiking, and photography with his family and friends in and around the San Lorenzo Valley in central California. When he's able, he also provides public service through amateur radio as the licensed Amateur Extra station KF6GPE.

He is the author of *Microsoft Mapping with Carmen Au*, by Apress (published in 2013) and *Application Development with Qt Creator, Second Edition*, by *Packt* (published in 2014). He has written several other books, including *Beginning Java ME Platform* (Beginning from Novice to Professional), by Apress (published in 2008), *Software Development for the QUALCOMM BREW Platform*, by Apress (published in 2003), *Wireless Web Development, First Edition*, by Apress (published in 2002), and *Wireless Web Development, Second Edition*, by Apress (published in 2004).

*I'd like to thank my wife, Meg Given, for her patience as I worked on yet another book project.*

# www.PacktPub.com

For support files and downloads related to your book, please visit www.PacktPub.com.

Did you know that Packt offers eBook versions of every book published, with PDF and ePub files available? You can upgrade to the eBook version at www.PacktPub.com and as a print book customer, you are entitled to a discount on the eBook copy. Get in touch with us at service@packtpub.com for more details.

At www.PacktPub.com, you can also read a collection of free technical articles, sign up for a range of free newsletters and receive exclusive discounts and offers on Packt books and eBooks.

https://www.packtpub.com/mapt

Get the most in-demand software skills with Mapt. Mapt gives you full access to all Packt books and video courses, as well as industry-leading tools to help you plan your personal development and advance your career.

## Why subscribe?

- Fully searchable across every book published by Packt
- Copy and paste, print, and bookmark content
- On demand and accessible via a web browser

# Table of Contents

# Preface

C++ is a powerful language. Coupled with Qt, you have in your hands a cross-platform framework that allies performance and ease of use. Qt is a vast framework that provides tools in many areas (GUI, threads, networking, and so on). 25 years after its inception, Qt continues to evolve and grow with each release.

This book aims to teach you how to squeeze the best out of Qt with the new C++14 additions (lambdas, smart pointers, enum classes, and so on). These two technologies together bring you a safe and powerful development toolbox. Throughout the book, we try to emphasize a clean architecture that lets you create and maintain your application in a complex environment.

Each chapter is based on an example project that is the basis of all the discussion. Here are some tasters about what we will see in this book:

- Uncover qmake secrets
- Take a deep dive in the model/view architecture and study how you can build a complex application with this pattern
- Study QML and Qt Quick applications in mobile
- Develop Qt 3D components using QML and JavaScript
- Show how to develop plugins and SDKs using Qt
- Cover the multi-threading technologies provided by Qt
- Build an IPC mechanism using sockets
- Serialize data using XML, JSON, and binary format

We'll cover all this and much, much more.

Note that you can take a look at `Chapter 14`, *Qt Hat Tips and Tricks*, whenever you want if you want to get some development candies and see some code snippets that might make your development more pleasurable.

And most importantly, have fun writing Qt applications!

# What this book covers

Chapter 1, *Get Your Qt Feet Wet*, lays the fundamentals of Qt and refreshes your memory with a todo application. This chapter covers the Qt project structure, how to use the designer, basic principles of the signals and slots mechanism, and introduces new features of C++14.

Chapter 2, *Discovering QMake Secrets*, takes a deep dive in the heart of the Qt compilation system: qmake. This chapter will help you understand how it works, how to use it, and how you can structure a Qt application with platform-specific code by designing a system monitoring application.

Chapter 3, *Dividing Your Project and Ruling Your Code*, analyzes the Qt model/view architecture and how a project can be organized by developing a custom library with the core logic of the application. The project example is a persistent gallery application.

Chapter 4, *Conquering the Desktop UI*, studies the UI perspective of the model/view architecture with a Qt Widget application relying on the library completed in the previous chapter.

Chapter 5, *Dominating the Mobile UI*, adds the missing part of the gallery application with the mobile version (Android and iOS); the chapter covers it with the use of QML, Qt Quick controls, and QML / C++ interactions.

Chapter 6, *Even Qt Deserves a Slice of Raspberry Pi*, continues to the road on Qt Quick application with the Qt 3D perspective. This chapter covers how to build a 3D snake game targeted at the Raspberry Pi.

Chapter 7, *Third-Party Libraries Without a Headache*, covers how a third-party library can be integrated in a Qt project. OpenCV will be integrated with an image filter application that also provides a custom QDesigner plugin.

Chapter 8, *Animations, It's Alive, Alive!*, extends the image filter application by adding animations and the ability to distribute a custom SDK to let other developers add their own filters.

Chapter 9, *Keeping Your Sanity with Multithreading*, investigates the multithreading facilities provided by Qt by building a multithreaded Mandelbrot fractal drawing application.

Chapter 10, *Need IPC? Get Your Minions to Work*, broadens the Mandelbrot fractal application by moving the calculation to other processes and managing the communication using sockets.

Chapter 11, *Having Fun with Serialization*, covers multiple serialization formats (JSON, XML, and binary) inside a drum machine application in which you can record and load sound loops.

Chapter 12, *You Shall (Not) Pass with QTest*, adds tests to the drum machine application and studies how the Qt Test frameworks can be used to make unit tests, benchmarking, and GUI events simulation

Chapter 13, *All Packed and Ready to Deploy*, gives insights into how to package an application on all desktop OSes (Windows, Linux, and Mac OS) and mobile platforms (Android and iOS).

Chapter 14, *Qt Hat Tips and Tricks*, gathers some tips and tricks to develop with Qt with pleasure. It shows how to manage sessions in Qt Creator, useful Qt Creator keyboard shortcuts, how you can customize the logging, save it to disk, and much more.

# What you need for this book

All the code in this book can be compiled and run from Qt Creator using Qt 5.7. You can do it from your preferred OS: Windows, Linux, or Mac OS.

About the mobile-specific chapters, either an Android or an iOS device works, but it is not mandatory (the simulator/emulator can be enough).

Chapter 6, *Even Qt Deserves a Slice of Raspberry Pi*, offers to build an application running on a Raspberry Pi. Although it is more fun if we can do it with a real Raspberry Pi, it is not necessary to have one to complete the chapter.

# Who this book is for

This book will appeal to developers and programmers who would like to build GUI-based application. You should be fluent with C++ and the object-oriented paradigm. Qt knowledge is recommended, but is not necessary.

# Conventions

In this book, you will find a number of text styles that distinguish between different kinds of information. Here are some examples of these styles and an explanation of their meaning.

Code words in text, database table names, folder names, filenames, file extensions, pathnames, dummy URLs, user input, and Twitter handles are shown as follows: "The `qmake` command is executed with the project `.pro` file."

A block of code is set as follows:

```
void MemoryWidget::updateSeries()
{
    double memoryUsed = SysInfo::instance().memoryUsed();
    mSeries->append(mPointPositionX++, memoryUsed);
    if (mSeries->count() > CHART_X_RANGE_COUNT) {
        QChart* chart = chartView().chart();
        chart->scroll(chart->plotArea().width()
                    / CHART_X_RANGE_MAX, 0);
        mSeries->remove(0);
    }
}
```

When we wish to draw your attention to a particular part of a code block, the relevant lines or items are set in bold:

```
windows {
    SOURCES += SysInfoWindowsImpl.cpp
    HEADERS += SysInfoWindowsImpl.h

    debug {
        SOURCES += DebugClass.cpp
        HEADERS += DebugClass.h
    }
}
```

Any command-line input or output is written as follows:

```
/path/to/qt/installation/5.7/gcc_64/bin/qmake -makefile -o Makefile
/path/to/sysinfoproject/ch02-sysinfo.pro
```

**New terms** and **important words** are shown in bold. Words that you see on the screen, for example, in menus or dialog boxes, appear in the text like this: "In Qt Creator, when you click on the **Build** button, qmake is invoked."

Warnings or important notes appear in a box like this.

Tips and tricks appear like this.

# Reader feedback

Feedback from our readers is always welcome. Let us know what you think about this book-what you liked or disliked. Reader feedback is important for us as it helps us develop titles that you will really get the most out of. To send us general feedback, simply e-mail feedback@packtpub.com, and mention the book's title in the subject of your message. If there is a topic that you have expertise in and you are interested in either writing or contributing to a book, see our author guide at www.packtpub.com/authors.

# Customer support

Now that you are the proud owner of a Packt book, we have a number of things to help you to get the most from your purchase.

## Downloading the example code

You can download the example code files for this book from your account at http://www.packtpub.com. If you purchased this book elsewhere, you can visit http://www.packtpub.com/support and register to have the files e-mailed directly to you.

You can download the code files by following these steps:

1. Log in or register to our website using your e-mail address and password.
2. Hover the mouse pointer on the **SUPPORT** tab at the top.
3. Click on **Code Downloads & Errata**.
4. Enter the name of the book in the **Search** box.
5. Select the book for which you're looking to download the code files.
6. Choose from the drop-down menu where you purchased this book from.
7. Click on **Code Download**.

Once the file is downloaded, please make sure that you unzip or extract the folder using the latest version of:

- WinRAR / 7-Zip for Windows
- Zipeg / iZip / UnRarX for Mac
- 7-Zip / PeaZip for Linux

The code bundle for the book is also hosted on GitHub at `https://github.com/PacktPubl ishing/masteringqt5`. We also have other code bundles from our rich catalog of books and videos available at `https://github.com/PacktPublishing/`. Check them out!

# Errata

Although we have taken every care to ensure the accuracy of our content, mistakes do happen. If you find a mistake in one of our books-maybe a mistake in the text or the code-we would be grateful if you could report this to us. By doing so, you can save other readers from frustration and help us improve subsequent versions of this book. If you find any errata, please report them by visiting `http://www.packtpub.com/submit-errata`, selecting your book, clicking on the **Errata Submission Form** link, and entering the details of your errata. Once your errata are verified, your submission will be accepted and the errata will be uploaded to our website or added to any list of existing errata under the Errata section of that title.

To view the previously submitted errata, go to `https://www.packtpub.com/books/conten t/support`and enter the name of the book in the search field. The required information will appear under the **Errata** section.

# Piracy

Piracy of copyrighted material on the Internet is an ongoing problem across all media. At Packt, we take the protection of our copyright and licenses very seriously. If you come across any illegal copies of our works in any form on the Internet, please provide us with the location address or website name immediately so that we can pursue a remedy.

Please contact us at `copyright@packtpub.com` with a link to the suspected pirated material.

We appreciate your help in protecting our authors and our ability to bring you valuable content.

# Questions

If you have a problem with any aspect of this book, you can contact us at `questions@packtpub.com`, and we will do our best to address the problem.

# 1
# Get Your Qt Feet Wet

If you know C++ but have never touched Qt, or if you have made some intermediate Qt applications, this chapter will ensure that your Qt foundations are safe before studying advanced concepts in the following chapters.

We will teach you to create a simple todo application using Qt Creator. This application will display a list of tasks that you can create/update/delete. We will cover the Qt Creator and Qt Designer interfaces, an introduction to the signal/slot mechanism, the creation of a custom widget with custom signals/slots, and its integration into your application.

You will implement a todo app using new C++14 semantics: lambdas, auto variables, and for loops. Each one of these concepts will be explained in depth and will be used throughout the book.

At the end of this chapter, you will be able to create a desktop application with a flexible UI using Qt widgets and new C++ semantics.

In this chapter, we will cover the following topics:

- Qt project basic structure
- Qt Designer interface
- UI fundamentals
- Signals and slots
- Custom `QWidget`
- C++14 lambda, auto, for each

# Creating a project

The first thing to do is to start Qt Creator.

In Qt Creator, you can create a new Qt project via **File | New File or Project | Application | Qt Widgets Application | Choose**.

The wizard will then guide you through four steps:

1. **Location**: You must choose a project name and a location.
2. **Kits**: Target platforms that your project aims at (Desktop, Android, and so on).
3. **Details**: Base class information and name for the generated class.
4. **Summary**: Allows you to configure your new project as a subproject and automatically add it to a version control system.

Even if all default values can be kept, please at least set a useful project name such as "todo" or "TodoApp." We won't blame you if you want to call it "Untitled" or "Hello world."

Once done, Qt Creator will generate several files that you can see in the **Projects** hierarchy view:

The .pro file is Qt's configuration project file. As Qt adds specific file formats and C++ keywords, an intermediate build step is performed, parsing all files to generate final files. This process is done by qmake, an executable from the Qt SDK. It will also generate the final Makefiles for your project.

A basic .pro file generally contains:

- Qt modules used (core, gui, and so on)
- Target name (todo, todo.exe, and so on)
- Project template (app, lib, and so on)
- Sources, headers, and forms

There are some great features that come with Qt and C++14. This book will showcase them in all its projects. For GCC and CLANG compilers, you must add CONFIG += c++14 to the .pro file to enable C++14 on a Qt project, as shown in the following code:

```
QT       += core gui
CONFIG   += c++14

greaterThan(QT_MAJOR_VERSION, 4): QT += widgets

TARGET = todo
TEMPLATE = app

SOURCES += main.cpp \
           MainWindow.cpp

HEADERS  += MainWindow.h \

FORMS    += MainWindow.ui \
```

The MainWindow.h and MainWindow.cpp files are the headers/sources for the MainWindow class. These files contain the default GUI generated by the wizard.

The MainWindow.ui file is your UI design file in XML format. It can be edited more easily with Qt Designer. This tool is a **WYSIWYG (What You See Is What You Get)** editor that helps you to add and adjust your graphical components (widgets).

Here is the main.cpp file, with its well-known function:

```
#include "MainWindow.h"
#include <QApplication>

int main(int argc, char *argv[])
{
    QApplication a(argc, argv);
    MainWindow w;
    w.show();

    return a.exec();
```

```
}
```

As usual, the `main.cpp` file contains the program entry point. It will, by default, perform two actions:

- Instantiate and show your main window
- Instantiate a `QApplication` and execute the blocking main event loop

This is the bottom-left toolbar for Qt Creator:

Use it to build and start your `todo` application in debug mode:

1. Check that the project is in **Debug** build mode.
2. Use the hammer button to build your project.
3. Start debugging using the green Play button with a little blue bug.

You will discover a wonderful and beautifully empty window. We will rectify this after explaining how this `MainWindow` is constructed:

An empty **MainWindow** screenshot

**Qt tip**

- Press *Ctrl + B* (for Windows/Linux) or *Command + B* (for Mac) to build your project
- Press *F5* (for Windows / Linux) or *Command +R* (for Mac) to run your application in debug mode

# MainWindow structure

This generated class is a perfect yet simple example of Qt framework usage; we will dissect it together. As mentioned previously, the MainWindow.ui file describes your UI design and MainWindow.h/ MainWindow.cpp is the C++ object where you can manipulate the UI with code.

It is important to take a look at the header file MainWindow.h. Our MainWindow object inherits from Qt's QMainWindow class:

```
#include <QMainWindow>

namespace Ui {
class MainWindow;
}
```

```
class MainWindow : public QMainWindow
{
    Q_OBJECT

public:
    explicit MainWindow(QWidget *parent = 0);
    ~MainWindow();
private:
    Ui::MainWindow *ui;
};
```

As our class inherits from the QMainWindow class, on top of the header file, we add the corresponding include. The second part is the forward declaration of the Ui::MainWindow, as we only declare a pointer.

The Q_OBJECT can look a little strange to a non-Qt developer. This macro allows the class to define its own signals/slots and more globally Qt's meta-object system. These features will be covered later in this chapter.

This class defines a public constructor and destructor. The latter is pretty common. But the constructor takes a parameter parent. This parameter is a QWidget pointer that is null by default.

A QWidget is a UI component. It can be a label, a textbox, a button, and so on. If you define a parent-child relationship between your window, layout, and other UI widgets, memory management of your application will be easier. Indeed, in this case, deleting the parent is enough because its destructor will take care of also deleting its child, which in turn will delete its children and so on.

Our MainWindow class extends QMainWindow from the Qt framework. We have a ui member variable in the private fields. The type is a pointer of Ui::MainWindow, which is defined in the ui_MainWindow.h file generated by Qt. It's the C++ transcription of the UI design file MainWindow.ui. The ui member variable will allow you to interact with your UI components (QLabel, QPushButton, and so on) from C++, as shown in the following figure:

**C++ tip**
If your class only uses pointers or references for a class type, you can avoid including the header by using forward declaration. That will drastically reduce compilation time.

Now that the header part is done, we can talk about the `MainWindow.cpp` source file.

In the following code snippet, the first include is our class header. The second one is the include required by the generated class `Ui::MainWindow`. This include is required as we only use a forward declaration in the header:

```
#include "MainWindow.h"
#include "ui_MainWindow.h"

MainWindow::MainWindow(QWidget *parent) :
    QMainWindow(parent),
    ui(new Ui::MainWindow)
{
    ui->setupUi(this);
```

In many cases, Qt generates a good piece of code using the initializer list. The `parent` argument is used to call the superclass constructor `QMainWindow`. Our private member variable `ui` is also initialized now.

Now that `ui` is initialized, we must call the `setupUi` function to initialize all widgets used by the `MainWindow.ui` design file:

As we initialize a pointer in the constructor, it must be cleaned in the destructor:

```
MainWindow::~MainWindow()
{
    delete ui;
}
```

# Qt Designer

Qt Designer is a major tool for developing Qt applications. This WYSIWYG editor will help you easily design your GUI. If you switch between **Edit** mode and **Design** mode for the `MainWindow.ui` file, you will see the real XML content and the designer:

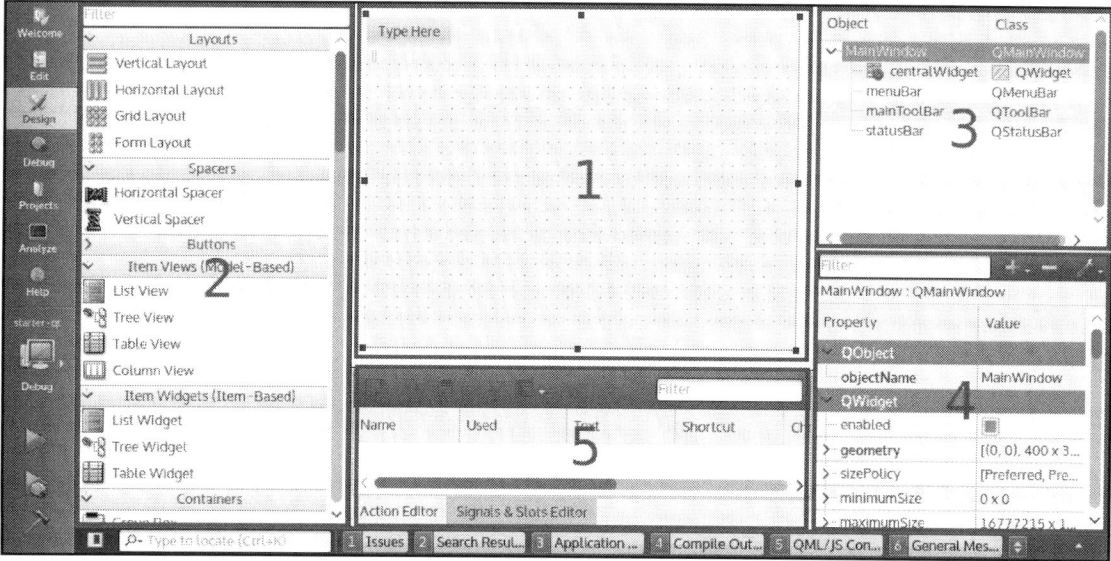

The designer displays several parts:

- **Form Editor**: This is a visual representation of the form (empty for now)
- **Widget Box**: This contains all widgets that can be used with your form
- **Object Inspector**: This displays your form as a hierarchical tree
- **Property Editor**: This enumerates the properties of the selected widget
- **Action Editor/Signal & Slots Editor**: This handles connections between your objects

It's time to embellish this empty window! Let's drag and drop a **Label** widget from the **Display Widgets** section on the form. You can change the name and the text properties from the properties editor.

As we are making a `todo` application, we suggest these properties:

- `objectName`: `statusLabel`
- `text`: `Status: 0 todo/0 done`

This label will later display the count of `todo` tasks and the count of tasks already done. OK, save, build, and start your application. You should now see your new label in the window.

You can now add a push button with those properties:

- `objectName`: `addTaskButton`
- `text`: `Add task`

You should get a result close to this:

**Qt tip**
You can edit the text property of a widget directly on your form by double-clicking on it!

# Signals and slots

The Qt framework brings a flexible message exchange mechanism through three concepts: signals, slots, and connections:

- A `signal` is a message sent by an object
- A `slot` is a function that will be called when this signal is triggered
- The `connect` function specifies which `signal` is linked to which `slot`

Qt already provides signals and slots for its classes, which you can use in your application. For example, `QPushButton` has a `signal clicked()`, which will be triggered when the user clicks on the button. The `QApplication` class has a `slot quit()` function, which can be called when you want to terminate your application.

Here is why you will love Qt signals and slots:

- A slot remains an ordinary function, so you can call it yourself
- A single signal can be linked to different slots
- A single slot can be called by different linked signals
- A connection can be made between a signal and a slot from different objects, and even between objects living inside different threads!

Keep in mind that, to be able to connect a `signal` to a `slot`, their methods' signatures must match. The count, order, and type of arguments must be identical. Note that signals and slots never return values.

This is the syntax of a Qt connection:

```
connect(sender, &Sender::signalName,
    receiver, &Receiver::slotName);
```

The first test that we can do to use this wonderful mechanism is to connect an existing `signal` with an existing `slot`. We will add this connect call to the `MainWindow` constructor:

```
MainWindow::MainWindow(QWidget *parent) :
    QMainWindow(parent),
    ui(new Ui::MainWindow)
{
    ui->setupUi(this);
    connect(ui->addTaskButton, &QPushButton::clicked,
    QApplication::instance(), &QApplication::quit);
}
```

Let's analyze how a connection is done:

- sender: This is the object that will send the signal. In our example, it is the QPushButton named addTaskButton added from the UI designer.
- &Sender::signalName: This is the pointer to the member signal function. Here, we want do something when the clicked signal is triggered.
- receiver: This is the object that will receive and handle the signal. In our case, it is the QApplication object created in main.cpp.
- &Receiver::slotName: This is a pointer to one of the receiver's member slot functions. In this example, we use the built-in quit() slot from Qapplication, which will exit the application.

You can now compile and run this short example. You will terminate the application if you click on the addTaskButton of your MainWindow.

**Qt tip**
You can connect a signal to another signal. The second signal will be emitted when the first one is triggered.

Now that you know how to connect a signal to an existing slot, let's see how to declare and implement a custom addTask() slot in our MainWindow class. This slot will be called when the user clicks on ui->addTaskButton.

This is the updated MainWindow.h:

```
class MainWindow : public QMainWindow
{
    Q_OBJECT

public:
    explicit MainWindow(QWidget *parent = 0);
    ~MainWindow();

public slots:
    void addTask();

private:
    Ui::MainWindow *ui;
};
```

Qt uses a specific `slot` keyword to identify slots. Since a slot is a function, you can always adjust the visibility (`public`, `protected` or `private`) depending on your needs.

Add this slot implementation in the `MainWindow.cpp` file:

```
void MainWindow::addTask()
{
    qDebug() << "User clicked on the button!";
}
```

Qt provides an efficient way of displaying debug information with the `QDebug` class. An easy way to obtain a `QDebug` object is to call the `qDebug()` function. Then, you can use the stream operator to send your debug information.

Update the top of the file like this:

```
#include <QDebug>

MainWindow::MainWindow(QWidget *parent) :
    QMainWindow(parent),
    ui(new Ui::MainWindow)
{
    ui->setupUi(this);
    connect(ui->addTaskButton, &QPushButton::clicked,
    this, &MainWindow::addTask);
}
```

Since we now use `qDebug()` in out slot, we must include `<QDebug>`. The updated connect now calls our custom slot instead of quitting the application.

Build and run the application. If you click on the button, you will see your debug message inside the Qt Creator `Application Output` tab.

# Custom QWidget

We now have to create the `Task` class that will hold our data (task name and completed status). This class will have its form file separated from `MainWindow`. Qt Creator provides an automatic tool to generate a base class and the associated form.

Click on **File** | **New File or Project** | **Qt** | **Qt Designer Form Class**. There are several form templates; you will recognize Main Window, which Qt Creator created for us when we started the `todo` app project. Select **Widget** and name the class `Task`, then click on **Next**. Here is a summary of what Qt Creator will do:

1. Create a `Task.h` file and a `Task.cpp` file.
2. Create the associated `Task.ui` and do the plumbing to connect it to `Task.h`.
3. Add these three new files to `todo.pro` so they can be compiled.

Finish and, voilà, the `Task` class is ready to be filled. We will jump into the `Task.ui` first. Start by dragging and dropping a `Check Box` (put `checkbox` in the `objectName`) and a `Push Button` (`objectName` = `removeButton`):

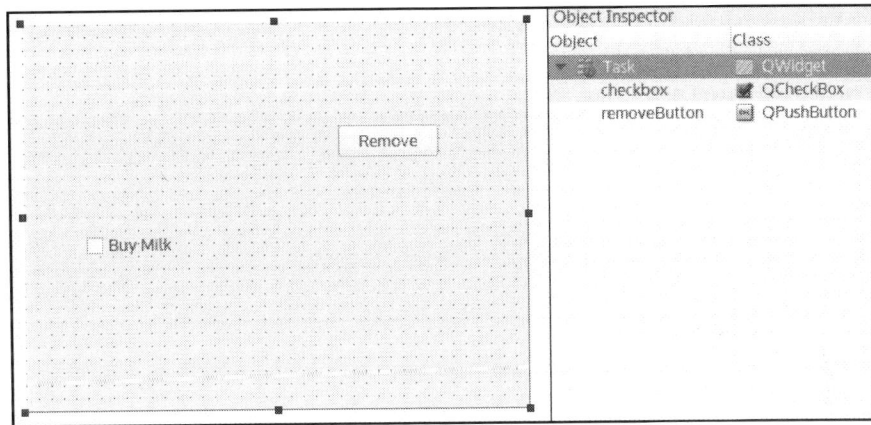

My alignment looks great, let's ship this to the customers!

Unless you have a pixel-perfect eye, your items are not very well aligned. You need to indicate how your widgets should be laid out and how they should react when the window geometry changes (for example, when the user resizes the window). For this, Qt has several default layout classes:

- `Vertical Layout`: In this layout, widgets are vertically stacked
- `Horizontal Layout`: In this layout, widgets are horizontally stacked
- `Grid Layout`: In this layout, widgets are arranged in a grid that can be subdivided into smaller cells
- `Form Layout`: In this layout, widgets are arranged like a web form, a label, and an input

Every layout will try to constrain all widgets to occupy equal surfaces. It will either change the widgets' shape or add extra margins, depending on each widget's constraints. A `Check Box` will not be stretched but a `Push Button` will.

In our `Task` object, we want this to be horizontally stacked. In the **Form Editor** tab, right-click on the window and select **Lay out | Lay out Horizontally**. Each time you add a new widget in this layout, it will be arranged horizontally.

Now add a `Push Button (objectName = editButton)` line just after the `checkbox` object.

The **Form Editor** window offers a realistic preview of how your UI will render. If you stretch the window now, you can observe how each widget will react to this event. When resizing horizontally, you can note that the push buttons are stretched. It looks bad. We need something to "hint" to the layout that these buttons should not be stretched. Enter the `Spacer` widget. Take the `Horizontal Spacer` in the widget box and drop it after the `checkbox` object:

A spacer is a special widget that tries to push (horizontally or vertically) adjacent widgets to force them to take up as little space as possible. The `editButton` and `removeButton` objects now take up only the space of their text and will be pushed to the edge of the window when it is resized.

You can add sub layouts of any type in a form (vertical, horizontal, grid, form) and create a complex-looking application with a combination of widgets, spacers, and layouts. These tools are targeted at designing a good-looking desktop application that can react properly to different window geometries.

The Designer part is finished, so we can switch to the `Task` source code. Since we created a Qt Designer Form class, `Task` is closely linked to its UI. We will use this as leverage to store our model in a single place. When we create a `Task` object, it has to have a name:

```
#ifndef TASK_H
#define TASK_H
```

```
#include <QWidget>
#include <QString>

namespace Ui {
class Task;
}

class Task : public QWidget
{
    Q_OBJECT

public:
    explicit Task(const QString& name, QWidget *parent = 0);
    ~Task();

    void setName(const QString& name);
    QString name() const;
    bool isCompleted() const;
private:
    Ui::Task *ui;
};

#endif // TASK_H
```

The constructor specifies a name, and as you can see there are no private fields storing any state of the object. All this will be done in the form part. We also added some getters and setters that will interact with the form. It is better to have a model completely separated from the UI, but our example is simple enough to merge them. Moreover, Task implementation details are hidden from the outside world and can still be refactored later on. Here is the content of the Task.cpp file:

```
#include "Task.h"
#include "ui_Task.h"

Task::Task(const QString& name, QWidget *parent) :
        QWidget(parent),
        ui(new Ui::Task)
{
    ui->setupUi(this);
    setName(name);
}

Task::~Task()
{
    delete ui;
}
```

```
void Task::setName(const QString& name)
{
    ui->checkbox->setText(name);
}

QString Task::name() const
{
    return ui->checkbox->text();
}

bool Task::isCompleted() const
{
    return ui->checkbox->isChecked();
}
```

The implementation is straightforward; we store the information in our `ui->checkbox` and the `name()` and `isCompleted()` getters take their data from the `ui->checkbox`.

# Adding a task

We will now rearrange the layout of `MainWindow` to be able to display our todo tasks. Right now, there is no widget where we can display our tasks. Open the `MainWindow.ui` file and edit it to get the following result:

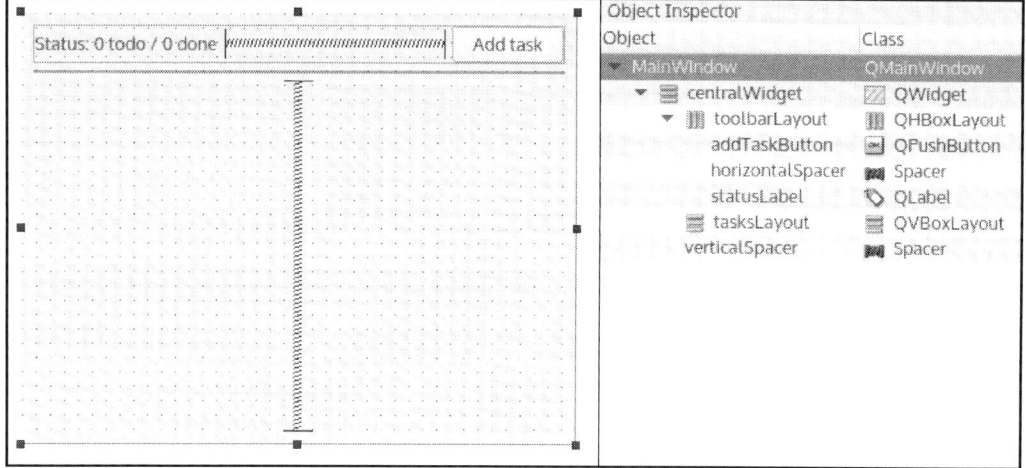

If we detail the content, we have:

- A vertical layout for `centralWidget` containing the `toolbarLayout` file and the `tasksLayout` file.
- A vertical spacer pushing these layouts to the top, forcing them to take up the smallest possible space.
- We got rid of `menuBar`, `mainToolBar`, and `statusBar`. Qt Creator created them automatically, we simply don't need them for our purposes. You can guess their uses from their names.

Do not forget to rename the `MainWindow` title to `Todo` by selecting the **MainWindow** in the **Object Inspector** window and editing the **Qwidget | windowTitle** property. Your app deserves to be named properly.

**Qt Tip**
Press *Shift + F4* in Designer mode to switch between the form editor and the source.

Now that the `MainWindow` UI is ready to welcome tasks, let's switch to the code part. The application has to keep track of the new tasks. Add the following in the `MainWindow.h` file:

```
#include <QVector>

#include "Task.h"

class MainWindow : public QMainWindow
{
    // MAINWINDOW_H

public slots:
    void addTask();

private:
    Ui::MainWindow *ui;
    QVector<Task*> mTasks;
};
```

The `QVector` is the Qt container class providing a dynamic array, which is an equivalent of the `std::vector`. As a general rule, STL containers are more customizable but might miss some features compared to Qt containers. If you use C++11 smart pointers, you should favor `std` containers, but we will get into that later.

In the Qt documentation of QVector, you might stumble upon the following statement: *"For most purposes,* QList *is the right class to use"*. There is a debate about this in the Qt community:

- Do you often need to insert objects larger than a pointer at the beginning or in the middle of your array? Use a QList class.
- Need contiguous memory allocation? Less CPU and memory overhead? Use a QVector class.

The already added slot addTask() will now be called each time we want to add a new Task object to the mTasks function.

Let's fill our QVector tasks each time addTaskButton is clicked. First, we connect the clicked() signal in the MainWindow.cpp file:

```
MainWindow::MainWindow(QWidget *parent) :
    QMainWindow(parent),
    ui(new Ui::MainWindow),
    mTasks()
{
    ui->setupUi(this);
    connect(ui->addTaskButton, &QPushButton::clicked,
    this, &MainWindow::addTask);
};
```

**C++ tip**

As a best practice, try to always initialize member variables in the initializer list and respect the order of variable declarations. Your code will run faster and you will avoid unnecessary variable copies. Take a look at the standard C++ documentation at https://isocpp.org/wiki/faq/ctors#init-lists.

The body of the addTask() function should look like this:

```
void MainWindow::addTask()
{
        qDebug() << "Adding new task";
        Task* task = new Task("Untitled task");
        mTasks.append(task);
        ui->tasksLayout->addWidget(task);
}
```

We created a new task and added it to our `mTask` vector. Because Task is a `QWidget`, we also added it directly to the `tasksLayout`. An important thing to note here is that we never managed this new task's memory. Where is the `delete task` instruction? This is a key feature of the Qt Framework we started to broach earlier in the chapter; the `QObject` class parenting automatically handles object destruction.

In our case, the `ui->tasksLayout->addWidget(task)` call has an interesting side-effect; the ownership of the task is transferred to `tasksLayout`. The `QObject *` parent defined in `Task` constructor is now `tasksLayout`, and the `Task` destructor will be called when `tasksLayout` releases its own memory by recursively iterating through its children and calling their destructor.

This will happen at this precise moment:

```
MainWindow::~MainWindow()
{
    delete ui;
}
```

When `MainWindow` is released (remember, it's a stack variable allocated in the `main.cpp` file), it will call `delete ui`, which in turn will bring down the whole `QObject` hierarchy. This feature has interesting consequences. First, if you use the `QObject` parenting model in your application, you will have much less memory to manage. Second, it can collide with some new C++11 semantics, specifically the smart pointers. We will get into that in later chapters.

# Using a QDialog

We deserve something better than an untitled task. The user needs to define its name when it's created. The easiest path would be to display a dialog where the user can input the task name. Fortunately Qt offers us a very configurable dialog that fits perfectly in `addTask()`:

```
#include <QInputDialog>
...
void MainWindow::addTask()
{
    bool ok;
    QString name = QInputDialog::getText(this,
        tr("Add task"),
        tr("Task name"),
        QLineEdit::Normal,
        tr("Untitled task"),                    &ok);
    if (ok && !name.isEmpty()) {
```

```
        qDebug() << "Adding new task";
        Task* task = new Task(name);
        mTasks.append(task);
        ui->tasksLayout->addWidget(task);
    }
}
```

The `QinputDialog::getText` function is a static blocking function that displays the dialog. When the user validates/cancels the dialog, the code continues. If we run the application and try to add a new task, we'll see this:

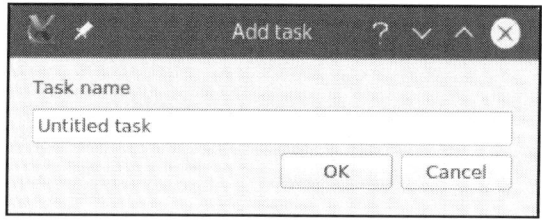

The `QInputDialog::getText` signature looks like this:

```
QString QinputDialog::getText(
  QWidget* parent,
      const QString& title,
      const QString& label,
      QLineEdit::EchoMode mode = QLineEdit::Normal,
      const QString& text = QString(),
      bool* ok = 0, ...)
```

Let's break it down:

- `parent`: This is the parent widget (`MainWindow`) to which the `QinputDialog` is attached. This is another instance of the `QObject` class's parenting model.
- `title`: This is the title displayed in the window title. In our example, we use `tr("Add task")`, which is how Qt handles i18n in your code. We will see later on how to provide multiple translations for a given string.
- `label`: This is the label displayed right above the input text field.
- `mode`: This is how the input field is rendered (password mode will hide the text).
- `ok`: This is a pointer to a variable that is set to true if the user presses **OK** and to false if the user presses **Cancel**.
- `QString`: The returned `QString` is what the user has typed.

There are a few more optional parameters we can safely ignore for our example.

# Distributing code responsibility

Great, the user can now specify the task name when it's created. What if he makes an error when typing the name? The next logical step is to rename the task after we created it. We'll take a slightly different approach. We want our `Task` to be as autonomous as possible. If we attach it to another component (rather than `MainWindow`), this renaming feature has to keep working. Thus, this responsibility has to be given to the `Task` class:

```cpp
// In Task.h
public slots:
    void rename();

// In Task.cpp
#include <QInputDialog>

Task::Task(const QString& name, QWidget *parent) :
        QWidget(parent),
        ui(new Ui::Task)
{
    ui->setupUi(this);
    setName(name);
    connect(ui->editButton, &QPushButton::clicked, this, &Task::rename);
}
...
void Task::rename()
{
    bool ok;
    QString value = QInputDialog::getText(this, tr("Edit task"),
                                  tr("Task name"),
                                  QLineEdit::Normal,
                                  this->name(), &ok);

    if (ok && !value.isEmpty()) {
        setName(value);
    }
}
```

We add a public slot `rename()` to connect it to a signal. The body of `rename()` reuses what we had previously covered with `QInputDialog`. The only difference is the `QInputDialog` default value, which is the current task name. When `setName(value)` is called, the UI is instantly refreshed with the new value; there's nothing to synchronize or update, the Qt main loop will do its job.

The nice thing is that `Task::rename()` is completely autonomous. Nothing has been modified in `MainWindow`, so we have effectively zero coupling between our `Task` and the parent `QWidget`.

# Emitting a custom signal using lambdas

The remove task is straightforward to implement, but we'll study some new concepts along the way. The `Task` has to notify its owner and parent (`MainWindow`) that the `removeTaskButtonQPushButton` has been clicked. We'll implement this by defining a custom signal `removed` in `Task.h` files:

```
class Task : public QWidget
{
    ...
public slots:
    void rename();
signals:
    void removed(Task* task);
    ...
};
```

Like we did for the slots, we have to add the Qt keyword signals in our header. Since a `signal` is used only to notify another class, the `public` keyword is not needed (it even raises a compilation error). A `signal` is simply a notification sent to the receiver (the connected `slot`); it implies that there is no function body for the `removed(Task* task)` function. We added the `task` parameter to allow the receiver to know which task asked to be removed. The next step is to emit the `removed` signal upon the `removeButton` click. This is done in the `Task.cpp` file:

```
Task::Task(const QString& name, QWidget *parent) :
        QWidget(parent),
        ui(new Ui::Task)
{
    ui->setupUi(this);
    ...
    connect(ui->removeButton, &QPushButton::clicked, [this] {
        emit removed(this);
    });
}
```

This code excerpt shows a very interesting feature of C++11: `lambdas`. In our example, the `lambda` is the following part:

```
[this] {
        emit removed(this);
    });
```

What we did here is to connect the clicked signal to an anonymous inline function, a `lambda`. Qt allows signal relaying by connecting a signal to another signal if their signatures match. It's not the case here; the `clicked` signal has no parameter and the `removed` signal needs a `Task*`. A `lambda` avoids the declaration of a verbose `slot` in `Task`. Qt 5 accepts a `lambda` instead of a slot in a `connect`, and both syntaxes can be used.

Our `lambda` executes a single line of code: `emit removed(this)`. `Emit` is a Qt macro that will immediately trigger the connected `slot` with what we passed in a parameter. As we said earlier, `removed(Task* this)` has no function body, its purpose is to notify the registered slot of an event.

Lambdas are a great addition to C++. They offer a very practical way of defining short functions in your code. Technically, a `lambda` is the construction of a closure capable of capturing variables in its scope. The full syntax goes like this:

```
[ capture-list ] ( params ) -> ret { body }
```

Let's study each part of this statement:

- `capture-list`: This defines what variables will be visible inside the `lambda` scope.
- `params`: This is the function parameters type list that can be passed to the `lambda` scope. There are no parameters in our case, We might have written `[this] () { ... }`, but C++11 lets us skip the parentheses altogether.
- `ret`: This is the return type of the `lambda` function. Just like `params`, this parameter can be omitted if the return type is `void`.
- `body`: This is obviously your code body where you have access to your `capture-list`, and `params`, and which must return a variable with a type `ret`.

In our example, we captured the `this` pointer to be able to:

- Have a reference on the `removed()` function, which is a part of the `Task` class. If we did not capture `this`, the compiler would have shouted `error: 'this' was not captured for this lambda function emit removed(this);`.
- Pass `this` to the `removed` signal; the caller needs to know which task triggered `removed`.

The `capture-list` relies on standard C++ semantics: capture variables by copy or by reference. Let us say that we wanted to print a log of the constructor parameter `name` and we capture it by reference in our `lambda`:

```
connect(ui->removeButton, &QPushButton::clicked, [this, &name] {
        qDebug() << "Trying to remove" << name;
        this->emit removed(this);
    });
```

This code will compile fine. Unfortunately, the runtime will crash with a dazzling segmentation fault when we try to remove a `Task`. What happened? As we said, our `lambda` is an anonymous function that will be executed when the `clicked()` signal has been emitted. We captured the `name` reference, but this reference may be – and is – invalid once we get out of `Task` constructor (more precisely, from the caller scope). The `qDebug()` function will then try to display an unreachable code and crash.

You really want to be careful with what you capture and the context in which your lambda will be executed. In this example, the segmentation fault can be amended by capturing the `name` by copy:

```
connect(ui->removeButton, &QPushButton::clicked, [this, name] {
        qDebug() << "Trying to remove" << name;
        this->emit removed(this);
    });
```

### C++ Tip

- You can capture by copy or reference all variables that are reachable in the function where you define your lambda with the syntax [=] and [&].
- The `this` variable is a special case of the capture list. You cannot capture it by reference [&this] and the compiler will warn you if you are in this situation: [=, this]. Don't do this. Kittens will die.

Our `lambda` is passed directly as a parameter to the connect function. In other words, the `lambda` is variable. This has many consequences: we can call it, assign it, and return it. To illustrate a "fully formed" `lambda`, we can define one that returns a formatted version of the task name. The sole purpose of this snippet is to investigate the `lambda` function's machinery. Don't include the following code in your `todo` app, your colleagues might call you something like a "functional zealot":

```
connect(ui->removeButton, &QPushButton::clicked, [this, name] {
```

```
    qDebug() << "Trying to remove" <<
        [] (const QString& taskName) -> QString {
            return "-------- " + taskName.toUpper();
    }(name);
    this->emit removed(this);
});
```

Here we did a tricky thing. We called `qDebug()`; inside this call we defined a `lambda` which is immediately executed. Let's analyze it:

- `[]`: We performed no capture. The `lambda` does not depend on the enclosing function.
- `(const Qstring& taskName)`: When this lambda is called, it will expect a `QString` to work on.
- `-> QString`: The returned value of the lambda will be a `QString`.
- `return "------- " + taskName.toUpper()`: the body of our `lambda`. We return a concatenation of a string and the uppercase version of the parameter `taskName`. As you can see, string manipulation becomes a lot easier with Qt.
- `(name)`: Here comes the catch. Now that the `lambda` function is defined, we can call it passing the `name` parameter. In a single instruction, we define it and call it. The `QDebug()` function will simply print the result.

The real benefit of this `lambda` will emerge if we are able to assign it to a variable and call it multiple times. C++ is statically typed, so we must provide the type of our `lambda` variable. In the language specification, a `lambda` type cannot be explicitly defined. We'll see soon how we can do it with C++11. For now, let's finish our remove feature.

Task now emits the `removed()` signal. This signal has to be consumed by `MainWindow`:

```
// in MainWindow.h
public slots:
    void addTask();
    void removeTask(Task* task);

// In MainWindow.cpp
void MainWindow::addTask()
{
    ...
    if (ok && !name.isEmpty()) {
        qDebug() << "Adding new task";
        Task* task = new Task(name);
        connect(task, &Task::removed,
        this, &MainWindow::removeTask);
```

```
        . . .
    }
}

void MainWindow::removeTask(Task* task)
{
    mTasks.removeOne(task);
    ui->tasksLayout->removeWidget(task);
    task->setParent(0);
    delete task;
}
```

The `MainWindow::removeTask()` must match the signal signature. The connection is made when the task is created. The interesting part comes in the implementation of `MainWindow::removeTask()`.

The task is first removed from the `mTasks` vector. It is then removed from `tasksLayout`. Here, `tasksLayout` releases its ownership of `task` (that is, `tasksLayout` ceases to be the `task` class's parent).

So far so good. The next two lines are interesting. The ownership transfer does not completely release the `task` class ownership. If we commented these lines, here is how `removeTask()` will look:

```
void MainWindow::removeTask(Task* task)
{
    mTasks.removeOne(task);
    ui->tasksLayout->removeWidget(task);
    // task->setParent(0);
    // delete task;
}
```

If you add a log message in `Task` destructor and execute the program, this log message will be displayed. Nonetheless, the Qt documentation tells us in `Qlayout::removeWidget` part: *The ownership of a widget remains the same as when it was added.*

Instead, what really happens is that the `task` class's parent becomes `centralWidget`, the `tasksLayout` class's parent. We want Qt to forget everything about `task`, that's why we call `task->setParent(0)`. We can then safely delete it and call it a day.

# Simplifying with the auto type and a range-based for loop

The final step to a complete CRUD of our tasks is to implement the completed task feature. We'll implement the following:

- Click on the checkbox to mark the task as completed
- Strike the task name
- Update the status label in `MainWindow`

The checkbox click handling follows the same pattern as `removed`:

```cpp
// In Task.h
signals:
    void removed(Task* task);
    void statusChanged(Task* task);
private slots:
    void checked(bool checked);

// in Task.cpp
Task::Task(const QString& name, QWidget *parent) :
        QWidget(parent),
        ui(new Ui::Task)
{
    ...

    connect(ui->checkbox, &QCheckBox::toggled,
    this, &Task::checked);
}

...

void Task::checked(bool checked)
{
    QFont font(ui->checkbox->font());
    font.setStrikeOut(checked);
    ui->checkbox->setFont(font);
    emit statusChanged(this);
}
```

We define a slot `checked(bool checked)` that will be connected to
the `checkbox::toggled` signal. In our `slot checked()`, we strike out the `checkbox` text
according to the `bool checked` value. This is done using the `QFont` class. We create a copy
font from the `checkbox->font()`, modify it, and assign it back to `ui->checkbox`. If the
original `font` was in bold, with a special size, its appearance would be guaranteed to stay
the same.

Play around with the font object in Qt Designer. Select the `checkbox` in
the `Task.ui` file and go to **Properties Editor** | **QWidget** | **font**.

The last instruction notifies `MainWindow` that the `Task` status has changed. The signal name
is `statusChanged`, rather than `checkboxChecked`, to hide the implementation details of
the task. Add the following code in the `MainWindow.h` file:

```
// In MainWindow.h
public:
    void updateStatus();
public slots:
    void addTask();
    void removeTask(Task* task);
    void taskStatusChanged(Task* task);

// In MainWindow.cpp
MainWindow::MainWindow(QWidget *parent) :
    QMainWindow(parent),
    ui(new Ui::MainWindow),
    mTasks()
{
    ...
    updateStatus();
    }
}

void MainWindow::addTask()
{
    ...
    if (ok && !name.isEmpty()) {
        ...
        connect(task, &Task::removed, this,
                &MainWindow::removeTask);
        connect(task, &Task::statusChanged, this,
                &MainWindow::taskStatusChanged);
        mTasks.append(task);
        ui->tasksLayout->addWidget(task);
```

```
            updateStatus();
    }
}

void MainWindow::removeTask(Task* task)
{
    ...
    delete task;
    updateStatus();
}

void MainWindow::taskStatusChanged(Task* /*task*/)
{
    updateStatus();
}

void MainWindow::updateStatus()
{
    int completedCount = 0;
    for(auto t : mTasks)  {
        if (t->isCompleted()) {
            completedCount++;
        }
    }
    int todoCount = mTasks.size() - completedCount;

    ui->statusLabel->setText(
        QString("Status: %1 todo / %2 completed")
                        .arg(todoCount)
                        .arg(completedCount));
}
```

We defined a slot taskStatusChanged, which is connected when a task is created. The single instruction of this slot is to call updateStatus(). This function iterates through the tasks and updates the statusLabel. The updateStatus() function is called upon task creation and deletion.

In updateStatus(), we meet more new C++11 semantics:

```
for(auto t : mTasks)  {
    ...
}
```

The `for` keyword lets us loop over a range-based container. Because `QVector` is an iterable container, we can use it here. The range declaration (`auto t`) is the type and variable name that will be assigned at each iteration. The range expression (`mTasks`) is simply the container on which the process will be done. Qt provides a custom implementation of the `for` (namely `foreach`) loop targeted at prior versions of C++; you don't need it anymore.

The `auto` keyword is another great new semantic. The compiler deduces the variable type automatically based on the initializer. It relieves a lot of pain for cryptic iterators such as this:

```
std::vector::const_iterator iterator = mTasks.toStdVector()
                                    .stdTasks.begin();

// how many neurones did you save?
auto autoIter = stdTasks.begin();
```

Since C++14, `auto` can even be used for function return types. It's a fabulous tool, but use it sparingly. If you put `auto`, the type should be obvious from the signature name/variable name.

The `auto` keyword can be combined with `const` and references. You can write a for loop like this: `for (const auto & t : mTasks) { ... }`.

Remember our half bread `lambda`? With all the covered features, we can write:

```
auto prettyName = [] (const QString& taskName) -> QString {
    return "-------- " + taskName.toUpper();
};
connect(ui->removeButton, &QPushButton::clicked,
    [this, name, prettyName] {
        qDebug() << "Trying to remove" << prettyName(name);
        this->emit removed(this);
});
```

Now that's something beautiful. Combining `auto` with `lambda` makes very readable code and opens up a world of possibilities.

The last item to study is the `QString` API. We used it in `updateStatus()`:

```
ui->statusLabel->setText(
        QString("Status: %1 todo / %2 completed")
                        .arg(todoCount)
                        .arg(completedCount));
```

The people behind Qt put a lot of work into making string manipulation bearable in C++. This is a perfect example, where we replace the classic C `sprintf` with a more modern and robust API. Arguments are position-based only, no need to specify the type (less error-prone), and the `arg(...)` function accepts all kinds of types.

> Take some time to skim through the `QString` documentation at `http://d oc.qt.io/qt-5/qstring.html`. It shows how much you can do with this class and you'll see yourself using fewer and fewer examples of `std string` or even `cstring`.

# Summary

In this chapter, we created a desktop Qt application from scratch. Qt is well known for its signal/slot mechanism and you must be confident with this paradigm. We also introduced some important C++14 features that will be used all through this book.

It's now time to discover some qmake secrets and what is really done when you build your Qt project. In the next chapter, we will also talk about how to create and organize an application with some platform-dependent code that must run on Windows, Mac OS, and Linux.

# 2
# Discovering QMake Secrets

This chapter addresses the issue of creating a cross-platform application that relies on platform-specific code. We will see the impact of qmake on the compilation of your project.

You will learn how to create a system monitoring application that retrieves the average CPU load and the memory used from Windows, Linux, and Mac. For this kind of OS dependent application, architecture is the key to keeping your application reliable and maintainable.

At the end of this chapter, you will be able to create and organize a cross-platform application that uses platform-specific code and displays Qt Charts widgets. Moreover, qmake will not be a mystery anymore.

This chapter covers the following topics:

- Platform-specific code organization
- Design patterns, strategy, and singleton
- Abstract class and pure virtual function
- Qt Charts
- The qmake tool

# Designing a cross-platform project

We want to display some visual gauges and chart widgets, so create a new **Qt widgets Application** called ch02-sysinfo. As already discussed in Chapter 1, *Get Your Qt Feet Wet*, Qt Creator will generate some files for us: main.cpp, MainWindow.h, MainWindow.cpp, and MainWindow.ui.

Before diving into the C++ code, we must think about the software's architecture. This project will handle multiple desktop platforms. Thanks to the combination of C++ and Qt, most of the source code will be common to all targets. However, to retrieve both the CPU and memory usage from the OS (operating system), we will use some platform-specific code.

To successfully achieve this task, we will use two design patterns:

- **Strategy pattern**: This is an interface that describes functionalities (for example, retrieve CPU usage), and specific behaviors (retrieve CPU usage on Windows/Mac OS/Linux) will be performed into subclasses that implement this interface.
- **Singleton pattern**: This pattern guarantees a single instance for a given class. This instance will be easily accessible with a unique access point.

As you can see in the following diagram, the class `SysInfo` is our interface with the strategy pattern, and is also a singleton. The specific behavior from the strategy pattern is performed in the classes `SysInfoWindowsImpl`, `SysInfoMacImpl`, and `SysInfoLinuxImpl`, subclassing `SysInfo`:

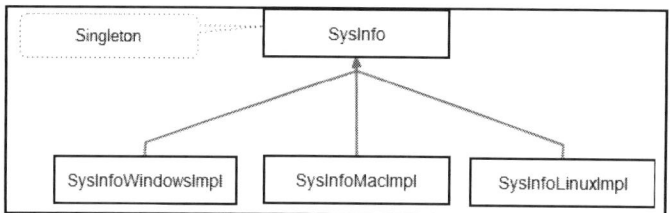

The UI part will only know and use the `SysInfo` class. The platform-specific implementation class is instantiated by the `SysInfo` class, and the caller doesn't need to know anything about the `SysInfo` child classes. As the `SysInfo` class is a singleton, access will be easier for all widgets.

Let's begin by creating the `SysInfo` class. On Qt Creator, you can create a new C++ class from the contextual menu, accessible with a right click on the project name in the hierarchy view. Then click on the **Add new** option, or from the menu, go to **File | New file or project | Files and classes**. Then perform the following steps:

1. Go to **C++ Class | Choose**.
2. Set the **Class** name field to `SysInfo`. As this class does not inherit from another class, we do not need to use the `Base` class field.
3. Click on **Next**, then **Finish** to generate an empty C++ class.

We will now specify our interface by adding three pure virtual functions:
`init()`, `cpuLoadAverage()`, and `memoryUsed()`:

```cpp
// In SysInfo.h
class SysInfo
{
public:
    SysInfo();
    virtual ~SysInfo();

    virtual void init() = 0;
    virtual double cpuLoadAverage() = 0;
    virtual double memoryUsed() = 0;
};

// In SysInfo.cpp
#include "SysInfo.h"

SysInfo::SysInfo()
{
}

SysInfo::~SysInfo()
{
}
```

Each of these functions has specific roles:

- `init()`: This function allows the derived class to perform any initialization process depending on the OS platform
- `cpuLoadAverage()`: This function calls some OS-specific code to retrieve the average CPU load and returns it as a percentage value
- `memoryUsed()`: This function calls some OS-specific code to retrieve the memory used and returns it as a percentage value

The `virtual` keyword indicates that the function can be overridden in a derived class. The `= 0` syntax means that this function is pure virtual, and must be overridden in any concrete derived class. Moreover, this makes `SysInfo` an abstract class that cannot be instantiated.

We also added an empty virtual destructor. This destructor must be virtual to ensure that any deletion of an instance of a derived class–from a base class pointer–will call the derived class destructor and not only the base class destructor.

Now that our `SysInfo` class is an abstract class and ready to be derived, we will describe three implementations: Windows, Mac OS, and Linux. You can also perform only one implementation if you would rather not use the other two. We will not make any judgment on this. The `SysInfo` class will be transformed into a singleton after adding the implementations.

# Adding the Windows implementation

Remember the UML diagram at the beginning of this chapter? The `SysInfoWindowsImpl` class is one of the classes derived from the `SysInfo` class. The main purpose of this class is to encapsulate the Windows-specific code to retrieve CPU and memory usage.

It's time to create the `SysInfoWindowsImpl` class. To do that, you need to perform the following steps:

1. Right click on the `ch02-sysinfo` project name in the hierarchy view.
2. Click on **Add New** | **C++ Class** | **Choose**.
3. Set the **Class name** field to `SysInfoWindowsImpl`.
4. Set the **Base class** field to **<Custom>** and write under the `SysInfo` class.
5. Click on **Next** then **Finish** to generate an empty C++ class.

These generated files are a good starting point, but we must tune them:

```
#include "SysInfo.h"

class SysInfoWindowsImpl : public SysInfo
{
public:
    SysInfoWindowsImpl();

    void init() override;
    double cpuLoadAverage() override;
    double memoryUsed() override;
};
```

The first thing to do is to add the `include` directive to our parent class, `SysInfo`. You can now override virtual functions defined in the base class.

**Qt Tip**

Put your cursor on a derived class name (after the keyword `class`) and press *Alt + Enter* (Windows / Linux) or *Command + Enter* (Mac) to automatically insert virtual functions of the base class.

The `override` keyword comes from C++11. It ensures that the function is declared as virtual in the base class. If the function signature marked as `override` does not match any parent class' `virtual` function, a compile-time error will be displayed.

Retrieving the current memory used on Windows is easy. We will begin with this feature in the `SysInfoWindowsImpl.cpp` file:

```
#include "SysInfoWindowsImpl.h"

#include <windows.h>

SysInfoWindowsImpl::SysInfoWindowsImpl() :
    SysInfo(),
{
}

double SysInfoWindowsImpl::memoryUsed()
{
    MEMORYSTATUSEX memoryStatus;
    memoryStatus.dwLength = sizeof(MEMORYSTATUSEX);
    GlobalMemoryStatusEx(&memoryStatus);
    qulonglong memoryPhysicalUsed =
        memoryStatus.ullTotalPhys - memoryStatus.ullAvailPhys;
    return (double)memoryPhysicalUsed /
        (double)memoryStatus.ullTotalPhys * 100.0;
}
```

Don't forget to include the `windows.h` file so that we can use the Windows API! Actually, this function retrieves the total and the available physical memory. A simple subtraction gives us the amount of memory used. As required by the base class `SysInfo`, this implementation will return the value as a `double` type; for example, the value `23.0` for 23% memory used on a Windows OS.

Retrieving the total memory used is a good start, but we cannot stop now. Our class must also retrieve the CPU load. The Windows API can be messy sometimes. To make our code more readable, we will create two private helper functions. Update your `SysInfoWindowsImpl.h` file to match the following snippet:

```
#include <QtGlobal>
#include <QVector>

#include "SysInfo.h"

typedef struct _FILETIME FILETIME;

class SysInfoWindowsImpl : public SysInfo
{
public:
    SysInfoWindowsImpl();

    void init() override;
    double cpuLoadAverage() override;
    double memoryUsed() override;

private:
    QVector<qulonglong> cpuRawData();
    qulonglong convertFileTime(const FILETIME& filetime) const;

private:
    QVector<qulonglong> mCpuLoadLastValues;
};
```

Let's analyze these changes:

- The `cpuRawData()` is the function that will perform the Windows API call to retrieve system timing information and return values in a generic format. We will retrieve and return three values: the amount of time that the system has spent in idle, in Kernel, and in User mode.
- The `convertFileTime()` function is our second helper. It will convert a Windows `FILETIME` struct syntax to a `qulonglong` type. The `qulonglong` type is a Qt `unsigned long long int`. This type is guaranteed by Qt to be 64-bit on all platforms. You can also use the typedef `quint64`.
- The `mCpuLoadLastValues` is a variable that will store system timing (idle, Kernel, and User) at a given moment.

- Don't forget to include the `<QtGlobal>` tag to use the `qulonglong` type, and the `<QVector>` tag to use the `QVector` class.
- The syntax `typedef struct _FILETIME FILETIME` is a kind of forward declaration for `FILENAME` syntax. As we only use a reference, we can avoid including the `<windows.h>` tag in our file `SysInfoWindowsImpl.h` and keep it in the CPP file.

We can now switch to the file `SysInfoWindowsImpl.cpp` and implement these functions to finish the CPU load average feature on Windows:

```
#include "SysInfoWindowsImpl.h"

#include <windows.h>

SysInfoWindowsImpl::SysInfoWindowsImpl() :
    SysInfo(),
    mCpuLoadLastValues()
{
}

void SysInfoWindowsImpl::init()
{
    mCpuLoadLastValues = cpuRawData();
}
```

When the `init()` function is called, we store the return value from the `cpuRawData()` function in our class variable `mCpuLoadLastValues`. It will be helpful for the `cpuLoadAverage()` function process.

You may be wondering why we do not perform this task in the initialization list of the constructor. That is because when you call a function from the initialization list, the object is not yet fully constructed! In some circumstances, it may be unsafe because the function can try to access a member variable that has not been constructed yet. However, in this `ch02-sysinfo` project, the `cpuRawData` function does not use any member variables, so you are safe, if you really want to do it. Add the `cpuRawData()` function to the `SysInfoWindowsImpl.cpp` file:

```
QVector<qulonglong> SysInfoWindowsImpl::cpuRawData()
{
    FILETIME idleTime;
    FILETIME kernelTime;
    FILETIME userTime;

    GetSystemTimes(&idleTime, &kernelTime, &userTime);
```

```
        QVector<qulonglong> rawData;

        rawData.append(convertFileTime(idleTime));
        rawData.append(convertFileTime(kernelTime));
        rawData.append(convertFileTime(userTime));
        return rawData;
    }
```

Here we are: the Windows API call to the `GetSystemTimes` function! This function will give us the amount of time that the system has spent idle, and in the Kernel and User modes. Before filling the `QVector` class, we convert each value with our helper `convertFileTime` described in the following code:

```
    qulonglong SysInfoWindowsImpl::convertFileTime(const FILETIME& filetime)
    const
    {
        ULARGE_INTEGER largeInteger;
        largeInteger.LowPart = filetime.dwLowDateTime;
        largeInteger.HighPart = filetime.dwHighDateTime;
        return largeInteger.QuadPart;
    }
```

The Windows structure `FILEFTIME` stores 64-bit information on two 32-bit parts (low and high). Our function `convertFileTime` uses the Windows structure `ULARGE_INTEGER` to correctly build a 64-bit value in a single part before returning it as a `qulonglong` type. Last but not least, the `cpuLoadAverage()` implementation:

```
    double SysInfoWindowsImpl::cpuLoadAverage()
    {
        QVector<qulonglong> firstSample = mCpuLoadLastValues;
        QVector<qulonglong> secondSample = cpuRawData();
        mCpuLoadLastValues = secondSample;

        qulonglong currentIdle = secondSample[0] - firstSample[0];
        qulonglong currentKernel = secondSample[1] - firstSample[1];
        qulonglong currentUser = secondSample[2] - firstSample[2];
        qulonglong currentSystem = currentKernel + currentUser;

        double percent = (currentSystem - currentIdle) * 100.0 /
            currentSystem ;
        return qBound(0.0, percent, 100.0);
    }
```

There are three important points to note here:

- Keep in mind that a sample is an absolute amount of time, so subtracting two different samples will give us instantaneous values that can be processed to get the current CPU load.
- The first sample comes from our member variable mCpuLoadLastValues, probed the first time by the init() function. The second one is retrieved when the cpuLoadAverage() function is called. After initializing the samples, the mCpuLoadLastValues variable can store the new sample that will be used for the next call.
- The percent equation can be a little tricky because the Kernel value retrieved from the Windows API also contains the idle value.

If you want to learn more about the Windows API, take a look at the MSDN documentation at https://msdn.microsoft.com/library.

The final step to finish the Windows implementation is to edit the file ch02-sysinfo.pro so that it resembles the following snippet:

```
QT       += core gui
CONFIG   += C++14

greaterThan(QT_MAJOR_VERSION, 4): QT += widgets

TARGET = ch02-sysinfo
TEMPLATE = app

SOURCES += main.cpp \
    MainWindow.cpp \
    SysInfo.cpp

HEADERS += MainWindow.h \
    SysInfo.h

windows {
    SOURCES += SysInfoWindowsImpl.cpp
    HEADERS += SysInfoWindowsImpl.h
}

FORMS     += MainWindow.ui
```

As we did in the `ch01-todo` project, we also use C++14 with the `ch02-sysinfo` project. The really new point here is that we removed the files `SysInfoWindowsImpl.cpp` and `SysInfoWindowsImpl.h` from the common `SOURCES` and `HEADERS` variables. Indeed, we added them into a `windows` platform scope. When building for other platforms, those files will not be processed by qmake. That is why we can safely include a specific header such as `windows.h` in the source file `SysInfoWindowsImpl.cpp` without harming the compilation on other platforms.

# Adding the Linux implementation

Let's make the Linux implementation of our `ch02-sysinfo` project. If you have already done the Windows implementation, it will be a piece of cake! If you have not, you should take a look at it. Some information and tips will not be repeated in this part, such as how to create a `SysInfo` implementation class, keyboard shortcuts, and details about the `SysInfo` interface.

Create a new C++ class called `SysInfoLinuxImpl` that inherits from the `SysInfo` class, and insert virtual functions from the base class:

```
#include "SysInfo.h"

class SysInfoLinuxImpl : public SysInfo
{
public:
    SysInfoLinuxImpl();

    void init() override;
    double cpuLoadAverage() override;
    double memoryUsed() override;
};
```

We will start by implementing the `memoryUsed()` function in the file `SysInfoLinuxImpl.cpp`:

```
#include "SysInfoLinuxImpl.h"

#include <sys/types.h>
#include <sys/sysinfo.h>

SysInfoLinuxImpl::SysInfoLinuxImpl() :
    SysInfo(),
{
}
```

```
double SysInfoLinuxImpl::memoryUsed()
{
    struct sysinfo memInfo;
    sysinfo(&memInfo);

    qulonglong totalMemory = memInfo.totalram;
    totalMemory += memInfo.totalswap;
    totalMemory *= memInfo.mem_unit;

    qulonglong totalMemoryUsed = memInfo.totalram - memInfo.freeram;
    totalMemoryUsed += memInfo.totalswap - memInfo.freeswap;
    totalMemoryUsed *= memInfo.mem_unit;

    double percent = (double)totalMemoryUsed /
        (double)totalMemory * 100.0;
    return qBound(0.0, percent, 100.0);
}
```

This function uses Linux-specific API. After adding the required includes, you can use the Linux `sysinfo()` function that returns information on the overall system statistics. With the total memory and the total memory used, we can easily return the `percent` value. Note that swap memory has been taken into account.

The CPU load feature is a little more complex than the memory feature. Indeed, we will retrieve from Linux the total amount of time the CPU spent performing different kinds of work. That is not exactly what we want. We must return the instantaneous CPU load. A common way to get it is to retrieve two sample values in a short period of time and use the difference to get the instantaneous CPU load:

```
#include <QtGlobal>
#include <QVector>

#include "SysInfo.h"

class SysInfoLinuxImpl : public SysInfo
{
public:
    SysInfoLinuxImpl();

    void init() override;
    double cpuLoadAverage() override;
    double memoryUsed() override;

private:
    QVector<qulonglong> cpuRawData();

private:
```

```
    QVector<qulonglong> mCpuLoadLastValues;
};
```

In this implementation, we will only add one helper function and one member variable:

- The `cpuRawData()` is a function that will perform the Linux API call to retrieve system timing information and return values in a `QVector` class of `qulonglong` type. We retrieve and return four values containing the time the CPU has spent on the following: normal processes in User mode, nice processes in User mode, processes in Kernel mode, and idle.
- The `mCpuLoadLastValues` is a variable that will store a sample of system timing at a given moment.

Let's go to the `SysInfoLinuxImpl.cpp` file to update it:

```
#include "SysInfoLinuxImpl.h"

#include <sys/types.h>
#include <sys/sysinfo.h>

#include <QFile>

SysInfoLinuxImpl::SysInfoLinuxImpl() :
    SysInfo(),
    mCpuLoadLastValues()
{
}

void SysInfoLinuxImpl::init()
{
    mCpuLoadLastValues = cpuRawData();
}
```

As discussed before, the `cpuLoadAverage` function will need two samples to be able to compute an instantaneous CPU load average. Calling the `init()` function allows us to set `mCpuLoadLastValues` for the first time:

```
QVector<qulonglong> SysInfoLinuxImpl::cpuRawData()
{
    QFile file("/proc/stat");
    file.open(QIODevice::ReadOnly);

    QByteArray line = file.readLine();
    file.close();
    qulonglong totalUser = 0, totalUserNice = 0,
        totalSystem = 0, totalIdle = 0;
```

```
std::sscanf(line.data(), "cpu %llu %llu %llu %llu",
    &totalUser, &totalUserNice, &totalSystem,
    &totalIdle);

QVector<qulonglong> rawData;
rawData.append(totalUser);
rawData.append(totalUserNice);
rawData.append(totalSystem);
rawData.append(totalIdle);

return rawData;
}
```

To retrieve the CPU raw information on a Linux system, we chose to parse information available in the /proc/stat file. All we need is available on the first line, so a single readLine() is enough. Even though Qt provides some useful features, sometimes the C standard library functions are simpler. This is the case here; we are using std::sscanf to extract variables from a string. Now let's look at the cpuLoadAvearge() body:

```
double SysInfoLinuxImpl::cpuLoadAverage()
{
    QVector<qulonglong> firstSample = mCpuLoadLastValues;
    QVector<qulonglong> secondSample = cpuRawData();
    mCpuLoadLastValues = secondSample;

    double overall = (secondSample[0] - firstSample[0])
        + (secondSample[1]   firstSample[1])
        + (secondSample[2] - firstSample[2]);

    double total = overall + (secondSample[3] - firstSample[3]);
    double percent = (overall / total) * 100.0;
    return qBound(0.0, percent, 100.0);
}
```

This is where the magic happens. In this last function, we put all the puzzle pieces together. This function uses two samples of the CPU raw data. The first sample comes from our member variable mCpuLoadLastValues, set the first time by the init() function. The second sample is requested by the cpuLoadAverage() function. Then the mCpuLoadLastValues variable will store the new sample that will be used as the first sample on the next cpuLoadAverage() function call.

The `percent` equation should be easy to understand:

- `overall` is equal to user + nice + kernel
- `total` is equal to overall + idle

> You can find more information about `/proc/stat` in the Linux Kernel documentation at `https://www.kernel.org/doc/Documentation/filesy stems/proc.txt`.

Like the other implementations, the last thing to do is to edit the `ch02-sysinfo.pro` file like this:

```
QT          += core gui
CONFIG      += C++14

greaterThan(QT_MAJOR_VERSION, 4): QT += widgets

TARGET = ch02-sysinfo
TEMPLATE = app

SOURCES += main.cpp \
    MainWindow.cpp \
    SysInfo.cpp \
    CpuWidget.cpp \
    MemoryWidget.cpp \
    SysInfoWidget.cpp

HEADERS += MainWindow.h \
    SysInfo.h \
    CpuWidget.h \
    MemoryWidget.h \
    SysInfoWidget.h

windows {
    SOURCES += SysInfoWindowsImpl.cpp
    HEADERS += SysInfoWindowsImpl.h
}

linux {
    SOURCES += SysInfoLinuxImpl.cpp
    HEADERS += SysInfoLinuxImpl.h
}

FORMS       += MainWindow.ui
```

With this Linux scope condition in the ch02-sysinfo.pro file, our Linux-specific files will not be processed by the qmake command on other platforms.

# Adding the Mac OS implementation

Let's take a look at the Mac implementation of the SysInfo class. Start by creating a new C++ class named SysInfoMacImpl that inherits from the SysInfo class. Override SysInfo virtual functions and you should have a SysInfoMacImpl.h file like this:

```
#include "SysInfo.h"

#include <QtGlobal>
#include <QVector>

class SysInfoMacImpl : public SysInfo
{
public:
    SysInfoMacImpl();

    void init() override;
    double cpuLoadAverage() override;
    double memoryUsed() override;
};
```

The first implementation we will do will be the memoryUsed() function, in the SysInfoMacImpl.cpp file:

```
#include <mach/vm_statistics.h>
#include <mach/mach_types.h>
#include <mach/mach_init.h>
#include <mach/mach_host.h>
#include <mach/vm_map.h>

SysInfoMacImpl::SysInfoMacImpl() :
    SysInfo()
{

}

double SysInfoMacImpl::memoryUsed()
{
    vm_size_t pageSize;
    vm_statistics64_data_t vmStats;

    mach_port_t machPort = mach_host_self();
```

```
        mach_msg_type_number_t count = sizeof(vmStats)
                                    / sizeof(natural_t);
        host_page_size(machPort, &pageSize);

        host_statistics64(machPort,
                        HOST_VM_INFO,
                        (host_info64_t)&vmStats,
                        &count);

        qulonglong freeMemory = (int64_t)vmStats.free_count
                            * (int64_t)pageSize;

        qulonglong totalMemoryUsed = ((int64_t)vmStats.active_count +
                            (int64_t)vmStats.inactive_count +
                            (int64_t)vmStats.wire_count)
                            * (int64_t)pageSize;

        qulonglong totalMemory = freeMemory + totalMemoryUsed;

        double percent = (double)totalMemoryUsed
                        / (double)totalMemory * 100.0;
        return qBound(0.0, percent, 100.0);
    }
```

We start by including the different headers for the Mac OS kernel. Then we initialize machPort with the call to the mach_host_self() function. A machPort is a kind of special connection to the kernel that enables us to request information about the system. We then proceed to prepare other variables so that we can retrieve virtual memory statistics with host_statistics64().

When the vmStats class is filled with the information needed, we extract the relevant data: the freeMemory and the totalMemoryUsed.

Note that Mac OS has a peculiar way of managing its memory: it keeps a lot of memory in cache, ready to be flushed when needed. This implies that our statistics can be misled; we see the memory as used, whereas it was simply kept "just in case".

The percentage calculation is straightforward; we still return a min/max clamped value to avoid any crazy values in our future graph.

Next comes the cpuLoadAverage() implementation. The pattern is always the same; take samples at regular intervals and compute the growth on this interval. Therefore, we have to store intermediate values to be able to calculate the difference with the next sample:

```
// In SysInfoMacImpl.h
#include "SysInfo.h"
```

```
#include <QtGlobal>
#include <QVector>

...

private:
    QVector<qulonglong> cpuRawData();

private:
    QVector<qulonglong> mCpuLoadLastValues;
};

// In SysInfoMacImpl.cpp
void SysInfoMacImpl::init()
{
    mCpuLoadLastValues =  cpuRawData();
}

QVector<qulonglong> SysInfoMacImpl::cpuRawData()
{
    host_cpu_load_info_data_t cpuInfo;
    mach_msg_type_number_t cpuCount = HOST_CPU_LOAD_INFO_COUNT;
    QVector<qulonglong> rawData;
    qulonglong totalUser = 0, totalUserNice = 0, totalSystem = 0,
totalIdle = 0;
    host_statistics(mach_host_self(),
                    HOST_CPU_LOAD_INFO,
                    (host_info_t)&cpuInfo,
                    &cpuCount);

    for(unsigned int i = 0; i < cpuCount; i++) {
        unsigned int maxTicks = CPU_STATE_MAX * i;
        totalUser += cpuInfo.cpu_ticks[maxTicks + CPU_STATE_USER];
        totalUserNice += cpuInfo.cpu_ticks[maxTicks
                                            + CPU_STATE_SYSTEM];
        totalSystem += cpuInfo.cpu_ticks[maxTicks
                                            + CPU_STATE_NICE];
        totalIdle += cpuInfo.cpu_ticks[maxTicks + CPU_STATE_IDLE];
    }

    rawData.append(totalUser);
    rawData.append(totalUserNice);
    rawData.append(totalSystem);
    rawData.append(totalIdle);
    return rawData;
}
```

As you can see, the pattern used is strictly equivalent to the Linux implementation. You can even copy-paste the body of the cpuLoadAverage() function from the SysInfoLinuxImpl.cpp file. They do exactly the same thing.

Now, the implementation is different for the cpuRawData() function. We load cpuInfo and cpuCount with host_statistics() and then we loop through each CPU to have the totalUser, totalUserNice, totalSystem, and totalIdle functions filled. Finally, we append all this data to the rawData object before returning it.

The very last part is to compile the SysInfoMacImpl class only on Mac OS. Modify the .pro file to have the following body:

```
...

linux {
    SOURCES += SysInfoLinuxImpl.cpp
    HEADERS += SysInfoLinuxImpl.h
}

macx {
    SOURCES += SysInfoMacImpl.cpp
    HEADERS += SysInfoMacImpl.h
}

FORMS     += MainWindow.ui
```

# Transforming SysInfo into a singleton

Promises are made to be kept: we will now transform the SysInfo class into a singleton. C++ offers many ways to implement the singleton design pattern. We will explain one of them here. Open the SysInfo.h file and make the following changes:

```
class SysInfo
{
public:
    static SysInfo& instance();
    virtual ~SysInfo();

    virtual void init() = 0;
    virtual double cpuLoadAverage() = 0;
    virtual double memoryUsed() - 0;

protected:
    explicit SysInfo();
```

```
private:
    SysInfo(const SysInfo& rhs);
    SysInfo& operator=(const SysInfo& rhs);
};
```

The singleton must guarantee that there will be only one instance of the class and that this instance will be easily accessible from a single access point.

So the first thing to do is to change the visibility of the constructor to `protected`. This way, only this class and the child classes will be allowed to call the constructor.

Since only one instance of the object must exist, allowing the copy constructor and the assignment operator is nonsense. One way to solve the problem is to make them `private`.

**C++ tip**

Since C++11, you can define a function as deleted with the syntax void `myFunction()` = `delete`. Any use of a deleted function will display a compile-time error. It's another way to prevent the use of the copy constructor and the assignment operator with a singleton.

The last change is the "unique access point" with a `static` function instance that will return a reference of the `SysInfo` class.

It is now time to commit singleton changes to the `SysInfo.cpp` file:

```cpp
#include <QtGlobal>

#ifdef Q_OS_WIN
    #include "SysInfoWindowsImpl.h"
#elif defined(Q_OS_MAC)
    #include "SysInfoMacImpl.h"
#elif defined(Q_OS_LINUX)
    #include "SysInfoLinuxImpl.h"
#endif

SysInfo& SysInfo::instance()
{
    #ifdef Q_OS_WIN
        static SysInfoWindowsImpl singleton;
    #elif defined(Q_OS_MAC)
        static SysInfoMacImpl singleton;
    #elif defined(Q_OS_LINUX)
        static SysInfoLinuxImpl singleton;
    #endif

    return singleton;
```

```
}

SysInfo::SysInfo()
{
}

SysInfo::~SysInfo()
{
}
```

Here you can see another Qt cross-OS trick. Qt provides some macro `Q_OS_WIN`, `Q_OS_LINUX`, or `Q_OS_MAC`. A Qt OS macro will be defined only on the corresponding OS. By combining these macros with a conditional preprocessor directive `#ifdef`, we can always include and instantiate the correct `SysInfo` implementation on all OSes.

Declaring the `singleton` variable as a static variable in the `instance()` function is a way to make a singleton in C++. We tend to prefer this version because you do not need to worry about the singleton memory management. The compiler will handle the instantiation the first time as well as the destruction. Moreover, since C++11 this method is thread safe.

# Exploring Qt Charts

The core part is ready. It's now time to create a UI for this project, and Qt Charts can help us with this task. Qt Charts is a module that provides a set of easy-to-use chart components, such as line chart, area chart, spline chart, pie chart, and so on.

Qt Charts was previously a commercial-only Qt module. Since Qt 5.7, the module is now included in Qt on GPLv3 license for open source users. If you are stuck on Qt 5.6, you can build the module by yourself from sources. More information can be found at `https://git hub.com/qtproject/qtcharts`.

The aim now is to create two Qt widgets, `CpuWidget` and `MemoryWidget`, to display nice Qt charts of the CPU and the memory used. These two widgets will share a lot of common tasks, so we will first create an abstract class, `SysInfoWidget`:

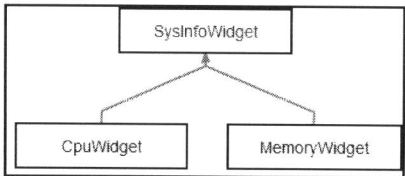

Then the two actual widgets will inherit from the `SysInfoWidget` class and perform their specific tasks.

Create a new C++ class called `SysInfoWidget` with `QWidget` as a base class. Some enhancements must be processed in the `SysInfoWidget.h` file:

```
#include <QWidget>
#include <QTimer>
#include <QtCharts/QChartView>

class SysInfoWidget : public QWidget
{
    Q_OBJECT
public:
    explicit SysInfoWidget(QWidget *parent = 0,
                           int startDelayMs = 500,
                           int updateSeriesDelayMs = 500);

protected:
    QtCharts::QChartView& chartView();

protected slots:
    virtual void updateSeries() = 0;

private:
    QTimer mRefreshTimer;
    QtCharts::QChartView mChartView;
};
```

The `QChartView` is the generic widget that can display many types of chart. This class will handle the layout and display the `QChartView`. A `QTimer` will call the slot function `updateSeries()` regularly. As you can see, this is a pure virtual slot. That is the reason why the `SysInfoWidget` class is abstract. The slot `updateSeries()` will be overridden by child classes to retrieve a system value and define how the chart should be drawn. Note that the parameters `startDelayMs` and `updateSeriesDelayMs` have default values that can be customized by the caller if required.

We can now proceed to the `SysInfoWidget.cpp` file to correctly prepare this `SysInfoWidget` class before creating the child widgets:

```
#include <QVBoxLayout>

using namespace QtCharts;

SysInfoWidget::SysInfoWidget(QWidget *parent,
                             int startDelayMs,
```

```
                                      int updateSeriesDelayMs) :
        QWidget(parent),
        mChartView(this)
{
        mRefreshTimer.setInterval(updateSeriesDelayMs);
        connect(&mRefreshTimer, &QTimer::timeout,
                this, &SysInfoWidget::updateSeries);
        QTimer::singleShot(startDelayMs,
            [this] { mRefreshTimer.start(); });

        mChartView.setRenderHint(QPainter::Antialiasing);
        mChartView.chart()->legend()->setVisible(false);

        QVBoxLayout* layout = new QVBoxLayout(this);
        layout->addWidget(&mChartView);
        setLayout(layout);
}

QChartView& SysInfoWidget::chartView()
{
        return mChartView;
}
```

All tasks in the `SysInfoWidget` constructor are common tasks required by the child widgets, `CpuWidget`, and `MemoryWidget`. The first step is the `mRefreshTimer` initialization to define the timer interval and the slot to call whenever a timeout signal is triggered. Then the static function `QTimer::singleShot()` will start the real timer after a delay defined by `startDelayMs`. Here again, Qt combined with lambda functions will give us a powerful code in just a few lines. The next part enables the antialiasing to smooth the chart drawing. We hide the chart's legend to get a minimalist display. The last part handles the layout to display the `QChartView` widget in our `SysInfoWidget` class.

# CpuWidget using QCharts

Now that the base class `SysInfoWidget` is ready, let's implement its first child class: `CpuWidget`. We will now use the Qt Charts API to display a good-looking widget. The average CPU load will be displayed in a pie graph with a hole in the center, like a partly eaten donut where the eaten part is the percentage of the CPU used. The first step is to add a new C++ class named `CpuWidget` and make it inherit `SysInfoWidget`:

```
#include "SysInfoWidget.h"

class CpuWidget : public SysInfoWidget
{
```

```
public:
    explicit CpuWidget(QWidget* parent = 0);
};
```

In the constructor, the only parameter needed is a `QWidget* ` parent. Since we provided default values for the `startDelayMs` and `updateSeriesDelayMs` variables in `SysInfoWidget` class, we get the best possible behavior; there is no need to remember it when subclassing `SysInfoWidget`, but it is still easy to override it if need be.

The next step is to override the `updateSeries()` function from the `SysInfoWidget` class and start using the Qt Charts API:

```
#include <QtCharts/QpieSeries>

#include "SysInfoWidget.h"

class CpuWidget : public SysInfoWidget
{
    Q_OBJECT
public:
    explicit CpuWidget(QWidget* parent = 0);

protected slots:
    void updateSeries() override;

private:
    QtCharts::QPieSeries* mSeries;
};
```

Since we overrode the `SysInfoWidget::updateSeries()` slot, we have to include the Q_OBJECT macro to allow `CPUWidget` to respond to the `SysInfoWidgetmRefreshTimer::timeout()` signal.

We include `QPieSeries` from the Qt Charts module so that we can create a member `QPieSeries*` named `mSeries`. The `QPieSeries` is a subclass of `QAbstractSeries`, which is the base class of all Qt Charts series (`QLineSeries`, `QAreaSeries`, `QPieSeries`, and so on). In Qt Charts, a `QAbstractSeries` subclass holds the data you want to display and defines how it should be drawn, but it does not define where the data should be displayed inside your layout.

We can now proceed to `CpuWidget.cpp` to investigate how we can tell Qt where the drawing takes place:

```
using namespace QtCharts;

CpuWidget::CpuWidget(QWidget* parent) :
    SysInfoWidget(parent),
    mSeries(new QPieSeries(this))
{
    mSeries->setHoleSize(0.35);
    mSeries->append("CPU Load", 30.0);
    mSeries->append("CPU Free", 70.0);

    QChart* chart = chartView().chart();
    chart->addSeries(mSeries);
    chart->setTitle("CPU average load");
}
```

All Qt Charts classes are defined in the `QtCharts` namespace. This is why we start with `using namespace QtCharts`.

First, we initialize `mSeries` in the constructor initializer list. We then proceed to configure it. We carve the donut with `mSeries->setHoleSize(0.35)` and we append two data sets to `mSeries`: a fake `CPU Load` and `Cpu Free`, which are expressed in percentages. The `mSeries` function is now ready to be linked to the class managing its drawing: `QChart`.

The `QChart` class is retrieved from the `SysInfoWidget::chartView()` function. When calling `chart->addSeries(mSeries)`, `chart` takes the ownership of `mSeries` and will draw it according to the series type–in our case, a `QPieSeries`. `QChart` is not a `QWidget`: it is a subclass of `QGraphicsWidget`. `QGraphicsWidget` can be described as a lighter `QWidget` with some differences (its coordinates and geometry are defined with `doubles` or `floats` instead of `integers`, a subset of `QWidget` attributes are supported: custom drag, drop framework, and so on). The `QGraphicsWidget` class is designed to be added in a `QGraphicsScene` class, a high-performance Qt component used to draw hundreds of items on screen at the same time.

In our `SysInfo` application, the `QChart` has to be displayed in a `QVBoxLayout` in `SysInfoWidget`. Here, the `QChartView` class comes in very handy. It lets us add `chart` in a `QWidget` layout.

Up to now, `QPieSeries` has seemed rather abstract. Let's add it to the `MainWindow` file to see how it looks:

```
// In MainWindow.h
```

```
#include "CpuWidget.h"

...

private:
    Ui::MainWindow *ui;
    CpuWidget mCpuWidget;
};

// In MainWindow.cpp
MainWindow::MainWindow(QWidget *parent) :
    QMainWindow(parent),
    ui(new Ui::MainWindow),
    mCpuWidget(this)
{
    ui->setupUi(this);
    SysInfo::instance().init();
    ui->centralWidget->layout()->addWidget(&mCpuWidget);
}
```

We simply declare `mCpuWidget` in the `MainWindow.h` file, initialize it, and add it to `MainWindow->centralWidget->layout`. If you now run the application, you should see something like this:

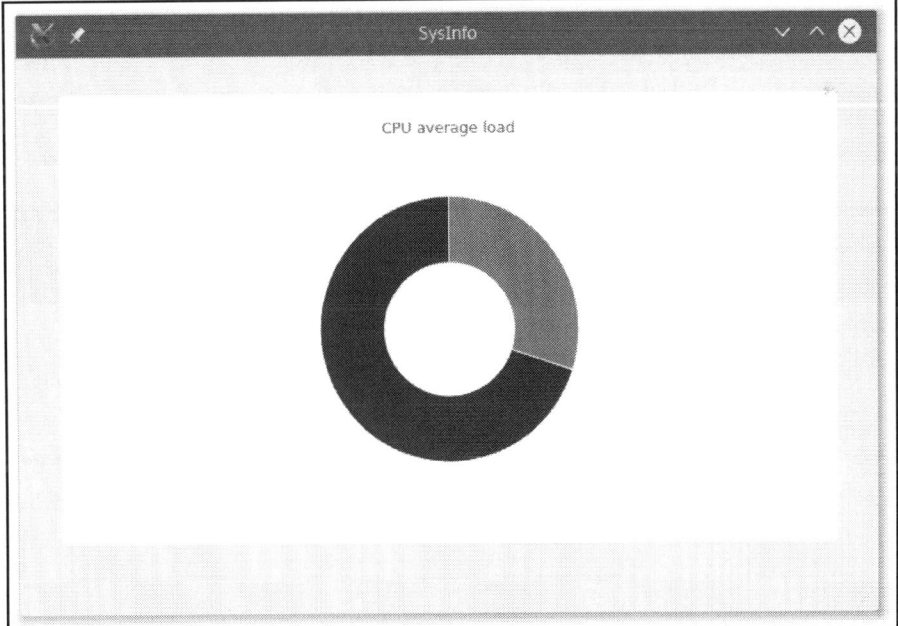

Even though it looks cool, this donut is a bit static and does not reflect the CPU usage. Thanks to the architecture we built with the `SysInfo` and `SysInfoWidget` classes, the remaining part will be implemented swiftly.

Switch back to the `CpuWidget.cpp` file and implement the `updateSeries()` function with the following body:

```
void CpuWidget::updateSeries()
{
    double cpuLoadAverage = SysInfo::instance().cpuLoadAverage();
    mSeries->clear();
    mSeries->append("Load", cpuLoadAverage);
    mSeries->append("Free", 100.0 - cpuLoadAverage);
}
```

First, we get a reference to our `SysInfo` singleton. We then retrieve the current average CPU load in the `cpuLoadAverage` variable. We have to feed this data to our `mSeries`. The `mSeries` object is a `QPieCharts`, which implies that we just want a snapshot of the current CPU average load. Past history is not meaningful with this kind of graph; that's why we clear the `mSeries` data with the `mSeries->clear()` syntax, and append the `cpuLoadAverage` variable and then the free part (`100.0 - cpuLoadAverage`).

The nice thing to note is that, in the `CpuWidget` class, we don't have to worry about refreshing. All the work is done in the `SysInfoWidget` subclass with all the whistles and bells of the `QTimer` class. In a `SysInfoWidget` subclass, we only have to concentrate on the valuable specific code: what data should be displayed and what kind of graph is used to display it. If you look at the whole `CpuWidget` class, it is very short. The next `SysInfoWidget` subclass, `MemoryWidget`, will also be very concise, as well as quick to implement.

# Memory using Qcharts

Our second `SysInfoWidget` is a `MemoryWidget` class. This widget will display a history of the data so that we can see how the memory consumption evolves over time. To display this data, we will use a `QLineSeries` class from the Qt Chart module. Create the `MemoryWidget` class and follow the same pattern we used for `CpuWidget`:

```
#include <QtCharts/QLineSeries>

#include "SysInfoWidget.h"

class MemoryWidget : public SysInfoWidget
```

```
{
    Q_OBJECT
public:
    explicit MemoryWidget(QWidget *parent = 0);

protected slots:
    void updateSeries() override;

private:
    QtCharts::QLineSeries* mSeries;
    qint64 mPointPositionX;
};
```

Instead of a being a QPieSeries*, mSeries is a type of QLineSeries* which will be linked to the chart object in a very similar fashion to MemoryWidget.cpp:

```
#include "MemoryWidget.h"
#include <QtCharts/QAreaSeries>

using namespace QtCharts;

const int CHART_X_RANGE_COUNT = 50;
const int CHART_X_RANGE_MAX = CHART_X_RANGE_COUNT - 1;

MemoryWidget::MemoryWidget(QWidget *parent) :
    SysInfoWidget(parent),
    mSeries(new QlineSeries(this)),
    mPointPositionX(0)
{
    QAreaSeries* areaSeries = new QAreaSeries(mSeries);

    QChart* chart = chartView().chart();
    chart->addSeries(areaSeries);
    chart->setTitle("Memory used");
    chart->createDefaultAxes();
    chart->axisX()->setVisible(false);
    chart->axisX()->setRange(0, CHART_X_RANGE_MAX);
    chart->axisY()->setRange(0, 100);
}

void MemoryWidget::updateSeries()
{
}
```

The `mSeries` data is, as usual, initialized in the initializer list. The `mPointPositionX` is an `unsigned long long` (using the Qt notation `qint64`) variable that will track the last X position of our data set. This huge value is used to make sure that `mPointPositionX` never overflows.

We then use an intermediate `areaSeries` that takes ownership of `mSeries` upon its initialization in `QAreaSeries* areaSeries = new QareaSeries(mSeries)`. `areaSeries` is then added to the `chart` object at `chart->addSeries(areaSeries)`. We do not want to display a single line in our `QChart`; instead we want to display an area that represents the used memory percentage. That is why we use an `areaSeries` type. Nonetheless, we will still update the `mSeries` data when adding new points to the dataset in the `updateSeries()` function. The `areaSeries` type will automatically handle them and deliver them to the `chart` object.

After `chart->addSeries(areaSeries)`, we configure the chart display:

- The `chart->createDefaultAxes()` function creates an X and Y axis based on the `areaSeries` type. If we used a 3D series, the `createDefaultAxes()` function would have added a Z axis.
- Hide the X axis tick values with `chart->axisX()->setVisible(false)` (intermediate values displayed at the bottom of the axis). In our `MemoryWidget` class, this information is not relevant.
- To define the number of points we want to display–the size of the display history–we call `chart->axisX()->setRange(0, CHART_X_RANGE_MAX)`. Here we use a constant to make it easier to modify this value afterwards. Seeing the value at the top of the file, we avoid having to skim through `MemoryWidget.cpp`, searching where this value is used to update it.
- `chart->axisY()->setRange(0, 100)` defines the maximum range of the Y axis, which is a percentage, based on the value returned by the `SysInfo::memoryUsed()` function.

The chart is now properly configured. We now have to feed it by filling the `updateSeries()` body:

```
void MemoryWidget::updateSeries()
{
    double memoryUsed = SysInfo::instance().memoryUsed();
    mSeries->append(mPointPositionX++, memoryUsed);
    if (mSeries->count() > CHART_X_RANGE_COUNT) {
        QChart* chart = chartView().chart();
        chart->scroll(chart->plotArea().width()
                    / CHART_X_RANGE_MAX, 0);
```

```
            mSeries->remove(0);
        }
    }
}
```

We first retrieve the latest memory percentage used and append it to `mSeries` at the *X* coordinate `mPointPositionX` (we post-increment it for the next `updateSeries()` call) and *Y* coordinate `memoryUsed`. As we want to keep a history of `mSeries`, `mSeries->clear()` is never called. However, what will happen when we add more than `CHART_X_RANGE_COUNT` points? The visible "window" on the chart is static and the points will be added outside. This means that we will see the memory usage only for the first `CHART_X_RANGE_MAX` points and then, nothing.

Fortunately, `QChart` provides a function to scroll inside the view to move the visible window. We start to handle this case only when the dataset is bigger than the visible window, meaning `if (mSeries->count() > CHART_X_RANGE_COUNT)`. We then remove the point at the index 0 with `mSeries->remove(0)` to ensure that the widget will not store an infinite dataset. A SysInfo application that monitors the memory usage and has itself a memory leak is a bit sad.

The syntax `chart->scroll(chart->plotArea().width() / CHART_X_RANGE_MAX, 0)` will then scroll to the latest point on the *X* axis and nothing on *Y*. The `chart->scroll(dx, dy)` expects coordinates expressed in our series coordinates. That is the reason why we have to retrieve the `char->plotArea()` divided by `CHART_X_RANGE_MAX`, the *X* axis unit.

We can now add the `MemoryWidget` class in `MainWindow`:

```cpp
// In MainWindow.h
#include "CpuWidget.h"
#include "MemoryWidget.h"

...

private:
    Ui::MainWindow *ui;
    CpuWidget mCpuWidget;
    MemoryWidget mMemoryWidget;
};

// In MainWindow.cpp
MainWindow::MainWindow(QWidget *parent) :
    QMainWindow(parent),
    ui(new Ui::MainWindow),
    mCpuWidget(this),
    mMemoryWidget(this)
```

```
{
    ui->setupUi(this);
    SysInfo::instance().init();
    ui->centralWidget->layout()->addWidget(&mCpuWidget);
    ui->centralWidget->layout()->addWidget(&mMemoryWidget);
}
```

Just as we did for `CPUWidget`, add a new member named `mMemoryWidget` to `MainWindow` and add it to the `centralWidget` layout with the `ui->centralWidget->layout()->addWidget(&mMemoryWidget)` syntax.

Compile, run the application, and wait a few seconds. You should see something close to this:

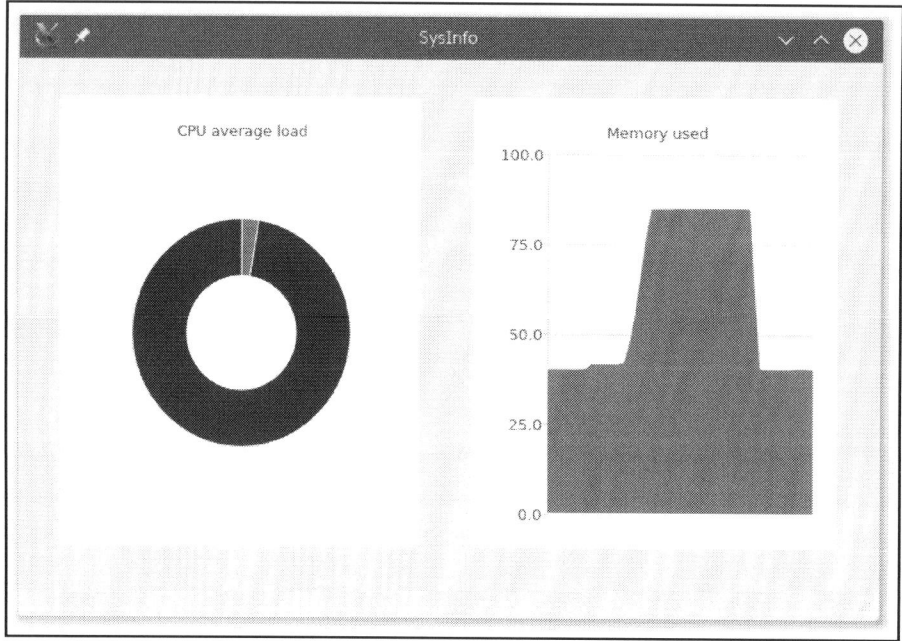

The `MemoryWidget` class works fine, but it looks a bit dull. We can customize it very easily with Qt. The goal is to have a bold line at the top of the memory area and a nice gradient from top to bottom. We just have to modify the `areaSeries` class in the `MemoryWidget.cpp` file:

```
#include <QtCharts/QAreaSeries>
#include <QLinearGradient>
#include <QPen>
```

```
#include "SysInfo.h"

using namespace QtCharts;

const int CHART_X_RANGE_MAX = 50;
const int COLOR_DARK_BLUE = 0x209fdf;
const int COLOR_LIGHT_BLUE = 0xbfdfef;
const int PEN_WIDTH = 3;

MemoryWidget::MemoryWidget(QWidget *parent) :
    SysInfoWidget(parent),
    mSeries(new QLineSeries(this))
{
    QPen pen(COLOR_DARK_BLUE);
    pen.setWidth(PEN_WIDTH);

    QLinearGradient gradient(QPointF(0, 0), QPointF(0, 1));
    gradient.setColorAt(1.0, COLOR_DARK_BLUE);
    gradient.setColorAt(0.0, COLOR_LIGHT_BLUE);
    gradient.setCoordinateMode(QGradient::ObjectBoundingMode);

    QAreaSeries* areaSeries = new QAreaSeries(mSeries);
    areaSeries->setPen(pen);
    areaSeries->setBrush(gradient);

    QChart* chart = chartView().chart();
    ...
}
```

The QPen pen function is a part of the QPainter API. It is the foundation on which Qt relies to do most of the GUI drawing. This includes the whole QWidget API (QLabel, QPushButton, QLayout, and so on). For the pen, we just have to specify its color and width, and then apply it to the areaSeries class with areaSeries->setPen(pen).

The principle is the same for the gradient. We define the starting point (QPointF(0, 0)) and the final point (QPointF(0, 1)) before specifying the color at each end of the vertical gradient. The QGradient::ObjectBoundingMode parameter defines how the start/final coordinates are mapped to the object. With the QAreaSeries class, we want the gradient coordinates to match the whole QareaSeries class. These coordinates are normalized coordinates, meaning that 0 is the start and 1 is the end of the shape:

- The [0.0] coordinates will point to the top left corner of the QAreaSeries class
- The [1.0] coordinates will point to the bottom left corner of the QAreaSeries class

A last build and run, and the `SysInfo` application will look like this:

A memory leak or starting a virtual machine is a great way to make your memory go crazy

The `SysInfo` application is now finished, and we even added some visual polish. You can explore the `QGradient` classes and the `QPainter` API if you want to further customize the widget to your taste.

# The .pro file in depth

When you click on the **Build** button, what exactly is Qt Creator doing? How does Qt handle the compilation of the different platforms with a single `.pro` file? What does the `Q_OBJECT` macro imply exactly? We will dig into each of these questions in the following sections. Our example case will be the `SysInfo` application we just completed, and we will study what Qt is doing under the hood.

We can start this study by digging into the `.pro` file. It is the main entry point in compiling any Qt project. Basically, a `.pro` file is a qmake project file describing the sources and headers used by the project. It is a platform-agnostic definition of a `Makefile`. First, we can cover the different qmake keywords used in the `ch02-sysinfo` application:

```
#-------------------------------------------------
#
# Project created by QtCreator 2016-03-24T16:25:01
#
#-------------------------------------------------
QT += core gui charts
CONFIG += C++14

greaterThan(QT_MAJOR_VERSION, 4): QT += widgets

TARGET = ch02-sysinfo
TEMPLATE = app
```

Each of these functions has specific roles:

- `#`: This is the prefix needed to comment on a line. Yes, we generated the project on 2016-03-24-crazy, huh?
- `QT`: This is a list of the Qt modules used in the project. In the platform-specific Makefile, each of the values will include the module headers and the corresponding library link.
- `CONFIG`: This is a list of configuration options for the project. Here, we configure the support of C++14 in the Makefile.
- `TARGET`: This is the name of the target output file.
- `TEMPLATE`: This is the project template used when generating the `Makefile.app` tells qmake to generate a Makefile targeted for a binary. If you are building a library, use the `lib` value.

In the `ch02-sysinfo` application, we started to use platform-specific compilation rules using the intuitive scope mechanism:

```
windows {
    SOURCES += SysInfoWindowsImpl.cpp
    HEADERS += SysInfoWindowsImpl.h
}
```

If you had to do this with a `Makefile`, you would probably lose some hair before doing it right (being bald is not an excuse). This syntax is simple yet powerful, and is also used for conditional statements. Let's say you wanted to build some files on debug only. You would have written the following:

```
windows {
    SOURCES += SysInfoWindowsImpl.cpp
    HEADERS += SysInfoWindowsImpl.h
    debug {
        SOURCES += DebugClass.cpp
        HEADERS += DebugClass.h
    }
}
```

Nesting the `debug` scope inside `windows` is the equivalent of `if (windows && debug)`. The scoping mechanism is even more flexible; you can have the OR Boolean operator condition with this syntax:

```
windows|unix {
    SOURCES += SysInfoWindowsAndLinux.cpp
}
```

You can even have else if/else statements:

```
windows|unix {
    SOURCES += SysInfoWindowsAndLinux.cpp
} else:macx {
    SOURCES += SysInfoMacImpl.cpp
} else {
    SOURCES += UltimateGenericSources.cpp
}
```

In this code snippet, we also see the use of the `+=` operator. The qmake tool provides a wide range of operators to modify the behavior of variables:

- `=`: This operator sets the variable to the value. The syntax `SOURCES = SysInfoWindowsImpl.cpp` would have assigned the single `SysInfoWindowsImpl.cpp` value to the `SOURCES` variable.
- `+=`: This operator adds the value to a list of values. This is what we commonly use in `HEADERS`, `SOURCES`, `CONFIG`, and so on.
- `-=`: This operator removes the value from the list. You can, for example, add a `DEFINE = DEBUG_FLAG` syntax in the common section and in a platform-specific scope (say a Windows release) remove it with the `DEFINE -= DEBUG_FLAG` syntax.

- *=: This operator adds the value to the list only if it is not already present. The DEFINE *= DEBUG_FLAG syntax adds the DEBUG_FLAG value only once.
- ~=: This operator replaces any values that match a regular expression with the specified value, DEFINE ~= s/DEBUG_FLAG/debug.

You can also define variables in the .pro file and reuse them in different places. We can simplify this with the use of the qmake message() function:

```
COMPILE_MSG = "Compiling on"

windows {
    SOURCES += SysInfoWindowsImpl.cpp
    HEADERS += SysInfoWindowsImpl.h
    message($$COMPILE_MSG windows)
}

linux {
    SOURCES += SysInfoLinuxImpl.cpp
    HEADERS += SysInfoLinuxImpl.h
    message($$COMPILE_MSG linux)
}

macx {
    SOURCES += SysInfoMacImpl.cpp
    HEADERS += SysInfoMacImpl.h
    message($$COMPILE_MSG mac)
}
```

If you build the project, you will see your platform-specific message each time you build the project in the **General Messages** tab (you can access this tab from **Window** | **Output Panes** | **General Messages**). Here, we defined a COMPILE_MSG variable and referenced it when calling message($$COMPILE_MSG windows). This offers interesting possibilities when you need to compile external libraries from your .pro file. You can then aggregate all the sources in a variable, combine it with the call to a specific compiler, and so on.

If your scope-specific statement is a single line, you can use the following syntax to describe it:

```
windows:message($$COMPILE_MSG windows)
```

Besides `message()`, there are a few other helpful functions:

- `error(string)`: This function displays the string and exits the compilation immediately.
- `exists(filename)`: This function tests the existence of the `filename`. qmake also provides the `!` operator, which means you can write `!exist(myfile) { ... }`.
- `include(filename)`: This function includes the content of another `.pro` file. It gives you the ability to slice your `.pro` files into more modular components. This will prove very useful when you have multiple `.pro` files for a single big project.

All the built-in functions are described at `http://doc.qt.io/qt-5/qmake -test-function-reference.html`.

# Under the hood of qmake

As we said earlier, qmake is the foundation of the Qt framework compilation system. In Qt Creator, when you click on the **Build** button, qmake is invoked. Let's study what qmake is exactly doing by calling it ourselves on the **CLI** (**Command Line Interface**).

Create a temporary directory where you will store the generated files. We are working on a Linux box, but this is transposable on any OS. We chose `/tmp/sysinfo`. Using the CLI, navigate to this new directory and execute the following command:

```
/path/to/qt/installation/5.7/gcc_64/bin/qmake -makefile -o Makefile
/path/to/sysinfoproject/ch02-sysinfo.pro
```

This command will execute qmake in the `-makefile` mode to generate a Makefile based on your `sysinfo.pro` file. If you skim through the Makefile content, you will see many things we covered earlier in the `.pro` section. The link to Qt modules, headers of different modules, inclusion of the headers and sources files of your project, and so on.

Now, let's build this Makefile by simply typing the `make` command.

This command will generate the binary `ch02-sysinfo` (based on the `TARGET` value of the `.pro` file). If you look at the list of files now present in `/tmp/sysinfo`:

```
$ ls -1
ch02-sysinfo
CpuWidget.o
main.o
MainWindow.o
Makefile
MemoryWidget.o
moc_CpuWidget.cpp
moc_CpuWidget.o
moc_MainWindow.cpp
moc_MainWindow.o
moc_MemoryWidget.cpp
moc_MemoryWidget.o
moc_SysInfoWidget.cpp
moc_SysInfoWidget.o
SysInfoLinuxImpl.o
SysInfo.o
SysInfoWidget.o
ui_MainWindow.h
```

Now this is very interesting, we find all our sources compiled in the usual `.o` extension (`SysInfo.o`, `SysInfoWidget.o`, and so on) but there are also a lot of other files prefixed with `moc_`. Here lies another keystone of the Qt framework: the Meta Object Compiler.

Every time you use the signal/slot system, you have to include the macro `Q_OBJECT` in your header. Each time you emit a signal or receive one in a slot and you did not write any specific code to handle it, Qt took care of it. This is done by generating an intermediate implementation of your class (the `moc_*.cpp` file) containing everything Qt needs to properly handle your signals and slots.

A picture is worth a thousand words. Here is the complete compilation pipeline for a standard qmake project:

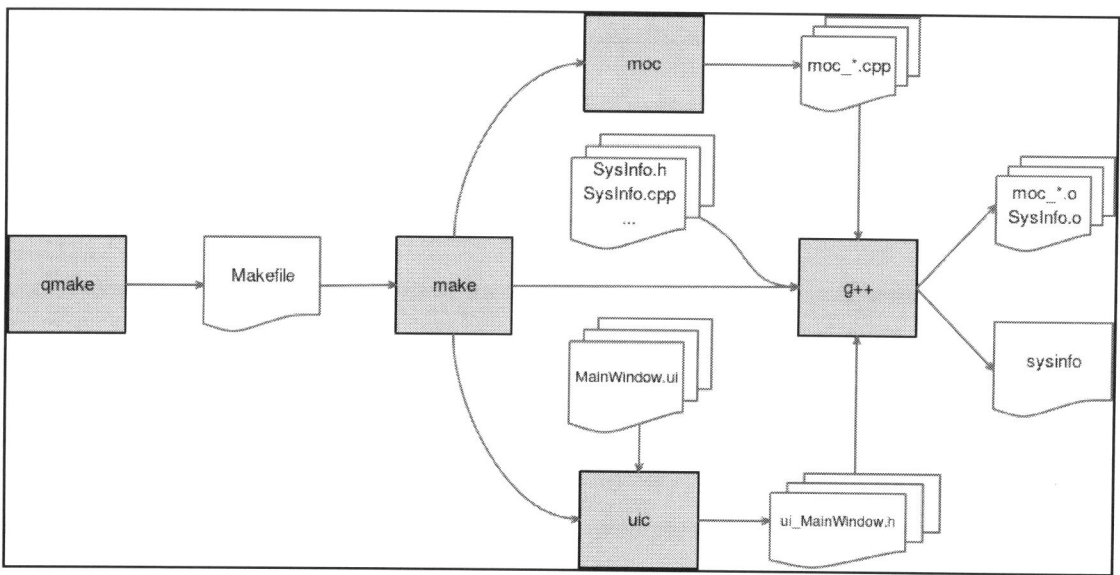

The blue boxes refer to commands and the wavy boxes are documents (sources or final binary). Let's walk through the steps:

1. The qmake command is executed with the project .pro file. It generates a Makefile based on the project file.

2. The make command is executed, which will call other commands to generate intermediate files.

3. The uic command stands for User Interface Compiler. It takes all the .ui files (which are basically an XML description of your interface) and generates the corresponding ui_*.h header that you include in your own .cpp (in our ch02-sysinfo project, it is in MainWindow.cpp).

4. The moc command takes every class containing the Q_OBJECT macro (paired with the superclass QObject) and generates the intermediate moc_*.cpp files, which include everything needed to make the signal/slot framework work.

5. The g++ command is executed, compiling all your sources' files and intermediate moc files into .o files before finally linking everything in the binary ch02-sysinfo.

Note that if you add a Q_OBJECT macro after the creation of a class, sometimes the compiler will complain about your signals and slots. To fix this, simply run the qmake command from **Build | Run qmake**.
You can now see that this stems from the fact that the Makefile has to be regenerated to include the generation of the new intermediate moc file.

Generally, source code generation is regarded as bad practice in the developer community. Qt has been criticized on this topic for a long time. We always fear that the machines does some kind of voodoo behind our back. Unfortunately, C++ does not offer any practical way of doing code introspection (namely reflection), and the signal and slots mechanism needs some kind of metadata about your class to resolve your signals and slots. This could have been done partly with the C++ template system, but this solution seemed to Qt to be much less readable, portable, usable, and robust. You also need an excellent compiler support for templates. This cannot be assumed in the wild world of C++ compilers.

The moc system is now fully mature. There are some very specific edge cases where it could bring trouble (some have reported problems in very specific situations with Visual Studio), but even so, we think that the gain of this feature largely outweighs the possibly encountered issues. The signal/slot system is a marvel to work with, and if you look at the beginnings of Qt, the system has been present from the very first releases. Adding the functor notation in Qt 5 (which gives a compile time check of the validity of your connect()) combined with C++11 lambas makes it a real delight.

# Beneath Q_OBJECT and signals/slots

The Qt building system should be clearer now. Still, the Q_OBJECT macro and the signal/slot/emit keywords are still black boxes. Let's dive into Q_OBJECT.

The truth lies in the source code; Q_OBJECT is defined in the file qobjectdefs.h (in Qt 5.7):

```
#define Q_OBJECT \
public: \
    // skipped details
    static const QMetaObject staticMetaObject; \
    virtual const QMetaObject *metaObject() const; \
    virtual void *qt_metacast(const char *); \
    virtual int qt_metacall(QMetaObject::Call, int, void **); \
    QT_TR_FUNCTIONS \
private: \
    // skipped details
qt_static_metacall(QObject *, QMetaObject::Call, int, void **);
```

This macro defines some static functions and a `static QMetaObject`. The body of these static functions is implemented in the generated `moc` file. We will not drown you in the gory details of the `QMetaObject` class. The role of this class is to store all the metainformation for the `QObject` subclass. It also maintains a correspondence table between the signals and slots of your class, and to the signals and slots of any connected class. Each signal and each slot is assigned with a unique index:

- The `metaObject()` function returns the `&staticMetaObject` for a normal Qt class and a `dynamicMetaObject` when working with QML objects.
- The `qt_metacast()` function performs a dynamic cast using the name of the class. This function is required because Qt does not rely on standard C++ **RTTI (Runtime Type Information)** to retrieve meta data about an object or a class.
- The `qt_metacall()` directly calls an internal signal or slot by its index. Because an index is used rather than a pointer, there is no pointer dereferencing, and the generated switch case can be heavily optimized by the compiler (the compiler can directly include the `jump` instruction to the specific case very early on, avoiding a lot of branch evaluation). Thus, the execution of the signal/slot mechanism is quite fast.

Qt also adds non-standard C++ keywords to manage the signal/slot mechanism, namely `signals`, `slots`, and `emit`. Let's see what is behind each one and see how everything fits inside a `connect()` function.

The `slots` and `signals` keywords are also defined in `qobjectdefs.h`:

```
#    define slots
#    define signals public
```

That is right: `slots` points to nothing and the `signals` keyword is just a placeholder for the `public` keyword. All your `signals`/`slots` are just... functions. The `signals` keyword is forced to be `public` to make sure that your signal functions are visible outside of your class (what is the point of a `private signal` anyway?). The Qt magic is simply the ability to emit a `signal` keyword to any connected `slot` keyword without knowing the detail of the class implementing this `slot`. Everything is done through the `QMetaObject` class implementation in the `moc` file. When a `signal` keyword is emitted, the function `QMetaObject::activate()` is called with the changed value and the signals index.

The last definition to study is `emit`:

```
# define emit
```

So many definitions of nothing, it is almost absurd! The `emit` keyword is completely useless from a code perspective; `moc` plainly ignores it and nothing particular happens with it afterwards. It is merely a hint for the developer to notice he is working with signal/slots rather than plain functions.

To trigger a `slot`, you must connect your `signal` keyword to it using the `QObject::connect()` function. This function creates a new `Connection` instance that is defined in `qobject_p.h`:

```
struct Connection
    {
        QObject *sender;
        QObject *receiver;
        union {
            StaticMetaCallFunction callFunction;
            QtPrivate::QSlotObjectBase *slotObj;
        };
        // The next pointer for the singly-linked ConnectionList
        Connection *nextConnectionList;
        //senders linked list
        Connection *next;
        Connection **prev;
        ...
    };
```

The `Connection` instance stores a pointer to the signal emitter class (`sender`), the slot receiver class (`receiver`), and the indexes of the connected `signal` and `slot` keywords. When a signal is emitted, every connected slot must be called. To be able to do this, every `QObject` has a linked list of `Connection` instances for each of its `signal`, and the same linked list of `Connection` for each of its `slot` keywords.

This pair of linked lists allows Qt to properly walk through each dependent `slot`/`signal` couple to trigger the right functions using the indexes. The same reasoning is used to handle the `receiver` destruction: Qt walks through the double linked list and removes the object from where it was connected.

This walk happens in the famous UI thread, where the whole message loop is processed and every connected signal/slot is triggered according to the possible events (mouse, keyboard, network, and so on). Because the `QThread` class inherits the `QObject`, any `QThread` can use the signal/slot mechanism. Additionally, the `signals` keyword can be posted to other threads where they will be processed in the receiving threads' event loop.

# Summary

In this chapter, we created a cross-platform `SysInfo` application. We covered the singleton and the strategy pattern to have a neat code organization with platform-specific code. You learned to use the Qt Charts module to display system information in real time. Finally, we took a deep dive into the `qmake` command to see how Qt implements the signal/slot mechanism, and to see what is hidden behind Qt-specific keywords (`emit`, `signals`, and `slots`).

By now, you should have a clear picture of how Qt works and how you can tackle a cross-platform application. In the next chapter, we will look at how you can split a bigger project in order to keep your sanity as a maintainer. We will study a fundamental pattern in Qt–the Model/View–and discover how to use a database with Qt.

# 3
# Dividing Your Project and Ruling Your Code

The last chapter delved into qmake to study what lies beneath the signal/slot system and covered a reasonable approach to implementing platform-specific code. This chapter wants to show you how a project can be properly divided to enjoy the maximum leverage from the Qt framework.

To do this, you will create a gallery application that handles albums and pictures. You will be able to create, read, update and delete any album and display the pictures in a grid of thumbnails or in full resolution. Everything will be persisted in a SQL database.

This chapter lays the foundations of the gallery by creating a core library that will be used in the following two chapters: Chapter 4, *Conquering the Desktop UI*, and Chapter 5, *Dominating the Mobile UI*.

This chapter covers the following topics:

- Application/library project separation
- Database interaction with Qt
- Smart pointers with C++14
- Model/View architecture in Qt with an implementation of the model

# Designing a maintainable project

The first step in designing a maintainable project is to properly split it in clearly defined modules. A common approach is to separate the engine from the user interface. This separation forces you to reduce coupling between the different parts of your code and make it more modular.

This is exactly the approach we will take with the `gallery` application. The project will be divided into three sub-projects:

The sub-projects are as follows:

- **gallery-core**: This is a library containing the core of the application logic: the data classes (or business classes), persistent storage (in SQL), and the model that makes the storage available to the UI through a single entry point.
- **gallery-desktop**: This is a Qt widgets application that will depend on the `gallery-core` library to retrieve data and display it to the user. This project will be covered in `Chapter 4`, *Conquering the Desktop UI*.
- **gallery-mobile**: This is a QML application targeted at mobile platforms (Android and iOS). It will also rely on `gallery-core`. This project will be covered in `Chapter 5`, *Dominating the Mobile UI*.

As you can see, each layer has a single responsibility. This principle is applied to both the project structure and the code organization. Throughout these three projects, we will endeavor to live up to the motto of the chapter: "Divide your project and rule your code".

To separate your Qt project this way, we will create a different kind of project, a **Subdirs** project:

1. Click on **File | New File or Project**.
2. In the **Projects** types, select **Other Project | Subdirs Project | Choose**.

3. Name it `ch03-gallery-core` and then click on **Choose**.

4. Select your latest Qt Desktop Kit, and then click on **Next** | **Finish & Add Subproject**.

Here, Qt Creator created the parent project, `ch03-gallery-core`, which will host our three sub-projects (`gallery-core`, `gallery-desktop`, and `gallery-mobile`). The parent project has neither code nor a compilation unit in itself, it is simply a convenient way to group multiple `.pro` projects and express the dependencies between them.

The next step is to create the first `subdir` project, which Qt Creator proposed immediately when you clicked on **Finish & Add Subproject**. We will start with `gallery-core`:

1. Select **Library** in the **Projects** tab.

2. Select **C++ Library**.

3. Choose the **Shared Library** type, and name it `gallery-core`, and click on **Next**.

4. Select the modules, **QtCore**, and **QtSql**, and then click on **Next**.

5. Type **Album** in the **Class name** field, and click on **Next**. Qt Creator will generate the basic skeleton of a library with this class as an example.

6. Check that the project is properly added as a sub-project of `ch03-gallery-core.pro` and click on **Finish**.

Before delving into `gallery-core` code, let's study what Qt Creator just made for us. Open the parent `.pro` file, `ch03-gallery-core.pro`:

```
TEMPLATE = subdirs

SUBDIRS += \
    gallery-core
```

Until now, we used the `TEMPLATE = app` syntax in our `.pro` files. The `subdirs` project template indicates to Qt that it should search for sub-projects to compile. When we added the `gallery-core` project to `ch03-gallery-core.pro`, Qt Creator added it to the `SUBDIRS` variable. As you can see, `SUBDIRS` is a list, so you can add as many sub-projects as you want.

When compiling `ch03-gallery-core.pro`, Qt will scan each `SUBDIRS` value to compile them. We can now switch to `gallery-core.pro`:

```
QT       += sql
QT       -= gui

TARGET = gallery-core
TEMPLATE = lib

DEFINES += GALLERYCORE_LIBRARY
SOURCES += Album.cpp
HEADERS += Album.h\
        gallery-core_global.h

unix {
    target.path = /usr/lib
    INSTALLS += target
}
```

Let's see how this works:

- The `QT` has appended the `sql` module and removed the `gui` module. By default, **QtGui** is always included and has to be removed explicitly.
- The `TEMPLATE` value is different, again. We use `lib` to tell qmake to generate a Makefile that will output a shared library named `gallery-core` (as specified by the `TARGET` variable).
- The `DEFINES += GALLERY_CORE_LIBRARY` syntax is a compilation flag that lets the compiler know when it should import or export library symbols. We will come back soon to this notion.
- The `HEADERS` contains our first class `Album.h`, but also another generated header: `gallery-core_global.h`. This file is syntactic sugar provided by Qt to ease the pain of a cross-platform library.
- The `unix { ... }` scope specifies the installation destination of the library. This platform scope is generated because we created the project on Linux. By default it will try to install the library in the system library path (`/usr/lib`).

Please remove the `unix` scope altogether, we don't need to make the library available system-wide.

To have a better understanding of the cross-platform shared object issue, you can open `gallery-core_global.h`:

```
#include <QtCore/qglobal.h>

#if defined(GALLERYCORE_LIBRARY)
#   define GALLERYCORESHARED_EXPORT Q_DECL_EXPORT
#else
#   define GALLERYCORESHARED_EXPORT Q_DECL_IMPORT
#endif
```

We encounter again the GALLERYCORE_LIBRARY defined in `gallery-core.pro` file. Qt Creator generated a useful piece of code for us: the cross-platform way to handle symbol visibility in a shared library.

When your application links to a shared library, symbol functions, variables, or classes must be marked in a special way to be visible by the application using the shared library. The default visibility of a symbol depends on the platform. Some platforms will hide symbols by default, other platforms will make them public. Of course, each platform and compiler has its own macros to express this public/private notion.

To obviate the whole `#ifdef windows #else` boilerplate code, Qt provides a Q_DECL_EXPORT (if we are compiling the library) and Q_DECL_IMPORT (if we are compiling your application using the shared library). Thus, throughout the symbols you want to mark as public, you just have to use the GALLERYCORESHARED_EXPORT macro.

An example is available in the `Album.h` file:

```
#ifndef ALBUM_H
#define ALBUM_H

#include "gallery-core_global.h"

class GALLERYCORESHARED_EXPORT Album
{

public:
    Album();
};

#endif // ALBUM_H
```

You include the proper `gallery-core_global.h` file to have access to the macro and you use it just after the `class` keyword. It does not pollute your code too much and is still cross-platform.

 Another possibility is to make a **Statically Linked Library**. This path is interesting if you want fewer dependencies to handle (a single binary is always easier to deploy). There are several downsides:

- Increased compilation time: each time you modify the library, the application will have to be recompiled as well.
- Tighter coupling, multiple applications cannot link to your library. Each one of them must embed it.

# Defining data classes

We are building our gallery from the ground up. We will start with the implementation of our data classes to be able to properly write the database layer. The application aims to organize pictures into albums. Hence, the two obvious classes are `Album` and `Picture`. In our example, an album simply has a name. A `Picture` class must belong to an `Album` class and has a file path (the path on your filesystem where the original file is located).

The `Album` class has already been created on project creation. Open the `Album.h` file and update it to include the following implementation:

```
#include <QString>

#include "gallery-core_global.h"

class GALLERYCORESHARED_EXPORT Album
{
public:
    explicit Album(const QString& name = "");

    int id() const;
    void setId(int id);
    QString name() const;
    void setName(const QString& name);

private:
    int mId;
    QString mName;
};
```

As you can see, the `Album` class contains only a `mId` variable (the database ID) and a `mName` variable. In a typical **OOP (Object Oriented Paradigm)** fashion, the `Album` class would have had a `QVector<Picture>mPictures` field. We did not do it on purpose. By decoupling these two objects, we will have more flexibility when we want to load an album without pulling the potential thousands of associated pictures. The other problem in having `mPictures` in the `Album` class is that the developer (you or anybody else) using this code will ask himself: when is `mPictures` loaded? Should I do a partial load of the `Album` and have an incomplete `Album` or should I always load `Album` with every picture in it?

By completely removing the field, the question ceases to exist, and the code is simpler to grasp. The developer knows intuitively that he will have to explicitly load the pictures if he want them; otherwise, he can continue with this simple `Album` class.

The getters and setters are obvious enough; we will let you implement them without showing them to you. We will only take a look at the `Album` class' constructor in `Album.cpp`:

```
Album::Album(const QString& name) :
    mId(-1),
    mName(name)
{
}
```

The `mId` variable is initialized to –1 to be sure that, by default, an invalid id is used, and the `mName` variable is assigned a `name` value.

We can now proceed to the `Picture` class. Create a new C++ class named `Picture` and open `Picture.h` to modify it like so:

```
#include <QUrl>
#include <QString>

#include "gallery-core_global.h"

class GALLERYCORESHARED_EXPORT Picture
{
public:
    Picture(const QString& filePath = "");
    Picture(const QUrl& fileUrl);

    int id() const;
    void setId(int id);

    int albumId() const;
    void setAlbumId(int albumId);
```

```
    QUrl fileUrl() const;
    void setFileUrl(const QUrl& fileUrl);
private:
    int mId;
    int mAlbumId;
    QUrl mFileUrl;
};
```

Do not forget to add the GALLERYCORESHARED_EXPORT macro right before the `class` keyword to export the class from the library. As a data structure, `Picture` has a `mId` variable, belongs to a `mAlbumId` variable, and has a `mUrl` value. We use the `QUrl` type to make path manipulation easier to use depending on the platform (desktop or mobile).

Let's take a look at `Picture.cpp`:

```
#include "Picture.h"
Picture::Picture(const QString& filePath) :
    Picture(QUrl::fromLocalFile(filePath))
{
}

Picture::Picture(const QUrl& fileUrl) :
    mId(-1),
    mAlbumId(-1),
    mFileUrl(fileUrl)
{
}

QUrl Picture::fileUrl() const
{
    return mFileUrl;
}

void Picture::setFileUrl(const QUrl& fileUrl)
{
    mFileUrl = fileUrl;
}
```

In the first constructor, the static function, `QUrl::fromLocalFile`, is called to provide a `QUrl` object to the other constructor, which takes a `QUrl` parameter.

The ability to call other constructors is a nice addition in C++11.

# Storing your data in a database

Now that the data classes are ready, we can proceed to implement the database layer. Qt provides a ready-to-use `sql` module. Various databases are supported in Qt using SQL database drivers. In `gallery-desktop`, we will use the `SQLITE3` driver, which is included in the `sql` module and perfectly fits the use case:

- **A very simple database schema**: No need for complex queries
- **Very few or no concurrent transactions**: No need for a complex transaction model
- **A single-purpose database**: No need to spawn a system service, the database is stored in a single file and does not need to be accessed by multiple applications

The database will be accessed from multiple locations; we need to have a single entry point for it. Create a new C++ class named `DatabaseManager` and modify `DatabaseManager.h` to look like this:

```
#include <QString>

class QSqlDatabase;

const QString DATABASE_FILENAME = "gallery.db";

class DatabaseManager
{
public:
    static DatabaseManager& instance();
    ~DatabaseManager();

protected:
    DatabaseManager(const QString& path = DATABASE_FILENAME);
    DatabaseManager& operator=(const DatabaseManager& rhs);

private:
    QSqlDatabase* mDatabase;
};
```

The first thing to notice is that we implement the singleton pattern in the `DatabaseManager` class, like we did in the *Transforming SysInfo in a singleton* section from `Chapter 2`, *Discovering QMake Secrets*. The `DatabaseManager` class will open the connection in the `mDatabase` field and lend it to other possible classes.

Also, QSqlDatabase is forward-declared and used as a pointer for the mDatabase field. We could have included the QSqlDatabase header, but we would have had a non-desired side-effect: every file, which includes DatabaseManager, must also include QSqlDatabase. Thus, if we ever have some transitive inclusion in our application (which links to the gallery-core library), the application is forced to enable the sql module. As a consequence, the storage layer leaks through the library. The application should not have any knowledge about the storage layer implementation. For all the application cares, it could be in SQL, XML, or anything else; the library is a black box that should honor the contract and persist the data.

Let's switch to DatabaseManager.cpp and open the database connection:

```cpp
#include "DatabaseManager.h"

#include <QSqlDatabase>

DatabaseManager& DatabaseManager::instance()
{
    static DatabaseManager singleton;
    return singleton;
}

DatabaseManager::DatabaseManager(const QString& path) :
    mDatabase(new QSqlDatabase(QSqlDatabase::addDatabase("QSQLITE")))
{
    mDatabase->setDatabaseName(path);
    mDatabase->open();
}

DatabaseManager::~DatabaseManager()
{
    mDatabase->close();
    delete mDatabase;
}
```

The correct database driver is selected on the mDatabase field initialization with the QSqlDatabase::addDatabase("QSQLITE") function call. The following steps are just a matter of configuring the database name (which is incidentally the file path in SQLITE3) and opening the connection with the mDatabase->open() function. In the DatabaseManager destructor, the connection is closed and the mDatabase pointer is properly deleted.

The database link is now opened; all we have to do is to execute our Album and Picture queries. Implementing the **CRUD (Create/Read/Update/Delete)** for both our data classes in DatabaseManager would quickly push DatabaseManager.cpp to be several hundreds of lines long. Add a few more tables and you can already see what a monster DatabaseManager would turn into.

For this reason, each of our data classes will have a dedicated database class, responsible for all the database CRUD operations. We will start with the Album class; create a new C++ class named AlbumDao (data access object) and update AlbumDao.h:

```cpp
class QSqlDatabase;

class AlbumDao
{
public:
    AlbumDao(QSqlDatabase& database);
    void init() const;

private:
    QSqlDatabase& mDatabase;
};
```

The AlbumDao class's constructor takes a QSqlDatabase& parameter. This parameter is the database connection that will be used for all the SQL queries done by the AlbumDao class. The init() function aims to create the albums table and should be called when mDatabase is opened.

Let's see the implementation of AlbumDao.cpp:

```cpp
#include <QSqlDatabase>
#include <QSqlQuery>

#include "DatabaseManager.h"

AlbumDao::AlbumDao(QSqlDatabase& database) :
    mDatabase(database)
{
}

void AlbumDao::init() const
{
    if (!mDatabase.tables().contains("albums")) {
        QSqlQuery query(mDatabase);
        query.exec("CREATE TABLE albums (id INTEGER PRIMARY KEY
AUTOINCREMENT, name TEXT)");
    }
```

```
    }
```

As usual, the `mDatabase` field is initialized with the database parameter. In the `init()` function, we can see a real SQL request in action. If the table `albums` class does not exist, a `QSqlQuery` query is created that will use the `mDatabase` connection to be executed. If you omit `mDatabase`, the query will use a default anonymous connection. The `query.exec()` function is the simplest manner of executing a query: you simply pass the `QString` type of your query and it's done. Here we create the `albums` table with the fields matching the data class `Album` (`id` and `name`).

The `QSqlQuery::exec()` function returns a `bool` value that indicates if the request has been successful. In your production code, always check this value. You can further investigate the error with `QSqlQuery::lastError()`. An example is available in the source code of the chapter in `DatabaseManager::debugQuery()`.

The skeleton of `AlbumDao` class is done. The next step is to link it to the `DatabaseManager` class. Update the `DatabaseManager` class like so:

```
// In DatabaseManager.h
#include "AlbumDao.h"

...

private:
    QSqlDatabase* mDatabase;

public:
    const AlbumDao albumDao;
};

// In DatabaseManager.cpp
DatabaseManager::DatabaseManager(const QString& path) :
    mDatabase(new QSqlDatabase(QSqlDatabase::addDatabase("QSQLITE"))),
    albumDao(*mDatabase)
{
    mDatabase->setDatabaseName(path);
    mDatabase->open();

    albumDao.init();
}
```

The `albumDao` field is declared as a `public const AlbumDao` in the `DatabaseManager.h` file. This needs some explanation:

- The `public` visibility is to give access to `DatabaseManager` clients to the `albumDao` field. The API becomes intuitive enough; if you want to make a database operation on an `album`, just call `DatabaseManager::instance().albumDao`.
- The `const` keyword is to make sure that nobody can modify `albumDao`. Because it is `public`, we cannot guarantee the safety of the object (anybody could modify the object). As a side-effect, we force every public function of `AlbumDao` to be `const`. This makes sense; after all, the `AlbumDao` field could have been a namespace with a bunch of functions. It is more convenient for it to be a class because we can keep the reference to the database connection with the `mDatabase` field.

In the `DatabaseManager` constructor, the `albumDao` class is initialized with the `mDatabase` dereferenced pointer. The `albumDao.init()` function is called after the database connection has opened.

We can now proceed to implement more interesting SQL queries. We can start with the creation of a new album in the `AlbumDao` class:

```
// In AlbumDao.h
class QSqlDatabase;
class Album;

class AlbumDao
{
public:
    AlbumDao(QSqlDatabase& database);
    void init() const;
    void addAlbum(Album& album) const;
    ...
};

// In AlbumDao.cpp

#include <QSqlDatabase>
#include <QSqlQuery>
#include <QVariant>

...

void AlbumDao::addAlbum(Album& album) const
```

```
{
    QSqlQuery query(mDatabase);
    query.prepare("INSERT INTO albums (name) VALUES (:name)");
    query.bindValue(":name", album.name());
    query.exec();
    album.setId(query.lastInsertId().toInt());
}
```

The `addAlbum()` function takes an `album` parameter to extract its information and execute the corresponding query. Here, we approach the prepared query notion: the `query.prepare()` function takes a `query` parameter which contains placeholders for parameters provided later. We will provide the `name` parameter with the syntax `:name`. Two syntaxes are supported: Oracle style with a colon-name (for example, `:name`) or ODBC style with a question mark (for example, `?name`).

We then bind the bind `:name` syntax to the value of the `album.name()` function. Because `QSqlQuery::bind()` expects a `QVariant` as a parameter value, we have to add the `include` directive to this class.

In a nutshell, a `QVariant` is a generic data holder that accepts a wide range of primitive types (`char`, `int`, `double`, and so on) and complex types (`QString`, `QByteArray`, `QUrl`, and so on).

When the `query.exec()` function is executed, the bound values are properly replaced. The `prepare()` statement technique makes the code more robust to SQL injection (injecting a hidden request would fail) and more readable.

The execution of the query modifies the state of the object query itself. The `QSqlQuery` query is not simply a SQL query executor, it also contains the state of the active query. We can retrieve information about the query with the `query.lastInsertId()` function, which returns a `QVariant` value containing the ID of the album row we just inserted. This `id` is given to the `album` provided in the `addAlbum()` parameter. Because we modify `album`, we cannot mark the parameter as `const`. Being strict about the `const` correctness of your code is a good hint for a fellow developer, who can deduce that your function might (or not) modify the passed parameter.

The remaining update and delete operations follow strictly the same pattern used for `addAlbum()`. We will just provide the expected function signatures in the next code snippet. Please refer to the source code of the chapter for the complete implementation. However, we need to implement the request to retrieve all the albums in the database. This one deserves a closer look:

```
// In AlbumDao.h
```

```
#include <QVector>

    ...
    void addAlbum(Album& album) const;
    void updateAlbum(const Album& album) const;
    void removeAlbum(int id) const;
    QVector<Album*> albums() const;
    ...
};

// In AlbumDao.cpp
QVector<Album*> AlbumDao::albums() const
{
    QSqlQuery query("SELECT * FROM albums", mDatabase);
    query.exec();
    QVector<Album*> list;
    while(query.next()) {
        Album* album = new Album();
        album->setId(query.value("id").toInt());
        album->setName(query.value("name").toString());
        list.append(album);
    }
    return list;
}
```

The `albums()` function must return a `QVector<Album*>` value. If we take a look at the
body of the function, we see yet another property of `QSqlQuery`. To walk through multiple
rows for a given request, `query` handles an internal cursor pointing to the current row. We
can then proceed to create a `new Album*()` function and fill it with the row data with
the `query.value()` statement, which takes a column name parameter and returns
a `QVariant` value that is casted to the proper type. This new `album` parameter is appended
to the `list` and, finally, this `list` is returned to the caller.

The `PictureDao` class is very similar to the `AlbumDao` class, both in usage and
implementation. The main difference is that a picture has a foreign key to an album.
The `PictureDao` function must be conditioned by an `albumId` parameter. The following
code snippet shows the `PictureDao` header and the `init()` function:

```
// In PictureDao.h
#include <QVector>

class QSqlDatabase;
class Picture;

class PictureDao
{
```

```
public:
    explicit PictureDao(QSqlDatabase& database);
    void init() const;

    void addPictureInAlbum(int albumId, Picture& picture) const;
    void removePicture(int id) const;
    void removePicturesForAlbum(int albumId) const;
    QVector<Picture*> picturesForAlbum(int albumId) const;

private:
    QSqlDatabase& mDatabase;
};

// In PictureDao.cpp
void PictureDao::init() const
{
    if (!mDatabase.tables().contains("pictures")) {
        QSqlQuery query(mDatabase);
        query.exec(QString("CREATE TABLE pictures")
        + " (id INTEGER PRIMARY KEY AUTOINCREMENT, "
        + "album_id INTEGER, "
        + "url TEXT)");
    }
}
```

As you can see, multiple functions take an `albumId` parameter to make the link between the picture and the owning `album` parameter. In the `init()` function, the foreign key is expressed in the `album_id INTEGER` syntax. SQLITE3 does not have a proper foreign key type. It is a very simple database and there is no strict constraint for this type of field; a simple integer is used.

Finally, the `PictureDao` function is added in the `DatabaseManager` class exactly as we did for `albumDao`. One could argue that, if there are a lot of `Dao` classes, adding a `const Dao` member in the `DatabaseManager` class and calling the `init()` function quickly becomes cumbersome.

A possible solution could be to make an abstract `Dao` class, with a pure virtual `init()` function. The `DatabaseManager` class would have a `Dao` registry, which maps each `Dao` to a `QString` key with a `QHash<QString, const Dao> mDaos`. The `init()` function call would then be called in a `for` loop and a `Dao` object would be accessed using the `QString` key. This is outside the scope of this project, but is nevertheless an interesting approach.

# Protecting your code with a smart pointer

The code we just described is fully functional, but, it can be strengthened, specifically with the function, `AlbumDao::albums()`. In this function, we iterate through the database rows and create a new `Album` to fill a list. We can zoom in on this specific code section:

```
QVector<Album*> list;
while(query.next()) {
    Album* album = new Album();
    album->setId(query.value("id").toInt());
    album->setName(query.value("name").toString());
    list.append(album);
}
return list;
```

Let's say that the `name` column has been renamed to `title`. If you forget to update `query.value("name")`, you might run into trouble. The Qt framework does not rely on exceptions, but this cannot be said for every API available in the wild. An exception here would cause a memory leak: the `Album* album` function has been allocated on the heap but not released. To handle this, you would have to surround the risky code with a `try catch` statement and deallocate the `album` parameter if an exception has been thrown. Maybe this error should bubble up; hence, your `try catch` statement is only there to handle the potential memory leak. Can you picture the spaghetti code weaving in front of you?

The real issue with pointers is the uncertainty of their ownership. Once it has been allocated, who is the owner of a pointer? Who is responsible for deallocating the object? When you pass a pointer as a parameter, when does the caller retain the ownership or release it to the callee?

Since C++11, a major milestone has been reached in memory management: the smart pointer feature has been stabilized and can greatly improve the safety of your code. The goal is to explicitly indicate the ownership of a pointer through simple template semantics. There are three types of smart pointer:

- The `unique_ptr` pointer indicates that the owner is the only owner of the pointer
- The `shared_ptr` pointer indicates that the pointer's ownership is shared among several clients
- The `weak_ptr` pointer indicates that the pointer does not belong to the client

For now, we will focus on the `unique_ptr` pointer to understand smart pointer mechanics.

A `unique_ptr` pointer is simply a variable allocated on the stack that takes the ownership of the pointer you provide with it. Let's allocate an `Album` with this semantic:

```
#include <memory>
void foo()
{
    Album* albumPointer = new Album();
    std::unique_ptr<Album> album(albumPointer);
    album->setName("Unique Album");
}
```

The whole smart pointer API is available in the `memory` header. When we declared `album` as a `unique_ptr`, we did two things:

- We allocated on the stack a `unique_ptr<Album>`. The `unique_ptr` pointer relies on templates to check at compile time the validity of the pointer type.
- We granted the ownership of `albumPointer` memory to `album`. From this point on, `album` is the owner of the pointer.

This simple line has important ramifications. First and foremost, you do not have to worry anymore about the pointer life cycle. Because a `unique_ptr` pointer is allocated on the stack, it will be destroyed as soon as it goes out of scope. In this example, when we exit `foo()`, `album` will be removed from the stack. The `unique_ptr` implementation will take care of calling the `Album` destructor and deallocating the memory.

Secondly, you explicitly indicate the ownership of your pointer at compile time. Nobody can deallocate the `albumPointer` content if they do not voluntarily fiddle with your `unique_ptr` pointer. Your fellow developers will also know with a single glance who is the owner of your pointer.

Note that, even though `album` is a type of `unique_ptr<Album>`, you can still call `Album` functions (for example, `album->setName()`) using the `->` operator. This is possible thanks to the overload of this operator. The usage of the `unique_ptr` pointer becomes transparent.

Well, this use case is nice, but the purpose of a pointer is to be able to allocate a chunk of memory and share it. Let's say the `foo()` function allocates the `album` `unique_ptr` pointer and then transfers the ownership to `bar()`. This would look like this:

```
void foo()
{
    std::unique_ptr<Album> album(new Album());
    bar(std::move(album));
}
```

```
void bar(std::unique_ptr<Album> barAlbum)
{
    qDebug() << "Album name" << barAlbum->name();
}
```

Here, we introduce the `std::move()` function: its goal is to transfer the ownership of a `unique_ptr` function. Once `bar(std::move(album))` has been called, `album` becomes invalid. You can test it with a simple `if` statement: `if (album) { ... }`.

From now on, the `bar()` function becomes the owner of the pointer (through `barAlbum`) by allocating a new `unique_ptr` on the stack and it will deallocate the pointer on its exit. You do not have to worry about the cost of a `unique_ptr` pointer, as these objects are very lightweight and it is unlikely that they will affect the performance of your application.

Again, the signature of `bar()` tells the developer that this function expects to take the ownership of the passed `Album`. Trying to pass around `unique_ptr` without the `move()` function will lead to a compile error.

Another thing to note is the different meanings of the `.` (dot) and the `->` (arrow) when working with a `unique_ptr` pointer:

- The `->` operator dereferences to the pointer members and lets your call function on your real object
- The `.` operator gives you access to the `unique_ptr` object functions

The `unique_ptr` pointer provides various functions. Among the most important are:

- The `get()` function returns the raw pointer. The `album.get()` returns an `Album*` value.
- The `release()` function releases the ownership of the pointer and returns the raw pointer. The `album.release()` function returns an `Album*` value.
- The `reset(pointer p = pointer())` function destroys the currently managed pointer and takes ownership of the given parameter. An example would be the `barAlbum.reset()` function, which destroys the currently owned `Album*`. With a parameter, `barAlbum.reset(new Album())` also destroys the owned object and takes the ownership of the provided parameter.

Finally, you can dereference the object with the * operation, meaning *album will return an Album& value. This dereferencing is convenient, but you will see that the more a smart pointer is used, the less you will need it. Most of the time, you will replace a raw pointer with the following syntax:

```
void bar(std::unique_ptr<Album>& barAlbum);
```

Because we pass the unique_ptr by reference, bar() does not take ownership of the pointer and will not try do deallocate it upon its exit. With this, there is no need to use move(album) in foo(); the bar() function will just do operations on the album parameter but will not take its ownership.

Now, let's consider shared_ptr. A shared_ptr pointer keeps a reference counter on a pointer. Each time a shared_ptr pointer references the same object, the counter is incremented; when this shared_ptr pointer goes out of scope, the counter is decremented. When the counter reaches zero, the object is deallocated.

Let's rewrite our foo()/bar() example with a shared_ptr pointer:

```
#include <memory>
void foo()
{
    std::shared_ptr<Album> album(new Album()); // ref counter = 1
    bar(album); // ref counter = 2
} // ref counter = 0

void bar(std::shared_ptr<Album> barAlbum)
{
    qDebug() << "Album name" << barAlbum->name();
} // ref counter = 1
```

As you can see, the syntax is very similar to the unique_ptr pointer. The reference counter is incremented each time a new shared_ptr pointer is allocated and points to the same data, and is decremented on the function exit. You can check the current count by calling the album.use_count() function.

The last smart pointer we will cover is the weak_ptr pointer. As the name suggests, it does not take any ownership or increment the reference counter. When a function specifies a weak_ptr, it indicates to the callers that it is just a client and not an owner of the pointer. If we re implement bar() with a weak_ptr pointer, we get:

```
#include <memory>
void foo()
{
    std::shared_ptr<Album> album(new Album()); // ref counter = 1
```

```
        bar(std::weak_ptr<Album>(album)); // ref counter = 1
    } // ref counter = 0

    void bar(std::weak_ptr<Album> barAlbum)
    {
        qDebug() << "Album name" << barAlbum->name();
    } // ref counter = 1
```

If the story stopped here, there would not be any interest in using a weak_ptr versus a raw pointer. The weak_ptr has a major advantage for the dangling pointer issue. If you are building a cache, you typically do not want to keep strong references to your object. On the other hand, you want to know if the objects are still valid. By using weak_ptr, you know when an object has been deallocated. Now, consider the raw pointer approach: your pointer might be invalid but you do not know the state of the memory.

There is another semantic introduced in C++14 that we have to cover: make_unique. This keyword aims to replace the new keyword and construct a unique_ptr object in an exception-safe manner. This is how it is used:

```
    unique_ptr<Album> album = make_unique<Album>();
```

The make_unique keyword wraps the new keyword to make it exception-safe, specifically in this situation:

```
    foo(new Album(), new Picture())
```

This code will be executed in the following order:

1. Allocate and construct the Album function.
2. Allocate and construct the Picture function.
3. Execute the foo() function.

If new Picture() throws an exception, the memory allocated by new Album() will be leaked. This is fixed by using the make_unique keyword:

```
    foo(make_unique<Album>(), make_unique<Picture>())
```

The make_unique keyword returns a unique_ptr pointer; the C++ standard committee also provided an equivalent for shared_ptr in the form of make_shared, which follows the same principle.

All these new C++ semantics try very hard to get rid of `new` and `delete`. Yet, it may be cumbersome to write all the `unique_ptr` and `make_unique` stuff. The `auto` keyword comes to the rescue in our `album` creation:

```
auto album = make_unique<Album>()
```

This is a radical departure from the common C++ syntax. The variable type is deduced, there is no explicit pointer, and the memory is automatically managed. After some time with smart pointers, you will see fewer and fewer raw pointers in your code (and even fewer `delete`, which is such a relief). The remaining raw pointers will simply indicate that a client is using the pointer but does not own it.

Overall, C++11 and C++14 smart pointers are a real step up in C++ code writing. Before them, the bigger the code base, the more insecure we felt about memory management. Our brain is just bad at properly grasping complexity at such a level. Smart pointers simply make you feel safe about what you write. On the other hand, you retain full control of the memory. For performance-critical code, you can always handle the memory yourself. For everything else, smart pointers are an elegant way of explicitly indicating your object's ownership and freeing your mind.

We are now equipped to rewrite the little insecure snippet in the `AlbumDao::albums()` function. Update `AlbumDao::albums()` like so:

```
// In AlbumDao.h
std::unique_ptr<std::vector<std::unique_ptr<Album>>> albums() const;

// In AlbumDao.cpp
unique_ptr<vector<unique_ptr<Album>>> AlbumDao::albums() const
{
    QSqlQuery query("SELECT * FROM albums", mDatabase);
    query.exec();
    unique_ptr<vector<unique_ptr<Album>>> list(new
vector<unique_ptr<Album>>());
    while(query.next()) {
        unique_ptr<Album> album(new Album());
        album->setId(query.value("id").toInt());
        album->setName(query.value("name").toString());
        list->push_back(move(album));
    }
    return list;
}
```

Wow! The signature of the `album()` function has turned into something very peculiar. Smart pointers are supposed to make your life easier, right? Let's break it down to understand a major point of smart pointers with Qt: container behavior.

The initial goal of the rewrite was to secure the creation of `album`. We want the `list` to be the explicit owner of the `album`. This would have changed our `list` type (that is `albums()` return type) to `QVector<unique_ptr<Album>>`. However, when the `list` type is returned, its elements will be copied (remember, we previously defined the return type to `QVector<Album>`). A natural way out of this would be to return a `QVector<unique_ptr<Album>>*` type to retain the uniqueness of our `Album` elements.

Behold, here lies a major pain: the `QVector` class overloads the copy operator. Hence, when the `list` type is returned, the uniqueness of our `unique_ptr` elements cannot be guaranteed by the compiler and it will throw a compile error. This is why we have to resort to a `vector` object coming from the standard library and write the long type: `unique_ptr<vector<unique_ptr<Album>>>`.

 Take a look at the official response for support of the `unique_ptr` pointer in the Qt container. It is clear beyond any possible doubt: `http://lists.q t-project.org/pipermail/interest/2013-July/007776.html`. The short answer is: no, it will never be done. Do not even mention it. Ever.

If we translate this new `albums()` signature into plain English it will read: the `album()` function returns a vector of `Album`. This vector is the owner of the `Album` elements it contains and you will be the owner of the vector.

To finish covering this implementation of `albums()`, you may notice that we did not use the `auto` and `make_unique` keywords for the `list` declaration. Our library will be used on a mobile in *Chapter 5*, *Dominating the Mobile UI*, and C++14 is not yet supported on this platform. Therefore, we have to restrain our code to C++11.

We also encounter the use of the `move` function in the instruction `list->push_back(move(album))`. Until that line, the `album` is "owned" by the `while` scope, the move gives the ownership to the list. At the last instruction, `return list`, we should have written `move(list)`, but C++11 accepts the direct return and will automatically make the `move()` function for us.

What we covered in this section is that the `AlbumDao` class is completely matched in `PictureDao`. Please refer to the source code of the chapter to see the full `PictureDao` class implementation.

# Implementing the model

The data is ready to be exposed to potential clients (the applications that will display and edit its content). However, a direct connection between the client and the database will make a very strong coupling. If we decide to switch to another storage type, the view would have to be rewritten, partially at least.

This is where the model comes to our rescue. It is an abstract layer that communicates with the data (our database) and exposes this data to the client in a data-specific, implementation-agnostic form. This approach is a direct offspring of the **MVC (Model View Controller)** concept. Let's recapitulate how MVC works:

- The Model manages the data. It is responsible for requesting for the data and updating it.
- The View displays the data to the user.
- The Controller interacts with both the Model and the View. It is responsible for feeding the View with the correct data and sending commands to the Model based on the user interaction received from the View.

This paradigm enables swapping various parts without disturbing the others. Multiple views can display the same data, the data layer can be changed, and the upper parts will not be aware of it.

Qt combines the View and the Controller to form the Model/View architecture. The separation of the storage and the presentation is retained while being simpler to implement than a full MVC approach. To allow editing and view customization, Qt introduces the concept of Delegate, which is connected to both the Model and the View:

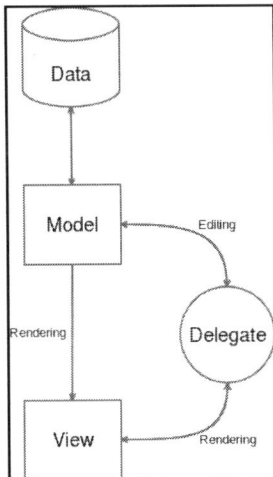

The Qt documentation about Model/View is truly plethoric. It is nevertheless easy to get lost in the details; it feels sometimes a bit overwhelming. We will try to clear things up by implementing the AlbumModel class and seeing how it works.

Qt offers various Model sub-classes that all extend from QAbstractItemModel. Before starting the implementation, we have to carefully choose which base class will be extended. Keep in mind that our data are variations on lists: we will have a list of albums, and each album will have a list of pictures. Let's see what Qt offers us:

- QAbstractItemModel: This class is the most abstract, and therefore, the most complex, to implement. We will have to redefine a lot of functions to properly use it.
- QStringListModel: This class is a model that supplies strings to views. It is too simple. Our model is more complex (we have custom objects).
- QSqlTableModel (or QSqlQueryModel): This class is a very interesting contender. It automatically handles multiple SQL queries. On the other hand, it works only for very simple table schemas. In the pictures table, for example, the album_id foreign key makes it very hard to fit this model. You might save some lines of code, but if feels like trying to shoehorn a round peg into a square hole.

- QAbstractListModel: This class provides a model that offers one-dimensional lists. This fits nicely with our requirements, saves a lot of key strokes, and is still flexible enough.

We will go with the QabstractListModel class and create a new C++ class named AlbumModel. Update the AlbumModel.h file to look like this:

```
#include <QAbstractListModel>
#include <QHash>
#include <vector>
#include <memory>

#include "gallery-core_global.h"
#include "Album.h"
#include "DatabaseManager.h"

class GALLERYCORESHARED_EXPORT AlbumModel : public QAbstractListModel
{
    Q_OBJECT
public:

    enum Roles {
        IdRole = Qt::UserRole + 1,
        NameRole,
    };

    AlbumModel(QObject* parent = 0);

    QModelIndex addAlbum(const Album& album);

    int rowCount(const QModelIndex& parent = QModelIndex()) const override;
    QVariant data(const QModelIndex& index, int role = Qt::DisplayRole)
const override;
    bool setData(const QModelIndex& index, const QVariant& value, int role)
override;
    bool removeRows(int row, int count, const QModelIndex& parent)
override;
    QHash<int, QByteArray> roleNames() const override;

private:
    bool isIndexValid(const QModelIndex& index) const;

private:
    DatabaseManager& mDb;
    std::unique_ptr<std::vector<std::unique_ptr<Album>>> mAlbums;
};
```

The AlbumModel class extends the QAbstractListModel class and has only two members:

- mDb: This is the link to the database. In the Model/View schema, the model will communicate with the data layer through mDb.
- mAlbums: This acts as a buffer that will avoid hitting the database too much. The type should remind you of what we wrote for AlbumDao::albums() with the smart pointers.

The only specific functions the AlbumModel class has are addAlbum() and isIndexValid(). The rest are overrides of QAbstractListModel functions. We will go through each of these functions to understand how a model works.

First, let's see how the AlbumModel class is constructed in the AlbumModel.cpp file:

```
AlbumModel::AlbumModel(QObject* parent) :
    QAbstractListModel(parent),
    mDb(DatabaseManager::instance()),
    mAlbums(mDb.albumDao.albums())
{
}
```

The mDb file is initialized with the DatabaseManager singleton address, and, after that, we see the now famous AlbumDao::albums() in action.

The vector type is returned and initializes mAlbums. This syntax make the ownership transfer automatic without any need for an explicit call to the std::move() function. If there are any stored albums in the database, mAlbums is immediately filled with those.

Each time the model interacts with the view (to notify us about changes or to serve data), mAlbums will be used. Because it is in memory only, reading will be very fast. Of course, we have to be careful about maintaining mAlbum coherently with the database state, but everything will stay inside the AlbumModel inner mechanics.

As we said earlier, the model aims to be the central point to interact with the data. Each time the data changes, the model will emit a signal to notify the view; each time the view wants to display data, it will request the model for it. The AlbumModel class overrides everything needed for read and write access. The read functions are:

- rowCount(): This function is used to get the list size
- data(): This function is used to get a specific piece of information about the data to display
- roleNames(): This function is used to indicate to the framework the name for each "role". We will explain in a few paragraphs what a role is

The editing functions are:

- `setData()`: This function is used to update data
- `removeRows()`: This function is used to remove data

We will start with the read part, where the view asks the model for the data.

Because we will display a list of albums, the first thing the view should know is how many items are available. This is done in the `rowCount()` function:

```
int AlbumModel::rowCount(const QModelIndex& parent) const
{
    return mAlbums->size();
}
```

Being our buffer object, using `mAlbums->size()` is perfect. There is no need to query the database, as `mAlbums` is already filled with all the albums of the database. The `rowCount()` function has an unknown parameter: a `const QModelIndex& parent`. Here, it is not used, but we have to explain what lies beneath this type before continuing our journey in the `AlbumModel` class.

The `QModelIndex` class is a central notion of the Model/View framework in Qt. It is a lightweight object used to locate data within a model. We use a simple `QAbstractListModel` class, but Qt is able to handle three representation types:

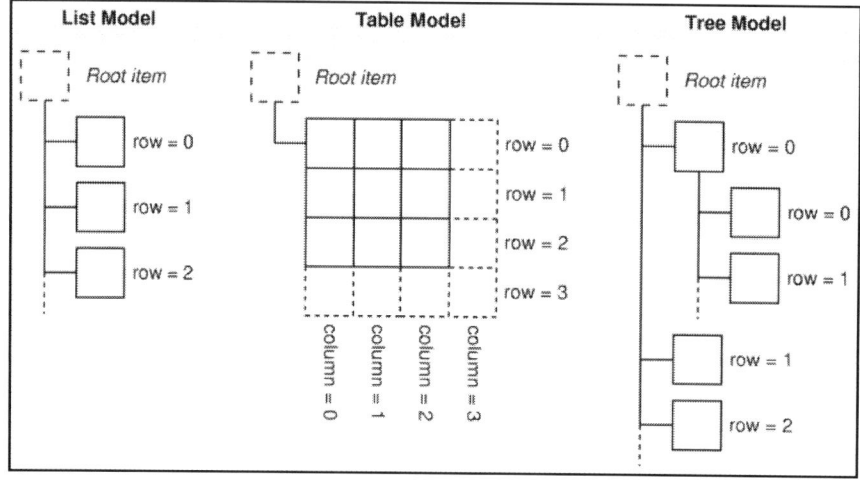

There is no better explanation than an official Qt diagram

Let's now see the models in detail:

- **List Model**: In this model, the data is stored in a one-dimensional array (rows)
- **Table Model**: In this model, the data is stored in a two-dimensional array (rows and columns)
- **Tree Model**: In this model, the data is stored in a hierarchical relationship (parent/children)

To handle all these model types, Qt came up with the QModelIndex class, which is an abstract way of dealing with them. The QModelIndex class has the functions for each of the use cases: row(), column(), and parent()/child(). Each instance of a QModelIndex is meant to be short-lived: the model might be updated and thus the index will become invalid.

The model will produce indexes according to its data type and will provide these indexes to the view. The view will then use them to query back new data to the model without needing to know if an index.row() function corresponds to a database row or a vector index.

We can see the index parameter in action with the implementation of data():

```
QVariant AlbumModel::data(const QModelIndex& index, int role) const
{
    if (!isIndexValid(index)) {
        return QVariant();
    }
    const Album& album = *mAlbums->at(index.row());

    switch (role) {
        case Roles::IdRole:
            return album.id();

        case Roles::NameRole:
        case Qt::DisplayRole:
            return album.name();

        default:
            return QVariant();
    }
}
```

The view will ask for data with two parameters: an index and a role. As we have already covered the index, we can focus on the role responsibility.

When the data is displayed, it will probably be an aggregation of multiple data. For example, displaying the picture will consist of a thumbnail and the picture name. Each one of these data elements needs to be retrieved by the view. The `role` parameter fills this need, it associates each data element to a tag for the view to know what category of data is shown.

Qt provides various default roles (`DisplayRole`, `DecorationRole`, `EditRole`, and so on) and you can define your own if needed. This is what we did in the `AlbumModel.h` file with the `enum Roles`: we added an `IdRole` and a `NameRole`.

The body of the `data()` function is now within our reach! We first test the validity of the `index` with a helper function, `isIndexValid()`. Take a look at the source code of the chapter to see what it does in detail. The view asked for data at a specific `index`: we retrieve the `album` row at the given `index` with `*mAlbums->at(index.row())`.

This returns a `unique_ptr<Album>` value at the `index.row()` index and we dereference it to have an `Album&`. The `const` modifier is interesting here because we are in a read function, and it makes no sense to modify the `album` row. The `const` modifier adds this check at compile time.

The `switch` on the `role` parameter tells us what data category should be returned. The `data()` function returns a `QVariant` value, which is the Awiss Army Knife of types in Qt. We can safely return the `album.id()`, `album.name()`, or a default `QVariant()` if we do not handle the specified role.

The last read function to cover is `roleNames()`:

```
QHash<int, QByteArray> AlbumModel::roleNames() const
{
    QHash<int, QByteArray> roles;
    roles[Roles::IdRole] = "id";
    roles[Roles::NameRole] = "name";
    return roles;
}
```

At this level of abstraction, we do not know what type of view will be used to display our data. If the views are written in QML, they will need some meta-information about the data structure. The `roleNames()` function provides this information so the role names can be accessed via QML. If you are writing for a desktop widget view only, you can safely ignore this function. The library we are currently building will be used for QML; this is why we override this function.

The reading part of the model is now over. The client view has everything it needs to properly query and display the data. We shall now investigate the editing part of `AlbumModel`.

We will start with the creation of a new album. The view will build a new `Album` object and pass it to `Album::addAlbum()` to be properly persisted:

```
QModelIndex AlbumModel::addAlbum(const Album& album)
{
    int rowIndex = rowCount();
    beginInsertRows(QModelIndex(), rowIndex, rowIndex);
    unique_ptr<Album> newAlbum(new Album(album));
    mDb.albumDao.addAlbum(*newAlbum);
    mAlbums->push_back(move(newAlbum));
    endInsertRows();
    return index(rowIndex, 0);
}
```

Indexes are a way to navigate within the model data. This first thing we do is to determinate what will be the index of this new album by getting the `mAlbums` size with `rowCount()`.

From here, we start to use specific model functions: `beginInsertRows()` and `endInsertRows()`. These functions wrap real data modifications. Their purpose is to automatically trigger signals for whoever might be interested:

- `beginInsertRows()`: This function informs that rows are about to change for the given indexes
- `endInsertRows()`: This function informs that rows have been changed

The first parameter of the `beginInsertRows()` function is the `parent` for this new element. The root for a model is always an empty `QModelIndex()` constructor. Because we do not handle any hierarchical relationship in `AlbumModel`, it is safe to always add the new element to the root. The following parameters are the first and last modified indexes. We insert a single element per call, so we provide `rowIndex` twice. To illustrate the usage of this signal, a view might, for example, display a loading message telling the user "Saving 5 new albums".

For `endInsertRows()`, the interested view might hide the saving message and display "Save finished".

This may look strange at first, but it enables Qt to handle automatically a lot of signaling for us and in a generic way. You will see very soon how well this works when designing the UI of the application in Chapter 4, *Conquering the Desktop UI*.

The real insertion begins after the beginInsertRows() instruction. We start by creating a copy of the album row with unique_ptr<Album> newAlbum. This object is then inserted in the database with mDb.albumDao.addAlbum(*newAlbum). Do not forget that the AlbumDao::addAlbum() function also modifies the passed album by setting its mId to the last SQLITE3-inserted ID.

Finally, newAlbum is added to mAlbums and its ownership is transferred as well with std::move(). The return gives the index object of this new album, which is simply the row wrapped in a QModelIndex object.

Let's continue the editing functions with setData():

```
bool AlbumModel::setData(const QModelIndex& index, const QVariant& value,
int role)
{
    if (!isIndexValid(index)
            || role != Roles::NameRole) {
        return false;
    }
    Album& album = *mAlbums->at(index.row());
    album.setName(value.toString());
    mDb.albumDao.updateAlbum(album);
    emit dataChanged(index, index);
    return true;
}
```

This function is called when the view wants to update the data. The signature is very similar to data(), with the additional parameter value.

The body also follows the same logic. Here, the album row is an Album&, without the const keyword. The only possible value to edit is the name, which is done on the object and then persisted to the database.

We have to emit ourselves the dataChanged() signal to notify whoever is interested that a row changed for the given indexes (the start index and end index). This powerful mechanism centralizes all the states of the data, enabling possible views (album list and current album detail for example) to be automatically refreshed.

The return of the function simply indicates if the data update was successful. In a production application, you should test the database processing success and return the relevant value.

Finally, the last editing function we will cover is removeRows():

```
bool AlbumModel::removeRows(int row, int count, const QModelIndex& parent)
{
    if (row < 0
            || row >= rowCount()
            || count < 0
            || (row + count) > rowCount()) {
        return false;
    }
    beginRemoveRows(parent, row, row + count - 1);
    int countLeft = count;
    while (countLeft--) {
        const Album& album = *mAlbums->at(row + countLeft);
        mDb.albumDao.removeAlbum(album.id());
    }
    mAlbums->erase(mAlbums->begin() + row,
                   mAlbums->begin() + row + count);
    endRemoveRows();
    return true;
}
```

The function signature should start to look familiar by now. When a view wants to remove rows, it has to provide the starting row, the number of rows to delete, and the parent of the row.

After that, just as we did for addAlbum(), we wrap the effective removal with two functions:

- The beginRemoveRows() function, which expects the parent, the starting index, and the last index
- The endRemoveRows() function, which simply triggers automatic signals in the model framework

The rest of the function is not very hard to follow. We loop on the rows left to delete and, for each one, we delete it from the database and remove it from mAlbums. We simply retrieve the album from our in-memory mAlbums vector and process the real database deletion with mDb.albumDao.removeAlbum(album.id()).

The AlbumModel class is now completely covered. You can now create a new C++ class and name it PictureModel.

We will not cover the PictureModel class in so much detail. The major parts are the same (you simply swap the data class Album for Picture). There is however one main difference: PictureModel always handles pictures for a given album. This design choice illustrates how two models can be linked with only some simple signals.

Here is the updated version of PictureModel.h:

```cpp
#include <memory>
#include <vector>

#include <QAbstractListModel>

#include "gallery-core_global.h"
#include "Picture.h"

class Album;
class DatabaseManager;
class AlbumModel;

class GALLERYCORESHARED_EXPORT PictureModel : public QAbstractListModel
{
    Q_OBJECT
public:

    enum PictureRole {
        FilePathRole = Qt::UserRole + 1
    };
    PictureModel(const AlbumModel& albumModel, QObject* parent = 0);

    QModelIndex addPicture(const Picture& picture);

    int rowCount(const QModelIndex& parent = QModelIndex()) const override;
    QVariant data(const QModelIndex& index, int role) const override;
    bool removeRows(int row, int count, const QModelIndex& parent)
override;

    void setAlbumId(int albumId);
    void clearAlbum();

public slots:
    void deletePicturesForAlbum();

private:
    void loadPictures(int albumId);
```

```
        bool isIndexValid(const QModelIndex& index) const;

private:
        DatabaseManager& mDb;
        int mAlbumId;
        std::unique_ptr<std::vector<std::unique_ptr<Picture>>> mPictures;
};
```

The interesting parts are those concerning the album. As you can see, the constructor expects an `AlbumModel`. This class also stores the current `mAlbumId` to be able to request the pictures for a given album only. Let's see what the constructor really does:

```
PictureModel::PictureModel(const AlbumModel& albumModel, QObject* parent) :
        QAbstractListModel(parent),
        mDb(DatabaseManager::instance()),
        mAlbumId(-1),
        mPictures(new vector<unique_ptr<Picture>>())
{
        connect(&albumModel, &AlbumModel::rowsRemoved,
                this, &PictureModel::deletePicturesForAlbum);
}
```

As you can see, the `albumModel` class is used only to connect a signal to our slot `deletePicturesForAlbum()` which is self-explanatory. This makes sure that the database is always valid: a picture should be deleted if the owning album is deleted. This will be done automatically when `AlbumModel` emits the `rowsRemoved` signal.

Now, `mPictures` is not initialized with all the pictures of the database. Because we chose to restrict `PictureModel` to work on the pictures for a given album, we do not know at the construction of `PictureModel` which album to choose. The loading can only be done when the album is selected, in `setAlbumId()`:

```
void PictureModel::setAlbumId(int albumId)
{
        beginResetModel();
        mAlbumId = albumId;
        loadPictures(mAlbumId);
        endResetModel();
}
```

When the album changes, we completely reload `PictureModel`. The reloading phase is wrapped with the `beginResetModel()` and `endResetModel()` functions. They notify any attached views that their state should be reset as well. Any previous data (for example, `QModelIndex`) reported from the model becomes invalid.

The `loadPictures()` function is quite straightforward:

```
void PictureModel::loadPictures(int albumId)
{
    if (albumId <= 0) {
        mPictures.reset(new vector<unique_ptr<Picture>>());
        return;
    }
    mPictures = mDb.pictureDao.picturesForAlbum(albumId);
}
```

By convention, we decided that, if a negative `album id` is provided, we clear the pictures. To do it, we reinitialize `mPictures` with the call `mPictures.reset(new vector<unique_ptr<Picture>>())`. This will call the destructor on the owned vector, which in turn will do the same for the `Picture` elements. We force `mPictures` to always have a valid vector object to avoid any possible null reference (in `PictureModel::rowCount()` for example).

After that, we simply assign the database pictures for the given `albumId` to `mPictures`. Because we work with smart pointers at every level, we do not even see any specific semantics here. Still, `mPicture` is a `unique_ptr<vector<unique_ptr<Picture>>>`. When the = operator is called, the `unique_ptr` pointer overloads it and two things happen:

- The ownership of the right-hand side (the pictures retrieved from the database) is transferred to `mPictures`
- The old content of `mPictures` is automatically deleted

It is effectively the same as calling `mPictures.reset()` and then `mPictures = move(mDb.pictureDao.picturesForAlbum(albumId))`. With the = overload, everything is streamlined and much more pleasant to read.

The `PictureModel` shows you how flexible the model paradigm can be. You can easily adapt it to your own use case without making any strong coupling. After all, the `albumModel` is only used to connect to a single signal; there are no retained references. The remainder of the class is available in the source code of the chapter.

# Summary

The chapter was a journey to create a well-defined `gallery-core` library. We studied advanced techniques with `.pro` files to split your project into sub-modules, persisted data in a SQLITE3 database with the help of smart pointers, and finally studied how the Model/View architecture works in Qt.

From now on, a project organization with Qt should hold no terrors for you. The next chapter will continue right where we stopped: the library is ready, now let's make great QWidgets to have a stunning gallery application and look at the other side of the model: the View layer.

# 4
# Conquering the Desktop UI

In the previous chapter, we built the brain of our gallery using Qt models. It is now time to build a desktop application using this engine. This software will use all the features offered by the `gallery-core` library, leading to a completely usable gallery on your computer.

The first task will be to link your project-shared library to this new application. Then you will learn how to create custom widgets, when to use Qt views, and how to synchronize them with the model.

The following topics will be covered in this chapter:

- Linking the application to a project library
- Qt model/view
- Qt resource file
- Promoting custom widgets

## Creating a GUI linked to a core shared library

The `gallery-core` shared library is now ready. Let's see how to create the desktop GUI project. We will create a Qt Widgets application sub-project called `gallery-desktop`. Only the first steps differ from a classic Qt Widgets application. Right-click on the main project, and select **ch04-gallery-desktop** | **New subproject** | **Application** | **Qt Widgets Application** | **Choose**.

You will get a nice multi-projects hierarchy like this:

It is now time to link this `gallery-desktop` application to the `gallery-core`. You can edit the file `gallery-desktop.pro` yourself or use the Qt Creator wizard like this: right-click on the project and select **gallery-desktop** | **Add library** | **Internal library** | **gallery-core** | **Next** | **Finish**. Here is the updated `gallery-desktop.pro`:

```
QT       += core gui

TARGET = desktop-gallery
TEMPLATE = app

SOURCES += main.cpp\
        MainWindow.cpp

HEADERS  += MainWindow.h

FORMS    += MainWindow.ui

win32:CONFIG(release, debug|release): LIBS += -L$$OUT_PWD/../gallery-
core/release/ -lgallery-core
else:win32:CONFIG(debug, debug|release): LIBS += -L$$OUT_PWD/../gallery-
core/debug/ -lgallery-core
else:unix: LIBS += -L$$OUT_PWD/../gallery-core/ -lgallery-core

INCLUDEPATH += $$PWD/../gallery-core
DEPENDPATH += $$PWD/../gallery-core
```

The `LIBS` variable specifies the libraries to link in this project. The syntax is very simple: you can provide library paths with the `-L` prefix and library names with the `-l` prefix.

```
LIBS += -L<pathToLibrary> -l<libraryName>
```

By default, compiling a Qt project on Windows will create a `debug` and `release` sub-directory. That is why a different `LIBS` edition is created depending on the platform.

Now that the application is linked to the library `gallery-core` and knows where to find it, we must indicate where the library header files are located. That is why we must add the `gallery-core` source path to `INCLUDEPATH` and `DEPENDPATH`.

To complete all those tasks successfully, qmake offers some useful variables:

- `$$OUT_PWD`: The absolute path to the output directory
- `$$PWD`: The absolute path of the current `.pro` file

To ensure that `qmake` will compile the shared library before the desktop application, we must update the `ch04-gallery-desktop.pro` file according the following snippet:

```
TEMPLATE = subdirs

SUBDIRS += \
    gallery-core \
    gallery-desktop

gallery-desktop.depends = gallery-core
```

The `depends` attribute explicitly indicates that `gallery-core` must be built before `gallery-desktop`.

Try to always use the `depends` attribute instead of relying on `CONFIG +=` `ordered`, which only specifies a simple list order. The `depends` attribute helps qmake process your projects in parallel, if it can be done.

Instead of rushing into coding blindly, we will take some time to think about the UI architecture. We have a lot of features to implement from the `gallery-core` library. We should split these features into independent QWidgets. The final application will look like this:

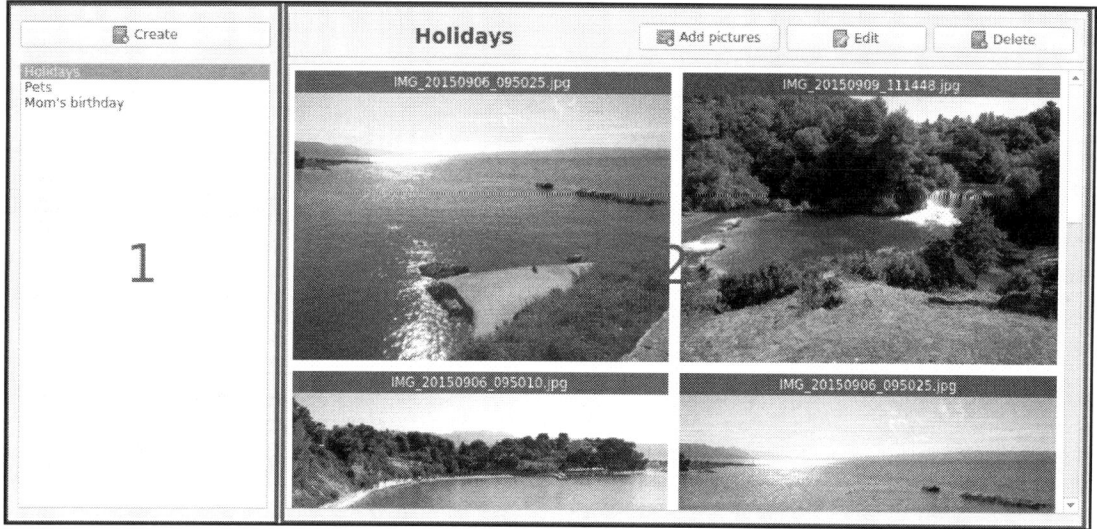

Our future gallery desktop is here!

The exapanded view of a photo will look like this:

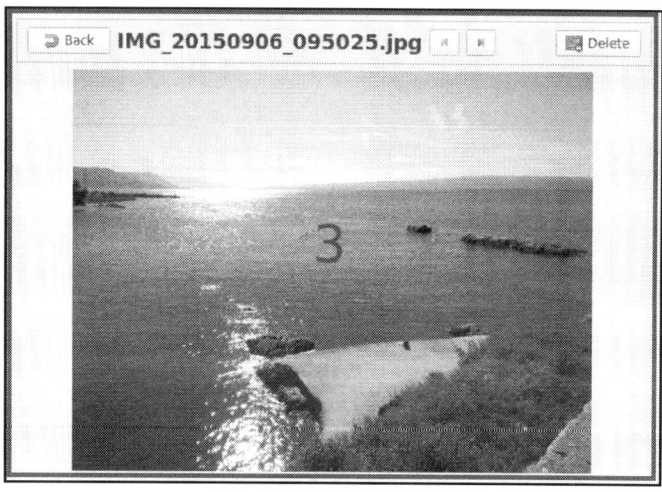

Double-click on a thumbnail to display it in full size.

To sum up the main UI components:

- `AlbumListWidget`: This component lists all existing albums
- `AlbumWidget`: This component shows the selected album and its thumbnails
- `PictureWidget`: This component displays the picture in full size

This is how we will organize it:

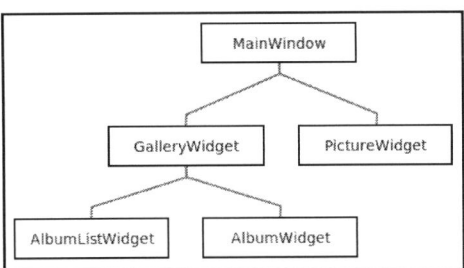

Each widget has a defined role and will handle specific features:

| Class name | Features |
|---|---|
| MainWindow | Handles the switch between the gallery and the current picture |
| GalleryWidget | • Displays existing albums<br>• Album selection<br>• Album creation |
| AlbumListWidget | • Displays existing albums<br>• Album selection<br>• Album creation |
| AlbumWidget | • Displays existing pictures as thumbnails<br>• Adds pictures in the album<br>• Album rename<br>• Album deletion<br>• Picture selection |
| PictureWidget | • Displays the selected picture<br>• Picture selection<br>• Picture deletion |

In the core shared library, we used smart pointers with standard containers (`vector`). Generally, in GUI projects, we tend to only use Qt containers and their powerful parent-child ownership system. This approach seems more appropriate to us. That is why we will rely on Qt containers for the GUI (and won't use smart pointers) in this chapter.

We can now safely begin to create our widgets; all of them are created from **Qt Designer Form Class**. If you have a memory lapse, you can check the *Custom QWidget* section in `Chapter 1`, *Get Your Qt Feet Wet*.

# Listing your albums with AlbumListWidget

This widget must offer a way to create a new album and display existing ones. Selecting an album must also trigger an event that will be used by other widgets to display the proper data. The `AlbumListWidget` component is the simplest widget in this project using the Qt View mechanism. Take the time to fully understand `AlbumListWidget` before jumping to the next widget.

The following screenshot shows the **Form Editor** view of the file, `AlbumListWidget.ui`:

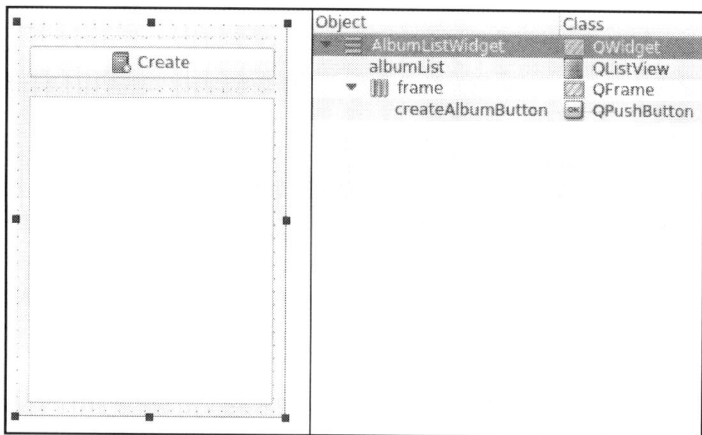

The layout is very simple. The components are described as follows:

- The `AlbumListWidget` component uses a vertical layout to display the **Create** button above the list
- The `frame` component contains an attractive button
- The `createAlbumButton` component handles album creation
- The `albumList` component displays the album list

You should have recognized most of the types used here. Let us take the time to talk about the really new one: `QListView`. As we already saw in the previous chapter, Qt provides a Model/View architecture. This system relies on specific interfaces that you must implement to provide generic data access via your model classes. That is what we did in the project `gallery-core` with the `AlbumModel` and `PictureModel` classes.

It is now time to deal with the view part. The view is in charge of the presentation of the data. It will also handle user interactions like selection, drag and drop, or item editing. Fortunately, to achieve these tasks, the view is helped by other Qt classes such as `QItemSelectionModel`, `QModelIndex`, or `QStyledItemDelegate`, which we will soon use in this chapter.

We can now enjoy one of the ready-to-use views offered by Qt:

- `QListView`: This view displays items from a model as a simple list
- `QTableView`: This view displays items from a model as a two-dimensional table
- `QTreeView`: This view displays items from a hierarchy of lists

Here, the choice is rather obvious because we want to display a list of album names. But in a more complex situation, a rule of thumb for choosing the proper view is to look for the model type; here we want to add a view for `AlbumModel` of type `QAbstractListModel` so the `QListView` class seems correct.

As you can see in the preceding screenshot, the `createAlbumButton` object has an icon. You can add one to a `QPushButton` class by selecting the widget **property: icon** | **Choose resource**. You can now choose a picture from the `resource.qrc` file.

A **Qt resource** file is a collection of files for embedding binary files in your application. You can store any types of file but we commonly use it to store pictures, sounds, or translation files. To create a resource file, right-click on the project name and then follow **Add New** | **Qt** | **Qt Resource File**. Qt Creator will create a default file, `resource.qrc`, and add this line in your file `gallery-desktop.pro`:

```
RESOURCES += resource.qrc
```

The resource file can be mainly displayed in two ways: **Resource Editor** and **Plain Text Editor**. You can choose an editor with by right-clicking on the resource file and selecting **Open With**.

The **Resource Editor** is a visual editor that helps you to easily add and remove files in your resource file, as shown in the following screenshot:

The**Plain Text Editor** will display this XML-based file `resource.qrc` like this:

```
<RCC>
    <qresource prefix="/">
        <file>icons/album-add.png</file>
        <file>icons/album-delete.png</file>
        <file>icons/album-edit.png</file>
        <file>icons/back-to-gallery.png</file>
        <file>icons/photo-add.png</file>
        <file>icons/photo-delete.png</file>
        <file>icons/photo-next.png</file>
        <file>icons/photo-previous.png</file>
    </qresource>
</RCC>
```

At the build time, `qmake` and `rcc` (Qt Resource Compiler) embed your resources into the application binary.

Now that the form part is clear, we can analyze the `AlbumListWidget.h` file:

```
#include <QWidget>
#include <QItemSelectionModel>

namespace Ui {
class AlbumListWidget;
}
```

```
class AlbumModel;

class AlbumListWidget : public QWidget
{
    Q_OBJECT

public:
    explicit AlbumListWidget(QWidget *parent = 0);
    ~AlbumListWidget();

    void setModel(AlbumModel* model);
    void setSelectionModel(QItemSelectionModel* selectionModel);

private slots:
    void createAlbum();

private:
    Ui::AlbumListWidget* ui;
    AlbumModel* mAlbumModel;
};
```

The `setModel()` and `setSelectionModel()` functions are the most important lines in this snippet. This widget require two things to work correctly:

- `AlbumModel`: This is the model class that provides access to data. We already created this class in the `gallery-core` project.
- `QItemSelectionModel`: This is a Qt class that handles the selection in a view. By default, views use their own selection model. Sharing the same selection model with different views or widgets will help us to synchronize album selection easily.

This is the main part of `AlbumListWidget.cpp`:

```
#include "AlbumListWidget.h"
#include "ui_AlbumListWidget.h"

#include <QInputDialog>

#include "AlbumModel.h"

AlbumListWidget::AlbumListWidget(QWidget *parent) :
    QWidget(parent),
    ui(new Ui::AlbumListWidget),
    mAlbumModel(nullptr)
{
    ui->setupUi(this);
```

```
        connect(ui->createAlbumButton, &QPushButton::clicked,
            this, &AlbumListWidget::createAlbum);
}

AlbumListWidget::~AlbumListWidget()
{
    delete ui;
}

void AlbumListWidget::setModel(AlbumModel* model)
{
    mAlbumModel = model;
    ui->albumList->setModel(mAlbumModel);
}

void AlbumListWidget::setSelectionModel(QItemSelectionModel*
selectionModel)
{
    ui->albumList->setSelectionModel(selectionModel);
}
```

The two setters will mainly be used to set the model and the selection model of the
albumList. Our QListView class will then automatically request the model (AlbumModel)
to get the row count and the Qt::DisplayRole (the album's name) for each one of them.

Let's now see the last part of the AlbumListWidget.cpp file that handles the album
creation:

```
void AlbumListWidget::createAlbum()
{
    if (!mAlbumModel) {
        return;
    }

    bool ok;
    QString albumName = QInputDialog::getText(this,
                            "Create a new Album",
                            "Choose an name",
                            QLineEdit::Normal,
                            "New album",
                            &ok);

    if (ok && !albumName.isEmpty()) {
        Album album(albumName);
        QModelIndex createdIndex = mAlbumModel->addAlbum(album);
        ui->albumList->setCurrentIndex(createdIndex);
    }
}
```

We already worked with the `QInputDialog` class in `Chapter 1`, *Get Your Qt Feet Wet*. This time we are using it to ask the user to enter an album's name. Then we create an `Album` class with the requested name. This object is just a "data holder;" `addAlbum()` will use it to create and store the real object with a unique ID.

The function `addAlbum()` returns us the `QModelIndex` value corresponding to the created album. From here, we can request the list view to select this new album.

# Creating a ThumbnailProxyModel

The future `AlbumWidget` view will display a grid of thumbnails with the pictures attached to the selected `Album`. In `Chapter 3`, *Dividing Your Project and Ruling Your Code*, we designed the `gallery-core` library to be agnostic of how a picture should be displayed: a `Picture` class contains only a `mUrl` field.

In other words, the generation of the thumbnails has to be done in `gallery-desktop` rather than `gallery-core`. We already have the `PictureModel` class that is responsible for retrieving the `Picture` information, so it would be great to be able to extend its behavior with the thumbnail data.

This is possible in Qt with the use of the `QAbstractProxyModel` class and its subclasses. The goal of this class is to process data from a base `QAbstractItemModel` (sorting, filtering, adding data, and so on) and present it to the view by proxying the original model. To take a database analogy, you can view it as a projection over a table.

The `QAbstractProxyModel` class has two subclasses:

- The `QIdentityProxyModel` subclass proxies its source model without any modification (all the indexes match). This class is suitable if you want to transform the `data()` function.
- The `QSortFilterProxyModel` subclass proxies its source model with the ability to sort and filter the passing data.

The former, QIdentityProxyModel, fits our requirements. The only thing we need to do is to extend the data() function with the thumbnail generation content. Create a new class named ThumbnailProxyModel. Here is the ThumbnailProxyModel.h file:

```
#include <QIdentityProxyModel>
#include <QHash>
#include <QPixmap>

class PictureModel;

class ThumbnailProxyModel : public QIdentityProxyModel
{
public:
    ThumbnailProxyModel(QObject* parent = 0);

    QVariant data(const QModelIndex& index, int role) const override;
    void setSourceModel(QAbstractItemModel* sourceModel) override;
    PictureModel* pictureModel() const;

private:
    void generateThumbnails(const QModelIndex& startIndex, int count);
    void reloadThumbnails();

private:
    QHash<QString, QPixmap*> mThumbnails;

};
```

This class extends QIdentityProxyModel and overrides a couple of functions:

- The data() function to provide the thumbnail data to the client of ThumbnailProxyModel
- The setSourceModel() function to register to signals emitted by sourceModel

The remaining custom functions have the following goals:

- The pictureModel() is a helper function that casts the sourceModel to a PictureModel*
- The generateThumbnails() function takes care of generating the QPixmap thumbnails for a given set of pictures
- The reloadThumbnails() is a helper function that clears the stored thumbnails before calling generateThumbnails()

As you might have guessed, the mThumbnails class stores the QPixmap\* thumbnails using the filepath for the key.

We now switch to the ThumbnailProxyModel.cpp file and build it from the ground up. Let's focus on generateThumbnails():

```
const unsigned int THUMBNAIL_SIZE = 350;
...
void ThumbnailProxyModel::generateThumbnails(
                                    const QModelIndex& startIndex,
int count)
{
    if (!startIndex.isValid()) {
        return;
    }

    const QAbstractItemModel* model = startIndex.model();
    int lastIndex = startIndex.row() + count;
    for(int row = startIndex.row(); row < lastIndex; row++) {
        QString filepath = model->data(model->index(row, 0),
PictureModel::Roles::FilePathRole).toString();
        QPixmap pixmap(filepath);
        auto thumbnail = new QPixmap(pixmap
                                .scaled(THUMBNAIL_SIZE,
THUMBNAIL_SIZE,
                                        Qt::KeepAspectRatio,
                                        Qt::SmoothTransformation));
        mThumbnails.insert(filepath, thumbnail);
    }
}
```

This function generates the thumbnails for a given range indicated by the parameters (startIndex and count). For each picture, we retrieve the filepath from the original model, using model->data(), and we generate a downsized QPixmap that is inserted in the mThumbnails QHash. Note that we arbitrarily set the thumbnail size using const THUMBNAIL_SIZE. The picture is scaled down to this size and respects the aspect ratio of the original picture.

Each time that an album is loaded, we should clear the content of the mThumbnails class and load the new pictures. This work is done by the reloadThumbnails() function:

```
void ThumbnailProxyModel::reloadThumbnails()
{
    qDeleteAll(mThumbnails);
    mThumbnails.clear();
    generateThumbnails(index(0, 0), rowCount());
```

```
    }
```

In this function, we simply clear the content of `mThumbnails` and call the `generateThumbnails()` function with parameters indicating that all the thumbnails should be generated. Let's see when these two functions will be used, in `setSourceModel()`:

```cpp
void ThumbnailProxyModel::setSourceModel(QAbstractItemModel* sourceModel)
{
    QIdentityProxyModel::setSourceModel(sourceModel);
    if (!sourceModel) {
        return;
    }

    connect(sourceModel, &QAbstractItemModel::modelReset,
                [this] {
        reloadThumbnails();
    });

    connect(sourceModel, &QAbstractItemModel::rowsInserted,
                [this] (const QModelIndex& parent, int first, int last) {
        generateThumbnails(index(first, 0), last - first + 1);
    });
}
```

When the `setSourceModel()` function is called, the `ThumbnailProxyModel` class is configured to know which base model should be proxied. In this function, we register lambdas to two signals emitted by the original model:

- The `modelReset` signal is triggered when pictures should be loaded for a given album. In this case, we have to completely reload the thumbnails.
- The `rowsInserted` signal is triggered each time new pictures are added. At this point, `generateThumbnails` should be called to update `mThumbnails` with these newcomers.

Finally, we have to cover the `data()` function:

```cpp
QVariant ThumbnailProxyModel::data(const QModelIndex& index, int role)
const
{
    if (role != Qt::DecorationRole) {
        return QIdentityProxyModel::data(index, role);
    }

    QString filepath = sourceModel()->data(index,
PictureModel::Roles::FilePathRole).toString();
```

```
        return *mThumbnails[filepath];
    }
```

For any role that is not `Qt::DecorationRole`, the parent class `data()` is called. In our case, this triggers the `data()` function from the original model, `PictureModel`. After that, when `data()` must return a thumbnail, the `filepath` of the picture referenced by the `index` is retrieved and used to return the `QPixmap` object of `mThumbnails`. Luckily for us, `QPixmap` can be implicitly cast to `QVariant`, so we do not have anything special to do here.

The last function to cover in the `ThumbnailProxyModel` class is the `pictureModel()` function:

```
    PictureModel* ThumbnailProxyModel::pictureModel() const
    {
        return static_cast<PictureModel*>(sourceModel());
    }
```

Classes that will interact with `ThumbnailProxyModel` will need to call some functions that are specific to `PictureModel` to create or delete pictures. This function is a helper to centralize the cast of the `sourceModel` to `PictureModel*`.

As a side note, we could have tried to generate thumbnails on-the-fly to avoid a possible initial bottleneck during the album loading (and the call to `generateThumbnails()`). However, `data()` is a `const` function, meaning that it cannot modify the `ThumbnailProxyModel` instance. This rules out any way of generating a thumbnail in the `data()` function and storing it in `mThumbnails`.

As you can see, `QIdentityProxyModel`, and more generally `QAbstractProxyModel`, are valuable tools to add behavior to an existing model without breaking it. In our case, this is enforced by design in so far as the `PictureModel` class is defined in `gallery-core` rather than `gallery-desktop`. Modifying `PictureModel` implies modifying `gallery-core` and potentially breaking its behavior for other users of the library. This approach lets us keep things cleanly separated.

# Displaying the selected album with AlbumWidget

This widget will display the data of the selected album from `AlbumListWidget`. Some buttons will allow us to interact with this album.

Here is the layout of the `AlbumWidget.ui` file:

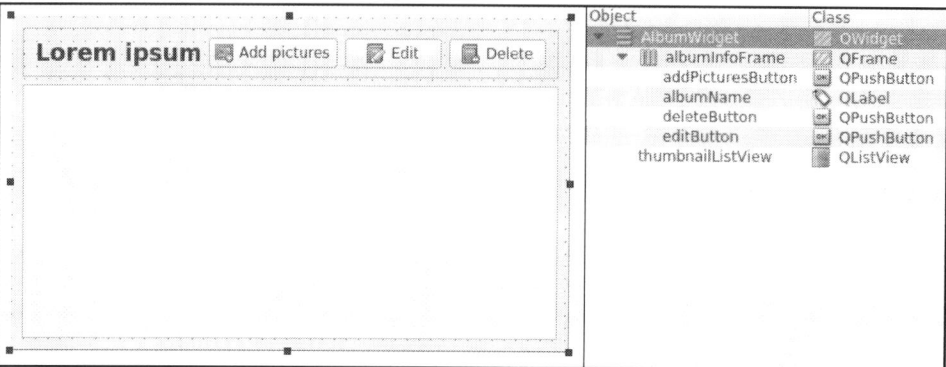

The top frame, `albumInfoFrame`, with a horizontal layout, contains:

- `albumName`: This object displays the album's name (**Lorem ipsum** in the designer)
- `addPicturesButton`: This object allows the user to add pictures selecting files
- `editButton`: This object is used to rename the album
- `deleteButton`: This object is used to delete the album

The bottom element, `thumbnailListView`, is a `QListView`. This list view represents items from `PictureModel`. By default, `QListView` is able to display a picture next to text requesting `Qt::DisplayRole` and `Qt::DecorationRole` from the model.

Take a look at the header `AlbumWidget.h` file:

```
#include <QWidget>
#include <QModelIndex>

namespace Ui {
class AlbumWidget;
}

class AlbumModel;
class PictureModel;
class QItemSelectionModel;
class ThumbnailProxyModel;

class AlbumWidget : public QWidget
{
    Q_OBJECT
```

```
public:
    explicit AlbumWidget(QWidget *parent = 0);
    ~AlbumWidget();

    void setAlbumModel(AlbumModel* albumModel);
    void setAlbumSelectionModel(QItemSelectionModel* albumSelectionModel);
    void setPictureModel(ThumbnailProxyModel* pictureModel);
    void setPictureSelectionModel(QItemSelectionModel* selectionModel);

signals:
    void pictureActivated(const QModelIndex& index);

private slots:
    void deleteAlbum();
    void editAlbum();
    void addPictures();

private:
    void clearUi();
    void loadAlbum(const QModelIndex& albumIndex);

private:
    Ui::AlbumWidget* ui;
    AlbumModel* mAlbumModel;
    QItemSelectionModel* mAlbumSelectionModel;

    ThumbnailProxyModel* mPictureModel;
    QItemSelectionModel* mPictureSelectionModel;
};
```

As this widget needs to deal with `Album` and `Picture` data, this class has `AlbumModel` and `ThumbnailProxyModel` setters. We also want to know and share the model selection with other widgets and views (that is, `AlbumListWidget`). That is why we also have `Album` and `Picture` model selection setters.

The signal `pictureActivated()` will be triggered when the user double-clicks on a thumbnail. We will see later how `MainWindow` will connect to this signal to display the picture at full size.

The private slots, `deleteAlbum()`, `editAlbum()`, and `addPictures()`, will be called when the user clicks on one of these buttons.

Finally, the `loadAlbum()` function will be called to update the UI for a specific album. The `clearUi()` function will be useful to clear all information displayed by this widget UI.

Take a look at the beginning of the implementation in the `AlbumWidget.cpp` file:

```cpp
#include "AlbumWidget.h"
#include "ui_AlbumWidget.h"

#include <QInputDialog>
#include <QFileDialog>

#include "AlbumModel.h"
#include "PictureModel.h"

AlbumWidget::AlbumWidget(QWidget *parent) :
    QWidget(parent),
    ui(new Ui::AlbumWidget),
    mAlbumModel(nullptr),
    mAlbumSelectionModel(nullptr),
    mPictureModel(nullptr),
    mPictureSelectionModel(nullptr)
{
    ui->setupUi(this);
    clearUi();

    ui->thumbnailListView->setSpacing(5);
    ui->thumbnailListView->setResizeMode(QListView::Adjust);
    ui->thumbnailListView->setFlow(QListView::LeftToRight);
    ui->thumbnailListView->setWrapping(true);

    connect(ui->thumbnailListView, &QListView::doubleClicked,
            this, &AlbumWidget::pictureActivated);

    connect(ui->deleteButton, &QPushButton::clicked,
            this, &AlbumWidget::deleteAlbum);

    connect(ui->editButton, &QPushButton::clicked,
            this, &AlbumWidget::editAlbum);

    connect(ui->addPicturesButton, &QPushButton::clicked,
            this, &AlbumWidget::addPictures);
}

AlbumWidget::~AlbumWidget()
{
    delete ui;
}
```

The constructor configures thumbnailListView, our QListView that will display thumbnails of the current selected album. We set here various parameters:

- setSpacing(): In this parameter, by default items are glued to each other. You can add spacing between them.
- setResizeMode(): This parameter dynamically lays out items when the view is resized. By default, items keep their original placement even if the view is resized.
- setFlow(): This parameter specifies the list direction. Here we want to display items from left to right. By default, the direction is TopToBottom.
- setWrapping(): This parameter allows an item to wrap when there is not enough space to display it in the visible area. By default, wrapping is not allowed and scrollbars will be displayed.

The end of the constructor performs all the signal connections related to the UI. The first one is a good example of signal relaying, explained in Chapter 1, *Get Your Qt Feet Wet*. We connect the QListView::doubleClicked signal to our class signal, AlbumWidget::pictureActivated. Other connections are common; we want to call a specific slot when the user clicks on a button. As always in the **Qt Designer Form Class**, the destructor will delete the member variable ui.

Let's see the AlbumModel setter implementation:

```
void AlbumWidget::setAlbumModel(AlbumModel* albumModel)
{
    mAlbumModel = albumModel;

    connect(mAlbumModel, &QAbstractItemModel::dataChanged,
        [this] (const QModelIndex &topLeft) {
            if (topLeft == mAlbumSelectionModel->currentIndex()) {
                loadAlbum(topLeft);
            }
    });
}

void AlbumWidget::setAlbumSelectionModel(QItemSelectionModel*
albumSelectionModel)
{
    mAlbumSelectionModel = albumSelectionModel;

    connect(mAlbumSelectionModel,
            &QItemSelectionModel::selectionChanged,
            [this] (const QItemSelection &selected) {
                if (selected.isEmpty()) {
```

```
                            clearUi();
                            return;
                    }
                    loadAlbum(selected.indexes().first());
        });
    }
```

If the selected album's data changed, we need to update the UI with the `loadAlbum()` function. A test is performed to ensure that the updated album is the currently selected one. Notice that the `QAbstractItemModel::dataChanged()` function has three parameters but the lambda slot syntax allows us to omit unused parameters.

Our `AlbumWidget` component must update its UI according to the currently selected album. As we share the same selection model, each time the user selects an album from `AlbumListWidget`, the signal `QItemSelectionModel::selectionChanged` is triggered. In this case, we update the UI by calling the `loadAlbum()` function. As we do not support album multi-selection, we can restrict the process to the first selected element. If the selection is empty, we simply clear the UI.

It is now the turn of the `PictureModel` setter implementation:

```
void AlbumWidget::setPictureModel(PictureModel* pictureModel)
{
    mPictureModel = pictureModel;
    ui->thumbnailListView->setModel(mPictureModel);
}

void AlbumWidget::setPictureSelectionModel(QItemSelectionModel*
selectionModel)
{
    ui->thumbnailListView->setSelectionModel(selectionModel);
}
```

It is very simple here. We set the model and the selection model of `thumbnailListView`, our `QListView` that will display the selected album's thumbnails. We also keep the picture model to manipulate the data later on.

We can now cover the features one by one. Let's start with album deletion:

```
void AlbumWidget::deleteAlbum()
{
    if (mAlbumSelectionModel->selectedIndexes().isEmpty()) {
        return;
    }
    int row = mAlbumSelectionModel->currentIndex().row();
    mAlbumModel->removeRow(row);
```

```
    // Try to select the previous album
    QModelIndex previousModelIndex = mAlbumModel->index(row - 1,
        0);
    if(previousModelIndex.isValid()) {
        mAlbumSelectionModel->setCurrentIndex(previousModelIndex,
            QItemSelectionModel::SelectCurrent);
        return;
    }

    // Try to select the next album
    QModelIndex nextModelIndex = mAlbumModel->index(row, 0);
    if(nextModelIndex.isValid()) {
        mAlbumSelectionModel->setCurrentIndex(nextModelIndex,
            QItemSelectionModel::SelectCurrent);
        return;
    }
}
```

The most important task in the `deleteAlbum()` function is to retrieve the current row index from `mAlbumSelectionModel`. Then, we can request `mAlbumModel` to delete this row. The rest of the function will only try to automatically select the previous or the next album. Once again, as we shared the same selection model, `AlbumListWidget` will automatically update its album selection.

The following snippet shows the album rename feature:

```
void AlbumWidget::editAlbum()
{
    if (mAlbumSelectionModel->selectedIndexes().isEmpty()) {
        return;
    }

    QModelIndex currentAlbumIndex =
        mAlbumSelectionModel->selectedIndexes().first();

    QString oldAlbumName = mAlbumModel->data(currentAlbumIndex,
        AlbumModel::Roles::NameRole).toString();

    bool ok;
    QString newName = QInputDialog::getText(this,
                                            "Album's name",
                                            "Change Album name",
                                            QLineEdit::Normal,
                                            oldAlbumName,
                                            &ok);

    if (ok && !newName.isEmpty()) {
```

```
            mAlbumModel->setData(currentAlbumIndex,
                            newName,
                            AlbumModel::Roles::NameRole);
    }
}
```

Here, again the `QInputDialog` class will help us to implement a feature. You should be confident with its behavior now. This function performs three steps:

1. Retrieve the current name from album model.
2. Generate a great input dialog.
3. Request the album model to update the name

As you can see, the generic functions `data()` and `setData()` from the models are very powerful when combined with `ItemDataRole`. As already explained, we do not directly update our UI; this will be automatically performed because `setData()` emits a signal, `dataChanged()`, which `AlbumWidget` handles.

The last feature allows us to add some new picture files in the current album:

```
void AlbumWidget::addPictures()
{
    QStringList filenames =
        QFileDialog::getOpenFileNames(this,
            "Add pictures",
             QDir::homePath(),
            "Picture files (*.jpg *.png)");

    if (!filenames.isEmpty()) {
        QModelIndex lastModelIndex;
        for (auto filename : filenames) {
            Picture picture(filename);
            lastModelIndex =
    mPictureModel->pictureModel()->addPicture(picture);
        }
        ui->thumbnailListView->setCurrentIndex(lastModelIndex);
    }
}
```

The QFileDialog class is used here to help the user select several picture files. For each filename, we create a Picture data holder, like we have already seen in this chapter for album creation. Then we can request mPictureModel to add this picture in the current album. Note that, because mPictureModel is a ThumbnailProxyModel class, we have to retrieve the real PictureModel using the helper function, pictureModel(). As the function addPicture() returns us the corresponding QModelIndex, we finally select the most recently added picture in thumbnailListView.

Let's complete AlbumWidget.cpp:

```
void AlbumWidget::clearUi()
{
    ui->albumName->setText("");
    ui->deleteButton->setVisible(false);
    ui->editButton->setVisible(false);
    ui->addPicturesButton->setVisible(false);
}

void AlbumWidget::loadAlbum(const QModelIndex& albumIndex)
{
    mPictureModel->pictureModel()->setAlbumId(mAlbumModel->data(albumIndex,
        AlbumModel::Roles::IdRole).toInt());

    ui->albumName->setText(mAlbumModel->data(albumIndex,
        Qt::DisplayRole).toString());

    ui->deleteButton->setVisible(true);
    ui->editButton->setVisible(true);
    ui->addPicturesButton->setVisible(true);
}
```

The clearUi() function clears the album's name and hides the buttons, while the loadAlbum() function retrieves the Qt::DisplayRole (the album's name) and displays the buttons.

# Enhancing thumbnails with PictureDelegate

By default, a `QListView` class will request `Qt::DisplayRole` and `Qt::DecorationRole` to display text and a picture for each item. Thus, we already have a visual result, for free, that looks like this:

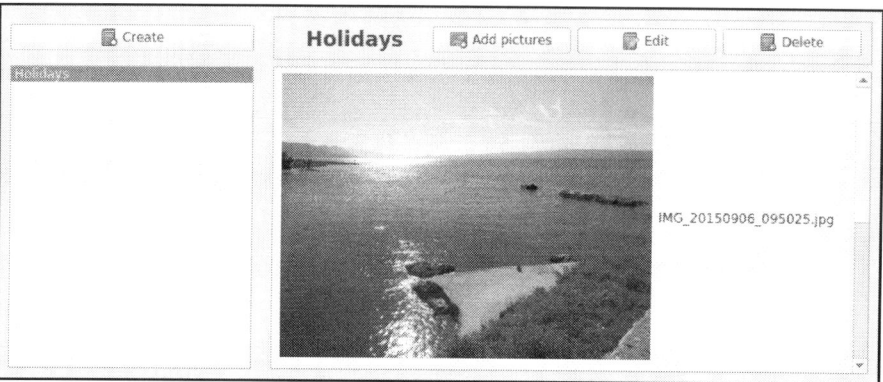

However, our **Gallery** application deserves better thumbnail rendering. Hopefully, we can easily customize it using the view's delegate concept. A `QListView` class provides a default item rendering. We can do our own item rendering by creating a class that inherits `QStyledItemDelegate`. The aim is to paint your dream thumbnails with a name banner like the following screenshot:

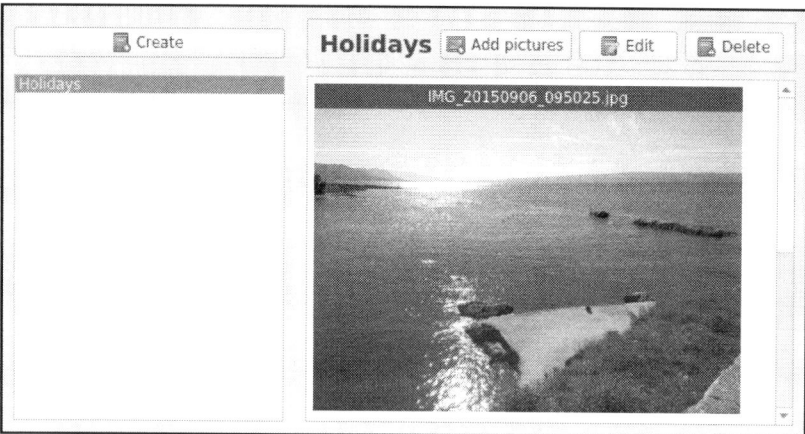

Let's take a look at `PictureDelegate.h`:

```
#include <QStyledItemDelegate>

class PictureDelegate : public QStyledItemDelegate
{
    Q_OBJECT
public:
    PictureDelegate(QObject* parent = 0);

    void paint(QPainter* painter, const QStyleOptionViewItem&
        option, const QModelIndex& index) const override;

    QSize sizeHint(const QStyleOptionViewItem& option,
        const QModelIndex& index) const override;
};
```

That is right, we only have to override two functions. The most important function, `paint()`, will allow us to paint the item like we want. The `sizeHint()` function will be used to specify the item size.

We can now see the painter work in `PictureDelegate.cpp`:

```
#include "PictureDelegate.h"

#include <QPainter>

const unsigned int BANNER_HEIGHT = 20;
const unsigned int BANNER_COLOR = 0x303030;
const unsigned int BANNER_ALPHA = 200;
const unsigned int BANNER_TEXT_COLOR = 0xffffff;
const unsigned int HIGHLIGHT_ALPHA = 100;

PictureDelegate::PictureDelegate(QObject* parent) :
    QStyledItemDelegate(parent)
{
}

void PictureDelegate::paint(QPainter* painter, const QStyleOptionViewItem&
option, const QModelIndex& index) const
{
    painter->save();

    QPixmap pixmap = index.model()->data(index,
        Qt::DecorationRole).value<QPixmap>();
    painter->drawPixmap(option.rect.x(), option.rect.y(), pixmap);

    QRect bannerRect = QRect(option.rect.x(), option.rect.y(),
```

```
        pixmap.width(), BANNER_HEIGHT);
    QColor bannerColor = QColor(BANNER_COLOR);
    bannerColor.setAlpha(BANNER_ALPHA);
    painter->fillRect(bannerRect, bannerColor);

    QString filename = index.model()->data(index,
        Qt::DisplayRole).toString();
    painter->setPen(BANNER_TEXT_COLOR);
    painter->drawText(bannerRect, Qt::AlignCenter, filename);

    if (option.state.testFlag(QStyle::State_Selected)) {
        QColor selectedColor = option.palette.highlight().color();
        selectedColor.setAlpha(HIGHLIGHT_ALPHA);
        painter->fillRect(option.rect, selectedColor);
    }

    painter->restore();
}
```

Each time `QListView` needs to display an item, this delegate's `paint()` function will be called. The paint system can be seen as layers that you paint one on top of each other. The `QPainter` class allows us to paint anything we want: circles, pies, rectangles, text, and so on. The item area can be retrieved with `option.rect()`. Here are the steps:

1. It is easy to break the `painter` state passed in the parameter list, thus we must save the painter state with `painter->save()` before doing anything, to be able to restore it when we have finished our drawing.
2. Retrieve the item thumbnail and draw it with the `QPainter::drawPixmap()` function.
3. Paint a translucent gray banner on top of the thumbnail with the `QPainter::fillRect()` function.
4. Retrieve the item display name and draw it on the banner using the `QPainter::drawText()` function.
5. If the item is selected, we paint a translucent rectangle on the top using the highlight color from the item.
6. We restore the painter state to its original state.

If you want to draw a more complex item, check the `QPainter` official documentation at `doc.qt.io/qt-5/qpainter.html`.

This is the `sizeHint()` function's implementation:

```
QSize PictureDelegate::sizeHint(const QStyleOptionViewItem& /*option*/,
const QModelIndex& index) const
{
    const QPixmap& pixmap = index.model()->data(index,
        Qt::DecorationRole).value<QPixmap>();
    return pixmap.size();
}
```

This one is easier. We want the item's size to be equal to the thumbnail size. As we kept the aspect ratio of the thumbnail during its creation in `Picture::setFilePath()`, thumbnails can have a different width and height. Hence, we basically retrieve the thumbnail and return its size.

> When you create an item delegate, avoid directly inheriting the `QItemDelegate` class and instead inherit `QStyledItemDelegate`. This last one supports Qt style sheets, allowing you to easily customize the rendering.

Now that `PictureDelegate` is ready, we can configure our `thumbnailListView` to use it, updating the `AlbumWidget.cpp` file like this:

```
AlbumWidget::AlbumWidget(QWidget *parent) :
    QWidget(parent),
    ui(new Ui::AlbumWidget),
    mAlbumModel(nullptr),
    mAlbumSelectionModel(nullptr),
    mPictureModel(nullptr),
    mPictureSelectionModel(nullptr)
{
    ui->setupUi(this);
    clearUi();

    ui->thumbnailListView->setSpacing(5);
    ui->thumbnailListView->setResizeMode(QListView::Adjust);
    ui->thumbnailListView->setFlow(QListView::LeftToRight);
    ui->thumbnailListView->setWrapping(true);
    ui->thumbnailListView->setItemDelegate(
        new PictureDelegate(this));
    ...
}
```

**Qt tip**
An item delegate can also manage the editing process with the
`QStyledItemDelegate::createEditor()` function.

# Displaying a picture with PictureWidget

This widget will be called to display a picture at its full size. We also add some buttons to
go to the previous/next picture or delete the current one.

Let's start to analyze the `PictureWidget.ui` form, here is the design view:

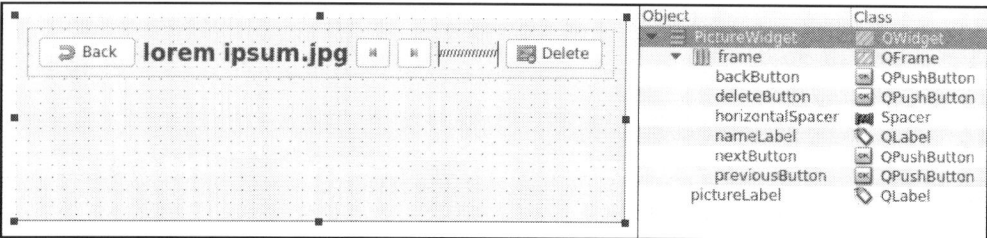

Here are the details:

- `backButton`: This object requests to display the gallery
- `deleteButton`: This object removes the picture from the album
- `nameLabel`: This object displays the picture name
- `nextButton`: This object selects the next picture in the album
- `previousButton`: This object selects the previous picture in the album
- `pictureLabel`: This object displays the picture

We can now take a look at the header `PictureWidget.h`:

```
#include <QWidget>
#include <QItemSelection>

namespace Ui {
class PictureWidget;
}

class PictureModel;
class QItemSelectionModel;
class ThumbnailProxyModel;
```

```
class PictureWidget : public QWidget
{
    Q_OBJECT

public:
    explicit PictureWidget(QWidget *parent = 0);
    ~PictureWidget();
    void setModel(ThumbnailProxyModel* model);
    void setSelectionModel(QItemSelectionModel* selectionModel);

signals:
    void backToGallery();

protected:
    void resizeEvent(QResizeEvent* event) override;

private slots:
    void deletePicture();
    void loadPicture(const QItemSelection& selected);

private:
    void updatePicturePixmap();

private:
    Ui::PictureWidget* ui;
    ThumbnailProxyModel* mModel;
    QItemSelectionModel* mSelectionModel;
    QPixmap mPixmap;
};
```

No surprises here, we have the `ThumbnailProxyModel*` and `QItemSelectionModel*` setters in the `PictureWidget` class. The signal `backToGallery()` is triggered when the user clicks on the `backButton` object. It will be handled by `MainWindow` to display again the gallery. We override `resizeEvent()` to ensure that we always use all the visible area to display the picture. The `deletePicture()` slot will process the deletion when the user clicks on the corresponding button. The `loadPicture()` function will be called to update the UI with the specified picture. Finally, `updatePicturePixmap()` is a helper function to display the picture according to the current widget size.

This widget is really similar to the others. As a result, we will not put the full implementation code of `PictureWidget.cpp` here. You can check the full source code example if needed.

Let's see how this widget is able to always display the picture at its full size in
`PictureWidget.cpp`:

```
void PictureWidget::resizeEvent(QResizeEvent* event)
{
    QWidget::resizeEvent(event);
    updatePicturePixmap();
}

void PictureWidget::updatePicturePixmap()
{
    if (mPixmap.isNull()) {
        return;
    }
    ui->pictureLabel->setPixmap(mPixmap.scaled(ui->pictureLabel->size(),
Qt::KeepAspectRatio));
}
```

So, every time the widget is resized, we call `updatePicturePixmap()`. The `mPixmap`
variable is the full-size picture from `PictureModel`. This function will scale the picture to
the `pictureLabel` size, keeping the aspect ratio. You can freely resize the window and
enjoy your picture with the biggest possible size.

# Composing your Gallery app

Alright, we completed `AlbumListWidget`, `AlbumWidget`, and `PictureWidget`. If you
remember correctly, `AlbumListWidget` and `AlbumWidget` are contained in a widget
called `GalleryWidget`.

Let's take a look at the `GalleryWidget.ui` file:

This widget does not contain any standard Qt widgets but only our created widgets. Qt provides two ways to use your own widgets in the Qt designer:

- **Promoting widgets**: This is the fastest and easiest way
- **Creating widget plugin for Qt designer**: This is more powerful but more complex

In this chapter, we will use the first way, which consists of placing a generic QWidget as a placeholder and then promoting it to our custom widget class. You can follow these steps to add the albumListWidget and the albumWidget objects to the GalleryWidget.ui file from the Qt designer:

1. Drag and drop a **Widget** from **Containers** to your form.
2. Set the **objectName** (for example, albumListWidget) from the **Property Editor**.
3. Select **Promote to...** from the widget contextual menu.
4. Set the promoted class name (for example, AlbumWidget).
5. Check that header file is correct (for example, AlbumWidget.h).
6. Click on the **Add** button and then click on **Promote**.

If you fail your widget promotion, you can always reverse it with **Demote to QWidget** from the contextual menu.

There is nothing really exciting in the header and implementation of GalleryWidget. We only provide setters for the model and model selection of Album and Picture to forward them to albumListWidget and albumWidget. This class also relays the signal pictureActivated from albumWidget. Please check the full source code if needed.

This is the final part of this chapter. We will now analyze MainWindow. Nothing is done in MainWindow.ui because everything is handled in the code. This is MainWindow.h:

```
#include <QMainWindow>
#include <QStackedWidget>

namespace Ui {
class MainWindow;
}

class GalleryWidget;
class PictureWidget;

class MainWindow : public QMainWindow
{
    Q_OBJECT
```

```
public:
    explicit MainWindow(QWidget *parent = 0);
    ~MainWindow();

public slots:
    void displayGallery();
    void displayPicture(const QModelIndex& index);

private:
    Ui::MainWindow *ui;
    GalleryWidget* mGalleryWidget;
    PictureWidget* mPictureWidget;
    QStackedWidget* mStackedWidget;
};
```

The two slots, `displayGallery()` and `displayPicture()`, will be used to switch the display between the gallery (album list with the album and thumbnail) and the picture ( full-size). The `QStackedWidget` class can contain various widgets but display only one at a time.

Let's take a look to the beginning of the constructor in the `MainWindow.cpp` file:

```
ui->setupUi(this);

AlbumModel* albumModel = new AlbumModel(this);
QItemSelectionModel* albumSelectionModel =
    new QItemSelectionModel(albumModel, this);
mGalleryWidget->setAlbumModel(albumModel);
mGalleryWidget->setAlbumSelectionModel(albumSelectionModel);
```

First, we initialize the UI by calling `ui->setupUi()`. Then we create `AlbumModel` and its `QItemSelectionModel`. Finally, we call the setters of `GalleryWidget` that will dispatch them to the `AlbumListWidget` and `AlbumWidget` objects.

Continuing our analysis of this constructor:

```
PictureModel* pictureModel = new PictureModel(*albumModel, this);
ThumbnailProxyModel* thumbnailModel = new ThumbnailProxyModel(this);
thumbnailModel->setSourceModel(pictureModel);

QItemSelectionModel* pictureSelectionModel =
    new QItemSelectionModel(pictureModel, this);

mGalleryWidget->setPictureModel(thumbnailModel);
mGalleryWidget->setPictureSelectionModel(pictureSelectionModel);
mPictureWidget->setModel(thumbnailModel);
mPictureWidget->setSelectionModel(pictureSelectionModel);
```

The behavior with `Picture` is close to the previous one with `Album`. But we also share `ThumbnailProxyModel`, which is initialized from `PictureModel`, and its `QItemSelectionModel` with `PictureWidget`.

The constructor now performs the signal/slot connections:

```
connect(mGalleryWidget, &GalleryWidget::pictureActivated,
        this, &MainWindow::displayPicture);

connect(mPictureWidget, &PictureWidget::backToGallery,
        this, &MainWindow::displayGallery);
```

Do you remember the `pictureActivated()` function? This signal is emitted when you double-click on a thumbnail in `albumWidget`. We can now connect it to our `displayPicture` slot, which will switch the display with the picture at its full size. Do not forget to also connect the `backToGallery` signal emitted when the user clicks on the `backButton` from `PictureWidget`. It will switch again to display the gallery.

The last part of the constructor is easy:

```
mStackedWidget->addWidget(mGalleryWidget);
mStackedWidget->addWidget(mPictureWidget);
displayGallery();

setCentralWidget(mStackedWidget);
```

We add our two widgets, `mGalleryWidget` and `mPictureWidget`, to the `mStackedWidget` class. When the application starts, we want to display the gallery, so we call our own slot `displayGallery()`. Finally, we define `mStackedWidget` as the main window's central widget.

To finish this chapter, let's see what happens in these two magic slots that allows to switch the display when the user requests it:

```
void MainWindow::displayGallery()
{
    mStackedWidget->setCurrentWidget(mGalleryWidget);
}

void MainWindow::displayPicture(const QModelIndex& /*index*/)
{
    mStackedWidget->setCurrentWidget(mPictureWidget);
}
```

That seems ridiculously easy. We just request `mStackedWidget` to select the corresponding widget. As `PictureWidget` shares the same selection model with other views, we can even ignore the `index` variable.

# Summary

The real separation between data and representation is not always an easy task. Dividing the core and the GUI in two different projects is a good practice. It will force you to design separated layers in your application. At first sight, the Qt model/view system can appear complex. But this chapter taught you how powerful it can be and how easy it is to use. Thanks to the Qt framework, the persistence of data in a database can be done without headaches.

This chapter built on top of the foundations laid with the `gallery-core` library. In the next chapter, we will reuse the same core library and create a mobile UI with Qt Quick in QML.

# 5
# Dominating the Mobile UI

In Chapter 3, *Dividing Your Project and Ruling Your Code*, we created a strong core library to handle a picture gallery. We will now use this gallery-core library to create a mobile application.

We will teach you how to create a Qt Quick project from scratch. You will create custom Qt Quick views with QML. This chapter will also cover how your QML views can communicate with the C++ library.

At the end of this chapter, your gallery application will run on your mobile (Android or iOS) with a dedicated GUI compliant with touch devices. This application will offer the same features as the desktop application.

This chapter covers the following topics:

- Creating a Qt Quick project
- QML
- Qt Quick controls
- Qt for mobile (Android and iOS)
- Calling C++ functions from QML

# Starting with Qt Quick and QML

Qt Quick is another way of creating applications with Qt. You can use it to create a complete application in place of Qt Widgets. The Qt Quick module provides transitions, animations, and visual effects. You can also customize graphical effects with shaders. This module is especially efficient at making software for devices using touchscreens. Qt Quick uses a dedicated language: Qt Modeling Language (QML). It is a declarative language; the syntax is close to the JSON (JavaScript Object Notation) syntax. Furthermore, QML also supports JavaScript expressions inline or in a separate file.

Let's begin with a simple example of a Qt Quick application using QML. Create a new file called `main.qml` with this code snippet:

```
import QtQuick 2.5
import QtQuick.Window 2.2

Window {
    visible: true
    width: 640; height: 480

    // A nice red rectangle
    Rectangle {
        width: 200; height: 200
        color: "red"
    }
}
```

Qt 5 provides a nice tool called `qmlscene` to prototype a QML user interface. You can find the binary file in your Qt installation folder, for example: `Qt/5.7/gcc_64/bin/qmlscene`. To load your `main.qml` file, you can run the tool and select the file, or use the CLI with the `.qml` file in an argument: `qmlscene main.qml`. You should see something like this:

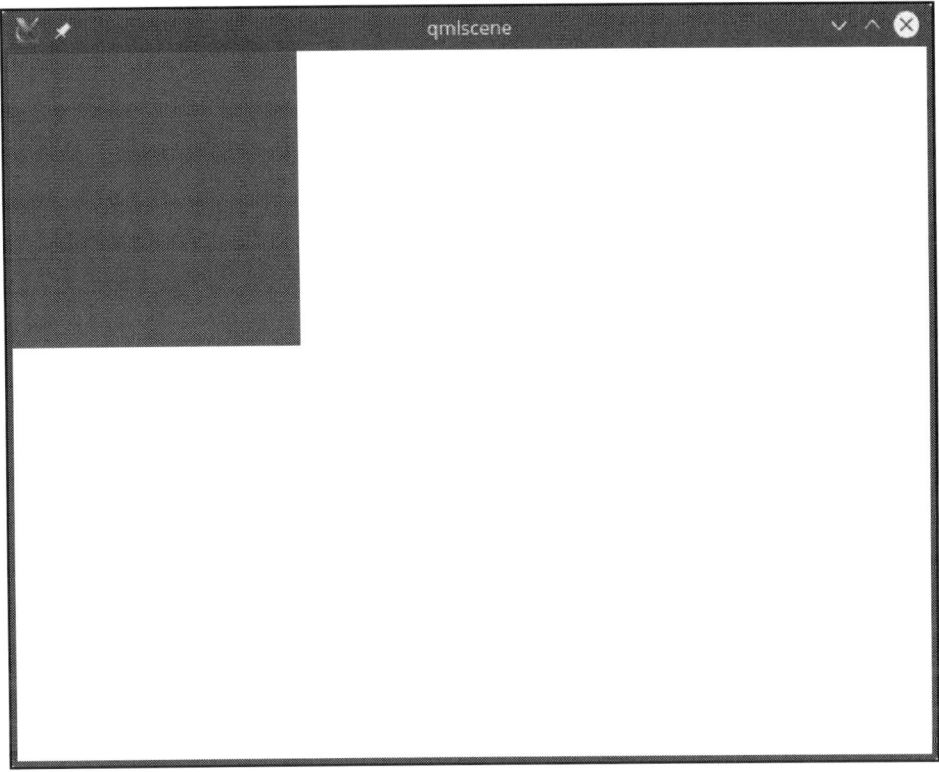

To use a Qt Quick module, you need to import it. The syntax is easy:

```
import <moduleName> <moduleVersion>
```

In this example we import `QtQuick`, which is the common module that will provide basic components (`Rectangle`, `Image`, `Text`) and we also import the `QtQuick.Window` module that will provide the main window application (`Window`).

A QML component can have properties. For example, we set the `width` property of the `Window` class to the value `640`. Here is the generic syntax:

```
<ObjectType> {
    <PropertyName>: <PropertyValue>
}
```

We can now update `main.qml` file with some new rectangles:

```
import QtQuick 2.5
import QtQuick.Window 2.2

Window {
    visible: true
    width: 640; height: 480

    Rectangle {
        width: 200; height: 200
        color: "red"
    }

    Rectangle {
        width: 200; height: 200
        color: "green"
        x: 100; y: 100

        Rectangle {
            width: 50; height: 50
            color: "blue"
            x: 100; y: 100
        }
    }
}
```

Here is the visual result:

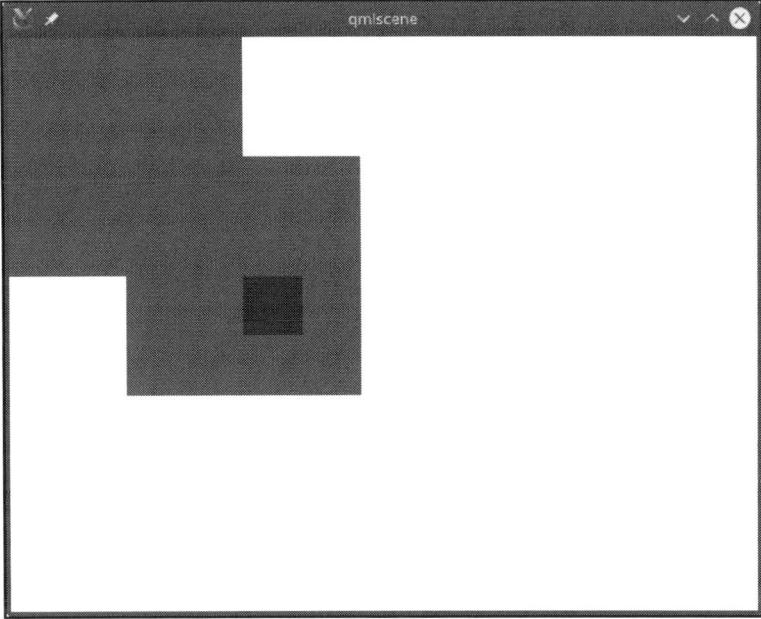

Your QML file describes the UI as a hierarchy of components. The hierarchy below the `Window` element is the following:

- **Red** `Rectangle`
- **Green** `Rectangle`
- **Blue** `Rectangle`

Each nested item will always have its x, y coordinates relative to its parent.

To structure your application, you can build reusable QML components. You can easily create a new component. All QML components must have a single root item. Let's build a new `MyToolbar` component by creating a new file called `MyToolbar.qml`:

```
import QtQuick 2.5

import QtQuick 2.5

Rectangle {
    color: "gray"
    height: 50
```

```
Rectangle {
    id: purpleRectangle
    width: 50; height: parent.height
    color: "purple"
    radius: 10
}

Text {
    anchors.left: purpleRectangle.right
    anchors.right: parent.right
    text: "Dominate the Mobile UI"
    font.pointSize: 30
}
}
```

The gray Rectangle element will be our root item used as background. We also created two items:

- A purple Rectangle element that can be identified with the ID purpleRectangle. The height of this item will be the height of its parent, that is, the gray Rectangle element.
- A Text item. In this case, we use anchors. It will help us to layout items without using hardcoded coordinates. The left of the Text item will be aligned with the right of purpleRectangle, and the right of the Text item will be aligned with the right of the parent (the gray Rectangle element).

Qt Quick provides a lot of anchors:
left, horizontalCenter, right, top, verticalCenter, and bottom. You can also use convenience anchors such as fill or centerIn. For more information on anchors, take a look at http://doc.qt.io/qt-5/qtq uick-positioning-anchors.html.

You can use MyToolbar in your window by updating your main.qml:

```
Window {
    ...
    MyToolbar {
        width: parent.width
    }
}
```

We set the width to the parent width. Like this, the toolbar fills the window's width. Here is the result:

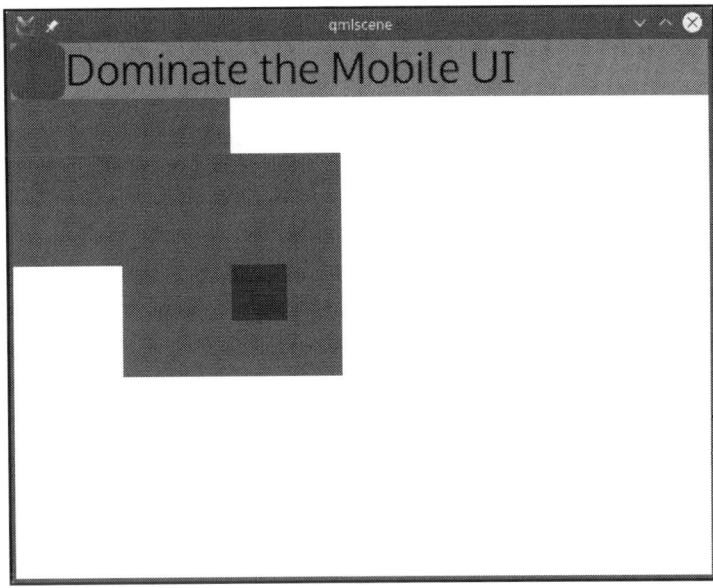

Anchors are great to align specific items, but if you want to layout several items in grid, row, or column fashion, you can use the QtQuick.layouts module. Here is an example of the updated main.qml:

```
import QtQuick 2.5
import QtQuick.Window 2.2
import QtQuick.Layouts 1.3

Window {
    visible: true
    width: 640; height: 480

    MyToolbar {
        id: myToolbar
        width: parent.width
    }

    RowLayout {
        anchors.top: myToolbar.bottom
        anchors.left: parent.left
        anchors.right: parent.right
        anchors.bottom: parent.bottom
```

```
                Rectangle { width: 200; height: 200; color: "red" }
                Rectangle { width: 200; height: 200 color: "green" }
                Rectangle { width: 50; height: 50; color: "blue" }
        }
    }
```

You should get something like this:

As you can see, we use a `RowLayout` element that fits under the `myToolbar` and to its parent, a `Window` element. This item provides a way to dynamically layout items in a row. Qt Quick also provides other layout items: `GridLayout` and `ColumnLayout`.

Your custom component can also expose custom properties that can be modified outside of the component itself. You can do it by adding the `property` attribute. Please update `MyToolbar.qml`:

```
import QtQuick 2.5

Rectangle {

    property color iconColor: "purple"
    property alias title: label.text

    color: "gray"
    height: 50

    Rectangle {
        id: purpleRectangle
        width: 50; height: parent.height
        color: iconColor
        radius: 10
    }

    Text {
        id: label
        anchors.left: purpleRectangle.right
        anchors.right: parent.right
        text: "Dominate the Mobile UI"
        font.pointSize: 30
    }
}
```

The `iconColor` is a really new property that is a fully-fledged variable. We also update the `Rectangle` attribute to use this property as `color`. The `title` property is only an `alias`, you can see it as a pointer to update the `label.text` property.

From outside you can use these attributes with the same syntax; please update the `main.qml` file with the following snippet:

```
import QtQuick 2.5
import QtQuick.Window 2.2
import QtQuick.Layouts 1.3

Window {
    visible: true
    width: 640; height: 480

    MyToolbar {
        id: myToolbar
```

```
            width: parent.width

            title: "Dominate Qt Quick"
            iconColor: "yellow"
        }
    ...
}
```

You should get a nice updated toolbar like this one:

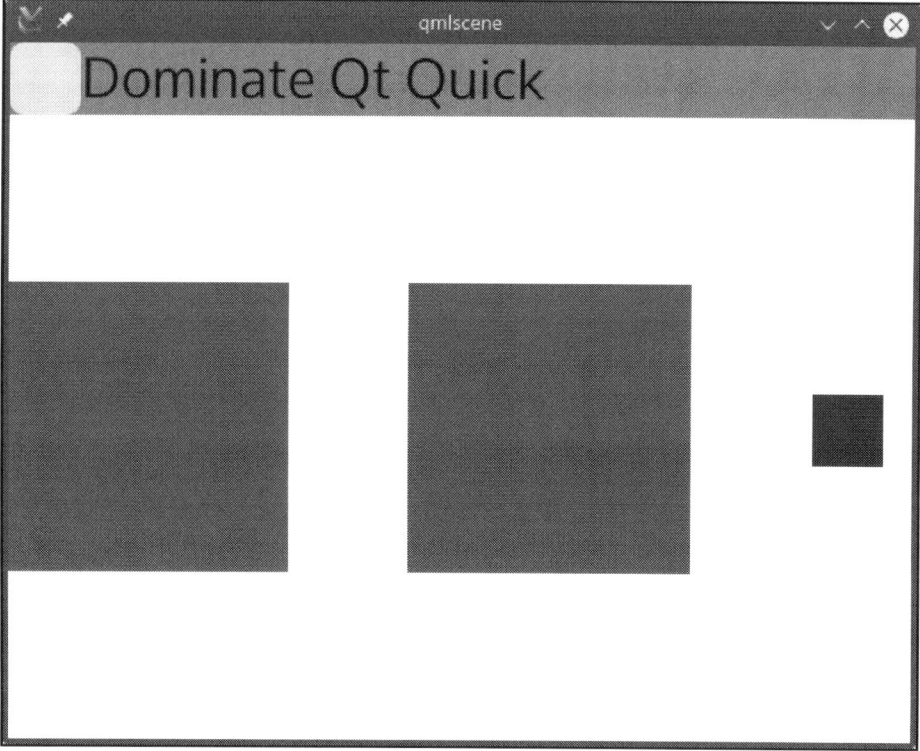

We have covered the basics of QML, now we are going to proceed to mobile application development using QML.

# Checking your development environment

To be able to create a Qt application for Android, you must have:

- A device with Android v2.3.3 (API 10) or later
- Android SDK
- Android NDK
- JDK
- Qt Prebuilt Components for Android x86 (from the Qt Maintenance Tool)
- Qt Prebuilt Components for Android ARMv7 (from the Qt Maintenance Tool)

To be able to create a Qt application for iOS, you must have:

- A device with iOS 5.0 or later
- A Mac desktop computer
- Xcode
- Qt for iOS (from Qt Maintenance Tool)

When starting, Qt Creator will detect and create Android and iOS Qt kits. You can check your existing kits from **Tools** | **Options** | **Build & Run** | **Kits**, as shown in the following screenshot:

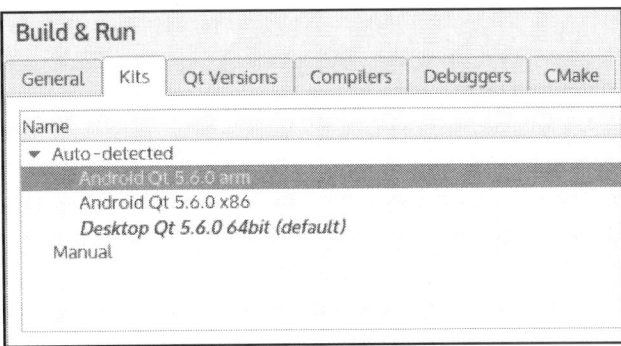

# Creating a Qt Quick project

This chapter will follow the same project structure we covered in Chapter 4, *Conquering the Desktop UI*: a parent project `ch05-gallery-mobile.pro` will host our two subprojects, `gallery-core` and the new `gallery-mobile`.

In Qt creator, you can create a Qt Quick subproject from **File** | **New File or Project** | **Application** | **Qt Quick Controls Application** | **Choose**.

The wizard will allow you to customize your project creation:

- Location
  - Choose a project name (`gallery-mobile`) and a location
- Details
  - Deselect **With ui.qml file**
  - Deselect **Enable native styling**
- Kits
  - Select your desktop kit
  - Select at least one mobile kit
- Summary
  - Be sure to add gallery-mobile as a subproject of `ch05-gallery-mobile.pro`

Let's take some time to explain why we created our project with these options.

The first thing to analyze is the application template. By default, Qt Quick only provides basic QML components (`Rectangle`, `Image`, `Text`, and so on). Advanced components will be handled by Qt Quick modules. For this project we will use Qt Quick Controls (`ApplicationWindow`, `Button`, `TextField`, and so on). That is why we chose to begin with a **Qt Quick Controls application**. Keep in mind that you can always import and use Qt Quick modules later.

In this chapter, we will not use the Qt Quick Designer. As a consequence, `.ui.qml` files are not required. Even if the designer can help a lot, it is good to understand and write QML files yourself.

The desktop "native styling" is disabled because this project mainly targets mobile platforms. Moreover, disabling "native styling" avoids heavy dependency on the Qt widgets module.

Finally, we select at least two kits. The first one is our desktop kit. The other kits are the mobile platforms you target. We usually use the following development workflow:

- Fast iterations on desktop
- Check and fix behavior on mobile emulator/simulator
- Real test on the mobile device

Deployment on a real device is generally longer so you can do most development with the desktop kit. The mobile kits will allow you to check your application behavior on a real mobile device or on an emulator (for example with a Qt Android x86 kit).

Let's talk about the files automatically generated by the wizard. Here is the `main.cpp` file:

```cpp
#include <QGuiApplication>
#include <QQmlApplicationEngine>

int main(int argc, char *argv[])
{
    QGuiApplication app(argc, argv);

    QQmlApplicationEngine engine;
    engine.load(QUrl(QStringLiteral("qrc:/main.qml")));

    return app.exec();
}
```

We use here `QGuiApplication` and not `QApplication` because we do not use Qt widgets in this project. Then, we create the QML engine and load `qrc:/mail.qml`. As you may have guessed (with the `qrc:/` prefix), this QML file is in a Qt resource file.

You can open the `qml.qrc` file to find the `main.qml`:

```qml
import QtQuick 2.5
import QtQuick.Controls 1.4

ApplicationWindow {
    visible: true
    width: 640
    height: 480
    title: qsTr("Hello World")

    menuBar: MenuBar {
        Menu {
            title: qsTr("File")
            MenuItem {
                text: qsTr("&Open")
```

```
                    onTriggered: console.log("Open action triggered");
            }
            MenuItem {
                text: qsTr("Exit")
                onTriggered: Qt.quit();
            }
        }
    }

    Label {
        text: qsTr("Hello World")
        anchors.centerIn: parent
    }
}
```

The first thing to do is to import types used in the file. Notice the module version at the end of each import. The `QtQuick` module will import basic QML elements (`Rectangle`, `Image`, and so on) while the `QtQuick.Controls` module will import advanced QML elements from the `QtQuick Controls` submodule (`ApplicationWindow`, `MenuBar`, `MenuItem`, `Label`, and so on).

Then, we define the root element of type `ApplicationWindow`. It provides a top-level application window with the following items: `MenuBar`, `ToolBar` and `StatusBar`. The properties `visible`, `width`, `height`, and `title` of `ApplicationWindow` are primitive types. The syntax is simple and intelligible.

The `menuBar` property is more complex. This `MenuBar` property is composed of a `Menu` file, itself composed of two `MenuItems`: `Open` and `Exit`. A `MenuItem` emits a `triggered()` signal each time it is activated. In this case, the `MenuItem` file will log a message on the console. The exit `MenuItem` terminates the application.

Finally, a `Label` displaying "Hello World" is added in the content area of our `ApplicationWindow` type. Positioning items with anchors is useful. In our case the label is centered vertically and horizontally in its parent, `ApplicationWindow`.

Before going ahead, check that this sample runs correctly on your desktop and on your mobile.

# Preparing your Qt Quick gallery entry point

First of all, you need to link this project to our `gallery-core` library. We already covered how to link an internal library in Chapter 4, *Conquering the Desktop UI*. For more details, refer to it. This is the updated `gallery-mobile.pro` file:

```
TEMPLATE = app

QT += qml quick sql svg

CONFIG += c++11

SOURCES += main.cpp

RESOURCES += gallery.qrc

LIBS += -L$$OUT_PWD/../gallery-core/ -lgallery-core
INCLUDEPATH += $$PWD/../gallery-core
DEPENDPATH += $$PWD/../gallery-core

contains(ANDROID_TARGET_ARCH,x86) {
    ANDROID_EXTRA_LIBS = \
        $$[QT_INSTALL_LIBS]/libQt5Sql.so
}
```

Please notice that we made several changes here:

- We added the `sql` module to deploy the dependency on your mobile device
- We added the `svg` module for the button icons
- The `qml.qrc` file has been renamed in `gallery.qrc`
- We linked the `gallery-core` library
- By default, the `sql` shared object (`libQt5Sql.so`) will not be deployed on your Android x86 device. You have to explicitly include it in your `.pro` file.

You can now use classes from the `gallery-core` library in our `gallery-mobile` application. Let's see how to bind C++ models with QML. This is the updated `main.cpp`:

```cpp
#include <QGuiApplication>
#include <QQmlApplicationEngine>
#include <QQmlContext>
#include <QQuickView>

#include "AlbumModel.h"
#include "PictureModel.h"
```

```
int main(int argc, char *argv[])
{
    QGuiApplication app(argc, argv);

    AlbumModel albumModel;
    PictureModel pictureModel(albumModel);

    QQmlApplicationEngine engine;

    QQmlContext* context = engine.rootContext();
    context->setContextProperty("albumModel", &albumModel);
    context->setContextProperty("pictureModel", &pictureModel);

    engine.load(QUrl(QStringLiteral("qrc:/qml/main.qml")));

    return app.exec();
}
```

Our models will be instantiated in C++ and exposed to QML using the root `QQmlContext` object. The `setContextProperty()` function allows us to bind a C++ `QObject` to a QML property. The first argument will be the QML property name. We are only binding a C++ object to a QML property; the context object does not take ownership of this object.

Let's now talk about the mobile application itself. We will define three pages with specific roles:

- `AlbumListPage`
  - Displays existing albums
  - Album creation
  - Album selection

- `AlbumPage`
  - Displays existing pictures as thumbnails
  - Adds pictures in album
  - Album rename
  - Album deletion
  - Picture selection

- `PicturePage`
  - Displays selected picture
  - Picture selection
  - Picture deletion

To handle the navigation, we will use a `StackView` component from Qt Quick Controls. This QML component implements a stack-based navigation. You can push a page when you want to display it. When the user requests to go back, you can pop it. Here is the workflow using a `StackView` component for our gallery mobile application. The page with the solid border is the page currently displayed on screen:

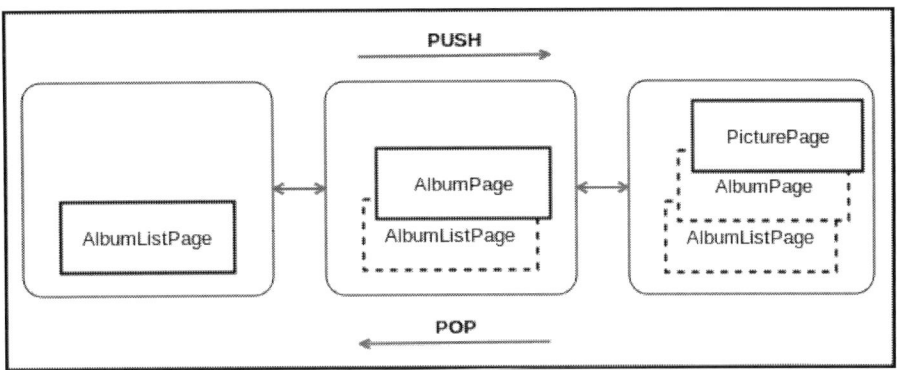

This is the implementation of `main.qml`:

```
import QtQuick 2.6
import QtQuick.Controls 2.0

ApplicationWindow {

    readonly property alias pageStack: stackView

    id: app
    visible: true
    width: 768
    height: 1280

    StackView {
        id: stackView
        anchors.fill: parent
        initialItem: AlbumListPage {}
    }

    onClosing: {
        if (Qt.platform.os == "android") {
            if (stackView.depth > 1) {
                close.accepted = false
                stackView.pop()
            }
        }
    }
```

```
        }
    }
```

This main file is really simple. The application is constructed around the `StackView` component. We set the `id` property to allow our `StackView` to be identified and referred to by other QML objects. The `anchors` property will set `stackView` to fill its parent, the `ApplicationWindow` type. Finally, we set the `initialItem` property to a page, `AlbumListPage` that will be implemented soon.

On Android, `onClosing` will be executed each time the user presses the back button. To mimic a native Android application, we will first pop the last stacked page before really closing the application.

At the top of the file, we define a `property alias` for the `stackView`. A `property alias` is a simple reference to another existing property. This alias will be useful to access `stackView` from other QML components. To prevent a QML component to crush the `stackView` we are using the `readonly` keyword. After initialization, the components can access the property but not change its value.

# Displaying albums with ListView

Let's make our first page for this mobile application! Create a file in `gallery.qrc` called `AlbumListPage.qml`. Here is the page header implementation:

```
import QtQuick 2.0
import QtQuick.Layouts 1.3

import QtQuick.Controls 2.0

Page {

    header: ToolBar {
        Label {
            Layout.fillWidth: true
            text: "Albums"
            font.pointSize: 30
        }
    }
    ...
}
```

A `Page` is a container control with a header and footer. In this application, we will only use the header item. We assign a `ToolBar` to the `header` property. The height of this toolbar will be handled by Qt and will be adjusted depending on the target platform. In this first simple implementation, we only put a `Label` displaying the text "Albums".

Add a `ListView` element to this page after the `header` initialization:

```
ListView {
    id: albumList
    model: albumModel
    spacing: 5
    anchors.fill: parent

    delegate: Rectangle {
        width: parent.width
        height: 120
        color: "#d0d1d2"

        Text {
            text: name
            font.pointSize: 16
            color: "#000000"
            anchors.verticalCenter: parent.verticalCenter
        }
    }
}
```

The Qt Quick `ListView` is the Qt Widget `QListView` equivalent. It displays a list of items from a provided model. We set the `model` property to value `albumModel`. This refers to the C++ model from `main.cpp` file accessible from QML because we used the `setContextProperty()` function. In Qt Quick, you must provide a delegate to describe how a row will be displayed. In this case, a row will only display the album's name with a `Text` item. Accessing the album's name in QML is easy because our `AlbumModel` model exposes its role list to QML. Let's refresh your memory concerning the overridden `roleNames()` function of `AlbumModel`:

```
QHash<int, QByteArray> AlbumModel::roleNames() const
{
    QHash<int, QByteArray> roles;
    roles[Roles::IdRole] = "id";
    roles[Roles::NameRole] = "name";
    return roles;
}
```

So each time your delegate from Qt Quick uses the `name` role, it will call the `AlbumModel` function `data()` with the correct role integer and return the correct album name string.

To handle the mouse, click on a row and add a `MouseArea` element on the delegate:

```
ListView {
    ...
    delegate: Rectangle {
        ...
        MouseArea {
            anchors.fill: parent
            onClicked: {
                albumList.currentIndex = index
                pictureModel.setAlbumId(id)
                pageStack.push("qrc:/qml/AlbumPage.qml",
                        { albumName: name, albumRowIndex: index })
            }
        }
    }
}
```

The `MouseArea` is an invisible item that can be used with any visible item to handle mouse events. This also applies to a simple touch on a phone touch screen. Here we tell the `MouseArea` element to take the full area of the parent `Rectangle`.

In our case, we only perform tasks on the `clicked` signal. We update the `currentIndex` of the `ListView` with `index`. This `index` is a special role containing the index of the item in the model.

When the user clicks, we will tell `pictureModel` to load the selected album with the `pictureModel.setAlbumId(id)` call. We will see soon how QML can call C++ methods.

Finally, we push `AlbumPage` on `pageStack` property. The `push()` function allows us to set a list of QML properties using a {key: value, ...} syntax. Each property will be copied into the pushed item. Here the `name` and the `index` will be copied in the `albumName` and `albumRowIndex` properties of `AlbumPage`. It is a simple yet powerful way to instantiate a QML page with properties arguments.

From your QML code, you can only call some specific C++ methods:

- Properties (using `Q_PROPERTY`)
- Public slot
- Function decorated as invokable (using `Q_INVOKABLE`)

In this case we will decorate `PictureModel::setAlbumId()` as `Q_INVOKABLE`, please update the `PictureModel.h` file:

```cpp
class GALLERYCORESHARED_EXPORT PictureModel : public QAbstractListModel
{
    Q_OBJECT
public:
    ...
    Q_INVOKABLE void setAlbumId(int albumId);
    ...
};
```

# Theming the application with a QML singleton

Styling and theming a QML application can be done in various ways. In this chapter, we will declare a QML singleton with the theme data used by custom components. Moreover, we will also create a custom `Page` component to handle the toolbar and its default item (back button and page's title).

Please create a new `Style.qml` file:

```qml
pragma Singleton
import QtQuick 2.0

QtObject {
    property color text: "#000000"

    property color windowBackground: "#eff0f1"
    property color toolbarBackground: "#eff0f1"
    property color pageBackground: "#fcfcfc"
    property color buttonBackground: "#d0d1d2"

    property color itemHighlight: "#3daee9"
}
```

We declare a `QtObject` component that will only contain our theme properties. A `QtObject` is a non-visual QML component.

Declaring a singleton type in QML requires two steps. First you need to use the `pragma singleton`, it will indicate the use of a single instance of the component. The second step is to register it. This can be done in C++ or by creating a `qmldir` file. Let's see the second step. Create a new plain-text file called `qmldir`:

```
singleton Style 1.0 Style.qml
```

This simple line will declare a QML `singleton` type named `Style` with the version 1.0 from the file named `Style.qml`.

It is now time to use these theme properties in custom components. Let's see a simple example. Create a new QML file called `ToolBarTheme.qml`:

```
import QtQuick 2.0
import QtQuick.Controls 2.0

import "."

ToolBar {
    background: Rectangle {
        color: Style.toolbarBackground
    }

}
```

This QML object describes a customized `ToolBar`. Here, the `background` element is a simple `Rectangle` with our color. We can easily access our singleton `Style` and its theme property using `Style.toolbarBackground`.

 QML Singletons require an explicit import to load the `qmldir` file. The `import "."` is a workaround for this Qt bug. For more information, please check https://bugreports.qt.io/browse/QTBUG-34418.

We will now create a QML file `PageTheme.qml`, with the aim of containing all the code related to the page's toolbar and theme:

```
import QtQuick 2.0

import QLQuick.Layouts 1.3
import Qt.labs.controls 1.0
import QtQuick.Controls 2.0
import "."

Page {
```

```
property alias toolbarButtons: buttonsLoader.sourceComponent
property alias toolbarTitle: titleLabel.text

header: ToolBarTheme {
    RowLayout {
        anchors.fill: parent
        ToolButton {
            background: Image {
                source: "qrc:/res/icons/back.svg"
            }
            onClicked: {
                if (stackView.depth > 1) {
                    stackView.pop()
                }
            }
        }

        Label {
            id: titleLabel
            Layout.fillWidth: true
            color: Style.text
            elide: Text.ElideRight
            font.pointSize: 30
        }

        Loader {
            Layout.alignment: Qt.AlignRight
            id: buttonsLoader
        }
    }
}

Rectangle {
    color: Style.pageBackground
    anchors.fill: parent
}
}
```

This PageTheme element will customize the page's header. We use our previously
created ToolBarTheme. This toolbar only contains a RowLayout element to display items
horizontally in one row. This layout contains three elements:

- ToolButton: This is the "back" that displays an image from gallery.qrc and
  pops the current page if required

- `Label`: This is the element that displays the page title
- `Loader`: This is the element that allows a page to dynamically add specific items in this generic toolbar

The `Loader` element owns a `sourceComponent` property. In this application, this property can be assigned by `PageTheme` pages to add specific buttons. These buttons will be instantiated at runtime.

The `PageTheme` pages also contain a `Rectangle` element that fits the parent and configures the page background color using the `Style.pageBackground`.

Now that our `Style.qml` and `PageTheme.qml` files are ready, we can update the `AlbumListPage.qml` file to use it:

```
import QtQuick 2.6
import QtQuick.Controls 2.0
import "."

PageTheme {

    toolbarTitle: "Albums"

    ListView {
        id: albumList
        model: albumModel
        spacing: 5
        anchors.fill: parent

        delegate: Rectangle {
            width: parent.width
            height: 120
            color: Style.buttonBackground

            Text {
                text: name
                font.pointSize: 16
                color: Style.text
                anchors.verticalCenter: parent.verticalCenter
            }
            ...
        }
    }
}
```

Now that `AlbumListPage` is a `PageTheme` element, we do not manipulate `header` directly. We only need to set the property `toolbarTitle` to display a nice "Albums" text in the toolbar. We can also enjoy nice colors using properties from the `Style` singleton.

By centralizing the theme properties in a single file, you can easily change the look and feel of your application. The source code of the project also contains a dark theme.

# Loading a database on mobile

Before continuing the UI implementation, we have to take care of the database deployment on mobile. Spoiler: this will not be fun.

We have to jump back to `DatabaseManager.cpp` in the `gallery-core` project:

```
DatabaseManager& DatabaseManager::instance()
{
    return singleton;
}

DatabaseManager::DatabaseManager(const QString& path) :
    mDatabase(new QSqlDatabase(QSqlDatabase::addDatabase("QSQLITE"))),
    albumDao(*mDatabase),
    pictureDao(*mDatabase)
{
    mDatabase->setDatabaseName(path);
    ...
}
```

Whereas on Desktop, the SQLite3 database is created at the instruction `mDatabase->setDatabaseName()`, on mobile it does not work at all. This is due to the fact that the filesystem is very specific on each mobile platform (Android and iOS). An application has only access to a narrow sandbox where it cannot mess with the rest of the filesystem. All the files inside the application directory must have specific file permissions. If we let SQLite3 create the database file, it will not have the right permission and the OS will block the database from opening.

As a consequence, the database will not be properly created and your data cannot be persisted. When using the native API, this is not a problem since the OS takes care of the proper configuration of the database. Because we are developing with Qt, we do not have easy access to this API (except by using JNI or other black magic). A workaround is to embed a "ready-to-use" database in the application's package and copy it at the right filesystem path with the correct rights.

This database should contain an empty created database without any content. The database is available in the source code of the chapter (you can also generate it from the source code of Chapter 4, *Conquering the Desktop UI*). You can add it to the gallery.qrc file.

Because our layers are clearly defined, we just have to modify the DatabaseManager::instance() implementation to handle this case:

```
DatabaseManager& DatabaseManager::instance()
{
#if defined(Q_OS_ANDROID) || defined(Q_OS_IOS)
    QFile assetDbFile(":/database/" + DATABASE_FILENAME);
    QString destinationDbFile = QStandardPaths::writableLocation(
                        QStandardPaths::AppLocalDataLocation)
                .append("/" + DATABASE_FILENAME);

        if (!QFile::exists(destinationDbFile)) {
            assetDbFile.copy(destinationDbFile);
            Qfile::setPermissions(destinationDbFile,
                        QFile::WriteOwner | QFile::ReadOwner);
        }
    }
    static DatabaseManager singleton(destinationDbFile);
#else
    static DatabaseManager singleton;
#endif
    return singleton;
}
```

We first retrieve the platform-specific path of the application with a nifty Qt class: QStandardPaths. This class return paths for multiple types (AppLocalDataLocation, DocumentsLocation, PicturesLocation, and so on). The database should be stored in the application data directory. If the file does not exist, we copy it from our assets.

Finally, the permissions of the file are modified to ensure that the OS does not block the opening of the database (due to permissions not being restrictive enough).

When everything is done, the DatabaseManager singleton is instantiated with the correct database file path and the constructor can open this database transparently.

 In the iOS Simulator, the QStandardPaths::writableLocation() function will not return the proper path. Since iOS 8, the simulator's storage path on the host has changed and Qt does not reflect this. For more information, please check out https://bugreports.qt.io/browse/QTCREATORBUG-13655.

These workarounds were not trivial. This shows the limitations of a cross-platform application on mobile. Each platform has its own very specific way of handling the filesystem and deploying its content. Even if we manage to write platform agnostic code in QML, we still have to deal with differences between the OSes.

# Creating a new album from a custom InputDialog

The `AlbumListPage` needs some data to display. The next step is to be able to add a new album. To do this, at some point we will have to call an `AlbumModel` function from QML to add this new album. Before building the UI, we have to make a small modification in `gallery-core`.

The `AlbumModel` function is already available in QML. However, we cannot directly call `AlbumModel::addAlbum(const Album& album)` from the QML code; the QML engine will not recognize the function and will throw an error **TypeError: Property 'addAlbum' of object AlbumModel(...) is not a function**. This can be fixed by simply decorating the desired function with the `Q_INVOKABLE` macro (as we did for `PictureModel::setAlbumId()`).

Nonetheless, there is another issue here: `Album` is a C++ class which is not recognized in QML. If we wanted to have full access to `Album` in QML, it would involve important modifications to the class:

- Force `Album` class to inherit from the `QObject` class.
- Add a `Q_PROPERTY` macro to specify which property of the class should be accessible from QML.
- Add multiple constructors (copy constructor, `QObject* parent`, and so on).
- Force `AlbumModel::addAlbum()` function to take an `Album*` rather than an `Album&`. For complex objects (that is, not primitive types), QML can only handle pointers. This is not a big problem, but using references instead of pointers tends to make the code safer.

These modifications are perfectly reasonable if the class is heavily manipulated in QML. Our use case is very limited: we only want to create a new album. Throughout the application, we will rely on the native Model/View API to display the album data and nothing specific to `Album` will be used.

For all these reasons, we will simply add a wrapper function in `AlbumModel`:

```
// In AlbumModel.h
...
QModelIndex addAlbum(const Album& album);
Q_INVOKABLE void addAlbumFromName(const QString& name);
...

// In AlbumModel.cpp
void AlbumModel::addAlbumFromName(const QString& name)
{
    addAlbum(Album(name));
}
```

The new function `addAlbumFromName()` just wraps the call to `addAlbum()` with the desired album `name` parameter. It can be called from the QML with the `Q_INVOKABLE` macro.

We can now switch back to the UI in the `gallery-mobile` project. We will add this album using a QML `Dialog`. QtQuick provides various default implementations of dialogs:

- `ColorDialog`: This dialog is used to choose a color
- `Dialog`: This dialog is uses the generic dialog with standard buttons (equivalent of a `QDialog`)
- `FileDialog`: This dialog is used to choose a file from the local filesystem
- `FontDialog`: This dialog is used to choose a font
- `MessageDialog`: This dialog is used to display a message

You would have expected to see an `InputDialog` in this list (as we used the `QInputDialog` widget in Chapter 4, *Conquering the Desktop UI*) but Qt Quick does not have it. Create a new **QML File (Qt Quick 2)** and name it `InputDialog.qml`. The content should look like so:

```
import QtQuick 2.6
import QtQuick.Layouts 1.3
import Qt.labs.controls 1.0
import QtQuick.Dialogs 1.2
import QtQuick.Window 2.2
import "."

Dialog {

    property string label: "New item"
    property string hint: ""
```

```
property alias editText : editTextItem

standardButtons: StandardButton.Ok | StandardButton.Cancel
onVisibleChanged: {
    editTextItem.focus = true
    editTextItem.selectAll()
}
onButtonClicked: {
    Qt.inputMethod.hide();
}
Rectangle {

    implicitWidth: parent.width
    implicitHeight: 100

    ColumnLayout {
        Text {
            id: labelItem
            text: label
            color: Style.text
        }

        TextInput {
            id: editTextItem
            inputMethodHints: Qt.ImhPreferUppercase
            text: hint
            color: Style.text
        }
    }
}
}
```

In this custom `InputDialog`, we take the generic Qt Quick `Dialog` and modify it to contain our `TextInput` item referenced by the ID `editTextItem`. We also added a `labelItem` just above `editTextItem` to describe the expected input. There are several things to note in this dialog.

First, because we want this dialog to be generic, it has to be configurable. The caller should be able to provide parameters to display its specific data. This is done with the three properties at the top of the `Dialog` element:

- `label`: This property configures the displayed text in `labelItem`.
- `hint`: This property is the default text displayed in `editTextItem`.
- `editText`: This property references the "local" `editTextItem` element. This will let the caller retrieve the value when the dialog is closed.

We also configure the `Dialog` element to automatically use the platform buttons to validate or cancel the dialog with `standardButtons: StandardButton.Ok | StandardButton.Cancel` syntax.

Finally, to make the dialog a bit more user-friendly, `editTextItem` has the focus when the `Dialog` element becomes visible and the text is selected. These two steps are done in the `onVisibleChanged()` callback function. When the dialog is hidden (that is, **Ok** or **Cancel** has been clicked), we hide the virtual keyboard with `Qt.InputMethod.hide()`.

The `InputDialog` is ready to be used! Open `AlbumListPage.qml` and modify it like so:

```
PageTheme {

    toolbarTitle: "Albums"
    toolbarButtons: ToolButton {
        background: Image {
            source: "qrc:/res/icons/album-add.svg"
        }
        onClicked: {
            newAlbumDialog.open()
        }
    }

    InputDialog {
        id: newAlbumDialog
        title: "New album"
        label: "Album name:"
        hint: "My Album"

        onAccepted: {
            albumModel.addAlbumFromName(editText.text)
        }
    }
```

We add `InputDialog` with the ID `newAlbumDialog` inside `PageTheme` element. We define all our custom properties: `title`, `label`, and `hint`. When the user clicks on the **Ok** button, the `onAccepted()` function is called. Here, it is a simple matter of calling the wrapper function `addAlbumFromName()` in the `AlbumModel` element with the entered text.

This `Dialog` element is not visible by default, we open it by adding a `ToolButton` in `toolbarButtons`. This `ToolButton` will be added at the far right of the header as we specified in the `PageTheme.qml` file. To match mobile standards, we simply use a custom icon inside that button rather than text.

Here you can see that it is possible to reference images stored in the `.qrc` file with the syntax `qrc:/res/icons/album-add.svg`. We use SVG files to have scalable icons, but you are free to use your own icons for the `gallery-mobile` application.

When the user clicks on the `ToolButton`, the `onClicked()` function is called, where we open `newAlbumDialog`. On our reference device, a Nexus 5X, this is how it looks:

When the user clicks on the **OK** button, the whole Model/View pipeline starts to work. This new album is persisted, the `AlbumModel` element emits the correct signals to notify our `ListView`, `albumList`, to refresh itself. We are starting to leverage the power of our `gallery-core`, which can be used in a desktop application and a mobile application without rewriting a significant portion of the engine code.

# Loading images with an ImageProvider

It is now time to display the thumbnails for our freshly persisted album. These thumbnails have to be loaded somehow. Because our application is targeted at mobile devices, we cannot afford to freeze the UI thread while loading thumbnails. We would either hog the CPU or be killed by the OS, neither of which are desirable destinies for `gallery-mobile`. Qt provides a very handy class to handle the image loading: `QQuickImageProvider`.

The `QQuickImageProvider` class provides an interface to load the `QPixmap` class in your QML code in an asynchronous manner. This class automatically spawns threads to load the `QPixmap` class and you simply have to implement the function `requestPixmap()`. There is more to it, `QQuickImageProvider` caches by default the requested pixmap to avoid hitting the data source too much.

Our thumbnails must be loaded from the `PictureModel` element, which gives access to the `fileUrl` of a given `Picture`. Our implementation of rQQuickImageProvider will have to get the `QPixmap` class for a row index in `Picture1Model`. Create a new C++ class named `PictureImageProvider`, and modify `PictureImageProvider.h` like this:

```
#include <QQuickImageProvider>

class PictureModel;

class PictureImageProvider : public QQuickImageProvider
{
public:

    PictureImageProvider(PictureModel* pictureModel);

    QPixmap requestPixmap(const QString& id, QSize* size,
            const QSize& requestedSize) override;

private:
    PictureModel* mPictureModel;
};
```

A pointer to the `PictureModel` element has to be provided in the constructor to be able to retrieve `fileUrl`. We override `requestPixmap()`, which takes an `id` parameter in its parameters list (the `size` and `requestedSize` can be safely ignored for now). This `id` parameter will be provided in the QML code when we want to load a picture. For a given `Image` in QML, the `PictureImageProvider` class will be called like so:

```
Image { source: "image://pictures/" + index }
```

Let's break it down:

- `image`: This is the scheme for the URL source of the image. This tells Qt to work with an image provider to load the image.
- `pictures`: This is the identifier of the image provider. We will link the `PictureImageProvider` class and this identifier at the initialization of `QmlEngine` in `main.cpp`.
- `index`: This is the ID of the image. Here it is the row index of the picture. This corresponds to the `id` parameter in `requestPixmap()`.

We already know that we want to display a picture in two modes: thumbnail and full resolution. In both cases, a `QQuickImageProvider` class will be used. These two modes have a very similar behavior: they will request `PictureModel` for `fileUrl` and return the loaded `QPixmap`.

There is a pattern here. We can easily encapsulate these two modes in
PictureImageProvider. The only thing we have to know is when the caller wants a
thumbnail or a full resolution QPixmap. This can be easily done by making the id
parameter more explicit.

We are going to implement the requestPixmap() function to be able to be called in two
ways:

- images://pictures/<index>/full: Using this syntax to retrieve the full
  resolution picture
- images://pictures/<index>/thumbnail: Using this syntax to retrieve the
  thumbnail version of the picture

If the index value was 0, these two calls would set the ID to 0/full or 0/thumbnail
in requestPixmap(). Let's see the implementation in PictureImageProvider.cpp:

```cpp
#include "PictureModel.h"

PictureImageProvider::PictureImageProvider(PictureModel* pictureModel) :
    QQuickImageProvider(QQuickImageProvider::Pixmap),
    mPictureModel(pictureModel)
{
}

QPixmap PictureImageProvider::requestPixmap(const QString& id, QSize*
/*size*/, const QSize& /*requestedSize*/)
{
    QStringList query = id.split('/');
    if (!mPictureModel || query.size() < 2) {
        return QPixmap();
    }

    int row = query[0].toInt();
    QString pictureSize = query[1];

    QUrl fileUrl = mPictureModel->data(mPictureModel->index(row, 0),
PictureModel::Roles::UrlRole).toUrl();
    return ?? // Patience, the mystery will be soon unraveled
}
```

We start by calling the QQuickImageProvider constructor with
the QQuickImageProvider::Pixmap parameter to configure QQuickImageProvider to
call requestPixmap(). The QQuickImageProvider constructor supports various image
types (QImage, QPixmap, QSGTexture, QQuickImageResponse) and each one has its
specific requestXXX() function.

In the `requestPixmap()` function, we start by splitting this ID with the / separator. From here, we retrieve the `row` values and the desired `pictureSize`. The `fileUrl` is loaded by simply calling the `mPictureModel::data()` function with the right parameters. We used the exact same call in Chapter 4, *Conquering the Desktop UI*.

Great, we know which `fileUrl` should be loaded and what the desired dimension is. However, we have one last thing to handle. Because we manipulate a row and not a database ID, we will have the same request URL for two different pictures, which are in different albums. Remember that `PictureModel` loads a list of pictures for a given `Album`.

We should picture (pun intended) the situation. For an album called `Holidays`, the request URL will be `images://pictures/0/thumbnail` to load the first picture. It will be the same URL for another album `Pets`, which will load the first picture with `images://pictures/0/thumbnail`. As we said earlier, `QQuickImageProvider` automatically generates a cache which will avoid subsequent calls to `requestPixmap()` for the same URL. Thus, we will always serve the same picture, no matter which album is selected.

This constraint forces us to disable the cache in `PictureImageProvider` and to roll out our own cache. This is an interesting thing to do; here is a possible implementation:

```
// In PictureImageProvider.h

#include <QQuickImageProvider>
#include <QCache>

...
public:
    static const QSize THUMBNAIL_SIZE;

    QPixmap requestPixmap(const QString& id, QSize* size, const QSize&
requestedSize) override;

    QPixmap* pictureFromCache(const QString& filepath, const QString&
pictureSize);

private:
    PictureModel* mPictureModel;
    QCache<QString, QPixmap> mPicturesCache;
};

// In PictureImageProvider.cpp
const QString PICTURE_SIZE_FULL = "full";
const QString PICTURE_SIZE_THUMBNAIL = "thumbnail";
const QSize PictureImageProvider::THUMBNAIL_SIZE = QSize(350, 350);
```

```
QPixmap PictureImageProvider::requestPixmap(const QString& id, QSize*
/*size*/, const QSize& /*requestedSize*/)
{
    ...
    return *pictureFromCache(fileUrl.toLocalFile(), pictureSize);
}

QPixmap* PictureImageProvider::pictureFromCache(const QString& filepath,
const QString& pictureSize)
{
    QString key = QStringList{ pictureSize, filepath }
                        .join("-");

    QPixmap* cachePicture = nullptr;
    if (!mPicturesCache.contains(pictureSize)) {
        QPixmap originalPicture(filepath);
        if (pictureSize == PICTURE_SIZE_THUMBNAIL) {
            cachePicture = new QPixmap(originalPicture
                                .scaled(THUMBNAIL_SIZE,
                                        Qt::KeepAspectRatio,
                                        Qt::SmoothTransformation));
        } else if (pictureSize == PICTURE_SIZE_FULL) {
            cachePicture = new QPixmap(originalPicture);
        }
        mPicturesCache.insert(key, cachePicture);
    } else {
        cachePicture = mPicturesCache[pictureSize];
    }

    return cachePicture;
}
```

This new `pictureFromCache()` function aims to store the generated `QPixmap`
in `mPicturesCache` and return the proper `QPixmap`. The `mPicturesCache` class relies on
a `QCache`; this class lets us store data in a key/value fashion with the possibility to assign a
cost for each entry. This cost should roughly map the memory cost of the object (by
default, `cost` = 1). When `QCache` is instantiated, it is initialized with a `maxCost` value (by
default 100). When the cost of the sum of all objects' exceeds the `maxCost`, `QCache` starts
deleting objects to make room for the new objects, starting with the less recently accessed
objects.

In the `pictureFromCache()` function, we first generate a key composed of the `fileUrl` and the `pictureSize` before trying to retrieve the `QPixmap` from the cache. If it is not present, the proper `QPixmap` (scaled to `THUMBNAIL_SIZE` macro if needed) will be generated and stored inside the cache. The `mPicturesCache` class becomes the owner of this `QPixmap`.

The last step to complete the `PictureImageProvider` class is to make it available in the QML context. This is done in `main.cpp`:

```cpp
#include "AlbumModel.h"
#include "PictureModel.h"
#include "PictureImageProvider.h"

int main(int argc, char *argv[])
{
    QGuiApplication app(argc, argv);
    ...

    QQmlContext* context = engine.rootContext();
    context->setContextProperty("thumbnailSize",
PictureImageProvider::THUMBNAIL_SIZE.width());
    context->setContextProperty("albumModel", &albumModel);
    context->setContextProperty("pictureModel", &pictureModel);

    engine.addImageProvider("pictures", new
                        PictureImageProvider(&pictureModel));
    ...
}
```

The `PictureImageProvider` class is added to the QML engine with `engine.addImageProvider()`. The first argument will be the provider identifier in QML. Note that the engine takes ownership of the passed `PictureImageProvider`. One last thing, the `thumbnailSize` parameter is also passed to `engine`, it will constrain the thumbnails to be displayed with the specified size in the QML code.

# Displaying thumbnails in a GridView

The next step is to display these thumbnails. Create a new QML file named `AlbumPage.qml`:

```qml
import QtQuick 2.6
import QtQuick.Layouts 1.3
import QtQuick.Controls 2.0
import "."
```

```
PageTheme {

    property string albumName
    property int albumRowIndex

    toolbarTitle: albumName

    GridView {
        id: thumbnailList
        model: pictureModel
        anchors.fill: parent
        anchors.leftMargin: 10
        anchors.rightMargin: 10
        cellWidth : thumbnailSize
        cellHeight: thumbnailSize

        delegate: Rectangle {
            width: thumbnailList.cellWidth - 10
            height: thumbnailList.cellHeight - 10
            color: "transparent"

            Image {
                id: thumbnail
                anchors.fill: parent
                fillMode: Image.PreserveAspectFit
                cache: false
                source: "image://pictures/" + index + "/thumbnail"
            }
        }
    }
}
```

This new `PageTheme` element defines two properties: `albumName` and `albumRowIndex`.
The `albumName` property is used to update the title in `toolbarTitle`; `albumRowIndex` will
be used to interact with `AlbumModel` in order to rename or delete the album from the
current page.

To display thumbnails, we rely on a `GridView` element which will layout the thumbnails in
a grid of cells. This `thumbnailList` item uses the `pictureModel` to request its data. The
delegate is simply a `Rectangle` element with a single `Image` inside. This `Rectangle`
element is slightly smaller than the `thumbnailList.cellWidth`
or `thumbnailList.cellHeight`. The `GridView` element does not provide a `spacing`
property (like `ListView`) for some room between each item. Thus, we simulate it by using a
smaller area to display the content.

The `Image` item will try to take all the available space with `anchors.fill: parent` but will still keep the aspect ratio of the provided picture with `fillMode: Image.PreserveAspectFit`. You recognize the `source` attribute where the current delegate `index` is provided to retrieve the thumbnail. Finally, the `cache: false` attribute ensures that the `PictureImageProvider` class will not try to use the native cache.

To display `AlbumPage.qml`, we have to update the `stackView` (located in `main.qml`). Remember that `stackView` has been declared as a property (`pageStack`), it is thus accessible from any QML file.

The `AlbumPage` element will be displayed when the user clicks on the `MouseArea` element for a given `Album` value in `AlbumListPage.qml`.

We will now give the ability to the user to add a new picture. To do this, we will rely on a QtQuick Dialog: `FileDialog`. Here is the updated version of `AlbumPage.qml`:

```
import QtQuick 2.6
import QtQuick.Layouts 1.3
import QtQuick.Controls 2.0
import QtQuick.Dialogs 1.2
import "."

PageTheme {

    property string albumName
    property int albumRowIndex

    toolbarTitle: albumName
    toolbarButtons: RowLayout {
        ToolButton {
            background: Image {
                source: "qrc:/res/icons/photo-add.svg"
            }
            onClicked: {
                dialog.open()
            }
        }
    }

    FileDialog {
        id: dialog
        title: "Open file"
        folder: shortcuts.pictures
        onAccepted: {
            var pictureUrl = dialog.fileUrl
            pictureModel.addPictureFromUrl(pictureUrl)
```

```
            dialog.close()
        }
    }

    GridView {
        ...
    }
}
```

The `FileDialog` element is straightforward to implement. By using the `folder:` `shortcuts.pictures` property, QtQuick will automatically position the `FileDialog` element in the platform-specific pictures directory. Even better, on iOS it will open the native photo application where you can pick your own picture.

When the user validates his picture choice, the path is available in the `onAccepted()` function with the `dialog.fileUrl` field, which we stored in the `pictureUrl` variable. This `pictureUrl` variable is then passed to a new wrapper function of `PictureModel: addPictureFromUrl()`. The pattern used is exactly the same as we did for `AlbumModel::addAlbumFromName()`: a `Q_INVOKABLE` wrapper function around `PictureModel::addPicture()`.

The only missing parts of `AlbumPage` are the delete album and rename album features. They follow patterns we already covered. The deletion will be done using a wrapper function in `AlbumModel`, and the rename reuses the `InputDialog` we created for `AlbumListPage.qml`. Please refer to the source code of the chapter to see the implementation for these features. This is how the thumbnails will look on an Android device:

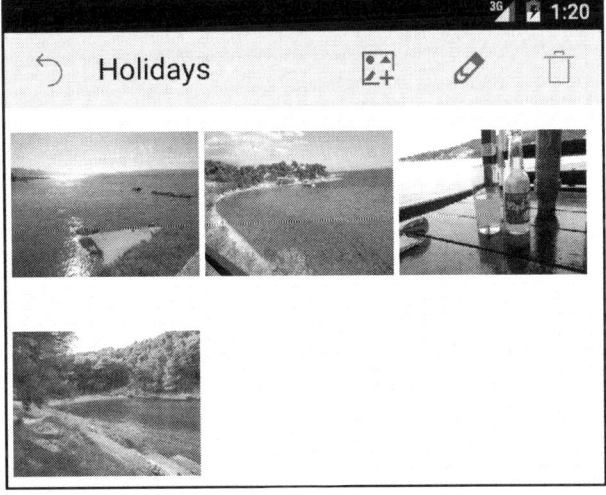

# Swiping through full resolution pictures

The last page we have to implement in `gallery-mobile` is the full resolution picture page. In Chapter 4, *Conquering the Desktop UI*, we navigated through the pictures using previous/next buttons. In this chapter, we target the mobile platform. Therefore, the navigation should be done using a touch-based gesture: a fling.

Here is the implementation of this new `PicturePage.qml` file:

```
import QtQuick 2.0
import QtQuick.Layouts 1.3
import QtQuick.Controls 2.0
import "."

PageTheme {

    property string pictureName
    property int pictureIndex

    toolbarTitle: pictureName

    ListView {
        id: pictureListView
        model: pictureModel
        anchors.fill: parent
        spacing: 5
        orientation: Qt.Horizontal
        snapMode: ListView.SnapOneItem
        currentIndex: pictureIndex

        Component.onCompleted: {
            positionViewAtIndex(currentIndex,
                                ListView.SnapPosition)
        }

        delegate: Rectangle {
            property int itemIndex: index
            property string itemName: name

            width: ListView.view.width == 0 ?
                   parent.width : ListView.view.width
            height: pictureListView.height
            color: "transparent"

            Image {
                fillMode: Image.PreserveAspectFit
                cache: false
```

```
                width: parent.width
                height: parent.height
                source: "image://pictures/" + index + "/full"
            }
        }
    }
}
```

We first define two properties, `pictureName` and `pictureIndex`. The current `pictureName` property is displayed in the `toolbarTitle` and `pictureIndex` is used to initialize the correct `currentIndex` in `ListView`, `currentIndex`: `pictureIndex`.

To be able to swipe through the pictures, we again use a `ListView`. Here, each item (a simple `Image` element) will take the full size of its parent. When the component is loaded, even if `currentIndex` is correctly set, the view has to be updated to be positioned at the correct index. This is what we do in `pictureListView` with this:

```
Component.onCompleted: {
    positionViewAtIndex(currentIndex, ListView.SnapPosition)
}
```

This will update the position of the current visible item to `currentIndex`. So far so good. Nonetheless, when a `ListView` is created, the first thing it does is to initialize its delegate. A `ListView` has a `view` property, which is filled with the `delegate` content. That implies that the `ListView.view` (yes, it hurts) does not have any width in `Component.onCompleted()`. As a consequence, the `positionViewAtIndex()` function does... absolutely nothing. To prevent this behavior, we have to provide a default initial width to the delegate with the ternary expression `ListView.view.width == 0 ? parent.width : ListView.view.width`. The view will then have a default width on the first load and the `positionViewAtIndex()` function can happily move until `ListView.view` is properly loaded.

To swipe through each picture, we set the `snapMode` value of the `ListView` to `ListView.SnapOneItem`. Each fling will snap to the next or previous picture without continuing the motion.

The `Image` item of the delegate looks very much like the thumbnail version. The sole difference is the source property, where we request `PictureImageProvider` class with the `full` resolution.

When `PicturePage` opens, the correct `pictureName` property is displayed in the header. However, when the user flings to another picture, the name is not updated. To handle this, we have to detect the motion state. Add the following callbacks in `pictureListView`:

```
onMovementEnded: {
    currentIndex = itemAt(contentX, contentY).itemIndex
}

onCurrentItemChanged: {
    toolbarTitleLabel.text = currentItem.itemName
}
```

The `onMovementEnded()` class is triggered when the motion started by the swipe has ended. In this function, we update the `ListViewcurrentIndex` with the `itemIndex` of the visible item at the `contentX` and `contentY` coordinates.

The second function, `onCurrentItemChanged()`, is called upon the `currentIndex` update. It will simply update the `toolbarTitleLabel.text` with the picture name of the current item.

To display `PicturePage.qml`, the same `MouseArea` pattern is used in the `thumbnailList` delegate of `AlbumPage.qml`:

```
MouseArea {
    anchors.fill: parent
    onClicked: {
        thumbnailList.currentIndex = index
        pageStack.push("qrc:/qml/PicturePage.qml",
    { pictureName: name, pictureIndex: index })
    }
}
```

Again, the `PicturePage.qml` file is pushed on the `pageStack` and the needed parameters (`pictureName` and `pictureIndex`) are provided in the same manner.

# Summary

This chapter brings closure to the development of the gallery application. We built a strong foundation with `gallery-core`, created a widget UI with `gallery-desktop`, and finally crafted a QML UI with `gallery-mobile`.

QML enables a very fast approach to UI development. Unfortunately, the technology is still young and rapidly changing. The integration with mobile OSes (Android, iOS) is under heavy development and we hope that it will lead to great mobile applications with Qt. For now, the inherent limits of a mobile cross-platform toolkit are still hard to overcome.

The next chapter will take QML technology to new shores: the development of a snake game running on a Raspberry Pi.

# 6
# Even Qt Deserves a Slice of Raspberry Pi

In the previous chapter, we created a QML UI targeted at Android and iOS. We will continue our journey in the embedded world by discovering how we can deploy a Qt application on a Raspberry Pi. The example project to illustrate this topic will be a snake game using the Qt3D modules. The player will control a snake trying to eat apples to get as big as possible.

In this chapter, you will learn:

- The architecture of the Qt3D modules
- The basic principles of cross-compilation
- How to build your own Qt Creator kit to compile and deploy your game on a Raspberry Pi
- How to handle the differences and limitations of various platforms (desktop, Raspberry Pi)
- The Factory design pattern
- How to write a complete game engine using JavaScript and QML
- The usage of the QML Profiler

# Discovering Qt3D

The example project of this chapter will rely on 3D rendering. For this, we will use Qt3D. This part of the framework is divided into various Qt modules that enable the application to have a near-real time simulation of a 3D environment. Built on OpenGL, Qt3D offers a high-level API to describe complex scenes without having to resort to writing low-level OpenGL instructions. Qt3D supports the following basic features:

* 2D and 3D rendering for C++ and Qt Quick
* Meshes
* Materials
* GLSL shaders
* Shadow mapping
* Deferred rendering
* Instance rendering
* Uniform Buffer Object

All these features are implemented in the **ECS** (**entity component system**) architecture. Each mesh, material, or shader that you define is a component. The aggregation of these components makes an entity. If you wanted to draw a 3D red apple, you would need the following components:

* A mesh component, holding the vertices of your apple
* A material component, applying a texture on the mesh or coloring it

These two components will then be regrouped to define the entity Apple. You see here the two parts of the ECS: entities and components. The overall architecture looks like this:

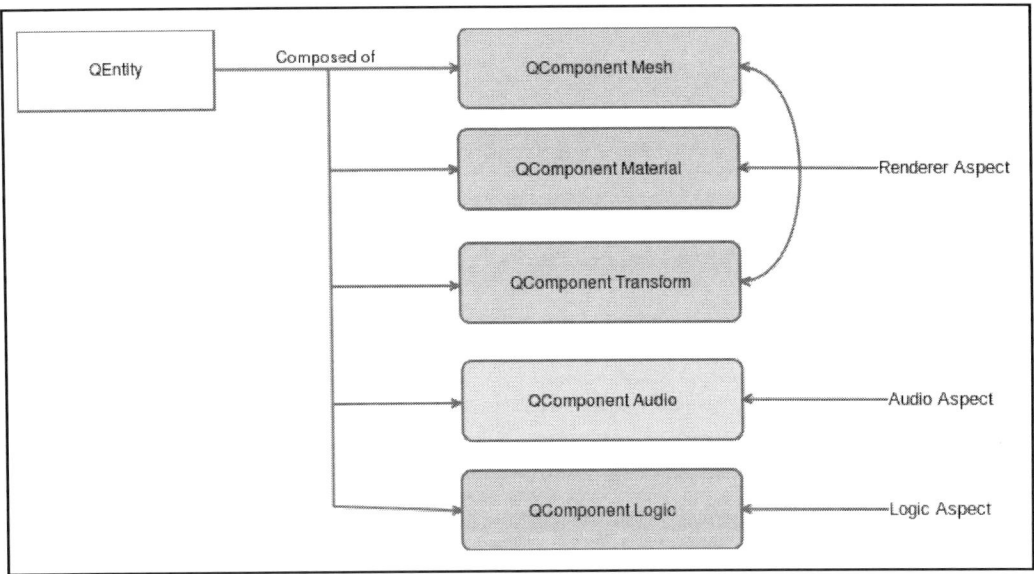

Each of these components can be regrouped in aspects. An aspect is a "slice" of multiple components working on the same part (rendering, audio, logic, and physics). When the graph of all your entities is processed by the Qt3D engine, each layer of aspects is processed sequentially.

The underlying approach is to favor composition over inheritance. In a game, an entity (an apple, a player, an enemy) can have various states during its life cycle: spawning, animating for a given state, dying animation, and so on. Using inheritance to describe these states will lead to a nerve-wracking tree: AppleSpawn, AppleAnimationShiny, AppleDeath, and so on. It would become quickly unmaintainable. Any modification to a class could have huge impact on many other classes and the number of possible combinations of states would get out of hand. Saying that a state is simply a component for a given entity, gives the flexibility to easily swap components and still keep the entity abstraction; an apple Entity element is still an apple, even though it is using the AnimationShinyComponent instead of the AnimationSpawnComponent.

Let's see how to define a basic Entity element in QML. Imagine that this is the apple we have been talking about. The Apple.qml file would look like this:

```
import Qt3D.Core 2.0
import Qt3D.Render 2.0
import Qt3D.Extras 2.0

Entity {
```

```
    property alias position: transform.translation
    PhongMaterial {
        id: material
        diffuse: "red"
    }

    SphereMesh {
        id: mesh
    }

    Transform {
        id: transform
    }

    components: [material, mesh, transform]
}
```

In a very few lines, you describe every aspect of the `Entity` element:

- `Entity`: This is the root object of the file; it follows the same QML pattern we studied in Chapter 5, *Dominating the Mobile UI*.
- `PhongMaterial`: This defines how the surface will be rendered. Here, it uses the Phong shading technique to achieve smooth surfaces. It inherits `QMaterial`, which is the base class for all the material classes.
- `CuboidMesh`: This defines what type of mesh will be used. It inherits `QGeometryRenderer`, which also gives the ability to load custom models (exported from 3D modeling software).
- `Transform`: This defines the transformation matrix of the component. It can customize the translation, scale, and position of the `Entity` element.
- `Position`: This is a property to expose `transform.translation` for a given caller/parent. This might quickly become handy if we want to move the apple around.
- `Components`: This is the array containing all the IDs of all the components for the `Entity` element.

If we want to make this `Apple` a child of another `Entity`, it is simply a matter of defining the Apple inside this new `Entity` element. Let's call it `World.qml`:

```
import Qt3D.Core 2.0
import Qt3D.Render 2.0
import Qt3D.Extras 2.0

Entity {
    id: sceneRoot
```

```
RenderSettings {
    id: frameFraph
    activeFrameGraph: ForwardRenderer {
        clearColor: Qt.rgba(0, 0, 0, 1)
    }
}

Apple {
    id: apple
    position: Qt.vector3d(3.0, 0.0, 2.0)
}

components: [frameGraph]
}
```

Here, the `World Entity` has no visual representation; we want it to be the root of our 3D scene. It only contains the `Apple` we defined earlier. The *x*, *y*, *z* coordinates of the apple are relative to the parent. When the parent makes a translation, the same translation will be applied to the apple.

This is how the hierarchy of entities/components is defined. If you write your Qt3D code in C++, the same logic applies to the equivalent C++ classes (`QEntity`, `QComponent`, and so on).

Because we decided to use the `World.qml` file as the root of our scene, it has to define how the scene will be rendered. The Qt3D rendering algorithm is data-driven. In other words, there is a clear separation between *what* should be rendered (the tree of entities and components) and *how* it should be rendered.

The *how* relies on a similar tree structure using `framegraph`. In Qt Quick, a single method of rendering is used and it covers the 2D drawing. On the other hand, in 3D, the need for flexible rendering makes it necessary to decouple the rendering techniques.

Consider this example: you play a game where you control your avatar and you encounter a mirror. The same 3D scene must be rendered from multiple viewports. If the rendering technique is fixed, this poses multiple problems: which viewport should be drawn first? Is it possible to parallelize the rendering of the viewports in the GPU? What if we need to make multiple passes for the rendering?

In this code snippet, we use the traditional OpenGL rendering technique with the `ForwardRenderer` tree, where each object is rendered directly on the back buffer, one at a time. Qt3D offers the possibility to choose the renderer (`ForwardRenderer`, `DeferredRenderer`, and so on) and configure how the scene should be rendered.

OpenGL typically uses the double-buffering technique to render its content. The front-buffer is what is displayed on the screen and the back-buffer is where the scene is being rendered. When the back-buffer is ready, the two buffers are swapped.

One last thing to notice at the top of each `Entity` element is that we specified the following:

```
import Qt3D.Core 2.0
import Qt3D.Render 2.0
import Qt3D.Extras 2.0
```

There are only Qt3D modules in the import section. Qt3D classes do not inherit `Item` so cannot be directly mixed with QML components. This inheritance tree of the basic Qt3D building blocks is:

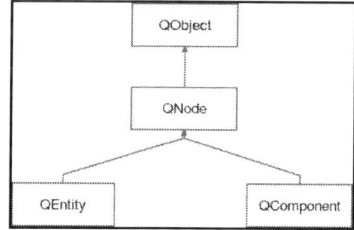

The `QNode` class is the base class of all Qt3D node classes. It relies on the `QObject` class to define the parenting relationship. Each `QNode` class instance also adds a unique `id` variable, which allows it to be recognized from other instances.

Even though `QNode` cannot be mixed with Qt Quick types, they can be added to a `Q3DScene` element (or `Scene3D` in QML), which serves as the canvas for Qt3D content and can be added to a Qt Quick `Item`. Adding `World.qml` to a scene is as simple as this:

```
Rectangle {

    Scene3D {
        id: scene
        anchors.fill: parent
        focus: true

        World { }
    }
}
```

The `Scene3D` element includes a `World` instance and defines common Qt Quick properties (`anchors`, `focus`).

# Configuring Qt for your Raspberry Pi

This project targets a new embedded platform: the Raspberry Pi. Qt officially supports the Raspberry Pi 2, but we got the project running without any trouble on a Raspberry Pi 3. If you do not have one of these devices, it might be nonetheless interesting to read this section to know how the cross-compilation works and how to configure your own kit in Qt Creator. The rest of the chapter will work on a Desktop platform anyway.

Before diving into the Raspberry Pi configuration, let's take a step back to understand our aim. Your computer is probably running on an x86 CPU architecture. This means that every program you run will be executed with the x86 instructions set of your CPU. In Qt Creator, this translates to your available kits. A kit must match your target platform. On startup, Qt Creator searches for available kits in your computer and loads them for you.

In `Chapter 5`, *Dominating the Mobile UI*, we targeted different platforms: Android and iOS. These platforms are running on a different CPU instruction set: ARM. Luckily, the people behind Qt automatically configured for us the necessary nuts and bolts to make it work.

The Raspberry Pi also runs on ARM but it is not ready for Qt by default. We have to prepare it before playing with it in Qt Creator. Note that the following commands are run from a Linux box, but you should be able to run them from Mac or Windows with Cygwin.

> Please follow the complete guide to prepare your Raspberry Pi for Qt at ht tps://wiki.qt.io/RaspberryPi2EGLFS, or simply download a precompiled bundle from http://www.qtrpi.com.

The complete Raspberry Pi installation guide is outside the scope of the book. It is interesting nonetheless to sum up the main steps:

1. Add development packages to the Raspberry Pi.
2. Retrieve the complete toolchain, including the cross-compiler that will be executed from your machine.
3. Create a `sysroot` folder on your machine that will mirror the necessary directories from the Raspberry Pi.
4. Compile Qt with the cross-compiler in the `sysroot` folder.
5. Synchronize this `sysroot` with the Raspberry Pi.

A `sysroot` is simply a directory containing a minimal filesystem for a given platform. It typically contains the `/usr/lib` and `/usr/include` directories. Having this directory on your machine enables the cross-compiler to properly compile and link the output binary without being executed from the Raspberry Pi.

All these steps are done to avoid compiling anything directly on the Raspberry Pi. Being a low-powered device, the execution of any compilation would take a very, very long time. Compiling Qt on a Raspberry Pi would easily take more than 40 hours. Knowing this, the time spent on configuring the cross-compiler seems much easier to bear.

The `qopenglwidget` example mentioned in the wiki should be properly running before proceeding. Once this has been done, we have to cross-compile a few more Qt modules to have our project running:

- `Qtdeclarative`: This model is used to access Qt Quick
- `qt3d`: This model is used to construct a 3D world
- `qtquickcontrols`: This model is used to include interesting controls (Label)
- `qtquickcontrols2`: This model is used to make some new layouts available

For each of these modules, execute the following commands (from your `~/raspi` directory):

```
git clone git://code.qt.io/qt/<modulename>.git -b 5.7
cd <modulename>
~/raspi/qt5/bin/qmake -r
make
make install
```

 You can speed up the compilation by adding the parameter `-j` (or `--jobs`) to `make`. The `make` command will try to parallelize the compilations jobs over your CPU cores, if you have four cores, use `make -j 4`, eight cores, `make -j 8`, and so on.

When everything has been compiled, synchronize your `sysroot` directory again with:

```
rsync -avz qt5pi pi@IP:/usr/local
```

In the previous command, you must replace the `IP` with the real Raspberry Pi address.

The Raspberry Pi is ready to execute our Qt code. However, we have to create our own kit in Qt Creator to be able to compile and deploy our program on it. A kit is composed of the following parts:

- A **compiler** that will compile your code using the CPU instruction set of the target platform
- A **debugger** that will know the instruction set of the target platform to properly break and read the memory content
- A **Qt version** compiled for the targeted platform to compile and link your binary to the target platform's shared objects
- A **device** to which Qt Creator can connect to deploy and execute your program

We will start with the compiler. In Qt Creator:

1. Go to **Tools** | **Options** | **Build & Run** | **Compilers**.
2. Click on **Add** | **GCC**.
3. Browse to `~/raspi/tools/arm-bcm2708/gcc-linaro-arm-linux-gnueabihf-raspbian/bin/arm-linux-gnueabihf-g++`.
4. Rename the compiler to `Rpi GCC`.

This strange binary name makes it easier for Qt to parse the **ABI** (**application binary interface**) to find out the platform architecture, file format, and so on. It should look like this:

Now for the debugger. As we said earlier, we are building this project from a Linux box (Ubuntu). Cross-compilation and embedded development tend to be easier on Linux but you should be able to do the same on a Windows or Mac with a few additional steps.

On Ubuntu Linux, just install a multi-architecture `gdb` with the command `sudo apt-get install gdb-multiarch`. In Qt Creator, add this new debugger in the **Debuggers** tab:

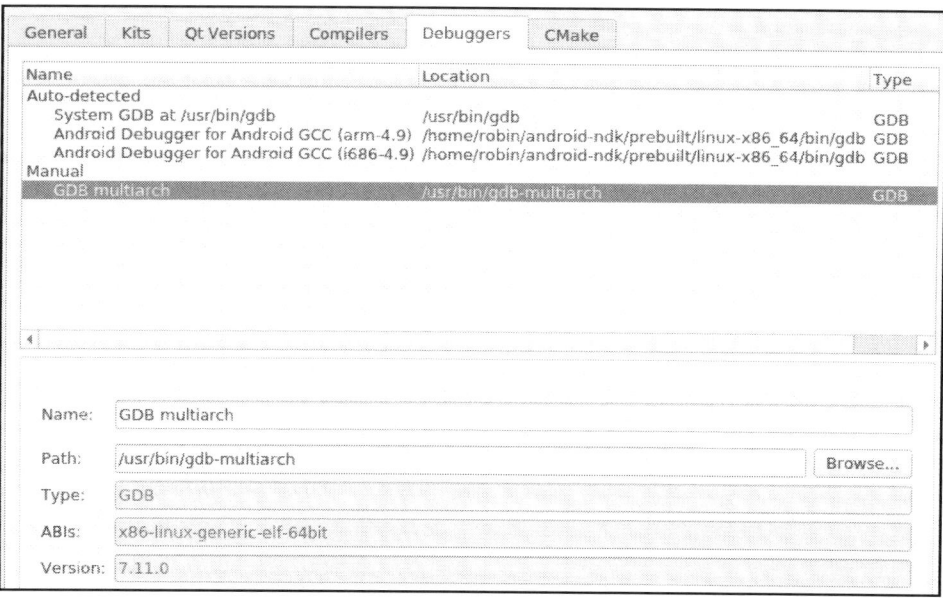

Next, add the cross-compiled Qt explained on the wiki page in the **Qt Versions** tab. Click on **Add** and browse to `~/raspi/qt5/bin/qmake`. This is the resulting Qt Version:

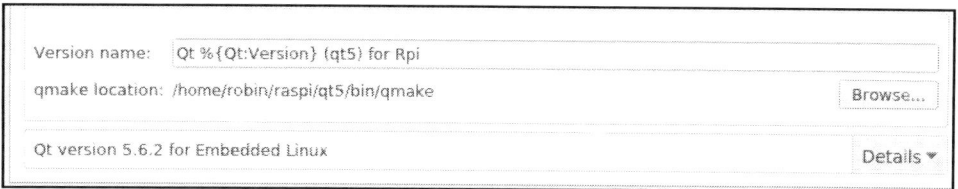

We are almost there! Before building the kit, we simply have to configure Raspberry Pi device access. In **Options | Devices**, follow this procedure:

1. Click on **Add.. | Generic Linux Device | Start Wizard**.
2. The name will be `Rpi 2` (or 3 if you have one).
3. Enter the IP address of your device (indeed, you have to be connected to your local network!).
4. The default username is **pi**.
5. The default password is "raspberry".
6. Click on **Next** to test the connection to the device.

If everything went well, this is your new device:

Finally, the kit will compose all these parts into a valid Qt Creator platform. Go back to **Build & Run | Kits**. From here you simply have to point to each of the parts we built previously. Here is the resulting kit:

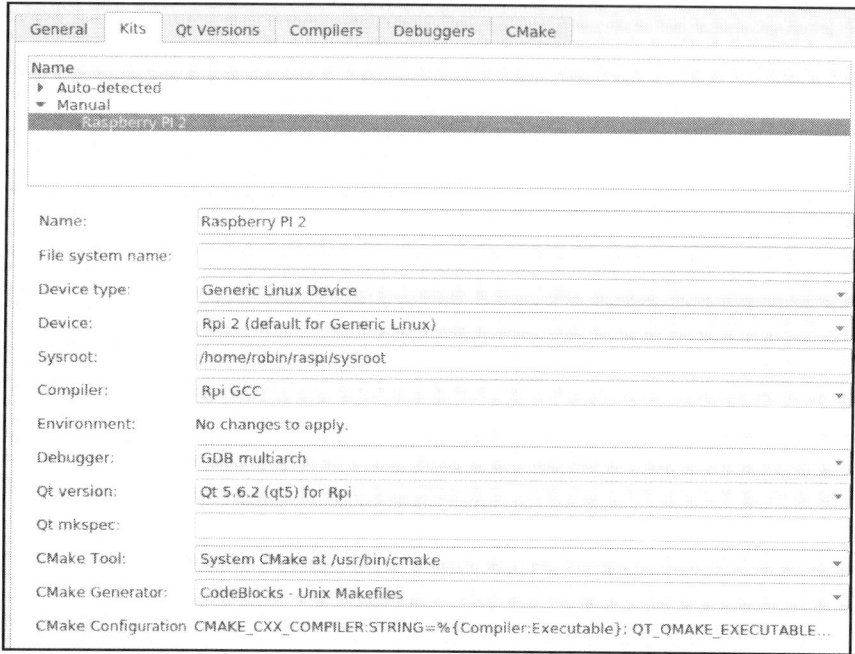

Note that the **Sysroot** filed should point to the `sysroot` folder we previously created at `~/raspi/sysroot`.

If you click on the button to the right of **Name**, you can choose a custom picture for a kit, such as the Raspberry Pi logo.

Everything is now ready to make an awesome snake game.

# Creating an entry point for your Qt3D code

For those who did not play the snake game in their youth, here is a quick reminder of the gameplay:

- You control a snake moving in an empty area

- This area is surrounded by walls
- An apple spawns randomly in the game area
- If the snake eats the apple, it grows and you gain a point. Right after, another apple spawns in the game area
- If the snake touches a wall or a part of its own body, you lose

The goal is to eat as many apples as possible to have the highest score. The longer the snake, the harder it will become to avoid the wall and its own tail. Oh, and the snake goes faster and faster each time it eats an apple. The architecture of the game will be the following:

- All the game items will be defined using Qt3D in QML
- All the game logic will be done in JavaScript, which will communicate with the QML elements

We will keep the 2D feel of the original snake game by placing the camera above the game area but we will spice things up with 3D models and some shaders.

Alright, we spent an awful lot of pages preparing for this moment. It is now time to begin the snake project. Create a new **Qt Quick Controls Application** named ch06-snake. In the project details:

1. Select **Qt 5.6** for the **minimal required Qt version** field.
2. Uncheck **With ui.qml file**.
3. Uncheck **Enable native styling**.
4. Click on **Next** and select the following kits:
   - RaspberryPi 2
   - **Desktop**

5. Click on **Next | Finish**.

We have to add the Qt3D modules. Modify ch06-snake.pro like this:

```
TEMPLATE = app

QT += qml quick 3dcore 3drender 3dquick 3dinput 3dextras
CONFIG += c++11

SOURCES += main.cpp

RESOURCES += \
    snake.qrc

HEADERS +=
```

```
target.files = ch06-snake
target.path = /home/pi
INSTALLS += target
```

We have to prepare the entry point of the application to have a proper OpenGL context with which Qt3D can work. Open and update `main.cpp` like so:

```cpp
#include <QGuiApplication>
#include <QtGui/QOpenGLContext>
#include <QtQuick/QQuickView>
#include <QtQml/QQmlEngine>

int main(int argc, char *argv[])
{
    QGuiApplication app(argc, argv);

    qputenv("QT3D_GLSL100_WORKAROUND", "");

    QSurfaceFormat format;
    if (QOpenGLContext::openGLModuleType() ==
        QOpenGLContext::LibGL) {
        format.setVersion(3, 2);
        format.setProfile(QSurfaceFormat::CoreProfile);
    }
    format.setDepthBufferSize(24);
    format.setStencilBufferSize(8);

    QQuickView view;
    view.setFormat(format);
    view.setResizeMode(QQuickView::SizeRootObjectToView);
    QObject::connect(view.engine(), &QQmlEngine::quit,
                     &app, &QGuiApplication::quit);
    view.setSource(QUrl("qrc:/main.qml"));
    view.show();

    return app.exec();
}
```

The idea is to configure a `QSurfaceFormat` to properly handle OpenGL and to give it to a custom `QQuickView view`. This `view` will use this format to paint itself.

The `qputenv("QT3D_GLSL100_WORKAROUND", "")` instruction is a workaround related to Qt3D shaders on some embedded Linux devices, such as the Raspberry Pi. It will enable a separate GLSL 1.00 snippet for the lights required by some embedded devices. If you do not use this workaround, you will get a black screen and will not be able to properly run the project on Raspberry Pi.

The details of the Qt3d lights workaround are here:
`https://codereview.qt-project.org/#/c/143136/`.

We chose to handle the view using Qt Quick. Another approach would be to create a C++ class that inherits `QMainWindow` and make it the parent of the QML content. This approach can be found in many Qt3D example projects. Both are valid and work. You tend to write more code with the `QMainWindow` approach, but it allows you to create 3D scenes with C++ only.

Note that `view` from the `main.cpp` file tries to load a `main.qml` file. You can see it coming; here is the `main.qml`:

```
import QtQuick 2.6
import QtQuick.Controls 1.4

Item {
    id: mainView

    property int score: 0
    readonly property alias window: mainView

    width: 1280; height: 768
    visible: true

    Keys.onEscapePressed: {
        Qt.quit()
    }

    Rectangle {
        id: hud

        color: "#31363b"
        anchors.left: parent.left
        anchors.right: parent.right
        anchors.top : parent.top
        height: 60

        Label {
            id: snakeSizeText
            anchors.centerIn: parent
            font.pointSize: 25
            color: "white"
            text: "Score: " + score
        }
```

```
        }
    }
```

Here we define the **HUD (heads up display)** at the top of the screen, where the score (the number of apples eaten) will be displayed. Note that we bound the Escape key to the Qt.quit() signal. This signal is connected in main.cpp to the QGuiApplication::quit() signal to quit the application.

The QML context is now ready to welcome Qt3D content. Modify main.qml like so:

```
import QtQuick 2.6
import QtQuick.Controls 1.4
import QtQuick.Scene3D 2.0

Item {
    ...

    Rectangle {
        id: hud
        ...
    }

    Scene3D {
        id: scene
        anchors.top: hud.bottom
        anchors.bottom: parent.bottom
        anchors.left: parent.left
        anchors.right: parent.right
        focus: true
        aspects: "input"
    }
}
```

The Scene3D element takes all the available space below the hud object. It takes the focus of the window to be able to intercept keyboard events. It also enables the input aspect to let the Qt3D engine process keyboard events in its graph traversal.

# Setting up the scene

We can now start writing Qt3D code. The first step is to define the root of the scene. Create a new file named GameArea.qml:

```
import Qt3D.Core 2.0
import Qt3D.Render 2.0
import Qt3D.Extras 2.0
```

```
Entity {
    id: root

    property alias gameRoot: root

    Camera {
        id: camera
        property real x: 24.5
        property real y: 14.0

        projectionType: CameraLens.PerspectiveProjection
        fieldOfView: 45
        aspectRatio: 16/9
        nearPlane : 0.1
        farPlane : 1000.0
        position: Qt.vector3d( x, y, 33.0 )
        upVector: Qt.vector3d( 0.0, 1.0, 0.0 )
        viewCenter: Qt.vector3d( x, y, 0.0 )
    }



    RenderSettings {
        id: frameFraph
        activeFrameGraph: ForwardRenderer {
            clearColor: Qt.rgba(0, 0, 0, 1)
            camera: camera
        }
    }

    components: [frameFraph]
}
```

The first thing we do is create a camera and position it. Remember that, in OpenGL, the coordinates follow the thumb on your right hand points left!:

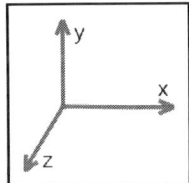

By placing the camera at `Qt.vector3d(x, y, 33)`, we make it come "out of the screen" to be able to express our yet-to-be-created entitiy's coordinates with the simple `x`, `y` axis. The `upVector: Qt.vector3d(0.0, 1.0, 0.0)` specifies the up vector of the camera, in our case it is the `Y` axis. Finally, we point at `Qt.vector(x, y, 0)`, meaning the center of the screen.

The overall goal is to simplify coordinate expression. By positioning the camera this way, placing an object at the coordinate 0, 0 will put it in the bottom-left part of the window, whereas the coordinates 50, 28 mean the top-right part of the window.

We also configure `RenderSettings` with a `ForwardRendered` that defines two properties:

- `clearColor`: This property `Qt.rgba(0, 0, 0, 1)` means that the background will be pitch-black
- `camera`: This property is used to determine the viewport to be rendered

The scene is ready to be rendered, but we need to handle user input, namely the keyboard. To capture keyboard events, modify `GameArea.qml` to look like this:

```
import Qt3D.Core 2.0
import Qt3D.Render 2.0
import Qt3D.Input 2.0

Entity {
    ...
    RenderSettings {
        ...
    }

    KeyboardDevice {
        id: keyboardController
    }

    InputSettings { id: inputSettings }

    KeyboardHandler {
        id: input
        sourceDevice: keyboardController
        focus: true
        onPressed: { }
    }

    components: [frameFraph, input]
}
```

The `KeyboardDevice` element is in charge of dispatching key events to the active `KeyboardHandler`, namely `input`. The `KeyboardHandler` component is attached to the controller and the `onPressed()` function will be called each time a key is pressed. The `KeyboardHandler` is a component; therefore it needs to be added to the list of components for `GameArea`.

The last missing part of `GameArea` is preapring the engine execution (initialization and update):

```
import Qt3D.Core 2.0
import Qt3D.Render 2.0
import Qt3D.Input 2.0
import QtQuick 2.6 as QQ2

Entity {
    id: root

    property alias gameRoot: root
    property alias timerInterval: timer.interval
    property int initialTimeInterval: 80
    property int initialSnakeSize: 5
    property string state: ""
    ...

    KeyboardDevice {
        id: keyboardController
    }

    QQ2.Component.onCompleted: {
        console.log("Start game...");
        timer.start()
    }

    QQ2.Timer {
        id: timer
        interval: initialTimeInterval
        repeat: true
        onTriggered: {}
    }

    components: [frameFraph, input]
}
```

Here we mix Qt Quick elements with Qt3D. Due to possible name collisions, we have to import the module using the alias `QQ2`. We already met `Component.onCompleted` in Chapter 5, *Dominating the Mobile UI*. Its job will be to start the game engine and start the `timer` defined right after.

This `timer` variable will repeat every 80 milliseconds (as defined in the `initialTimeInterval` property) and call the engine's `update()` function. This function will be covered when we build the engine code, later in this chapter. The goal is to emulate the original snake game as closely as possible. The whole game logic will be updated at this interval and not at the normal frame refresh interval. After each call to `update()`, the snake will advance. As a result, the snake's movement will not be smooth but rather jerky. This is clearly a design choice we made to have a retro-gaming feeling.

Each time the snake eats an apple, two things happen:

- The `interval` of the timer will be reduced by the engine (accessed by the `timerInterval` property).
- The snake will grow. Its initial size is defined in the `intialSnakeSize` property.

Reducing the timer interval will make the snake advance faster until it becomes very hard to manage its direction.

# Assembling your Qt3D entities

We will now proceed to create the building blocks of the game, each in the form of an `Entity` element:

- `Wall`: This represents the limit of where the snake cannot go
- `SnakePart`: This represents a part of the snake's body
- `Apple`: This represents the apple (no way!) spawned at a random location
- `Background`: This represents a good-looking background behind the snake and the apple

Each entity will be placed on a grid handled by the engine and will have a type identifier to make it easier to find. To factorize these properties, let's create a parent QML file named `GameEntity.qml`:

```
import Qt3D.Core 2.0

Entity {
    property int type: 0
```

```
    property vector2d gridPosition: Qt.vector2d(0, 0)
}
```

This `Entity` element only defines a `type` property and a `gridPosition` property , which
will be used by the engine to lay out the content on the grid.

The first item we will build is the `Wall.qml` file:

```
import Qt3D.Core 2.0

GameEntity {
    id: root

    property alias position: transform.translation

    Transform {
        id: transform
    }

    components: [transform]
}
```

As you can see, the `Wall` type does not have any visual representation. Because we target a
Raspberry Pi device, we have to be very careful with the CPU/GPU consumption. The game
area will be a grid where each cell contains an instance of one of our entities. The snake will
be surrounded by `Wall` instances. The Raspberry Pi is much slower than your average
computer, to the extent that the game would become unbearably slow if we displayed all
the walls.

To address this issue, the walls are invisible. They will be placed outside the visible
viewport and the borders of the window will act as the visual limit of the snake. Of course,
if you do not target the Raspberry Pi, but rather your computer, it is fine to display the
walls and make them look fancier than just nothing.

The next `Entity` element we will implement is `SnakePart.qml`:

```
import Qt3D.Core 2.0
import Qt3D.Render 2.0
import Qt3D.Extras 2.0

GameEntity {
    id: root

    property alias position: transform.translation

    PhongMaterial {
        id: material
```

```
            diffuse: "green"
        }

        CuboidMesh {
            id: mesh
        }

        Transform {
            id: transform
        }

        components: [material, mesh, transform]
    }
```

If added to the `GameArea` scene, the `SnakePart` block will display a single green cube. The `SnakePart` block is not the complete snake, rather a part of its body. Remember that the snake grows each time it eats an apple. Growing means adding a new instance of `SnakePart` to a list of `SnakePart`.

Let's proceed with the `Apple.qml`:

```
import Qt3D.Core 2.0
import Qt3D.Render 2.0
import Qt3D.Extras 2.0

GameEntity {
    id: root

    property alias position: transform.translation
    property alias color: material.diffuse

    Transform {
        id: transform
        scale: 0.5
    }

    Mesh {
        id: mesh
        source: "models/apple.obj"
    }

    DiffuseMapMaterial {
        id: material
        diffuse: "qrc:/models/apple-texture.png"
    }

    components: [material, mesh, transform]
```

```
    }
```

This snippet starts with introducing more complex yet easy-to-use features of Qt3D, namely a custom mesh and a texture applied to it. Qt3D supports the Wavefront `obj` format to load custom meshes. Here we added a home-cooked apple to the `.qrc` file of the application and we just have to provide the path to this resource to load it.

The same principle is applied for the `DiffuseMapMaterial` element. We added a custom texture and added it as a source of the component.

As you can see, the `Entity` definition and its components look very much the same. Yet we effortlessly traded a Qt3D `CuboidMesh` with a custom model.

We will push things even further with `Background.qml`:

```qml
import Qt3D.Core 2.0
import Qt3D.Render 2.0
import Qt3D.Extras 2.0

Entity {
    id: root

    property alias position: transform.translation
    property alias scale3D: transform.scale3D

    MaterialBackground {
        id: material
    }

    CuboidMesh {
        id: mesh
    }

    Transform {
        id: transform
    }

    components: [material, mesh, transform]
}
```

The `Background` block will be displayed behind the snake and the apple. At first sight, this entity looks very much like `SnakePart`. However, `Material` is not a Qt3D class. It is a custom defined `Material` that relies on shaders. Let's see `MaterialBackground.qml`:

```
import Qt3D.Core 2.0
import Qt3D.Render 2.0

Material {
    id: material

    effect: Effect {
        techniques: [
            Technique {
                graphicsApiFilter {
                    api: GraphicsApiFilter.OpenGL
                    majorVersion: 3
                    minorVersion: 2
                }
                renderPasses: RenderPass {
                    shaderProgram: ShaderProgram {
                        vertexShaderCode:
                        loadSource("qrc:/shaders/gl3/grass.vert")
                        fragmentShaderCode:
                        loadSource("qrc:/shaders/gl3/grass.frag")
                    }
                }
            }
        ]
    }
}
```

If you are not familiar with shaders, we can summarize them in the following statement: shaders are computer programs written in a C-style syntax that are executed by the GPU. Data from your logic will be fed by the CPU and made available to the GPU memory where your shaders will run. Here we manipulate two types of shader:

- **Vertex shader**, which is executed on each vertex of the source of your mesh
- **Fragment**, which is executed on each pixel to produce the final rendering

By being executed on the GPU, these shaders utilize the huge parallelization power of the GPU (which is orders-of-magnitude higher than your CPU). It enables modern games to have such stunning visual rendering. Covering shaders and the OpenGL pipeline is beyond the scope of this book (you can fill several bookshelves on this subject alone). We will limit ourselves to showing you how you can use shaders in Qt3D.

If you want to delve into OpenGL or sharpen your skills with shaders, we recommend the *OpenGL SuperBible*, by Graham Sellers, Richard S Wright Jr., and Nicholas Haemel.

Qt3D supports shaders in a very convenient way. Simply add your shader file to the .qrc resource file and load it in the effect property of a given Material.

In this snippet, we specify that this shader Technique should be run only on OpenGL 3.2. This is indicated in the graphicsApiFilter block. This version of OpenGL targets your desktop machine. Because the performance gap between your desktop and your Raspberry Pi is very marked, we have the ability to execute different shaders depending on the platform.

Thus, here is the Raspberry Pi-compatible technique:

```
Technique {
    graphicsApiFilter {
        api: GraphicsApiFilter.OpenGLES
        majorVersion: 2
        minorVersion: 0
    }

    renderPasses: RenderPass {
        shaderProgram: ShaderProgram {
            vertexShaderCode:
                loadSource("qrc:/shaders/es2/grass.vert")
            fragmentShaderCode:
                loadSource("qrc:/shaders/es2/grass.frag")
        }
    }
}
```

You just have to add it to the techniques property of the Material. Note that the targeted OpenGL version is OpenGLES 2.0, which will run fine on your Raspberry Pi and even your iOS/Android phone.

A last thing to cover is how parameters can be passed to shaders. Here is an example:

```
Material {
    id: material

    parameters: [
        Parameter {
            name: "score"; value: score
        }
```

```
    ]
    ...
}
```

The `score` variable will be accessible in the shader with this simple section. Please take a look at the source code for the chapter to see the complete content of this `Material` element. We had the fun of writing a shader displaying a moving and glowing wave over a grass texture.

The only fixed element of the game is the background. We can directly add it to `GameArea.qml`:

```
Entity {
    id: root
    ...

    Background {
        position: Qt.vector3d(camera.x, camera.y, 0)
        scale3D: Qt.vector3d(camera.x * 2, camera.y * 2, 0)
    }

    components: [frameFraph, input]
}
```

The `Background` element is positioned to cover the whole visible area behind the snake and the apple. Being defined inside `GameArea`, it will be automatically added to the entity/component tree and will be drawn right away.

# Preparing the board game

Even if our game has a 3D representation, we will implement 2D gameplay like the original snake game. Our game items are born, will live, and die in a 2D area. Like chess, this board will be composed of rows and columns. But in our snake game, each square can be:

- An apple
- A snake
- A wall
- Empty

Here is an example of a board representation from the point of view of the engine:

This is a small 10×8 board; even if the size does not matter, you will be able to define a bigger one. Your game, your rules! We have walls (**W**) surrounding the game area. An apple (**A**) is spawned at 7×2. Finally, we have a snake (**S**) beginning at 3×4 and ending at 5×5.

It is time to create our board class. Please create a JS file called `board.js`:

```
function Board(columnCount, rowCount, blockSize) {
    this.columnCount = columnCount;
    this.rowCount = rowCount;
    this.blockSize = blockSize;
    this.maxIndex = columnCount * rowCount;
    this.data = new Array(this.maxIndex);
}
```

This object constructor function required three parameters. The `columnCount` and `rowCount` parameters will help you to choose the board dimension. The last parameter, `blockSize`, is the size of a board square in the OpenGL world. For example, we can set `blockSize` to 10. In this case, the apple in 7×2 on the board we be displayed with x = 70 and y = 20 in the OpenGL world. In this chapter, we will use a `blockSize` of 1, so the board coordinates match OpenGL coordinates.

Let's add some utility functions to `board.js`:

```
Board.prototype.init = function() {
    for (var i = 0; i < this.data.length; i++) {
        this.data[i] = null;
    }
}

Board.prototype.index = function(column, row) {
    return column + (row * this.columnCount);
}
```

```
Board.prototype.setData = function(data, column, row) {
    this.data[this.index(column, row)] = data;
}

Board.prototype.at = function(column, row) {
    return this.data[this.index(column, row)];
}
```

Defining a class in JavaScript can be disturbing for a C++ developer. Every JavaScript object has a prototype object to which you can add functions. We are using it to add class methods to `Board`.

Here is a summary of the purpose of each function of the `Board` class:

- `init()`: This function initializes all array values to the `null` value
- `index()`: This function returns the array index from column/row coordinates
- `setData()`: This function assigns the `data` value on the board from column/row coordinates
- `at()`: This function retrieves the `data` value in an array from column/row coordinates

Please note that, in our case, a `null` square means an empty square.

# Crafting entities from the factory

Now that we have a board to receive items, we will create the game items factory. The factory is a design pattern that allows us to create an object without exposing the creation logic to the caller. This factory can be seen as a helper class that will handle all the dirty tasks required when you want to create a new game item from JavaScript. Do you remember `GameEntity.qml`? It is the parent class of `Apple.qml`, `Snake.qml`, and `Wall.qml`. The factory will be able to create a specific entity for a given a type and coordinates. We will use the property type to identify an entity kind. Here is the factory pattern schema used in our snake game:

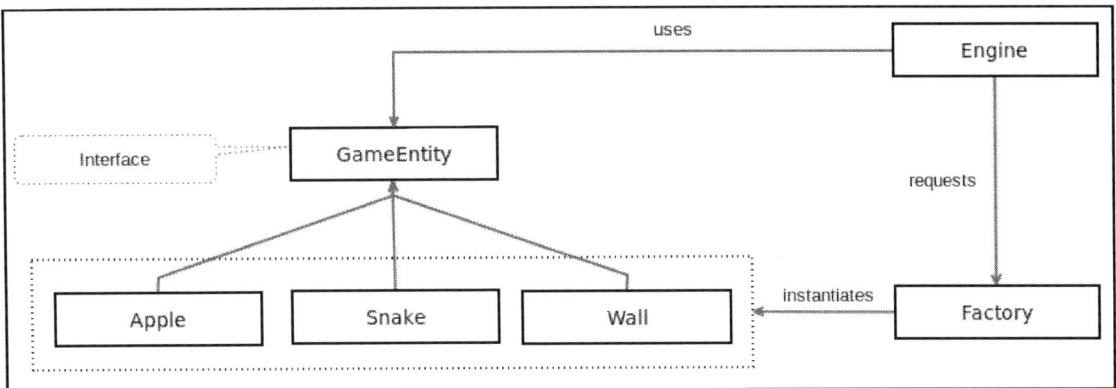

We can now create the `factory.js` file, which begins like this:

```
var SNAKE_TYPE = 1;
var WALL_TYPE  = 2;
var APPLE_TYPE = 3;

var snakeComponent = Qt.createComponent("Snake.qml");
var wallComponent = Qt.createComponent("Wall.qml");
var appleComponent = Qt.createComponent("Apple.qml");
```

First of all, we define all the game entity types. In our case we have apple, snake, and wall types. Then, we create game item components from QML files. These components will be use by the factory to dynamically create new game entities.

We can now add the constructor and a `removeAllEntities()` utility function to remove all instantiated entities:

```
function GameFactory() {

    this.board = null;
    this.parentEntity = null;
    this.entities = [];
}

GameFactory.prototype.removeAllEntities = function() {
    for(var i = 0; i < this.entities.length; i++) {
        this.entities[i].setParent(null);
    }
```

This factory has three member variables:

- A reference to the game `board` described in the previous section
- A reference to the `parentEntity` variable, that is, the game area
- An `entities` array that keeps a reference to created items

The `removeAllEntities()` function will remove the items from their parent (that is, the game area) and create a new empty entities array. This ensures that old entities are deleted by the garbage collector.

Let's add the core function `createGameEnity()` in the factory:

```
GameFactory.prototype.createGameEntity = function(type, column, row) {
    var component;
    switch(type) {
    case SNAKE_TYPE:
        component = snakeComponent;
        break;

    case WALL_TYPE:
        component = wallComponent;
        break;

    case APPLE_TYPE:
        component = appleComponent;
        break;
    }
    var gameEntity = component.createObject(this.parentEntity);
    gameEntity.setParent(this.parentEntity);

    this.board.setData(gameEntity, column, row);
    gameEntity.gridPosition = Qt.vector2d(column, row);
    gameEntity.position.x = column * this.board.blockSize;
    gameEntity.position.y = row * this.board.blockSize;

    this.entities.push(gameEntity);
    return gameEntity;
}
```

As you can see, the caller provides an entity `type` and board coordinates (`column` and `row`). The first part is a switch to select the correct QML component. Once we have the component, we can call `component.createObject()` to create an instance of this component. The parent of this new component will be `this.parentEntity`, in our case, `GameArea`. Then, we can update the board, update the entity position, and add this new entity in the `entities` array.

The last thing to do is to update our QML game entities with the proper factory type. Please open `Apple.qml` and update the file like this:

```
import "factory.js" as Factory

GameEntity {

    id: root
    type: Factory.APPLE_TYPE
    ...
}
```

You can now update `Snake.qml` with the `Factory.SNAKE_TYPE` type and `Wall.qml` with the `Factory.WALL_TYPE` type.

# Building a snake engine in JavaScript

It is time to get your hands dirty. Let's see how to create an engine in JavaScript to manage a snake game using our board, our factory, and the power of QML.

Please create a new `engine.js` file with the following snippet:

```
.import "factory.js" as Factory
.import "board.js" as Board

var COLUMN_COUNT = 50;
var ROW_COUNT = 29;
var BLOCK_SIZE = 1;

var factory = new Factory.GameFactory();
var board = new Board.Board(COLUMN_COUNT, ROW_COUNT, BLOCK_SIZE);

var snake = [];
var direction;
```

The first lines are the Qt way to import a JavaScript file from another JavaScript file. Then, we can easily instantiate a `factory` variable and a 50×29 `board` variable. The `snake` array contains all the snake game items instantiated. This array will be useful to move our snake. Finally, the `direction` variable is a 2d vector handling the current snake direction.

This is the first function of our engine:

```
function start() {
    initEngine();

    createSnake();
    createWalls();

    spawnApple();
    gameRoot.state = "PLAY";
}
```

This gives you a summary of what is done when we start the engine:

1. Initialize the engine.
2. Create the initial snake.
3. Create walls surrounding the game area.
4. Spawn the first apple.
5. Switch the GameArea state to PLAY.

Let's begin with the initEngine() function:

```
function initEngine() {
    timer.interval = initialTimeInterval;
    score = 0;

    factory.board = board;
    factory.parentEntity = gameRoot;
    factory.removeAllEntities();

    board.init();
    direction = Qt.vector2d(-1, 0);
}
```

This function initializes and resets all the variables. The first task is to set the GameArea timer interval to its initial value. Each time the snake eats an apple, this interval is reduced, increasing the game speed and thus the snake's movement speed. Logically, we reset the score of the player to 0. Then we initialize the factory, giving the board and gameRoot references. The gameRoot refers to the GameArea; this entity will be the parent of all items instantiated by the factory. Then, we remove all the existing entities from the factory and call the board's init() function to clear the board. Finally, we set a default direction for the snake. The vector -1, 0 means that the snake will begin moving to the left. If you want the snake to start moving up, you can set the vector to 0, 1.

The next function is creating the snake:

```
function createSnake() {
    snake = [];
    var initialPosition = Qt.vector2d(25, 12);
    for (var i = 0; i < initialSnakeSize; i++) {
        snake.push(factory.createGameEntity(Factory.SNAKE_TYPE,
                                 initialPosition.x + i,
                                 initialPosition.y));
    }
}
```

No big deal here, we reset and initialize the snake array. The first snake item will be created at 25×12. We then proceed to create as many snake items as we need to spawn a snake with the correct initial size. Please note that other snake items will be created to the right of the first item (26×12, 27×12, and so on). You can see how easy it is to call our factory and request a new snake item instance.

Let's add the createWalls() function to engine.js:

```
function createWalls() {
    for (var x = 0; x < board.columnCount; x++) {
        factory.createGameEntity(Factory.WALL_TYPE, x, 0);
        factory.createGameEntity(Factory.WALL_TYPE, x, board.rowCount - 1);
    }
    for (var y = 1; y < board.rowCount - 1; y++) {
        factory.createGameEntity(Factory.WALL_TYPE, 0, y);
        factory.createGameEntity(Factory.WALL_TYPE, board.columnCount - 1,
y);
    }
}
```

The first loop creates the top and bottom walls. The second loop creates the left and right walls. The indexes of the second loop are different from the first one to avoid creating the corners twice.

Let's see now how to implement the spawnApple() function in engine.js:

```
function spawnApple() {
    var isFound = false;
    var position;
    while (!isFound) {
        position = Qt.vector2d(Math.floor(Math.random()
                                 * board.columnCount),
                              Math.floor(Math.random()
                                 * board.rowCount));
        if (board.at(position.x, position.y) == null) {
```

```
            isFound = true;
        }
    }
    factory.createGameEntity(Factory.APPLE_TYPE, position.x, position.y);

    if (timerInterval > 10) {
        timerInterval -= 2;
    }
}
```

The first step is to find an empty square. The while loop will generate a random board position and check whether a square is empty. As soon as an empty square is found, we request the factory to create an apple entity at this position. Finally, we reduce the timerInverval value of GameArea to speed up the game.

We will now add some utility functions related to the snake position in engine.js:

```
function setPosition(item, column, row) {
    board.setData(item, column, row);
    item.gridPosition = Qt.vector2d(column, row);
    item.position.x = column * board.blockSize;
    item.position.y = row * board.blockSize;
}

function moveSnake(column, row) {
    var last = snake.pop();
    board.setData(null, last.gridPosition.x, last.gridPosition.y);
    setPosition(last, column, row);
    snake.unshift(last);
}
```

The setPosition() function handles all the necessary tasks when we want to move a game item. We first assign the game item to the correct board square, then we update the gridPosition property (from GameEntity) but also the OpenGL position.x and position.y.

The second function, moveSnake(), moves the snake to an adjacent square. Let's dissect all the steps performed by this function:

1. The snake is our global array containing all the snake items. The pop() method removes and returns the last element that we store in the last variable.
2. The last variable contains the snake's tail's grid position. We set this board square to null; that means an empty square for us.
3. The last variable is now put on the adjacent square requested by the caller.
4. The last variable is finally inserted at the beginning of the snake array.

The next schema illustrates the `moveSnake()` process when a snake is moving on the left. We also name snake items with a letter to visualize how the tail becomes the head, simulating a moving snake:

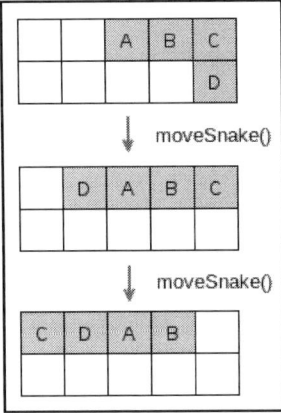

Now that we can move our snake, we must handle key events to move the snake in the correct direction. Please add this new function to `engine.js`:

```
function handleKeyEvent(event) {
    switch(event.key) {
        // restart game
        case Qt.Key_R:
            start();
            break;

        // direction UP
        case Qt.Key_I:
            if (direction != Qt.vector2d(0, -1)) {
                direction = Qt.vector2d(0, 1);
            }
            break;

        // direction RIGHT
        case Qt.Key_L:
            if (direction != Qt.vector2d(-1, 0)) {
                direction = Qt.vector2d(1, 0);
            }
            break;

        // direction DOWN
        case Qt.Key_K:
            if (direction != Qt.vector2d(0, 1)) {
                direction = Qt.vector2d(0, -1);
```

```
            }
            break;

        // direction LEFT
        case Qt.Key_J:
            if (direction != Qt.vector2d(1, 0)) {
                direction = Qt.vector2d(-1, 0);
            }
            break;
    }
}
```

In this game, we use the I-J-K-L keys to update the snake direction vector. Like the original snake game, you can't reverse your direction. A check is performed to avoid this behavior. Please notice that pressing the R key will call start() and so restart the game. We will see soon how to bind this function with the QML keyboard controller.

Here we are, the last (but not least) function, the update() function of engine.js:

```
function update() {
    if (gameRoot.state == "GAMEOVER") {
        return;
    }

    var headPosition = snake[0].gridPosition;
    var newPosition = Qt.vector2d(headPosition.x + direction.x,
                                  headPosition.y + direction.y);
    var itemOnNewPosition = board.at(newPosition.x,
                                     newPosition.y);

    ...
}
```

This function will be called at regular intervals by QML. As you can see, if the gameRoot (that is GameArea) state variable equals GAMEOVER, this function does nothing and returns immediately. Then, three important steps are performed:

1. Retrieve the grid position of the snake's head in headPosition.
2. Process where the snake goes using the direction vector in newPosition.
3. Put the item where the snake is going in itemOnNewPosition.

The second part of the `update()` function is the following snippet:

```
function update() {
    ...
    if(itemOnNewPosition == null) {
        moveSnake(newPosition.x, newPosition.y);
        return;
    }

    switch(itemOnNewPosition.type) {
        case Factory.SNAKE_TYPE:
            gameRoot.state = "GAMEOVER";
            break;

        case Factory.WALL_TYPE:
            gameRoot.state = "GAMEOVER";
            break;

        case Factory.APPLE_TYPE:
            itemOnNewPosition.setParent(null);
            board.setData(null, newPosition.x, newPosition.y);
            snake.unshift(factory.createGameEntity(
                    Factory.SNAKE_TYPE,
                    newPosition.x,
                    newPosition.y));
            spawnApple();
            score++;
            break;
    }
}
```

If the snake is going to an empty square (`itemOnNewPosition` is `null`), it is alright and we only move the snake to `newPosition`.

If the square is not empty, we must apply the correct rule depending on the item type. If the next square is a snake part or a wall, we update the state to GAMEOVER. On the other hand, if the next square is an apple, several steps are performed:

1. Detach the apple item from `GameArea`, setting its parent to `null`.
2. Remove the apple from the board, setting the board square to `null`.
3. Grow the snake, creating a snake part at the beginning of the `snake` array.
4. Spawn a new apple in a random empty square.
5. Increment the score.

Our snake engine is now complete. The last step is to call some engine functions from QML. Please update `GameArea.qml`:

```
...
import "engine.js" as Engine

Entity {
    ...
    QQ2.Component.onCompleted: {
        console.log("Start game...");
        Engine.start();
        timer.start()
    }

    QQ2.Timer {
        id: timer
        interval: initialTimeInterval
        repeat: true
        onTriggered: Engine.update()
    }

    KeyboardInput {
        id: input
        controller: keyboardController
        focus: true
        onPressed: Engine.handleKeyEvent(event)
    }
    ...
}
```

You can already play the game. If you eat an apple, the snake grows and you get one point. When you hit yourself or a wall, the game state switches to GAMEOVER and the game stops. Finally, if you press the R key, the game restarts. The game looks like the next screenshot on to null Raspberry Pi:

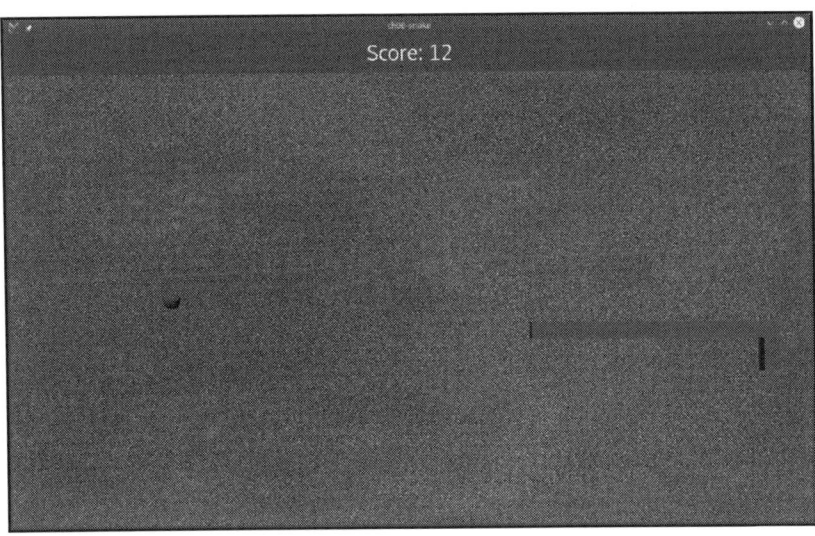

# Varying the HUD with QML states

We will now create a "Game Over" HUD, displayed when you lose the game. Create a new file GameOverItem.qml:

```
Item {
    id: root
    anchors.fill: parent

    onVisibleChanged: {
        scoreLabel.text = "Your score: " + score
    }

    Rectangle {
        anchors.fill: parent
        color: "black"
        opacity: 0.75
    }

    Label {
        id: gameOverLabel
        anchors.centerIn: parent
        color: "white"
        font.pointSize: 50
        text: "Game Over"
    }
```

```
        Label {
            id: scoreLabel
            width: parent.width
            anchors.top: gameOverLabel.bottom
            horizontalAlignment: "AlignHCenter"
            color: "white"
            font.pointSize: 20
        }

        Label {
            width: parent.width
            anchors.bottom: parent.bottom
            anchors.bottomMargin: 50
            horizontalAlignment: "AlignHCenter"
            color: "white"
            font.pointSize: 30
            text:"Press R to restart the game"
        }
    }
}
```

Let's examine the items of this Game Over screen:

- A black rectangle filling the entire screen with an `opacity` value of 75%. As a consequence, the game area will still be visible at 25% behind the game over screen.
- A `gameOverLabel` label displaying the text "Game Over". This is a traditional video game message but you can edit this label with text such as "Loser!" or "Too bad!".
- A dynamic `scoreLabel` label that will display the final score.
- A label explaining to the player how he can restart the game.

Please notice that, when the visibility of the root item changes, the `scoreLabel` text is updated with the current `score` variable from `main.qml`.

Qt Quick provides an interesting feature related to UI states. You can define several states for an item and describe the behaviors for each state. We will now use this feature and our `GameOverItem` in a new file called `OverlayItem.qml`:

```
Item {
    id: root

    states: [
        State {
            name: "PLAY"
            PropertyChanges { target: root; visible: false }
```

```
        },
        State {
            name: "GAMEOVER"
            PropertyChanges { target: root; visible: true }
            PropertyChanges { target: gameOver; visible: true }
        }
    ]

    GameOverItem {
        id: gameOver
    }
}
```

You can see that the `states` element is an `Item` property. By default, the `states` element contains an empty string state. Here we are defining two `State` items named PLAY and GAMEOVER. We are using the same naming convention as in `engine.js`. Afterwards we can bind property values to a state. In our case, when the state is GAMEOVER, we set the visibility to `true` for this `OverlayItem` and its `GameOverItem`. Otherwise, for the state PLAY, we hide it.

The overlay HUD and its "Game Over" screen are ready to be used. Please update your `mail.qml` with the following snippet:

```
Item {
    id: mainView
    property int score: 0
    readonly property alias window: mainView
    ...
    OverlayItem {
        id: overlayItem
        anchors.fill: mainView
        visible: false

        Connections {
            target: gameArea
            onStateChanged: {
                overlayItem.state = gameArea.state;
            }
        }
    }
}
```

Our `OverlayItem` element fits the screen and is not visible by default. Like a C++ Qt Widgets signal/slot connection, you can perform a QML connection. The target property contains the item that will send the signal. Then you can use the QML slot syntax:

```
on<PropertyName>Changed
```

In our case, the target is `gameArea`. This item contains the `state` variable, so we can be notified when the state variable is updated using `onStateChanged`. Then, we switch the state of `OverlayItem`. This assignation will trigger all `PropertyChanged` defined in `OverlayItem` element and display or hide our `GameOverItem`.

You can now lose the game and enjoy your Game Over overlay:

# Profiling your QML application

Qt Creator provides a QML profiler to collect useful data on your application during the runtime. You can use it on a desktop and also on a remote target such as our Raspberry Pi. Let's check that your debug build configuration allows QML debugging and profiling. Click on **Projects** | **Rpi 2** | **Build**. Then you can click on **Details** of **qmake** from **Build Steps**. You should also check it for your desktop kit:

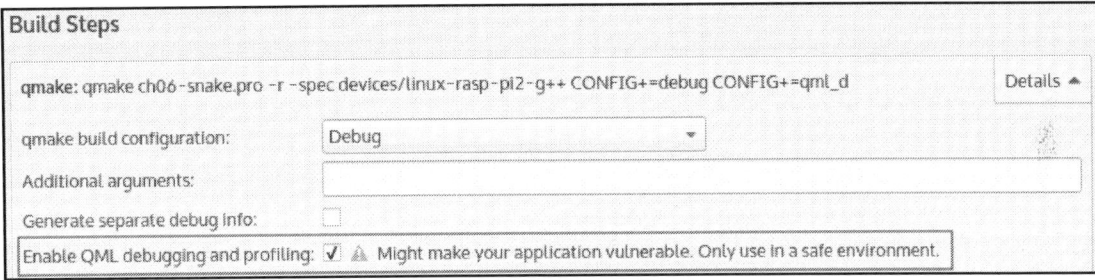

By default, data is only sent from target to host when you stop profiling. You can flush data periodically: **Tools** | **Options** | **Analyser** | **QML Profiler**.

Keep in mind that flushing data while profiling frees memory on the target device but takes time. Thus, it can affect your profiling result and analysis.

While we are using Qt Creator kits, we can start the QML profiler in the same way for desktops or remote devices. Switch to a kit and click on **Analyze** | **QML Profiler** to start the QML profiling. If you are profiling an application running on your desktop, Qt Creator starts your software with an argument such as this:

```
-qmljsdebugger=file:/tmp/QtCreator.OU7985
```

If you're profiling an application on a remote device (such as a Raspberry Pi), Qt Creator uses a TCP socket to retrieve data, adding an argument such as this:

```
-qmljsdebugger=port:10000
```

For both targets, the QML profiler will afterwards try to connect to your application. Another way to start the QML profiler on a remote device is to start the application yourself with the -qmljsdebugger argument, for example:

```
./ch06-snake -qmljsdebugger=port:3768
```

Then, you can click on **Analyze** | **QML Profiler (External)**. Select your remote kit (such as Rpi 2), set the **port** to 3768, and click on **OK**.

Great, the QML profiler is started, a new toolbar appears. You can play the game for a few seconds and click on the **Stop** button from the QML Profiler toolbar. Then the QML profiler processes data and displays something like this:

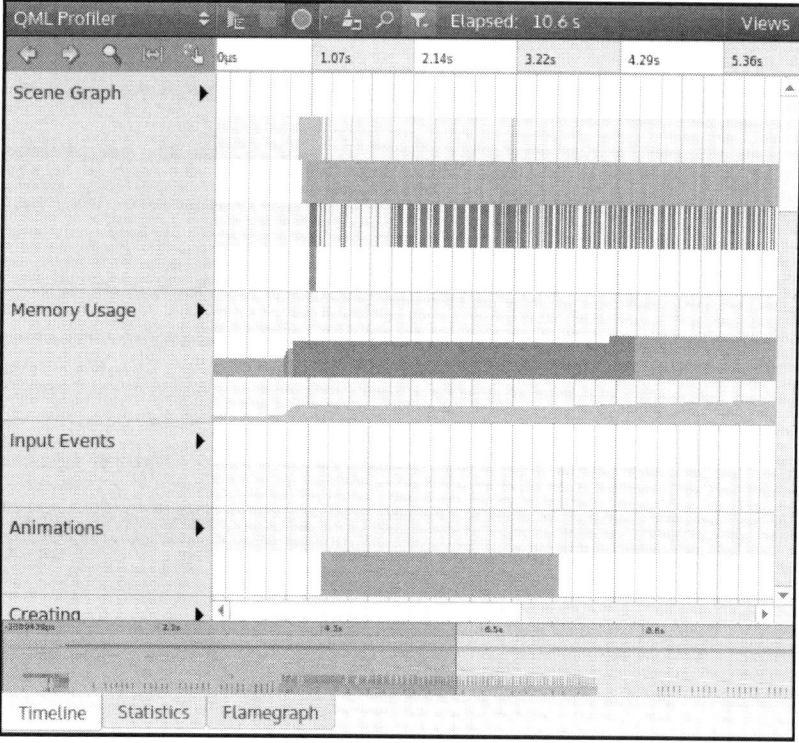

Let's begin analyzing the top buttons from left to right:

1. Start QML profiler.
2. Stop the application and the QML profiler.
3. Enable/disable profiling. You can also select an event to capture.
4. Discard data to clean your profiling session.
5. Search timeline event notes.
6. Hide or show event categories.
7. **Elapsed** indicates the session duration.
8. **Views** hides or shows the **Timeline**, **Statistics**, and **Flamegraph** tabs.

To learn to use the QML profiler, we will take a real case. Restarting the game is a little slow on the Raspberry Pi. Let's find with the QML profiler what requires several seconds to restart the game!

Please follow this operational mode to gather data from the QML profiler:

1. Select the Raspberry Pi kit.
2. Start the QML profiler.
3. Wait for the snake to hit a wall.
4. Press the *R* key to restart the game.
5. Wait for the game to restart and the snake to move again.
6. Stop the QML profiler.

Let's begin our investigation using the **timeline** tab. This view displays a chronological view of events, grouped by event type. The JavaScript row dissects your code and displays useful information. You can click on an item to get some details. Identify in the timeline when you restart the game. The JavaScript row can be read as a call stack, from top to bottom:

In our case, we restarted the game around 3.5 seconds after the application started. Here is the stack with durations provided by the QML profiler. Here is the stack with durations provided by the QML profiler. Let's track all functions called when we restart the game pressing the R key:

- The `onPressed()` function from `GameArea.qml`
- The `handleKetEvent()` function from `engine.js`
- The `start()` function from `engine.js` at 4.2 seconds
  - `initEngine()` at 80 ms
  - `createSnake()` at 120 ms
  - `createWalls()` at 4.025 seconds!

Here we are, `createWalls()` takes ~4 seconds on the Raspberry Pi when we restart the game.

Let's switch to the **Statistics** view:

The **Statistics** view displays numbers concerning the call count of an event. An event can be a QML binding, creation, signal triggered, or a JavaScript function. The bottom part shows QML callers and callees.

A caller is the source of a change in a binding. For example, the JS function `createWalls()` is a caller.

A callee is the affected item that a binding triggers. For example, the QML item `Wall.qml` is a callee.

Once again, `createWalls()` requesting many factory item creation seems responsible for the slow restart of the game on Raspberry Pi.

Take a look at the last view of the QML profiler, the **Flamegraph**:

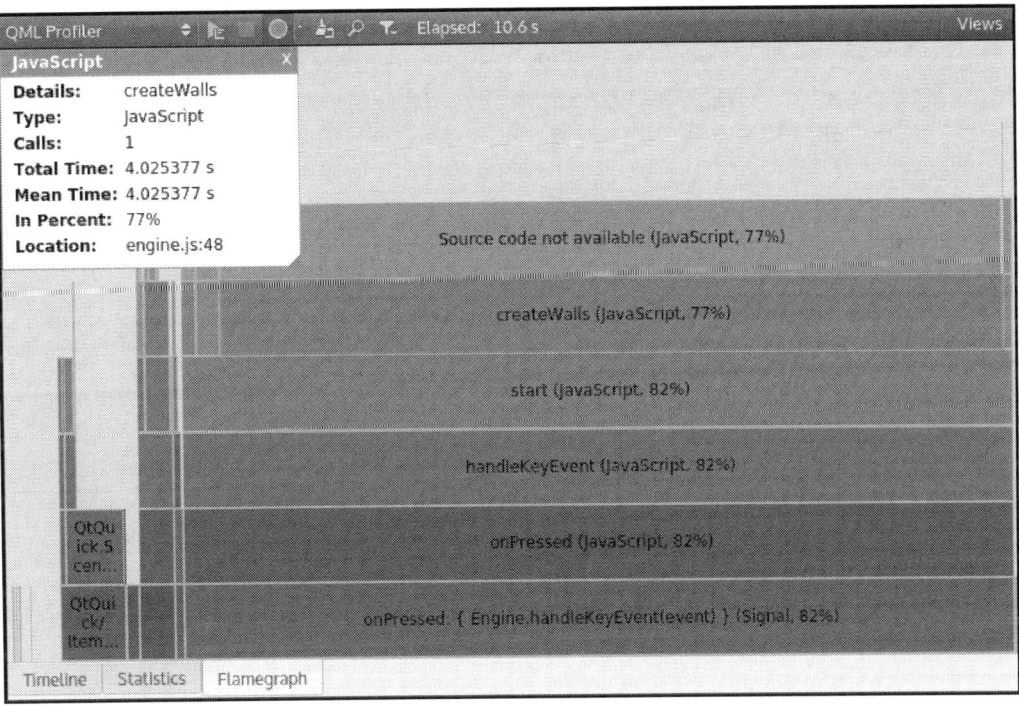

The **Flamegraph** view is a compact summary of your QML and JavaScript code while running the game. You can see the call count and the amount of time relative to the total duration. Like the **Timeline** view, you can see the call stack but from bottom to top!

Again, the profiler indicates `createWalls()` is a heavy function. On a profiling session of 10 seconds with one game restart, 77% of the time is spent in `engine.createWalls()`.

You will now be able to profile a QML application. You can try to edit the code to speed up the restart. Here are some hints:

- Create the walls only once at application startup; do not delete and recreate them on each restart.
- Implement a common design pattern in video games: an object pool of preloaded items. Request a wall when needed, and return the wall to the pool when you do not use it.

# Summary

In this chapter, we discovered how to use the Qt3D module. You also learned how to configure Qt Creator to create a new kit for an embedded Linux device. Your Raspberry Pi can now run your Qt applications. We created a snake game using QML views and an engine in JavaScript. We also covered the Factory design pattern to easily create new game items from the engine. Finally, you are now able to investigate the bad behavior of QML software using the powerful QML profiler.

Even if Qt is a powerful framework, sometimes you need to use a third-party library. In the next chapter, we will see how to integrate the OpenCV library into your Qt application.

# 7
# Third-Party Libraries Without a Headache

In previous chapters, we have used our own libraries or the ones provided by Qt. In this chapter, we will learn how to integrate the third-party library OpenCV with a Qt project. This library will give you an impressive image processing toolbox. For each platform, you will learn to use a different specific compiler link configuration.

Qt Designer is a powerful WYSIWYG editor. This is why this chapter will also teach you to build a Qt Designer plugin that can be dragged and dropped from the **Widget Box** to the **Form Editor**, and then configured directly from Qt Creator.

In the example project, the user can load a picture, select a filter from thumbnail previews, and save the result. This application will rely on OpenCV functions for image processing.

This chapter will cover the following topics:

- Prepare a cross-platform project to host a third-party library
- Link with a third party library
- Build a custom `QWidget` class using Qt Designer plugins
- How the OpenCV API can work with Qt
- Create a Qt application that relies on a custom `QWidget` class

# Creating your Qt Designer plugin

In Chapter 4, *Conquering the Desktop UI*, we created a custom Qt widget in Qt Designer using the promoting technique. It is now time to learn how to create a custom Qt widget by building a plugin for Qt Designer. Your widget will be available from the **Design mode** in the **Widget Box** alongside other regular Qt widgets. For this project example, we will create a FilterWidget class that processes an input image to apply a filter. The widget will also display the filter name and a dynamic thumbnail of the filtered picture.

This project is composed of two sub-projects:

- filter-plugin-designer: This is a Qt Designer plugin containing FilterWidget class and the image processing code. This plugin is a dynamic library that will be used by the Qt Creator to offer our new FilterWidget in the **Form Editor**.
- image-filter: This is a Qt Widget application using multiple FilterWidget. The user can open an image from their hard disk, select a filter (grayscale, blur, and so on), and save the filtered image.

Our filter-plugin-designer will use the third-party library **OpenCV** (**Open Source Computer Vision**). It is a powerful, cross-platform open source library to manipulate images. Here is an overview schema:

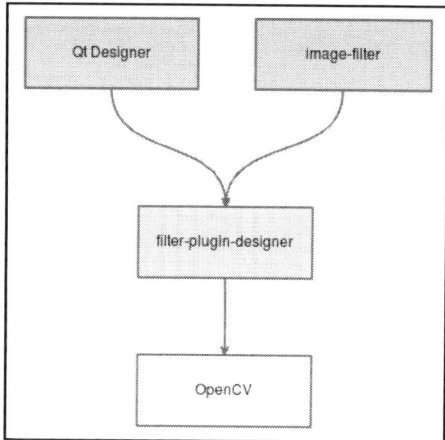

You can see a plugin as a kind of module, which can be easily added to an existing software. A plugin must respect a specific interface to be automatically called by the application. In our case, the Qt Designer is the application that loads Qt plugins. So creating a plugin allows us to enhance the application without the need to modify the Qt Designer source code and recompile it. A plugin is a generally dynamic library (.dll/.so), so it will be loaded at runtime by the application.

Now that you have a clear mind about the Qt Designer plugins, let's build one! First, create a Subdirs project called ch07-image-filter. Then, you can add a subproject, filter-plugin-designer. You can use the **Empty qmake Project** template because we start this project from scratch. Here is the filter-plugin-designer.pro file:

```
QT += widgets uiplugin
CONFIG += plugin
CONFIG += c++14
TEMPLATE = lib
DEFINES += FILTERPLUGINDESIGNER_LIBRARY

TARGET = $$qtLibraryTarget($$TARGET)
INSTALLS += target
```

Please note the uiplugin and plugin keywords for QT and CONFIG. They are required to create a Qt Designer plugin. We set the TEMPLATE keyword to lib because we are creating a dynamic library. The define, FILTERPLUGINDESIGNER_LIBRARY, will be used by the import/export mechanism of the library. We already covered this topic in Chapter 3, *Dividing Your Project and Ruling Your Code*. By default, our TARGET is filter-plugin-designer; the $$qtLibraryTarget() function will update it according to your platform. For example, the suffix "d" (standing for debug) will be appended on Windows. Finally, we append target to INSTALLS. Right now, this line does nothing, but we will describe a destination path for each platform soon; this way, executing the make install command will copy our target library file (.dll/.so) into the correct folder. To automatically perform this task on each compilation, you can add a new build step.

The deploy path is configured, but it will not be done automatically. Open the **Projects** tab and do the following:

1. Open the **Build Settings** | **Build Steps**.
2. Click on **Add Build Step** | **Make**.
3. In the **Make arguments** field, type install.

You should get something like this:

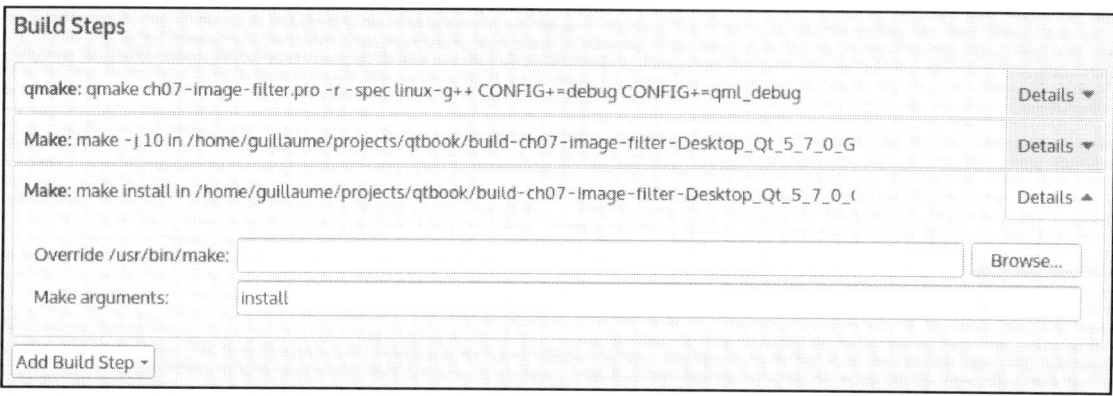

Each time you build the project, the `make install` command will be called and it will deploy the library in Qt Creator.

# Configuring the project for Windows

Before preparing this project on Windows, let's talk about the available choices when you develop a Qt application on a Windows host. The official Qt website provides multiple binary packages. We are mainly interested in the following:

- Qt for Windows 32-bit (MinGW)
- Qt for Windows 32-bit (VS 2013)

You may already be using one of these versions. The first one comes with a MinGW GCC compiler and the Qt framework. The second only provides the Qt framework and relies on the Microsoft Visual C++ compiler that will be installed with Visual Studio.

Both versions are fine when you want to create a common Qt application for Windows. However, for this chapter, we want to link our `filter-plugin-designer` project with OpenCV libraries. Qt Designer must also be able to dynamically load `filter-plugin-designer`, so we must use a consistent compiler version at all stages.

Please note that Qt Creator on Windows is always based on MSVC, even in the MinGW binary package! So if you create a Qt Designer plugin using a MinGW compiler, your Qt Creator will not be able to load it. OpenCV for Windows provides only MSVC libraries, compile for MSVC11 (which is VS 2012), and MSVC12 (VS 2013).

Here is a summary of the different solutions for building our project example in Windows:

| | MinGW GCC | MSVC |
|---|---|---|
| **OpenCV** | Binary not provided Recompilation required | Binary for msvc11 and msvc12 provided |
| **Qt Designer** | Binary not provided Recompilation required | Based on msvc12 32-bit |

Keep in mind that for open-source software such as Qt Creator and OpenCV you can always try to compile them from a source with a different compiler. So, if you absolutely want to use a MinGW compiler, you must recompile OpenCV and Qt Creator from sources. Otherwise, we suggest that you use Qt for Windows 32-bit (VS 2013) as explained shortly. Here are the steps to prepare your development environment:

1. Download and install Visual Studio Community Edition.
2. Download and install Qt for Windows 32-bit (VS 2013).
3. Download and extract OpenCV for Windows (for example: `C:\lib\opencv`).
4. Create a new `OPENCV_HOME`: `C:\lib\opencv\build\x86\vc12` environment variable.
5. Append to your system `Path`: `C:\lib\opencv\build\x86\vc12\bin` environment variable.

The `OPENCV_HOME` directory will be used in our `.pro` file. We also add an OpenCV libraries folder to the `Path` directory to easily resolve the dependencies at runtime.

You can now add the following snippet to the `filter-plugin-designer.pro` file:

```
windows {
target.path = $$(QTDIR)/../../Tools/QtCreator/bin/plugins/designer

debug:target_lib.files = $$OUT_PWD/debug/$${TARGET}.lib
release:target_lib.files = $$OUT_PWD/release/$${TARGET}.lib
target_lib.path = $$(QTDIR)/../../Tools/QtCreator/bin/plugins/designer
    INSTALLS += target_lib

    INCLUDEPATH += $$(OPENCV_HOME)/../../include
    LIBS += -L$$(OPENCV_HOME)/lib
        -lopencv_core2413
```

```
            -lopencv_imgproc2413
    }
```

The `target` path is set to the Qt Creator plugin folder. We also create a `target_lib` library to copy the `.lib` file generated by MSVC when we make a dynamic library (`.dll`). We add the OpenCV headers folder to the `INCLUDEPATH` to easily include them in our code. Finally, we update `LIBS` variable to link our plugin with the OpenCV modules (`core` and `imgproc`) from the OpenCV `lib` folder.

Please note that the standalone Qt Designer application and the Qt Creator are different software. Both programs use a different plugin path. In our case, we only used the form editor from the Qt Creator, so we are targeting the Qt Creator plugin path.

Just as we appended `target` and `target_lib` to `INSTALLS`, both `.dll` and `.lib` files will be copied in the Qt Creator plugin path on a `make install` command. Qt Creator only requires the `.dll` file to load the plugin at runtime. The `.lib` file is only used to resolve the links with `filter-plugin-designer` when building our `image-filter` application. For simplicity, we are using the same directory.

# Configuring the project for Linux

OpenCV binaries are certainly available in official software repositories. Depending on your distribution and your package manager, you can install it with commands such as the following:

```
apt-get install libopencv
yum install opencv
```

When OpenCV is installed on your Linux, you can add this snippet to the `filter-plugin-designer.pro` file:

```
linux {
target.path = $$(QTDIR)/../../Tools/QtCreator/lib/Qt/plugins/designer/

    CONFIG += link_pkgconfig
    PKGCONFIG += opencv
}
```

This time we do not use the `LIBS` variable but `PKGCONFIG`, which relies on `pkg-config`. It is a helper tool that will insert the correct options into the compile command line. In our case, we will request `pkg-config` to link our project with OpenCV.

> You can list all the libs managed by `pkg-config` with the `pkg-config --list-all` command.

# Configuring the project for Mac

The first step in making the project work on Mac OS is to install OpenCV. Fortunately, this is very easy using the `brew` command. If you develop on Mac OS and do not use it already, you should download it right now. In a nutshell, `brew` is an alternate package manager that gives you access to many packages (for developers and non-developers) that are not available on the Mac App Store.

> You can download and install brew from `http://brew.sh/`.

In a terminal, simply type the following command:

```
brew install opencv
```

This will download, compile, and install OpenCV on your machine. At the time of writing, the latest OpenCV version available on brew was version 2.4.13. Once this is done, open `filter-plugin-designer.pro` and add the following block:

```
macx {
target.path = "$$(QTDIR)/../../QtCreator.app/Contents/PlugIns/designer/"
target_lib.files = $$OUT_PWD/lib$${TARGET}.dylib
target_lib.path =
"$$(QTDIR)/../../QtCreator.app/Contents/PlugIns/designer/"
    INSTALLS += target_lib

    INCLUDEPATH += /usr/local/Cellar/opencv/2.4.13/include/

    LIBS += -L/usr/local/lib \
        -lopencv_core \
        -lopencv_imgproc
}
```

We add OpenCV headers and link the path with INCLUDEPATH and LIBS variables. The target definition and INSTALLS are used to automatically deploy the output shared object to the Qt Creator application plugins directory.

The last thing we have to do is to add an environment variable to let the Qt Creator know where it will find the library that will link it to the final application. In the **Projects** tab, go through the following steps:

1. Open the **Details** window in **Build Environment**.
2. Click on the **Add** Button.
3. Type DYLD_LIBRARY_PATH in the <VARIABLE> field.
4. Type the path of the build directory in <VALUE> (you can copy and paste it from the section **General | Build directory**).

# Implementing your OpenCV filters

Now that your development environment is ready, we can begin the fun part! We will implement three filters using OpenCV:

- FilterOriginal: This filter does nothing and returns the same picture (lazy!)
- FilterGrayscale: This filter converts a picture from color to grayscale
- FilterBlur: This filter smoothes the picture

The parent class of all these filters is Filter. Here is this abstract class:

```
//Filter.h
class Filter
{
public:
Filter();
virtual ~Filter();

virtualQImage process(constQImage& image) = 0;
};

//Filter.cpp
Filter::Filter() {}
Filter::~Filter() {}
```

As you can see, process() is a pure abstract method. All filters will implement a specific behavior with this function. Let's begin with the simple FilterOriginal class. Here is FilterOriginal.h:

```
class FilterOriginal : public Filter
{
public:
FilterOriginal();
    ~FilterOriginal();

QImageprocess(constQImage& image) override;
};
```

This class inherits Filter and we override the process() function. The implementation is also really simple. Fill FilterOriginal.cpp with the following:

```
FilterOriginal::FilterOriginal() :
Filter()
{
}

FilterOriginal::~FilterOriginal()
{
}

QImageFilterOriginal::process(constQImage& image)
{
return image;
}
```

No modification is performed; we return the same picture. Now that the filter structure is clear, we can create FilterGrayscale. The .h/.cpp files are close to FilterOriginalFilter, so let's jump to the process() function of FilterGrayscale.cpp:

```
QImageFilterGrayscale::process(constQImage& image)
{
    // QImage => cv::mat
cv::Mattmp(image.height(),
image.width(),
                CV_8UC4,
                (uchar*)image.bits(),
image.bytesPerLine());

cv::MatresultMat;
    cv::cvtColor(tmp, resultMat, CV_BGR2GRAY);
```

```
    // cv::mat =>QImage
QImageresultImage((constuchar *) resultMat.data,
resultMat.cols,
resultMat.rows,
resultMat.step,
QImage::Format_Grayscale8);
returnresultImage.copy();
}
```

In the Qt framework, we use the `QImage` class to manipulate pictures. In the OpenCV world, we use the `Mat` class, so the first step is to create a correct `Mat` object from the `QImage` source. OpenCV and Qt both handle many image formats. An image format describes the data bytes organization with information such as the following:

- `Channel count`: A grayscale picture only needs one channel (white intensity), while a color picture requires three channels (red, green, and blue). You will even need four channels to handle the opacity (alpha) pixel information.
- `Bit depth`: The number of bits used to store a pixel color.
- `Channel order`: The most common orders are RGB and BGR. Alpha can be placed before or after the color information.

For example, the OpenCV image format, `CV_8UC4`, means four channels of unsigned 8-bit, which is the perfect fit for an alpha color picture. In our case, we are using a compatible Qt and OpenCV image format to convert our `QImage` in `Mat`. Here is a little summary:

| Qt | | OpenCV | |
|---|---|---|---|
| Order | QImage | Order | cv::Mat |
| BGRX | Format_RGB32 | BGRA | CV_8UC4 |
| BGRA | Format_ARGB32 | | |
| RGBA | Format_RGBA8888 | | |
| RGB | Format_RGB888 | BGR | CV_8UC3 |
| Gray | Format_Grayscale8 | Gray | CV_8UC1 |

Please note that some `QImage` class formats also depend on your platform endianness. The preceding table is for a little endian system. For OpenCV, the order is always the same: `BGRA`. It is not required in our project example, but you can swap blue and red channels as follows:

```
// with OpenCV
cv::cvtColor(mat, mat, CV_BGR2RGB);
```

```
// with Qt
QImage swapped = image.rgbSwapped();
```

OpenCV `Mat` and Qt `QImage` classes perform shallow construction/copy by default. This means that only metadata is really copied; the pixel data is shared. To create a deep copy of a picture, you must call the `copy()` function:

```
// with OpenCV
mat.clone();
```

```
// with Qt
image.copy();
```

We created a `Mat` class called `tmp` from the `QImage` class. Note that `tmp` is not a deep copy of `image`; they share the same data pointer. Then, we can call the OpenCV function to convert the picture from color to grayscale using `cv::cvtColor()`. Finally, we create a `QImage` class from the grayscale `resultMat` element. In that case too, `resultMat` and `resultImage` share the same data pointer. Once we're done, we return a deep copy of `resultImage`.

It is now time to implement the last filter. Here is the `process()` function of `FilterBlur.cpp`:

```
QImageFilterBlur::process(constQImage& image)
{
    // QImage => cv::mat
cv::Mattmp(image.height(),
image.width(),
                CV_8UC4,
                (uchar*)image.bits(),
image.bytesPerLine());

int blur = 17;
cv::MatresultMat;
    cv::GaussianBlur(tmp,
resultMat,
                    cv::Size(blur, blur),
                    0.0,
                    0.0);

    // cv::mat =>QImage
QImageresultImage((constuchar *) resultMat.data,
resultMat.cols,
resultMat.rows,
resultMat.step,
QImage::Format_RGB32);
```

```
returnresultImage.copy();
}
```

The conversion from `QImage` to `Mat` is the same. The processing differs because we use the `cv::GaussianBlur()` OpenCV function to smooth the picture. The `blur` is the kernel size used by the Gaussian blur. You can increase this value to get a softer picture, but only use an odd and positive number. Finally, we convert the `Mat` to `QImage` and return a deep copy to the caller.

# Designing the UI with FilterWidget

Fine. Our filter classes are implemented, and we can now create our custom widget. This widget will take in input, a source, and a thumbnail picture. Then the thumbnail is immediately processed to display a preview of the filter. If the user clicks on the widget, it will process the source picture and trigger a signal with the filtered picture. Keep in mind that this widget will later be dragged and dropped in the **Form Editor** of Qt Creator. That's why we will provide properties with getters and setters to select a filter from Qt Creator. Please create a new widget called `FilterWidget` using the **Qt Designer Form Class** template. The `FilterWidget.ui` is really simple:

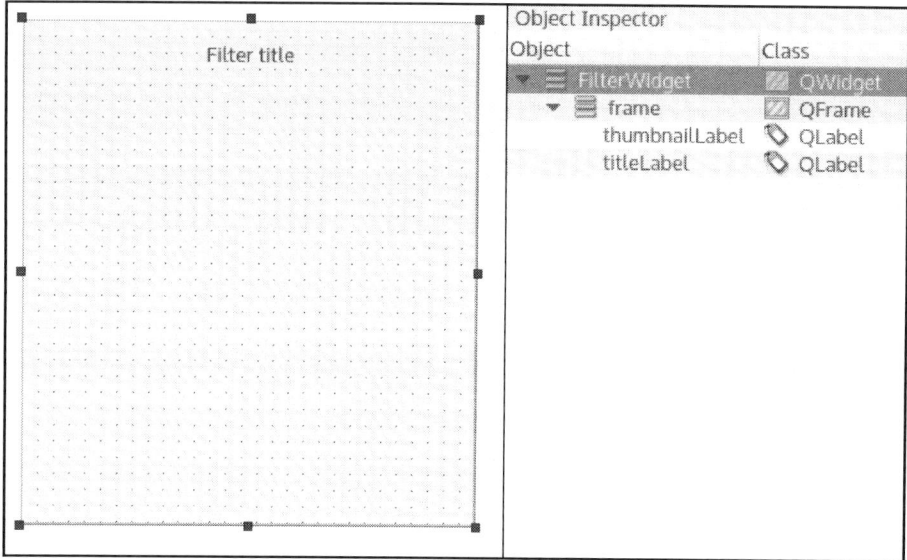

The `titleLabel` is a `QLabel` on top of the `QWidget`. Below, `thumbnailLabel` will display the filtered picture thumbnail. Let's switch to `FilterWidget.h`:

```
class FILTERPLUGINDESIGNERSHARED_EXPORT FilterWidget : public QWidget
{
    Q_OBJECT

    Q_ENUMS(FilterType)
    Q_PROPERTY(QString title READ title WRITE setTitle)
    Q_PROPERTY(FilterTypefilterType READ filterType WRITE setFilterType)

public:
enumFilterType { Original, Blur, Grayscale };

explicitFilterWidget(QWidget *parent = 0);
    ~FilterWidget();

void process();
voidsetSourcePicture(constQImage&sourcePicture);
voidupdateThumbnail(constQImage&sourceThumbnail);

QStringtitle() const;
FilterTypefilterType() const;

public slots:
voidsetTitle(constQString& tile);
voidsetFilterType(FilterTypefilterType);

signals:
voidpictureProcessed(constQImage& picture);

protected:
voidmousePressEvent(QMouseEvent*) override;

private:
Ui::FilterWidget *ui;
std::unique_ptr<Filter>mFilter;
FilterTypemFilterType;

QImagemDefaultSourcePicture;
QImagemSourcePicture;
QImagemSourceThumbnail;

QImagemFilteredPicture;
QImagemFilteredThumbnail;
};
```

The top part defines all the available filter types with the `enumFilterType`. We also use the Qtproperty system to expose the widget title and the current filter type to the **Property Editor** of Qt Creator. The syntax is like this:

```
Q_PROPERTY(<type><name> READ <getter> WRITE <setter>)
```

Please note that exposing an enumeration requires it to be registered using the `Q_ENUM()` macro, so the **Property Editor** will display a combo box that allows you to choose the filter type from Qt Creator.

The middle part lists all functions, slots, and signals. The most notable is the `process()` function that will use the current filter to modify the source picture.
The `pictureProcessed()` signal will notify the application with the filtered picture.

The bottom part lists the picture and thumbnail `QImage` variables used in this class. In both cases, we handle both source and filtered pictures. The default source picture is an embedded picture in the plugin. This allows you to display a default preview when no thumbnail has been provided. The `mFilter` variable is a smart pointer to the current `Filter` class.

Let's switch to the implementation with `FilterWidget.cpp`:

```
FilterWidget::FilterWidget(QWidget *parent) :
QWidget(parent),
ui(new Ui::FilterWidget),
mFilterType(Original),
mDefaultSourcePicture(":/lenna.jpg"),
mSourcePicture(),
mSourceThumbnail(mDefaultSourcePicture.scaled(QSize(256, 256),
Qt::KeepAspectRatio,
Qt::SmoothTransformation)),
mFilteredPicture(),
mFilteredThumbnail()
{
ui->setupUi(this);
setFilterType(Original);
}

FilterWidget::~FilterWidget()
{
deleteui;
}
```

Here are the constructor and the destructor. Please note that the default source picture loads an embedded picture of the gorgeous Lenna often used in image processing literature. The picture is in the resource file, `filter-plugin-designer.qrc`. The `mSourceThumbnail` function is initialized with a scaled picture of Lenna. The constructor calls the `setFilterType()` function to initialize an `Original` filter by default. Here is the core `process()` function:

```
voidFilterWidget::process()
{
mFilteredPicture = mFilter->process(mSourcePicture);
emitpictureProcessed(mFilteredPicture);
}
```

The `process()` function is powerful, but really simple. We call `process()` of the current filter to update our filtered picture from the current source picture. Then we trigger the `pictureProcessed()` signal with the filtered picture. We can now add our `QImage` setters:

```
voidFilterWidget::setSourcePicture(constQImage&sourcePicture)
{
mSourcePicture = sourcePicture;
}

voidFilterWidget::updateThumbnail(constQImage&sourceThumbnail)
{
mSourceThumbnail = sourceThumbnail;
mFilteredThumbnail = mFilter->process(mSourceThumbnail);
QPixmappixmap = QPixmap::fromImage(mFilteredThumbnail);
ui->thumbnailLabel->setPixmap(pixmap);
}
```

The `setSourcePicture()` function is a simple setter called by the application with a new source picture. The `updateThumbnail()` method will filter the new source thumbnail and display it. Let's add the setters used by `Q_PROPERTY`:

```
voidFilterWidget::setTitle(constQString& tile)
{
ui->titleLabel->setText(tile);
}

voidFilterWidget::setFilterType(FilterWidget::FilterTypefilterType)
{
if (filterType == mFilterType&&&mFilter) {
return;
    }
mFilterType = filterType;
```

```
switch (filterType) {
case Original:
mFilter = make_unique<FilterOriginal>();
break;

case Blur:
mFilter = make_unique<FilterBlur>();
break;

case Grayscale:
mFilter = make_unique<FilterGrayscale>();
break;

default:
break;
    }

updateThumbnail(mSourceThumbnail);
}
```

The setTitle() function is a simple setter used to customize the widget title. Let's talk about the setFilterType() function. As you can see, this function does not just update the current filter type, mFilterType. Depending on the type, the corresponding filter will be created. Do you remember the smart pointer from Chapter 3, *Dividing Your Project and Ruling Your Code*? Here we are using a unique_ptr pointer for the mFilter variable, so we can use make_unique instead of a new raw. The FilterWidget class takes the ownership of the Filter class, and we do not need to worry about the memory management. Upon the make_unique instruction, the old owned pointer (if there is any) will be automatically deleted.

Finally, we call the updateThumbnail() function to display a filtered thumbnail corresponding to the selected filter type. Here are the getters and the mouse event handler:

```
QStringFilterWidget::title() const
{
returnui->titleLabel->text();
}

FilterWidget::FilterTypeFilterWidget::filterType() const
{
returnmFilterType;
}

voidFilterWidget::mousePressEvent(QMouseEvent*)
{
process();
```

```
}
```

The `title()` and `filterType()` functions are getters used by the Qt Property System. We override the `mousePressEvent()` function to call our `process()` function each time the user clicks on the widget.

# Exposing your plugin to Qt Designer

The `FilterWidget` class is completed and ready to be used. We now have to register `FilterWidget` with the Qt Designer plugin system. This glue code is made using a child class of `QDesignerCustomWidgetInterface`.

Create a new C++ class named `FilterPluginDesigner` and update `FilterPluginDesigner.h` like so:

```
#include <QtUiPlugin/QDesignerCustomWidgetInterface>

class  FilterPluginDesigner : public QObject, public
QDesignerCustomWidgetInterface
{
    Q_OBJECT
    Q_PLUGIN_METADATA(IID
        "org.masteringqt.imagefilter.FilterWidgetPluginInterface")
    Q_INTERFACES(QDesignerCustomWidgetInterface)
public:
FilterPluginDesigner(QObject* parent = 0);
};
```

The `FilterPlugin` class inherits from two classes:

- The `QObject` class, to rely on the Qt parenting system
- The `QDesignerCustomWidgetInterface` class to properly expose the `FilterWidget` information to the plugin system

The `QDesignerCustomWidgetInterface` class brings two new macros:

- The `Q_PLUGIN_METADATA()` macro annotates the class to indicate a unique name for our filter to the meta-object system
- The `Q_INTERFACES()` macro tells the meta-object system which interface the current class has implemented

Qt Designer is now able to detect our plugin. We now have to provide information about the plugin itself. Update `FilterPluginDesigner.h`:

```
class  FilterPluginDesigner : public QObject, public
QDesignerCustomWidgetInterface
{
    ...
FilterPluginDesigner(QObject* parent = 0);

QStringname() const override;
QStringgroup() const override;
QStringtoolTip() const override;
QStringwhatsThis() const override;
QStringincludeFile() const override;
QIconicon() const override;
boolisContainer() const override;
QWidget* createWidget(QWidget* parent) override;
boolisInitialized() const override;
void initialize(QDesignerFormEditorInterface* core) override;

private:
boolmInitialized;
};
```

This is much less overwhelming than it looks. The body of each one of these functions usually takes a single line. Here is the implementation of the most straightforward functions:

```
QStringFilterPluginDesigner::name() const
{
return "FilterWidget";
}

QStringFilterPluginDesigner::group() const
{
return "Mastering Qt5";
}

QStringFilterPluginDesigner::toolTip() const
{
return "A filtered picture";
}

QStringFilterPluginDesigner::whatsThis() const
{
return "The filter widget applies an image effect";
}
```

```
QIconFilterPluginDesigner::icon() const
{
returnQIcon(":/icon.jpg");
}

boolFilterPluginDesigner::isContainer() const
{
return false;
}
```

As you can see, there isn't much to say about these functions. Most of them will simply return a `QString` value that will be displayed on the appropriate spot in the Qt Designer UI. We will focus only on the most interesting ones. Let's start with `includeFile()`:

```
QStringFilterPluginDesigner::includeFile() const
{
return "FilterWidget.h";
}
```

This function will be called by `uic` (**User Interface Compiler**) to generate the header corresponding to a `.ui` file. Continuing with `createWidget()`:

```
QWidget* FilterPluginDesigner::createWidget(QWidget* parent)
{
return new FilterWidget(parent);
}
```

This function makes the bridge between Qt Designer and `FilterWidget`. When you add the `FilterWidget` class in a `.ui` file, Qt Designer will call the `createWidget()` function to have an instance of the `FilterWidget` class and display its content. It also provides the `parent` element to which `FilterWidget` will be attached.

Let's finish with `initialize()`:

```
voidFilterPluginDesigner::initialize(QDesignerFormEditorInterface*)
{
if (mInitialized)
return;

mInitialized = true;
}
```

Nothing much is done in this function. However, the `QDesignerFormEditorInterface*` parameter is worth some explanation. This pointer, provided by Qt Designer, gives access to a few of Qt Designer's components via functions:

- `actionEditor()`: This function is the action editor (bottom panel of the designer)
- `formWindowManager()`: This function is the interface that enables you to create a new form window
- `objectInspector()`: This function is the hierarchical representation of your layout (top right panel of the designer)
- `propertyEditor()`: This function is the list of all the editable properties of the currently selected widget (bottom right panel of the designer)
- `topLevel()`: This function is the top-level widget of the designer

We covered each of these panels in `Chapter 1`, *Get Your Qt Feet Wet*. If your widget plugin needs to intervene in any of these areas, this function is the entry point to customize the behavior of Qt Designer.

# Using your Qt Designer plugin

Our custom plugin is now finished. Because we added a custom `Build` command to automatically deploy the filter-widget library, it should be visible in Qt Designer. The deploy path we specified is inside the Qt Creator directory. Qt Creator integrates Qt Designer via a plugin that displays the UI inside Qt Creator.

When Qt Creator starts, it will try to load every library available in its specific paths. This means that you have to restart Qt Creator each time you modify the plugin (if you want to see the result of your modifications in the designer).

To see the plugin in action, we now have to create the application project of the chapter. Create a **Qt Widgets Application** sub-project in the `ch07-image-filter` project named `image-filter`. In the wizard, let it generate the form, `MainWindow.ui`.

To properly use the plugin, just link the `filter-plugin-designer` library in `image-filter.pro` like so:

```
QT          += core gui

greaterThan(QT_MAJOR_VERSION, 4): QT += widgets

TARGET = image-filter
TEMPLATE = app

INCLUDEPATH += ../filter-plugin-designer

win32 {
    LIBS += -L$$(QTDIR)/../../Tools/QtCreator/bin/plugins/designer -
lfilter-plugin-designer
}

macx {
    LIBS += -L$$(QTDIR)/../../"QtCreator.app"/Contents/PlugIns/designer/ -
lfilter-plugin-designer
}

linux {
    LIBS += -L$$(QTDIR)/../../Tools/QtCreator/lib/Qt/plugins/designer/ -
lfilter-plugin-designer
}

SOURCES += main.cpp\
        MainWindow.cpp

HEADERS   += MainWindow.h

FORMS     += MainWindow.ui
```

To have access to the headers of `filter-plugin-designer`, we simply add it to the `INCLUDEPATH` directory. Finally, the linker is instructed to link to the library we deployed in Qt Creator. This ensures that the same library is used by Qt Designer and by our application.

Open the `MainWindow.ui` file and scroll to the bottom of the **Widget box**. Lo and behold, you should see this:

The `FilterWidget` plugin appears under the Mastering Qt5 section. It even displays the famous Lenna as a preview icon. If you do not see the `FilterWidget` plugin, then restart Qt Creator and make sure that the plugin is properly loaded. To check this (in the **Design** tab), go to **Tools** | **Form Editor** | **About Qt Designer Plugins**. This is what it should display:

If the `FilterWidget` plugin does not appear in this list, you should check the Qt Creator plugin directory content (the path is stated in `image-filter.pro`).

# Building the image-filter application

We can proceed to build the UI of the application. The idea is to open a picture from the filesystem and apply to it the various filters we developed in the `filter-designer-plugin` project. If you want to keep the result, you can save the resulting image.

We will start by designing the UI. Modify `MainWindow.ui` to look like this:

Here is the Object Inspector content to help you build this layout:

There are three elements of this UI:

- The `menuFile` element, which contains three possible actions: `actionOpenPicture`, `actionExit`, and `actionSaveAs`. You can see the details of these actions in the `Action Editor` window.
- The `pictureLabel` element, which will display the loaded picture in the empty top part.
- The `filtersLayout` element, which contains the three instances of our `FilterWidget` class in the bottom part.

As you add a `FilterWidget` class in `filtersLayout`, you can see that you can customize the `title` and the `filterType` in the **Property Editor** window. The preview will be automatically updated with the selected filter applied to our default picture. A dynamic preview like this is simply awesome, and you can foresee that your custom Qt Designer widgets can become quite powerful.

Let's implement the logic of our application. Update `MainWindow.h` like so:

```
#include <QMainWindow>
#include <QImage>
#include <QVector>

namespaceUi {
classMainWindow;
}

classFilterWidget;

classMainWindow : public QMainWindow
{
```

```
    Q_OBJECT

public:
explicitMainWindow(QWidget *parent = 0);
    ~MainWindow();

voidloadPicture();

private slots:
voiddisplayPicture(constQImage& picture);

private:
voidinitFilters();
voidupdatePicturePixmap();

private:
Ui::MainWindow *ui;
QImagemSourcePicture;
QImagemSourceThumbnail;
QPixmapmCurrentPixmap;
FilterWidget* mCurrentFilter;
QVector<FilterWidget*>mFilters;
};
```

Here are some elements that we have to explain:

- mSourcePicture: This element is the loaded picture.
- mSourceThumbnail: This element is the generated thumbnail from mSourcePicture. To avoid wasting CPU cycles, mSourcePicture will be resized only once, and each of the FilterWidget instances will process this thumbnail rather than the full-resolution picture.
- mCurrentPixmap: This element is the currently displayed QPixmap in the pictureLabel widget.
- mCurrentFilter: This element is the currently applied filter. Each time the user clicks on a different FilterWidget, this pointer will be updated.
- mFilters: This element is a QVector of the FilterWidget class that we added to MainWindow.ui. It is only a helper, introduced to easily apply the same instructions to each FilterWidget class.

Now for the functions, we will limit ourselves to a broad overview. The details will be covered when we look at the implementation of each function:

- `loadPicture()`: This function triggers the whole pipeline. It will be called when the user clicks on `actionOpenPicture`.
- `initFilters()`: This function is in charge of initializing `mFilters`.
- `displayPicture()`: This function is the slot called by `mCurrentWidget::pictureProcessed()` to display the filtered picture.
- `updatePicturePixmap()`: This function handles the display of `mCurrentPixmap` inside `pictureLabel`.

Let's look at the `MainWindow` class's constructor implementation in `MainWindow.cpp`:

```
#include <QFileDialog>
#include <QPixmap>
#include <QDir>

#include "FilterWidget.h"

MainWindow::MainWindow(QWidget *parent) :
QMainWindow(parent),
ui(new Ui::MainWindow),
mSourcePicture(),
mSourceThumbnail(),
mCurrentPixmap(),
mCurrentFilter(nullptr),
mFilters()
{
ui->setupUi(this);
ui->pictureLabel->setMinimumSize(1, 1);

connect(ui->actionOpenPicture, &QAction::triggered,
    this, &MainWindow::loadPicture);
connect(ui->actionExit, &QAction::triggered,
    this, &QMainWindow::close);
initFilters();
}
```

We connect the `actionOpenPicture::triggered()` signal to our yet-to-be-implemented `loadPicture()` function. The `actionExit` is straightforward; it is simply connected to the `QMainWindow::close()` slot. Finally, `initFilter()` is called. Let's see its body:

```
voidMainWindow::initFilters()
{
```

```
mFilters.push_back(ui->filterWidgetOriginal);
mFilters.push_back(ui->filterWidgetBlur);
mFilters.push_back(ui->filterWidgetGrayscale);

for (inti = 0; i<mFilters.size(); ++i) {
connect(mFilters[i], &FilterWidget::pictureProcessed,
this, &MainWindow::displayPicture);
    }
mCurrentFilter = mFilters[0];
}
```

Each `FilterWidget` instance is added to `mFilters`. We then proceed to connect the `pictureProcessed()` signal to the `MainWindow::displayPicture` instruction and `mCurrentFilter` is initialized to the original filter.

The class is now ready to load some pictures! This is the implementation of `loadPicture()`:

```
voidMainWindow::loadPicture()
{
QString filename = QFileDialog::getOpenFileName(this,
        "Open Picture",
        QDir::homePath(),
  tr("Images (*.png *.jpg)"));
if (filename.isEmpty()) {
return;
    }
mSourcePicture = QImage(filename);
mSourceThumbnail = mSourcePicture.scaled(QSize(256, 256),
  Qt::KeepAspectRatio,
Qt::SmoothTransformation);
for (inti = 0; i<mFilters.size(); ++i) {
mFilters[i]->setSourcePicture(mSourcePicture);
mFilters[i]->updateThumbnail(mSourceThumbnail);
    }

mCurrentFilter->process();
}
```

The `mSourcePicture` method is loaded using a `QFileDialog`, and `mSourceThumbnail` is generated from this input. Every `FilterWidget` class is updated with this new data and the `mCurrentFilter` element is triggered by calling its `process()` function.

When `FilterWidget::process()` is finished, it emits the `pictureProcessed()` signal, which is connected to our `displayPicture()` slot. Let's switch to this function:

```
voidMainWindow::displayPicture(constQImage& picture)
{
mCurrentPixmap = QPixmap::fromImage(picture);
updatePicturePixmap();
}
```

Nothing very fancy here: `mCurrentPixmap` is updated from the given picture and the `updatePicturePixmap()` function is in charge of updating the `pictureLabel` element. Here is the implementation of `updatePicturePixmap()`:

```
voidMainWindow::updatePicturePixmap()
{
if (mCurrentPixmap.isNull()) {
return;
    }
ui->pictureLabel->setPixmap(
mCurrentPixmap.scaled(ui->pictureLabel->size(),
     Qt::KeepAspectRatio,
Qt::SmoothTransformation));
}
```

This function simply creates a scaled version of `mCurrentPixmap` that fits inside `pictureLabel`.

The whole picture loading/filter processing is completed. If you run the application you should be able to load and modify your pictures. However, if you resize the window, you will see that the `pictureLabel` element does not scale very well.

To address this issue, we have to regenerate the scaled version of `mCurrentPixmap` each time the window is resized. Update `MainWindow` like so:

```
// In MainWindow.h
classMainWindow : public QMainWindow
{
    ...
voidloadPicture();

protected:
voidresizeEvent(QResizeEvent* event) override;
    ...
};

// In MainWindow.cpp
voidMainWindow::resizeEvent(QResizeEvent* /*event*/)
```

```
{
updatePicturePixmap();
}
```

Here, the separation of mCurrentPixmap and the pictureLabel element's pixmap makes sense. Because we always generate the scaled version from the full-resolution mCurrentPixmap, we are sure that the resulting pixmap will look good.

The image-filter application would not be complete without the ability to save your filtered picture. This will not take much effort. Here is the updated version of MainWindow.h:

```
classMainWindow : public QMainWindow
{
    ...

private slots:
voiddisplayPicture(constQImage& picture);
voidsaveAsPicture();
    ...

private:
Ui::MainWindow *ui;
QImagemSourcePicture;
QImagemSourceThumbnail;
QImage&mFilteredPicture;
    ...
};
```

Here, we simply added a saveAsPicture() function that will take the mFilteredPicture element and save it to a file. The implementation in MainWindow.cpp should not blow your mind:

```
// In MainWindow.cpp
MainWindow::MainWindow(QWidget *parent) :
QMainWindow(parent),
ui(new Ui::MainWindow),
mSourcePicture(),
mSourceThumbnail(),
mFilteredPicture(mSourcePicture),
    ...
{
ui->setupUi(this);
ui->actionSaveAs->setEnabled(false);
ui->pictureLabel->setMinimumSize(1, 1);

connect(ui->actionOpenPicture, &QAction::triggered,
this, &MainWindow::loadPicture);
```

```
connect(ui->actionSaveAs, &QAction::triggered,
this, &MainWindow::saveAsPicture);
    ...
}

voidMainWindow::loadPicture()
{
    ...
if (filename.isEmpty()) {
return;
    }
ui->actionSaveAs->setEnabled(true);
    ...
}

voidMainWindow::displayPicture(constQImage& picture)
{
mFilteredPicture = picture;
mCurrentPixmap = QPixmap::fromImage(picture);
updatePicturePixmap();
}

voidMainWindow::saveAsPicture()
{
QString filename = QFileDialog::getSaveFileName(this,
            "Save Picture",
QDir::homePath(),
tr("Images (*.png *.jpg)"));
if (filename.isEmpty()) {
return;
    }
mFilteredPicture.save(filename);
}
```

The code snippet is long, but not very complex. The `actionSaveAs` function is enabled only when a picture is loaded. When the picture has been processed, `mFilteredPicture` is updated with the given picture. Because it is a reference, it costs absolutely nothing to store this filtered picture.

Finally, the `saveAsPicture()` function asks the user for a path and saves it using the `QImage` API, which tries to deduce the picture type based on the file extension.

# Summary

In this chapter, you learned how to integrate a third-party library with each desktop OS (Windows, Linux, and Mac). We chose the OpenCV library, which has been included in a custom Qt Designer plugin, and which can display a live preview of your image processing result in Qt Designer. We created an image filtering application that can open pictures, apply filters to them, and save the result on your machine.

We had a good look at how you can integrate third-party libraries and how to make a Qt Designer plugin. In the next chapter, we will push things forward by making the `image-filter` application ready to load filter plugins that could be implemented by third-party developers. To make things even cooler, we will cover the Qt animation framework to make the `image-filter` more spectacular.

# 8
# Animations - Its Alive, Alive!

In the previous chapter, you learned how to create a custom Qt Designer plugin. This chapter will push things further and teach you how to create a distributable Software Development Kit (SDK) to third-party developers, how the plugin system works with Qt, and how to make your application more attractive using fancy animations.

The example project will be a reimplementation of the project from Chapter 7, *Third-Party Libraries Without a Headache*. You will build the same image processing application, but with the ability to import the filters from plugins.

This chapter will teach you how to do the following:

* Create an SDK using the Qt Plugin system
* Implement custom plugins using the SDK
* Factorize build tasks using .pri
* Dynamically load plugins in your final application
* Understand the Qt Animation framework
* Use simple, sequential, and parallel animations
* Apply custom effects using QPropertyAnimation and QGraphics effects

## Preparing an SDK

Before diving into the code, we have to take a moment to reflect on how we are going to structure it. This chapter has two goals:

* Cover the Qt Plugin system in more depth
* Study and integrate the Qt Animation Framework

The first part of the chapter will focus on the plugin system. What we aim to do is provide a way to build plugins that can be integrated in our application to third-party developers. These plugins should be dynamically loaded. The application will be a direct offspring of the example project from `Chapter 7`, *Third-Party Libraries Without a Headache*. The features will be exactly the same, except it will be using this new plugin system and will have fancy animations.

The structure of the project will be as follows:

The parent project is `ch08-image-animation`, which is composed of the following:

- `filter-plugin-original`: A library project, which is the implementation of the original filter
- `filter-plugin-grayscale`: A library project, which is the implementation of the grayscale filter
- `filter-plugin-blur`: A library project, which is the implementation of the blur filter
- `image-animation`: A Qt Widgets application, which will load the plugins needed to display them and make it possible to apply each one to a loaded picture

We will develop each one of these plugins, but keep in mind that they might have been created by a third-party developer. To achieve this openness, an SDK will be available for each plugin. This SDK relies on the Qt Plugin system.

It is crucial to think about what should be handled by the plugin. Our application is an image processing piece of software. We chose to limit the responsibility of the plugin to the picture processing part, but this is definitely a design choice.

Another approach could have been to let the plugin developer provide its own UI to configure the plugin (for example, to vary the intensity of the blur). In this chapter, we have kept it simple by focusing only on the plugin development itself. It is really up to you and how you want to design your application. By opening up the range of what the plugin can do, you also increase the burden for the plugin developer. There is always a trade-off; giving more choice tends to increase the complexity. It is a well-known fact that we developers are a bunch of lazy people. At least, we want to be lazy while the computer is working for us.

We will start by building the SDK that will be deployed in each plugin. Execute the following steps:

1. Create a **Subdirs project** named `ch08-image-animation` (do not add a sub-project at the end of the wizard).
2. In your filesystem explorer, open the `ch08-image-animation` directory and create an `sdk` directory.
3. Inside `sdk`, create an empty `Filter.h` file.

Our SDK will consist of a single file, `Filter.h`, the interface (or header) that should be implemented with each plugin. Each plugin is responsible for returning the modified picture according to its desired features. Because this SDK is not linked to any particular project, we will simply display it in Qt Creator under the special folder **Other files**. To do so, update `ch08-image-animation.pro`:

```
TEMPLATE = subdirs

CONFIG += c++14

OTHER_FILES += \
            sdk/Filter.h
```

After `ch08-image-animation.pro` has been parsed by Qt Creator, you should see the
following in the **Projects** tab:

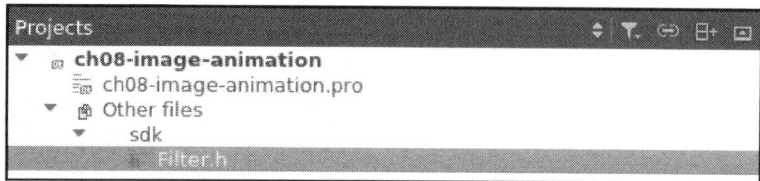

The `Filter.h` file is available at the parent project level. As a result, it will be easier to
factorize the SDK plumbing code between our various plugins. Let's implement `Filter.h`:

```
#include <QImage>

class Filter
{
public:
    virtual ~Filter() {}
    virtual QString name() const = 0;
    virtual QImage process(const QImage& image) = 0;
};

#define Filter_iid "org.masteringqt.imageanimation.filters.Filter"
Q_DECLARE_INTERFACE(Filter, Filter_iid)
```

Let's break down this interface: a `Filter` subclass must provide a name by
implementing `name()` and returning a processed image when implementing `process()`.
As you can see, `Filter.h` is indeed very close to the version seen in Chapter 7, *Third-Party
Libraries Without a Headache*.

However, the really new stuff comes right after the class definition:

```
#define Filter_iid "org.masteringqt.imageanimation.filters.Filter"
Q_DECLARE_INTERFACE(Filter, Filter_iid)
```

The `Filter_iid` is a unique identifier to let Qt know the interface name. This will be
enforced on the implementer side, which will also have to state this identifier.

For a real-world use case, you should add a version number to this unique
identifier. This will let you properly handle the versioning of your SDK
and the attached plugins.

The `Q_DECLARE_INTERFACE` macro associates the class to the given identifier. It will give Qt the ability to check that the loaded plugin can be safely casted to the `Filter` type.

In production code, it is safer to declare your interfaces inside a namespace. You never know the code environment in which your SDK will be deployed. This, way, you avoid potential name collision. If you do declare in a namespace, make sure that the `Q_DECLARE_INTERFACE` macro is outside the namespace scope.

# Creating your plugins

The SDK was painless to create. We can now proceed to create our first plugin. We already know that all our plugins will include the SDK we just completed. Fortunately, this can be easily factorized in a `.pri` file (PRoject Include). A `.pri` file behaves exactly like a `.pro` file; the only difference is that it is intended to be included inside `.pro` files.

In the `ch08-image-animation` directory, create a file named `plugins-common.pri` that contains the following code:

```
INCLUDEPATH += $$PWD/sdk
DEPENDPATH += $$PWD/sdk
```

This file will be included in each `.pro` plugin. It aims to tell the compiler where it can find the headers of the SDK and where to look to resolve dependencies between headers and sources. This will enhance the modification detection and properly compile the sources when needed.

To see this file in the project, we have to add it to the `OTHER_FILES` macro in `ch08-image-animation.pro`:

```
OTHER_FILES += \
        sdk/Filter.h \
        plugins-common.pri
```

The most straightforward plugin to build is `filter-plugin-original` as it does not perform any specific processing on the image. Let's create this plugin with the following steps:

1. Create a new **Subproject** in `ch08-image-animation`.
2. Select **Library** | **C++ Library** | **Choose...**.
3. Choose a **Shared Library**, name it `filter-plugin-original`, and then click on **Next**.

4. Select **QtCore** and go to **QtWidgets** | **Next**.

5. Name the created class `FilterOriginal` and click on **Next**.

6. Add it as a **subproject** to `ch08-image-animation` then click on **Finish**.

Qt Creator creates a lot of boilerplate code for us, but in this case, we do not need it. Update `filter-plugin-original.pro` like so:

```
QT          += core widgets

TARGET = $$qtLibraryTarget(filter-plugin-original)
TEMPLATE = lib
CONFIG += plugin

SOURCES += \
    FilterOriginal.cpp

HEADERS += \
    FilterOriginal.h

include(../plugins-common.pri)
```

We start by specifying that the `TARGET` should be properly named according to the OS convention with `$$qtLibraryTarget()`. The `CONFIG` property adds the `plugin` directive, which tells the generated `Makefile` to include the necessary instructions to compile a dll/so/dylib (pick your OS).

We removed the unnecessary `DEFINES` and `FilterOriginal_global.h`. Nothing specific to the plugin should be exposed to the caller, and therefore, there is no need to handle the symbol export.

We can now proceed to `FilterOriginal.h`:

```
#include <QObject>

#include <Filter.h>

class FilterOriginal : public QObject, Filter
{
    Q_OBJECT
    Q_PLUGIN_METADATA(IID "org.masteringqt.imageanimation.filters.Filter")
    Q_INTERFACES(Filter)

public:
    FilterOriginal(QObject* parent = 0);
    ~FilterOriginal();
```

```
    QString name() const override;
    QImage process(const QImage& image) override;
};
```

The `FilterOriginal` class must first inherit `QObject`; when the plugin will be loaded, it will first be a `QObject` class before being casted to the real type, `Filter`.

The `Q_PLUGIN_METADATA` macro is stated to export the proper implemented interface identifier to Qt. It annotates the class to let the Qt metasystem know about it. We meet the unique identifier we defined in `Filter.h` again.

The `Q_INTERFACES` macro tells the Qt metaobject system which interface the class implements.

Finally, the `FilterOriginal.cpp` barely deserves to be printed:

```
FilterOriginal::FilterOriginal(QObject* parent) :
    QObject(parent)
{
}

FilterOriginal::~FilterOriginal()
{
}

QString FilterOriginal::name() const
{
    return "Original";
}

QImage FilterOriginal::process(const QImage& image)
{
    return image;
}
```

As you can see, its implementation is a no-op. The only thing we added to the version from `Chapter 7`, *Third-Party Libraries Without a Headache*, is the `name()` function, which returns `Original`.

We will now implement the grayscale filter. As we did in `Chapter 7`, *Third-Party Libraries Without a Headache*, we will rely on the OpenCV library to process the picture. The same can be said for the following plugin, the blur.

Since these two projects have their own .pro file, you can already foresee that the OpenCV linking will be the same. This is a perfect use-case for a .pri file.

Inside the ch08-image-animation directory, create a new file called plugins-common-opencv.pri. Do not forget to add it to OTHER_FILES in ch08-image-animation.pro:

```
OTHER_FILES += \
            sdk/Filter.h \
            plugins-common.pri \
            plugins-common-opencv.pri
```

Here is the content of plugins-common-opencv.pri:

```
windows {
    INCLUDEPATH += $$(OPENCV_HOME)/../../include
    LIBS += -L$$(OPENCV_HOME)/lib \
        -lopencv_core2413 \
        -lopencv_imgproc2413
}

linux {
    CONFIG += link_pkgconfig
    PKGCONFIG += opencv
}

macx {
    INCLUDEPATH += /usr/local/Cellar/opencv/2.4.13/include/

    LIBS += -L/usr/local/lib \
        -lopencv_core \
        -lopencv_imgproc
}
```

The content of plugins-common-opencv.pri is a direct copy of what we made in Chapter 7, *Third-Party Libraries Without a Headache*.

All the plumbing is now ready; we can now go ahead with the filter-plugin-grayscale project. As with filter-plugin-original, we will build it the following way:

1. Create a **C++ Library Subproject** of ch08-image-animation with the **Shared Library** type.
2. Create a class named FilterGrayscale.
3. In the **Required Modules**, select **QtCore** and **QWidgets**.

Here is the updated version of `filter-plugin-grayscale.pro`:

```
QT        += core widgets

TARGET = $$qtLibraryTarget(filter-plugin-grayscale)
TEMPLATE = lib
CONFIG += plugin

SOURCES += \
    FilterGrayscale.cpp

HEADERS += \
    FilterGrayscale.h

include(../plugins-common.pri)
include(../plugins-common-opencv.pri)
```

The content is very much like `filter-plugin-original.pro`. We only added `plugins-common-opencv.pri` to let our plugin link with OpenCV.

As for `FilterGrayscale`, the header is exactly like `FilterOriginal.h`. Here are the relevant pieces on `FilterGrayscale.cpp`:

```
#include <opencv/cv.h>

// Constructor & Destructor here
...

QString FilterOriginal::name() const
{
    return "Grayscale";
}

QImage FilterOriginal::process(const QImage& image)
{
    // QImage => cv::mat
    cv::Mat tmp(image.height(),
                image.width(),
                CV_8UC4,
                (uchar*)image.bits(),
                image.bytesPerLine());

    cv::Mat resultMat;
    cv::cvtColor(tmp, resultMat, CV_BGR2GRAY);

    // cv::mat => QImage
    QImage resultImage((const uchar *) resultMat.data,
                        resultMat.cols,
```

```
                              resultMat.rows,
                              resultMat.step,
                              QImage::Format_Grayscale8);
        return resultImage.copy();
    }
```

The inclusion of `plugins-common-opencv.pri` lets us properly include the `cv.h` header.

The last plugin we will implement is the blur plugin. Once again, create a **C++ Library Subproject** and create the `FilterBlur` class. The project structure and the content of the `.pro` file are the same. Here is `FilterBlur.cpp`:

```
QString FilterOriginal::name() const
{
    return "Blur";
}

QImage FilterOriginal::process(const QImage& image)
{
    // QImage => cv::mat
    cv::Mat tmp(image.height(),
                image.width(),
                CV_8UC4,
                (uchar*)image.bits(),
                image.bytesPerLine());

    int blur = 17;
    cv::Mat resultMat;
    cv::GaussianBlur(tmp,
                resultMat,
                cv::Size(blur, blur),
                0.0,
                0.0);

    // cv::mat => QImage
    QImage resultImage((const uchar *) resultMat.data,
                    resultMat.cols,
                    resultMat.rows,
                    resultMat.step,
                    QImage::Format_RGB32);
    return resultImage.copy();
}
```

The amount of blur is hard-coded at 17. In a production application, it could have been compelling to make this amount variable from the application.

 If you want to push the project further, try to include a layout in the SDK that contains a way to configure the plugin properties.

# Loading your plugins dynamically

We will now deal with the application loading these plugins:

1. Create a new **Subproject** inside ch08-image-animation.
2. Select the type **Qt Widgets Application**.
3. Name it image-animation and accept the default **Class Information settings**.

We have a few last things to do in the .pro files. First, image-animation will try to load the plugins from somewhere in its output directory. Because each filter plugin project is independent, its output directory is separated from image-animation. Thus, each time you modify a plugin, you will have to copy yourself the compiled shared library inside the proper image-animation directory. This works to make it available to the image-animation application, but we are lazy developers, right?

We can automate this by updating plugins-common-pri like so:

```
INCLUDEPATH += $$PWD/sdk
DEPENDPATH += $$PWD/sdk

windows {
    CONFIG(debug, debug|release) {
        target_install_path = $$OUT_PWD/../image-animation/debug/plugins/
    } else {
        target_install_path = $$OUT_PWD/../image-animation/release/plugins/
    }

} else {
    target_install_path = $$OUT_PWD/../image-animation/plugins/
}

# Check Qt file 'spec_post.prf' for more information about
'$$QMAKE_MKDIR_CMD'
createPluginsDir.path = $$target_install_path
createPluginsDir.commands = $$QMAKE_MKDIR_CMD $$createPluginsDir.path
```

```
INSTALLS += createPluginsDir

target.path = $$target_install_path
INSTALLS += target
```

In a nutshell, the output library is deployed in the output `image-animation/plugins` directory. Windows has a different output project structure; that is why we have to have a platform-specific section.

Even better, the `plugins` directory is automatically created with the instruction `createPluginsDir.commands = $$QMAKE_MKDIR_CMD $$createPluginsDir.path`. Instead of using a system command (`mkdir`), we have to use the special `$$QMAKE_MKDIR_CMD` command. Qt will then replace it with the correct shell command (depending on your OS) to create the directory only if it does not already exist. Do not forget to add the `make install` build step to execute this task!

The last thing to do in the `.pro` files concerns `image-animation`. The application will manipulate `Filter` instances. As a consequence, it needs to access the SDK. Add the following to `image-animation.pro`:

```
INCLUDEPATH += $$PWD/../sdk
DEPENDPATH += $$PWD/../sdk
```

Fasten your seatbelt. We will now load our freshly baked plugins. In `image-animation`, create a new class named `FilterLoader`. Here is the `FilterLoader.h` content:

```
#include <memory>
#include <vector>

#include <Filter.h>

class FilterLoader
{

public:
    FilterLoader();
    void loadFilters();

    const std::vector<std::unique_ptr<Filter>>& filters() const;

private:
    std::vector<std::unique_ptr<Filter>> mFilters;
};
```

This class is responsible for loading the plugins. Once again, we rely on C++11 smart pointers with `unique_ptr` to explicate the ownership of the `Filter` instances. The `FilterLoader` class will be the owner with `mFilters` and provides a getter to the `vector` with `filters()`.

Note that `filter()` returns a `const&` to the `vector`. This semantic brings two benefits:

- The reference makes sure that the `vector` is not copied. Without it, the compiler would have barked something like "`FilterLoader` is not the owner anymore of `mFilters` content!" at us. Of course, because it deals with C++ templates, the compiler error would have looked rather like an astounding insult to the English language.
- The `const` keyword makes sure that the `vector` type cannot be modified by callers.

Now we can create the `FilterLoader.cpp`: file:

```
#include "FilterLoader.h"

#include <QApplication>
#include <QDir>
#include <QPluginLoader>

FilterLoader::FilterLoader() :
    mFilters()
{
}

void FilterLoader::loadFilters()
{
    QDir pluginsDir(QApplication::applicationDirPath());
#ifdef Q_OS_MAC
    pluginsDir.cdUp();
    pluginsDir.cdUp();
    pluginsDir.cdUp();
#endif
    pluginsDir.cd("plugins");

    for(QString fileName: pluginsDir.entryList(QDir::Files)) {
        QPluginLoader pluginLoader(
                    pluginsDir.absoluteFilePath(fileName));
        QObject* plugin = pluginLoader.instance();
        if (plugin) {
            mFilters.push_back(std::unique_ptr<Filter>(
                    qobject_cast<Filter*>(plugin)
            ));
```

```
            }
        }
    }

    const std::vector<std::unique_ptr<Filter>>& FilterLoader::filters() const
    {
        return mFilters;
    }
```

The meat of the class lies in `loadFilter()`. We start by moving in the `plugins` directory with `pluginsDir`, located in the output directory of `image-animation`. A special case is handled for the Mac platform: `QApplication::applicationDirPath()` returns a path inside the bundle of the generated application. The only way to get out is to climb our way up three times with the `cdUp()` instruction.

For each `fileName` in this directory, we try to load a `QPluginLoader` loader. A `QPluginLoader` provides access to a Qt plugin. It is the cross-platform way to load a shared library. Moreover, the `QPluginLoader` loader has the following benefits:

- It checks that the plugin is linked with the same version of Qt as the host application
- It simplifies the loading of the plugin by providing direct access to the plugin via `instance()` rather than relying on C functions

We then proceed to try to load the plugin using `pluginLoader.instance()`. This will try to load the root component of the plugin. In our case, the root component is either `FilerOriginal`, `FilterGrayscale`, or `FilterBlur`. This function always returns a `QObject*`; if the plugin could not be loaded, it returns `0`. This is the reason why we inherited the `QObject` class in our custom plugins.

The call to `instance()` implicitly tries to load the plugin. Once this has been done, the `QPluginLoader` does not handle the memory of the `plugin`. From here, we cast the plugin to `Filter*` using `qobject_cast()`.

The `qobject_cast()` function behaves similarly to the standard C++ `dynamic_cast()`; the difference is that it does not require **RTTI (runtime type information)**.

Last but not least, the `Filter*` casted `plugin` is wrapped inside a `unique_ptr` and added to `mFilters` vector.

# Using the plugins inside the application

Now that the plugins are properly loaded, they have to be reachable from the UI of the application. To do so, we are going to take some inspiration (shameless stealing) from the `FilterWidget` class of Chapter 7, *Third-Party Libraries Without a Headache*.

Create a new Qt Designer **Form Class** using the **Widget** template named `FilterWidget`. The `FilterWidget.ui` file is exactly the same as the one completed in Chapter 7, *Third-Party Libraries Without a Headache*.

Create the `FilterWidget.h` file like this:

```
#include <QWidget>
#include <QImage>

namespace Ui {
class FilterWidget;
}

class Filter;

class FilterWidget : public QWidget
{
    Q_OBJECT

public:
    explicit FilterWidget(Filter& filter, QWidget *parent = 0);
    ~FilterWidget();

    void process();

    void setSourcePicture(const QImage& sourcePicture);
    void setSourceThumbnail(const QImage& sourceThumbnail);
    void updateThumbnail();

    QString title() const;

signals:
    void pictureProcessed(const QImage& picture);

protected:
    void mousePressEvent(QMouseEvent*) override;

private:
    Ui::FilterWidget *ui;
    Filter& mFilter;
```

```
        QImage mDefaultSourcePicture;
        QImage mSourcePicture;
        QImage mSourceThumbnail;

        QImage mFilteredPicture;
        QImage mFilteredThumbnail;
    };
```

Overall, we trimmed everything concerning the Qt Designer plugin and simply passed the `mFilter` value by reference to the constructor. The `FilterWidget` class is not the owner of the `Filter` anymore; it is rather the client that calls it. Remember that the owner of `Filter` (aka the plugin) is `FilterLoader`.

The other modification is the new `setThumbnail()` function. It should be called in place of the old `updateThumbnail()`. The new `updateThumbnail()` now only performs the thumbnail processing and does not touch the source thumbnail. This division is done to prepare the work for the coming animation section. The thumbnail update will be done only once the animation has been finished.

 Please refer to the source code of the chapter to see `FilterWidget.cpp`.

All the low layers have been completed. The next step is to fill `MainWindow`. Once again, it follows the same pattern we covered in Chapter 7, *Third-Party Libraries Without a Headache*. The sole difference with `MainWindow.ui` is that `filtersLayout` is empty. Obviously, the plugin is loaded dynamically, so we have nothing to put inside it at compile time.

Let's cover `MainWindow.h`:

```
        #include <QMainWindow>
        #include <QImage>
        #include <QVector>

        #include "FilterLoader.h"

        namespace Ui {
        class MainWindow;
        }

        class FilterWidget;

        class MainWindow : public QMainWindow
        {
            Q_OBJECT
```

```
public:
    explicit MainWindow(QWidget *parent = 0);
    ~MainWindow();

    void loadPicture();

protected:
    void resizeEvent(QResizeEvent* event) override;

private slots:
    void displayPicture(const QImage& picture);
    void saveAsPicture();

private:
    void initFilters();
    void updatePicturePixmap();

private:
    Ui::MainWindow *ui;
    QImage mSourcePicture;
    QImage mSourceThumbnail;
    QImage& mFilteredPicture;
    QPixmap mCurrentPixmap;

    FilterLoader mFilterLoader;
    FilterWidget* mCurrentFilter;
    QVector<FilterWidget*> mFilters;
};
```

The only notable thing is the addition of `mFilterLoader` as a member variable.
In `MainWindow.cpp`, we will focus on the changes only:

```
void MainWindow::initFilters()
{
    mFilterLoader.loadFilters();

    auto& filters = mFilterLoader.filters();
    for(auto& filter : filters) {
        FilterWidget* filterWidget = new FilterWidget(*filter);
        ui->filtersLayout->addWidget(filterWidget);
        connect(filterWidget, &FilterWidget::pictureProcessed,
                this, &MainWindow::displayPicture);
        mFilters.append(filterWidget);
    }

    if (mFilters.length() > 0) {
        mCurrentFilter = mFilters[0];
    }
```

```
}
```

The `initFilters()` function does not load the filters from the `ui` content. Rather, it starts by calling the `mFilterLoader.loadFilters()` function to dynamically load the plugins from the `plugins` directory.

After that, an `auto&` filter is assigned with `mFilterLoader.filters()`. Note that it is much more readable to use `auto` keyword. The real type is `std::vector<std::unique_ptr<Filter>>&`, which looks more like a cryptic incantation than a simple object type.

For each of these filters, we create a `FilterWidget*` and pass it the reference of the `filter`. Here, `filter` is effectively a `unique_ptr`. The people behind C++11 wisely modified the dereferencing operator, making it transparent to the new `FilterWidget(*filter)`. The combination of the `auto` keyword and the overload of the `->` operator, or the dereference operator, makes the use of new C++ features much more enjoyable.

Look at the for loop. For each `filter` we do the following tasks:

1. Create a `FilterWidget` template.
2. Add the `FilterWidget` template to the `filtersLayout` children.
3. Connect the `FilterWidget::pictureProcessed` signal to the `MainWindow::displayPicture` slot.
4. Add the new `FilterWidget` template to the `QVectormFilters`.

In the end, the first `FilterWidget` is selected.

The only other modification to `MainWindow.cpp` is the implementation of `loadPicture()`:

```
void MainWindow::loadPicture()
{
    ...
    for (int i = 0; i <mFilters.size(); ++i) {
        mFilters[i]->setSourcePicture(mSourcePicture);
        mFilters[i]->setSourceThumbnail(mSourceThumbnail);
        mFilters[i]->updateThumbnail();
    }
    mCurrentFilter->process();
}
```

The `updateThumbnail()` function has been split into two functions, and here is where it is used.

The application can now be tested. You should be able to execute it and see the dynamic plugins loaded and displaying the processed default Lenna picture.

# Discovering the Animation Framework

Your application works like a charm. It is now time to look at how we can make it jump and move, or, in a word, live. The Qt Animation Framework can be used to create and start animations of Qt properties. The property value will be smoothly interpolated by an internal global timer handle by Qt. You can animate anything as long as it is a Qt property. You can even create a property for your own object using `Q_PROPERTY`. If you forgot about `Q_PROPERTY`, please refer to `Chapter 7`, *Third-Party Libraries Without a Headache*.

Three main classes are provided to build animations:

- `QPropertyAnimation`: This class animates one Qt property animation
- `QParallelAnimationGroup`: This class animates multiple animations in parallel (all the animations start together)
- `QSequentialAnimationGroup`: This class animates multiple animations in sequence (the animations run one by one in a defined order)

All those classes inherit `QAbstractAnimation`. Here is a diagram from the official Qt documentation:

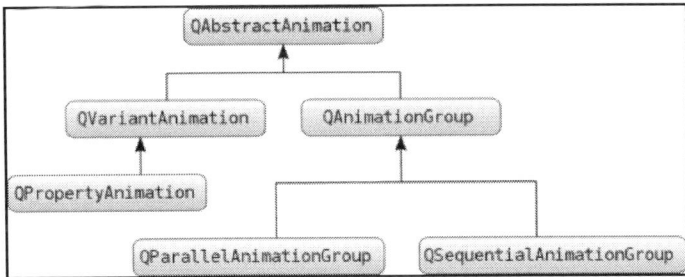

Please notice that QAbstractAnimation, QVariantAnimation, and QAnimationGroup are abstract classes. Here is a simple example of a Qt animation:

```
QLabel label;
QPropertyAnimation animation;

animation.setTargetObject(&label);
animation.setPropertyName("geometry");
animation.setDuration(4000);
animation.setStartValue(QRect(0, 0, 150, 50));
animation.setEndValue(QRect(300, 200, 150, 50));
animation.start();
```

The preceding snippet moves a QLabel label from the 0 x 0 position to 300 x 200 in four seconds. The first thing to do is to define the target object and its property. In our case, the target object is label and we want to animate the property called geometry. Then, we set the animation duration in milliseconds: 4000 milliseconds for four seconds. Finally, we can decide the start and end values of the geometry property, which is a QRect, defined like this:

```
QRect(x, y, width, height)
```

The label object starts with the 0 x 0 position and ends with 300 x 200. In this example, the size is fixed (150 x 50), but you can also animate the width and the height if you want.

Finally, we call the start() function to begin the animation. In four seconds, the animation smoothly moves the label from the 0 x 0 position to 300 x 200. By default, the animation uses a linear interpolation to provide intermediate values, so, after two seconds, the label will be at the 150 x 100 position. The linear interpolation of the value looks like the following schema:

In our case, the `label` object will move with a constant speed from the start to the end position. An easing function is a mathematical function that describes the evolution of a value over time. The easing curve is the visual representation of the mathematical function. The default linear interpolation is a good start, but Qt provides plenty of easing curves to control the speed behavior of your animation. Here is the updated example:

```
QLabel label;
QPropertyAnimation animation(&label, "geometry");
animation.setDuration(4000);
animation.setStartValue(QRect(0, 0, 150, 50));
animation.setEndValue(QRect(300, 200, 150, 50));
animation.setEasingCurve(QEasingCurve::InCirc);
animation.start();
```

You can set the target object and the property name directly using the `QPropertyAnimation` constructor. As a result, we removed the `setTargetObject()` and `setPropertyName()` functions. After that, we use `setEasingCurve()` to specify a curve for this animation. The `InCirc` looks like the following:

With this easing curve, the label starts to move really slowly but accelerates progressively during the animation.

Another way is to define the intermediate key steps yourself, using the `setKeyValueAt()` function. Let's update our example:

```
QLabel label;
QPropertyAnimation animation(&label, "geometry");
animation.setDuration(4000);
animation.setKeyValueAt(0, QRect(0, 0, 150, 50));
animation.setKeyValueAt(0.25, QRect(225, 112.5, 150, 50));
animation.setKeyValueAt(1, QRect(300, 200, 150, 50));
animation.start();
```

We are now setting key frames using `setKeyValueAt()`. The first argument is the time step in the range 0 to 1. In our case, step 1 means four seconds. The key frames at step 0 and step 1 provide the same positions as the start/end positions of the first example. As you can see, we also add a key frame at step 0.25 (that's one second for us) with the position 225 x 112.5. The next schema illustrates this:

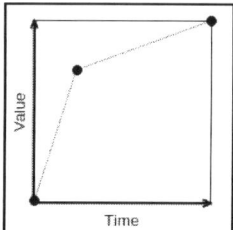

You can clearly distinguish the three key frames created with `setKeyValueAt()`. In our example, our `label` will quickly reach the 225 x 112.5 position in one second. Then the label will slowly move to the 300 x 200 position during the remaining three seconds.

If you have more than one `QPropertyAnimation` object, you can use groups to create more complex sequences. Let's see an example:

```
QPropertyAnimation animation1(&label1, "geometry");
QPropertyAnimation animation2(&label2, "geometry");
...
QSequentialAnimationGroup animationGroup;
animationGroup.addAnimation(&anim1);
animationGroup.addAnimation(&anim2);
animationGroup.start();
```

In this example, we are using a `QSequentialAnimationGroup` to run animations one by one. The first thing to do is to add animations to `animationGroup`. Then, when we call `start()` on our animation group, `animation1` is `launched`. When `animation1` is finished, `animationGroup` runs `animation2`. A `QSequentialAnimationGroup` is finished when the last animation of the list ends. The next schema depicts this behavior:

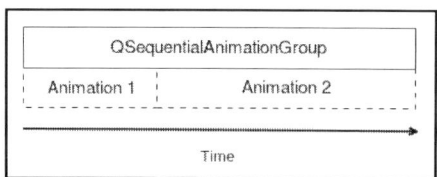

The second animation group, QParallelAnimationGroup, is initialized and started in the same way as QSequentialAnimationGroup. But the behavior is different: it starts all the animations in parallel, waiting for the longest animation to end. Here is an illustration of this:

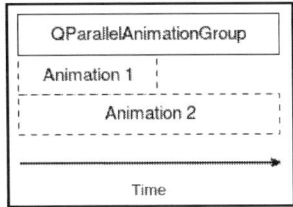

Keep in mind that an animation group is itself an animation (it inherits QAbstractAnimation). As a consequence, you can add animation groups to other animation groups to create a very complex animation sequence!

# Making your thumbnails jump

Let's apply what we learned about the Qt Animation Framework to our project. Each time the user clicks on a filter thumbnail, we want to poke it. All modifications will be done on the FilterWidget class. Let's start with FilterWidget.h:

```
#include <QPropertyAnimation>

class FilterWidget : public QWidget
{
    Q_OBJECT

public:
    explicit FilterWidget(Filter& filter, QWidget *parent = 0);
    ~FilterWidget();
    ...

private:
    void initAnimations();
    void startSelectionAnimation();

private:
    ...
    QPropertyAnimation mSelectionAnimation;
};
```

The first function, `initAnimations()`, initializes the animations used by `FilterWidget`. The second function, `startSelectionAnimation()`, performs tasks required to start this animation correctly. As you can see, we are also declaring a `QPropertyAnimation` class, as covered in the previous section.

We can now update `FilterWidget.cpp`. Let's update the constructor:

```
FilterWidget::FilterWidget(Filter& filter, QWidget *parent) :
    QWidget(parent),
    ...
    mSelectionAnimation()
{
    ...
    initAnimations();
    updateThumbnail();
}
```

We initialize our `QPropertyAnimation` called `mSelectionAnimation`. The constructor also calls `initAnimations()`. Here is its implementation:

```
void FilterWidget::initAnimations()
{
    mSelectionAnimation.setTargetObject(ui->thumbnailLabel);
    mSelectionAnimation.setPropertyName("geometry");
    mSelectionAnimation.setDuration(200);
}
```

You should be familiar with these animation initialization steps now. The target object is the `thumbnailLabel` displaying the filter plugin preview. The property name to animate is `geometry`, because we want to update the position of this `QLabel`. Finally, we set the animation duration to 200 ms. Like jokes, keep it short and sweet.

Update the existing mouse event handler like this:

```
void FilterWidget::mousePressEvent(QMouseEvent*)
{
    process();
    startSelectionAnimation();
}
```

Each time the user clicks on the thumbnail, the selection animation moving the thumbnail will be called. We can now add this most important function like this:

```
void FilterWidget::startSelectionAnimation()
{
    if (mSelectionAnimation.state() ==
        QAbstractAnimation::Stopped) {
```

```
QRect currentGeometry = ui->thumbnailLabel->geometry();
QRect targetGeometry = ui->thumbnailLabel->geometry();
targetGeometry.setY(targetGeometry.y() - 50.0);

mSelectionAnimation.setKeyValueAt(0, currentGeometry);
mSelectionAnimation.setKeyValueAt(0.3, targetGeometry);
mSelectionAnimation.setKeyValueAt(1, currentGeometry);
mSelectionAnimation.start();
    }
}
```

The first thing to do is to retrieve the current geometry of `thumbnailLabel` called `currentGeometry`. Then, we create a `targetGeometry` object with the same `x`, `width`, and `height` values. We only reduce the `y` position by 50, so the target position is always above the current position.

After that, we define our key frames:

- **At step 0**, the value is the current position.
- **At step 0.3** (60 ms, because the total duration is 200 ms), the value is the target position.
- **At step 1** (the end of the animation), we bring it to back the original position. The thumbnail will quickly reach the target position, then slowly fall down to its original position.

These key frames must be initialized before each animation starts. Because the layout is dynamic, the position (and so the geometry) could have been updated when the user resizes the main window.

Please note that we are preventing the animation from starting again if the current state is not stopped. Without this precaution, the thumbnail could move to the top again and again if the user clicks like a mad man on the widget.

You can now test your application and click on a filter effect. The filter thumbnail will jump to respond to your click!

# Fading the picture in

When the user opens a picture, we want to fade in the image by playing with its opacity. The classes `QLabel` or `QWidget` do not provide an opacity property. However, we can add a visual effect to any `QWidget` using a `QGraphicsEffect`. For this animation, we will use `QGraphicsOpacityEffect` to provide an `opacity` property.

Here is a schema to describe the role of each one:

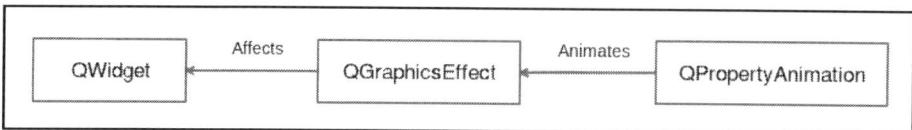

In our case, the QWidget class is our QLabel and the QGraphicsEffect class is
QGraphicsOpacityEffect. Qt provides the Graphics Effect system to alter the rendering
of a QWidget class. The abstract class QGraphicsEffect has a pure virtual method draw()
that is implemented by each graphics effect.

We can now update the MainWindow.h according to the next snippet:

```
#include <QPropertyAnimation>
#include <QGraphicsOpacityEffect>

class MainWindow : public QMainWindow
{
    ...
private:
    ...
    void initAnimations();
private:
    ...
    QPropertyAnimation mLoadPictureAnimation;
    QGraphicsOpacityEffect mPictureOpacityEffect;
};
```

The initAnimations() private function is in charge of all the animation initializations.
The mLoadPictureAnimation member variable performs the fade-in animation on the
loaded picture. Finally, we declare mPictureOpacityEffect, the
mandatory QGraphicsOpacityEffect.

Let's switch to the implementation part with the MainWindow.cpp constructor:

```
MainWindow::MainWindow(QWidget *parent) :
    QMainWindow(parent),
    ...
    mLoadPictureAnimation(),
    mPictureOpacityEffect()
{
    ...
    initFilters();
    initAnimations();
}
```

No surprises here. We use the initializer list to construct our two new member variables. The `MainWindow` constructor also calls `initAnimations()`.

Let's look at how this animation is initialized:

```
void MainWindow::initAnimations()
{
    ui->pictureLabel->setGraphicsEffect(&mPictureOpacityEffect);
    mLoadPictureAnimation.setTargetObject(&mPictureOpacityEffect);
    mLoadPictureAnimation.setPropertyName("opacity");
    mLoadPictureAnimation.setDuration(500);
    mLoadPictureAnimation.setStartValue(0);
    mLoadPictureAnimation.setEndValue(1);
    mLoadPictureAnimation.setEasingCurve(QEasingCurve::InCubic);
}
```

The first thing to do is to link our `QGraphicsOpacityEffect` with our `QLabel`. This can be easily done by calling the `setGraphicsEffect()` function on `pictureLabel`.

Now we can set our animation up. In this case, `mLoadPictureAnimation` targets `mPictureOpacityEffect` and will affect its property named `opacity`. The animation duration is `500` milliseconds. Next, we set the opacity value when the animation starts and ends:

- At the beginning, the picture is completely transparent (`opacity` value is `0`)
- At the end, the picture is fully visible (`opacity` value is `1`)

For this animation, we use the easing curve `InCubic`. This curve looks like this:

Feel free to try other curves to find the one that looks the best for you.

You can get the list of all easing curves with a visual preview here:
`http://doc.qt.io/qt-5/qeasingcurve.html`

The last step is to start the animation at the right place:

```
void MainWindow::loadPicture()
{
    ...
    mCurrentFilter->process();
    mLoadPictureAnimation.start();
}
```

You can now start your application and load a picture. You should see your picture fade in over 500 milliseconds!

# Flashing the thumbnail in a sequence

For this last animation, we want to display a blue flash on each filter preview when the thumbnail is updated. We do not want to flash all previews at the same time, but in a sequence, one by one. This feature will be achieved in two parts:

* Create a color animation in `FilterWidget` to display a blue flash
* Build a sequential animation group in `MainWindow` containing all `FilterWidget` color animations

Let's start to add the color animation. Update `FilterWidget.h` as shown in the following snippet:

```
#include <QGraphicsColorizeEffect>

class FilterWidget : public QWidget
{
    Q_OBJECT

public:
    explicit FilterWidget(Filter& filter, QWidget *parent = 0);
    ~FilterWidget();
    ...
    QPropertyAnimation* colorAnimation();

private:
    ...
```

```
    QPropertyAnimation mSelectionAnimation;
    QPropertyAnimation* mColorAnimation;
    QGraphicsColorizeEffect mColorEffect;
};
```

This time we do not want to affect the opacity, but rather colorize the thumbnail in blue. Thus, we use another Qt standard effect: QGraphicsColorizeEffect. We also declare a new QPropertyAnimation named mColorAnimation and its corresponding getter, colorAnimation(). We declare mColorAnimation as a pointer because the ownership will be taken by the animation group of MainWindow. This topic will be covered soon.

Let's update the constructor in FilterWidget.cpp:

```
FilterWidget::FilterWidget(Filter& filter, QWidget *parent) :
    QWidget(parent),
    . . .
    mColorAnimation(new QPropertyAnimation()),
    mColorEffect()
{
    . . .
}
```

We just have to construct our two new member variables, mColorAnimation and mColorEffect. Let's look at the amazing complexity of the getter:

```
QPropertyAnimation* FilterWidget::colorAnimation()
{
    return mColorAnimation;
}
```

It was a lie: we always try to write comprehensive code!

Now that the preliminaries are done, we can initialize the color animation by updating the initAnimations() function like this:

```
void FilterWidget::initAnimations()
{
    . . .
    mColorEffect.setColor(QColor(0, 150, 150));
    mColorEffect.setStrength(0.0);
    ui->thumbnailLabel->setGraphicsEffect(&mColorEffect);

    mColorAnimation->setTargetObject(&mColorEffect);
    mColorAnimation->setPropertyName("strength");
    mColorAnimation->setDuration(200);
    mColorAnimation->setStartValue(1.0);
```

```
        mColorAnimation->setEndValue(0.0);
    }
```

The first part sets the color filter up. Here, we chose a kind of turquoise color for the flash effect. The colorize effect is handled by its `strength` property. By default, the value is `1.0`, so, we set it to `0.0` to keep it from affecting our default thumbnail of Lenna. Finally, we link the `thumbnailLabel` with this `mColorEffect` calling `setGraphicsEffect()`.

The second part is the color animation preparation. This animation targets the color effect and its property, named `strength`. This is a short flash; `200` milliseconds is enough:

- We want to start with a full strength effect, so we put the start value at `1.0`
- During the animation, the colorize effect will decrease until it reaches `0.0`

The default linear interpolation is fine here, so we do not use any easing curve.

Here we are. The color effect/animation is initialized and we provided a `colorAnimation()` getter. We can now begin the second part of this feature, Updating `MainWindow.h`:

```
    #include <QSequentialAnimationGroup>

    class MainWindow : public QMainWindow
    {
        Q_OBJECT
        ...

    private:
        ...
        QSequentialAnimationGroup mFiltersGroupAnimation;
    };
```

We declare a `QSequentialAnimationGroup` class to trigger, one by one, all `FilterWidget` color animations displaying the blue flash. Let's update the constructor in `MainWindow.cpp`:

```
    MainWindow::MainWindow(QWidget *parent) :
        QMainWindow(parent),
        ...
        mFiltersGroupAnimation()
    {
        ...
    }
```

A new member variable means a new construction in the initializer list: that is the rule!

We can now update `initAnimations()` to prepare our animation group:

```
void MainWindow::initAnimations()
{
    ...
    for (FilterWidget* filterWidget : mFilters) {
        mFiltersGroupAnimation.addAnimation(
            filterWidget->colorAnimation());
    }
}
```

Do you remember that an animation group is only an animation container? As a consequence, we iterate on every `FilterWidget` to get its color animation and fill our `mFiltersGroupAnimation` calling `addAnimation()`. Thanks to C++11's range-based for loop, it is really readable. Keep in mind that when you add an animation to an animation group, the group takes ownership of this animation.

Our animation group is ready. We can now start it:

```
void MainWindow::loadPicture()
{
    ...
    mCurrentFilter->process();
    mLoadPictureAnimation.start();
    mFiltersGroupAnimation.start();
}
```

Start your application and open a picture. You can see that all filter thumbnails will flash one by one from left to right. This is what we intended, but it's still not perfect because all the thumbnails are already updated before the flashes. We have this behavior because the `loadPicture()` function actually sets and updates all thumbnails, and then finally starts the sequential animation group. Here is a schema illustrating the current behavior:

| set thumbnail 1 | update thumbnail 1 | set thumbnail 2 | update thumbnail 2 | flash thumbnail 1 | flash thumbnail 2 |
|---|---|---|---|---|---|

Time

The schema only describes the behavior for two thumbnails, but the principle is the same with three thumbnails. Here is the targeted behavior:

We must only update the thumbnail when the flash animation is over. Fortunately, QPropertyAnimation emits the finished signal when the animation is over, so we only have to make a few changes. Update loadPicture() function from MainWindow.cpp:

```
void MainWindow::loadPicture()
{
    ...
    for (int i = 0; i <mFilters.size(); ++i) {
        mFilters[i]->setSourcePicture(mSourcePicture);
        mFilters[i]->setSourceThumbnail(mSourceThumbnail);
        //mFilters[i]->updateThumbnail();
    }
    ...
}
```

As you can see, we kept the set and only removed the update thumbnail when a new picture is opened by the user. At this stage, all FilterWidget instances have the correct thumbnail, but they don't display it. Let's fix this by updating FilterWidget.cpp:

```
void FilterWidget::initAnimations()
{
    ...
    mColorAnimation->setTargetObject(&mColorEffect);
    mColorAnimation->setPropertyName("strength");
    mColorAnimation->setDuration(200);
    mColorAnimation->setStartValue(1.0);
    mColorAnimation->setEndValue(0.0);
    connect(mColorAnimation, &QPropertyAnimation::finished, [this]
    {
        updateThumbnail();
    });
}
```

We connect a `lambda` function to the finished signal of the color animation. This `lambda` simply updates the thumbnail. You can now start your application again and load a picture. You should see that we not only animate the sequential blue flash, but also the thumbnail update.

# Summary

In this chapter, you defined a `Filter` interface in your own SDK. Your filters are now plugins. You know how to create and load a new plugin, so your application is now modular and can be easily extended. We have also enhanced the application with the Qt Animation Framework. You know how to animate the position, the color, and the opacity of any `QWidget`, using `QGraphicsEffect` if necessary. We created a sequential animation that starts three animations one by one with `QSequentialAnimationGroup`.

In the next chapter, we will talk about a big subject: threading. The Qt framework can help you build a robust and reliable multithreading application. To illustrate the chapter, we will create a Mandelbrot fractal generator using threadpools.

# 9
# Keeping Your Sanity with Multithreading

In previous chapters, we managed to always write code without ever relying on threads. It is time to face the beast and truly understand how threading works in Qt. In this chapter, you will develop a multithreaded application that displays a Mandelbrot fractal. It is a heavy computational process that will bring tears to your CPU cores.

In the example project, the user can see the Mandelbrot fractal, zoom in the picture, and pan around to discover the magic of fractals.

The chapter covers the following topics:

- Deep understanding of the `QThread` framework
- Overview of all the available threading technologies in Qt
- Using a `QThreadPool` class to dispatch jobs and aggregate the results
- How to synchronize threads and minimize sharing states
- Low-level drawing to optimize the performances
- Common threading pitfalls and challenges

## Discovering QThread

Qt provides a sophisticated threading system. We assume you already know threading basics and the associated issues (deadlocks, threads synchronization, resource sharing, and so on) and we will focus on how Qt implements it.

The QThread is the central class of the Qt threading system. A QThread instance manages one thread of execution within the program.

You can subclass QThread to override the run() function, which will be executed in the QThread framework. Here is how you can create and start a QThread:

```
QThread thread;
thread.start();
```

The start() function calling will automatically call the run() function of the thread and emit the started() signal. Only at this point will the new thread of execution be created. When run() is completed, the thread object will emit the finished() signal.

This brings us to a fundamental aspect of QThread: it works seamlessly with the signal/slot mechanism. Qt is an event-driven framework, where a main event loop (or the GUI loop) processes events (user input, graphical, and so on) to refresh the UI.

Each QThread comes with its own event loop that can process events outside the main loop. If not overridden, run() calls the QThread::exec() function, which starts the thread object's event loop. You can also override QThread and call yourself exec(), like so:

```
class Thread : public QThread
{
Q_OBJECT
protected:
    void run()
    {
      Object* myObject = new Object();
        connect(myObject, &Object::started,
                this, &Thread::doWork);
        exec();
    }

private slots:
    void doWork();
};
```

The started() signal will be processed by the Thread event loop only upon the exec() call. It will block and wait until QThread::exit() is called.

A crucial thing to note is that a thread event loop delivers events for all QObjects that are living in that thread. This includes all objects created in that thread or moved to that thread. This is referred to as the thread affinity of an object. Let's see an example:

```
class Thread : public QThread
{
```

```
    Thread() :
        mObject(new QObject())
    {
    }
private :
    QObject* myObject;
};

// Somewhere in MainWindow
Thread thread;
thread.start();
```

In this snippet, `myObject` is constructed in `Thread` class's constructor, which is created in turn in `MainWindow`. At this point, `thread` is living in the GUI thread. Hence, `myObject` is also living in the GUI thread.

 An object created before a `QCoreApplication` object has no thread affinity. As a consequence, no event will be dispatched to it.

It is great to be able to handle signals and slots in our own `QThread`, but how can we control signals across multiple threads? A classic example is a long-running process that is executed in a separate thread that has to notify the UI to update some state:

```
class Thread : public QThread
{
    Q_OBJECT
    void run() {
        // long running operation
        emit result("I <3 threads");
    }
signals:
    void result(QString data);
};

// Somewhere in MainWindow
Thread* thread = new Thread(this);
connect(thread, &Thread::result, this, &MainWindow::handleResult);
connect(thread, &Thread::finished, thread, &QObject::deleteLater);
thread->start();
```

Intuitively, we assume that the first `connect` sends the signal across multiple threads (to have results available in `MainWindow::handleResult`), whereas the second `connect` should work on thread's event loop only.

Fortunately, this is the case due to a default argument in the `connect()` function signature: the connection type. Let's see the complete signature:

```
QObject::connect(
    const QObject *sender, const char *signal,
    const QObject *receiver, const char *method,
    Qt::ConnectionType type = Qt::AutoConnection)
```

The `type` keyword takes `Qt::AutoConnection` as a default value. Let's review the possible values of the `Qt::ConectionType` enum as the official Qt documentation states:

- `Qt::AutoConnection`: If the receiver lives in the thread that emits the signal, `Qt::DirectConnection` is used. Otherwise, `Qt::QueuedConnection` is used. The connection type is determined when the signal is emitted.
- `Qt::DirectConnection`: This slot is invoked immediately when the signal is emitted. The slot is executed in the signaling thread.
- `Qt::QueuedConnection`: This slot is invoked when control returns to the event loop of the receiver's thread. The slot is executed in the receiver's thread.
- `Qt::BlockingQueuedConnection`: This is the same as `Qt::QueuedConnection`, except that the signaling thread blocks until the slot returns. This connection must not be used if the receiver lives in the signaling thread, or else the application will deadlock.
- `Qt::UniqueConnection`: This is a flag that can be combined with any one of the previous connection types, using a bitwise OR. When `Qt::UniqueConnection` is set, `QObject::connect()` will fail if the connection already exists (that is, if the same signal is already connected to the same slot for the same pair of objects).

When using `Qt::AutoConnection`, the final `ConnectionType` is resolved only when the signal is effectively emitted. If you look again at our example, at the first `connect()`:

```
connect(thread, &Thread::result,
        this, &MainWindow::handleResult);
```

When `result()` is emitted, Qt will look at the `handleResult()` thread affinity, which is different from the thread affinity of the `result()` signal. The `thread` object is living in `MainWindow` (remember that it has been created in `MainWindow`), but the `result()` signal has been emitted in the `run()` function, which is running in a different thread of execution. As a result, a `Qt::QueuedConnection` slot will be used.

We can now take a look at the second `connect()`:

```
connect(thread, &Thread::finished, thread, &QObject::deleteLater);
```

Here, `deleteLater()` and `finished()` live in the same thread; therefore, a `Qt::DirectConnection` slot will be used.

It is crucial that you understand that Qt does not care about the emitting object thread affinity, it looks only at the signal "context of execution".

Loaded with this knowledge, we can take another look at our first `QThread` class example to have a full understanding of this system:

```
class Thread : public QThread
{
Q_OBJECT
protected:
    void run()
    {
        Object* myObject = new Object();
        connect(myObject, &Object::started,
                this, &Thread::doWork);
        exec();
    }

private slots:
    void doWork();
};
```

When the `Object::started()` function is emitted, a `Qt::QueuedConnection` slot will be used. This is where your brain freezes. The `Thread::doWork()` function lives in another thread than `Object::started()`, which has been created in `run()`. If Thread has been instantiated in the UI thread, this is where `doWork()` would have belonged.

This system is powerful, but complex. To make things simpler, Qt favors the worker model. It splits the threading plumbing from the real processing. Here is an example:

```
class Worker : public QObject
{
    Q_OBJECT
```

```
public slots:
    void doWork()
    {
        emit result("workers are the best");
    }

signals:
    void result(QString data);
};

// Somewhere in MainWindow
QThread* thread = new Thread(this);
Worker* worker = new Worker();
worker->moveToThread(thread);

connect(thread, &QThread::finished,
        worker, &QObject::deleteLater);
connect(this, &MainWindow::startWork,
        worker, &Worker::doWork);
connect(worker, &Worker::resultReady,
        this, handleResult);

thread->start();

// later on, to stop the thread
thread->quit();
thread->wait();
```

We start by creating a Worker class that has:

- A doWork() slot that will have the content of our old QThread::run()
- A result() signal that will emit the resulting data

Next in the MainWindow class, we create a simple thread object and an instance of Worker. The worker->moveToThread(thread) is where the magic happens. It changes the affinity of the worker object. The worker now lives in the thread object.

You can only push an object from your current thread to another thread. Conversely, you cannot pull an object that lives in another thread. You cannot change the thread affinity of an object if the object does not live in your thread. Once thread->start() is executed, we cannot call worker->moveToThread(this) unless we are doing it from this new thread.

After that, we do three `connect()`:

1. We handle the `worker` life cycle by reaping it when the thread is finished. This signal will use a `Qt::DirectConnection`.
2. We start the `Worker::doWork()` upon a possible UI event. This signal will use a `Qt::QueuedConnection`.
3. We process the resulting data in the UI thread with `handleResult()`. This signal will use a `Qt::QueuedConnection`.

To sum up, `QThread` can be either subclassed or used in conjunction with a `worker` class. Generally, the worker approach is favored because it separates more cleanly the threading affinity plumbing from the actual operation you want to execute in parallel.

# Flying over Qt multithreading technologies

Built upon `QThread`, several threading technologies are available in Qt. First, to synchronize threads, the usual approach is to use a mutual exclusion (mutex) to have a mutual exclusion for a given resource. Qt provides it by means of the `QMutex` class. Its usage is straightforward:

```
QMutex mutex;
int number = 1;

mutex.lock();
number *= 2;
mutex.unlock();
```

From the `mutex.lock()` instruction, any other thread trying to lock the `mutex` will wait until `mutex.unlock()` has been called.

The locking/unlocking mechanism is error-prone in complex code. You can easily forget to unlock a mutex in a specific exit condition, causing a deadlock. To simplify this situation, Qt provides a `QMutexLocker` that should be used where the `QMutex` needs to be locked:

```
QMutex mutex;
QMutexLocker locker(&mutex);

int number = 1;
number *= 2;
if (overlyComplicatedCondition) {
    return;
} else if (notSoSimple) {
```

```
        return;
    }
```

The `mutex` is locked when the `locker` object is created and will be unlocked when the `locker` object is destroyed; for example, when it goes out of scope. This is the case for every condition we stated where the `return` statement appears. It makes the code simpler and more readable.

You may need to create and destroy threads frequently, as managing `QThread` instances by hand can become cumbersome. For this, you can use the `QThreadPool` class, which manages a pool of reusable `QThreads`.

To execute code within threads managed by a `QThreadPool` class, you will use a pattern very close to the worker we covered earlier. The main difference is that the processing class has to extend the `QRunnable` class. Here is how it looks:

```
class Job : public QRunnable
{
    void run()
    {
        // long running operation
    }
}

Job* job = new Job();
QThreadPool::globalInstance()->start(job);
```

Just override the `run()` function and ask `QThreadPool` to execute your job in a separate thread. The `QThreadPool::globalInstance()` is a static helper function that gives you access to an application global instance. You can create your own `QThreadPool` if you need to have finer control over the `QThreadPool` life cycle.

Note that the `QThreadPool::start()` function takes the ownership of `job` and will automatically delete it when `run()` finishes. Watch out, this does not change the thread affinity like `QObject::moveToThread()` does with workers! A `QRunnable` class cannot be reused, it has to be a freshly baked instance.

If you fire up several jobs, `QThreadPool` automatically allocates the ideal number of threads based on the core count of your CPU. The maximum number of threads that the `QThreadPool` class can start can be retrieved with `QThreadPool::maxThreadCount()`.

If you need to manage threads by hand, but you want to base it on the number of cores of your CPU, you can use the handy static function, `QThreadPool::idealThreadCount()`.

Another approach to multi-threaded development is available with the Qt Concurrent framework. It is a higher-level API that avoids the use of mutexes/lock/wait conditions and promotes the distribution of the processing among CPU cores.

Qt Concurrent relies on the `QFuture` class to execute a function and expects a result later on:

```
void longRunningFunction();
QFuture<void> future = QtConcurrent::run(longRunningFunction);
```

The `longRunningFunction()` function will be executed in a separated thread obtained from the default `QThreadPool` class.

To pass parameters to a `QFuture` class and retrieve the result of the operation, use the following code:

```
QImage processGrayscale(QImage& image);
QImage lenna;

QFuture<QImage> future = QtConcurrent::run(processGrayscale,
    lenna);

QImage grayscaleLenna = future.result();
```

Here we pass `lenna` as a parameter to the `processGrayscale()` function. Because we want a `QImage` as a result, we declare the `QFuture` class with the template type, `QImage`. After that, `future.result()` blocks the current thread and waits for the operation to be completed to return the final `QImage`.

To avoid blocking, `QFutureWatcher` comes to the rescue:

```
QFutureWatcher<QImage> watcher;
connect(&watcher, &QFutureWatcher::finished,
        this, &QObject::handleGrayscale);

QImage processGrayscale(QImage& image);
QImage lenna;
QFuture<QImage> future = QtConcurrent::run(processImage, lenna);
watcher.setFuture(future);
```

We start by declaring a QFutureWatcher class with the template argument matching the one used for QFuture. Then simply connect the QFutureWatcher::finished signal to the slot you want to be called when the operation has been completed.

The last step is to tell the watcher object to watch the future object with watcher.setFuture(future). This statement looks almost like it comes from a science-fiction movie.

Qt Concurrent also provides a MapReduce and FilterReduce implementation. The MapReduce is a programming model that basically does two things:

- Maps or distributes the processing of the dataset among multiple cores of the CPU
- Reduces or aggregates the results to provide it to the caller

This technique was first promoted by Google to be able to process huge datasets within a cluster of CPUs.

Here is an example of a simple map operation:

```
QList images = ...;

QImage processGrayscale(QImage& image);
QFuture<void> future = QtConcurrent::mapped(
                                    images, processGrayscale);
```

Instead of QtConcurrent::run(), we use the mapped function that takes a list and the function to apply to each element in a different thread each time. The images list is modified in place, so there is no need to declare QFuture with a template type.

The operation can be made to block by using QtConcurrent::blockingMapped() instead of QtConcurrent::mapped().

Finally, a MapReduce operation looks like this:

```
QList images = ...;

QImage processGrayscale(QImage& image);
void combineImage(QImage& finalImage, const QImage& inputImage);

QFuture<void> future = QtConcurrent::mappedReduced(
                                    images,
                                    processGrayscale,
                                    combineImage);
```

Here we added a `combineImage()` function that will be called for each result returned by the map function, `processGrayscale()`. It will merge the intermediate data, `inputImage`, into the `finalImage`. This function is called only once at a time per thread, so there is no need to use a mutex to lock the result variable.

The `FilterReduce` follows exactly the same pattern; the filter function simply allows you to filter the input list instead of transforming it.

# Architecting the Mandelbrot project

The example project of this chapter is the multi-threaded calculation of a Mandelbrot fractal. The user will see the fractal and will be able to pan and zoom in that window.

Before diving into the code, we have to have a broad understanding of a fractal and how we are going to achieve its calculation.

The Mandelbrot fractal is a numerical set that works with complex numbers (a + bi). Each pixel is associated with a value calculated through iterations. If this iterated value diverges towards infinity then the pixel is out of the Mandelbrot set. If not, then the pixel is inside the Mandelbrot set. A visual representation of the Mandelbrot fractal looks like this:

Every black pixel in this image tends to diverge to an infinite value, whereas white pixels are bounded to a finite value. The white pixels belong to the Mandelbrot set.

What makes it interesting from a multi-threaded perspective, is that to determine if the pixel belongs or not to the Mandelbrot set, we have to iterate on a formula to be able to hypothesize its divergence or not. The more iterations we perform, the safer we are in claiming "yes, this pixel is in the Mandelbrot set, it is a white pixel".

Even more fun, we can take any value in the graphical plot and always apply the Mandelbrot formula to deduce if the pixel should be black or white. As a consequence, you can zoom endlessly inside the graphics of your fractal. There are only two main limitations:

- The power of your CPU hinders the picture generation speed.
- The floating number precision of your CPU architecture limits the zoom. If you keep zooming, you will get visual artifacts because the scale factor can only handle 15 to 17 significant digits.

The architecture of the application has to be carefully designed. Because we are working with threads, it is very easy to cause deadlock, starve threads, or even worse, freeze the UI.

We really want to maximize the use of the CPU. To do so, we will execute as many threads as possible on each core. Each thread will be responsible for calculating a part of the Mandelbrot set before giving back its result.

The architecture of the application is as follows:

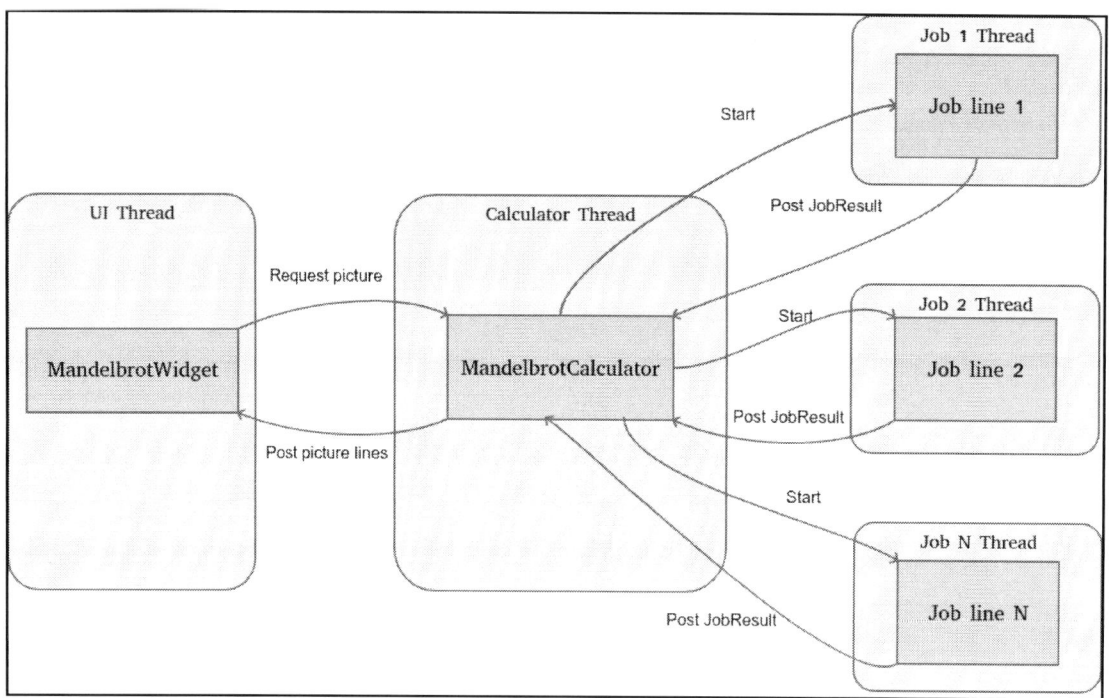

The application is divided into three parts:

- `MandelbrotWidget`: This requests a picture to display. It handles the drawing and the user interaction. This object lives in the UI thread.
- `MandelbrotCalculator`: This handles the picture requests and aggregates the resulting `JobResults` before sending it back to `MandelbrotWidget`. This object lives in its own thread.
- `Job`: This calculates a part of the final picture before transmitting the result back to `MandelbrotCalculator`. Each job lives in its own thread.

The `MandelbrotCalculator` thread will use a `QThreadPool` class to dispatch jobs in their own thread. This will scale perfectly according to your CPU cores. Each job will calculate a single line of the final picture before sending it back to `MandelbrotCalculator` through a `JobResult` object.

The `MandelbrotCalculator` thread is really the orchestrator of the calculation. Consider a user that zooms in the picture before the calculation is complete; `MandelbrotWidget` will request a new picture to `MandelbrotCalculator`, which in turn has to cancel all the current jobs before dispatching new jobs.

We will add a last constraint to this project: it has to be mutex free. Mutexes are very convenient tools, but they force threads to wait for each other and are error-prone. To do this, we will rely on multiple concepts and technologies provided by Qt: multi-threaded signal/slots, implicit sharing, and so on.

By minimizing the sharing state between our threads, we will be able to let them execute as fast as they possibly can. That is why we are here, to burn some CPU cores, right?

Now that the broad picture is clearer, we can start the implementation. Create a new **Qt Widget Application** project named `ch09-mandelbrot-threadpool`. Remember to add the `CONFIG += c++14` to the `.pro` file.

# Defining a Job class with QRunnable

Let's dive into the project's core. To speed up the Mandelbrot picture generation, we will split the whole computation into multiple jobs. A `Job` is a request of a task. Depending on your CPU architecture, several jobs will be executed simultaneously. A `Job` class produces a `JobResult` function containing result values. In our project, a `Job` class generates values for one line of the complete picture. For example, an image resolution of 800 x 600 requires 600 jobs, each one generating 800 values.

Please create a C++ header file called `JobResult.h`:

```cpp
#include <QSize>
#include <QVector>
#include <QPointF>

struct JobResult
{
    JobResult(int valueCount = 1) :
        areaSize(0, 0),
        pixelPositionY(0),
        moveOffset(0, 0),
        scaleFactor(0.0),
        values(valueCount)
    {
    }

    QSize areaSize;
    int pixelPositionY;
    QPointF moveOffset;
    double scaleFactor;

    QVector<int> values;
};
```

This structure contains two parts:

- Input data (`areaSize`, `pixelPositionY`, ...)
- Result `values` generated by a `Job` class

We can now create the `Job` class itself. Create a C++ class `Job` using the next snippet of `Job.h` for the content:

```cpp
#include <QObject>
#include <QRunnable>

#include "JobResult.h"
class Job : public QObject, public QRunnable
{
    Q_OBJECT
public:
    Job(QObject *parent = 0);
    void run() override;
};
```

This `Job` class is a `QRunnable`, so we can override `run()` to implement the Mandelbrot picture algorithm. As you can see, `Job` also inherits from `QObject`, allowing us to use the signal/slot feature of Qt. The algorithm requires some input data. Update your `Job.h` like this:

```cpp
#include <QObject>
#include <QRunnable>
#include <QPointF>
#include <QSize>
#include <QAtomicInteger>
class Job : public QObject, public QRunnable
{
    Q_OBJECT
public:
    Job(QObject *parent = 0);
    void run() override;

    void setPixelPositionY(int value);
    void setMoveOffset(const QPointF& value);
    void setScaleFactor(double value);
    void setAreaSize(const QSize& value);
    void setIterationMax(int value);

private:
    int mPixelPositionY;
    QPointF mMoveOffset;
    double mScaleFactor;
    QSize mAreaSize;
    int mIterationMax;
};
```

Let's talk about these variables:

- The `mPixelPositionY` variable is the picture height index. Because each `Job` generates data only for one picture line, we need this information.
- The `mMoveOffset` variable is the Mandelbrot origin offset. The user can pan the picture, so the origin will not always be (0, 0).
- The `mScaleFactor` variable is the Mandelbrot scale value. The user can also zoom into the picture.
- The `mAreaSize` variable is the final picture size in a pixel.
- The `mIterationMax` variable is the count of iterations allowed to determine the Mandelbrot result for one pixel.

We can now add a signal, `jobCompleted()`, and the abort feature to `Job.h`:

```
#include <QObject>
#include <QRunnable>
#include <QPointF>
#include <QSize>
#include <QAtomicInteger>

#include "JobResult.h"

class Job : public QObject, public QRunnable
{
    Q_OBJECT
public:
    ...
signals:
    void jobCompleted(JobResult jobResult);

public slots:
    void abort();

private:
    QAtomicInteger<bool> mAbort;
    ...
};
```

The `jobCompleted()` signal will be emitted when the algorithm is over. The `jobResult` parameter contains result values. The `abort()` slot will allow us to stop the job updating the `mIsAbort` flag value. Notice that `mAbort` is not a classic `bool`, but a `QAtomicInteger<bool>`. This Qt cross-platform type allows us to perform atomic operations without interruption. You could use a mutex or another synchronization mechanism to do the job, but using an atomic variable is a fast way to safely update and access a variable from different threads.

It is time to switch to the implementation part with `Job.cpp`. Here is the `Job` class's constructor:

```
#include "Job.h"

Job::Job(QObject* parent) :
    QObject(parent),
    mAbort(false),
    mPixelPositionY(0),
    mMoveOffset(0.0, 0.0),
    mScaleFactor(0.0),
    mAreaSize(0, 0),
    mIterationMax(1)
```

```
    {
    }
```

This is a classic initialization; do not forget to call the `QObject` constructor.

We can now implement the `run()` function:

```
void Job::run()
{
    JobResult jobResult(mAreaSize.width());
    jobResult.areaSize = mAreaSize;
    jobResult.pixelPositionY = mPixelPositionY;
    jobResult.moveOffset = mMoveOffset;
    jobResult.scaleFactor = mScaleFactor;
    ...
}
```

In this first part, we initialize a `JobResult` variable. The width of the area size is used to construct `JobResult::values` as a `QVector` with the correct initial size. Other input data is copied from `Job` to `JobResult` to let the receiver of `JobResult` get the result with the context input data.

Then we can update the `run()` function with the Mandelbrot algorithm:

```
void Job::run()
{
    ...
    double imageHalfWidth = mAreaSize.width() / 2.0;
    double imageHalfHeight = mAreaSize.height() / 2.0;
    for (int imageX = 0; imageX < mAreaSize.width(); ++imageX) {
        int iteration = 0;
        double x0 = (imageX - imageHalfWidth)
                    * mScaleFactor + mMoveOffset.x();
        double y0 = (mPixelPositionY - imageHalfHeight)
                    * mScaleFactor - mMoveOffset.y();
        double x = 0.0;
        double y = 0.0;
        do {
            if (mAbort.load()) {
                return;
            }

            double nextX = (x * x) - (y * y) + x0;
            y = 2.0 * x * y + y0;
            x = nextX;
            iteration++;

        } while(iteration < mIterationMax
```

```
                    && (x * x) + (y * y) < 4.0);

        jobResult.values[imageX] = iteration;
    }

    emit jobCompleted(jobResult);
}
```

The Mandelbrot algorithm itself is beyond the scope of this book. But you have to understand the main purpose of this `run()` function. Let's break it down:

- The for loop iterates over all x positions of pixels over one line
- The pixel position is converted into complex plane coordinates
- If the trial count exceeds the maximum authorized iteration, the algorithm ends with `iteration` to the `mIterationMax` value
- If the Mandelbrot check condition is true, the algorithm ends with `iteration < mIterationMax`
- In any case, for each pixel, the iteration count is stored in `values` of `JobResult`
- Finally, the `jobCompleted()` signal is emitted with result values of this algorithm
- We perform an atomic read with `mAbort.load()`; notice that if the return value is `true`, the algorithm is aborted and nothing is emitted

The last function is the `abort()` slot:

```
void Job::abort()
{
    mAbort.store(true);
}
```

This method performs an atomic write of the value, `true`. The atomic mechanism ensures that we can call `abort()` from multiple threads without disrupting the `mAbort` read in the `run()` function.

In our case, `run()` lives in the thread affected by the `QThreadPool` (we will cover it soon), while the `abort()` slot will be called in the `MandelbrotCalculator` thread context.

You might want to secure the operations on mAbort with a QMutex. However, keep in mind that locking and unlocking a mutex can become a costly operation if you do it often. Using a QAtomicInteger class here presents only the advantages: the access to mAbort is thread-safe and we avoid an expensive lock.

The end of the Job implementation only contains setter functions. Please refer to the complete source code if you have any doubt.

# Using QThreadPool in MandelbrotCalculator

Now that our Job class is ready to be used, we need to create a class to manage the jobs. Please create a new class, MandelbrotCalculator. Let's see what we need in the file, MandelbrotCalculator.h:

```cpp
#include <QObject>
#include <QSize>
#include <QPointF>
#include <QElapsedTimer>
#include <QList>

#include "JobResult.h"

class Job;

class MandelbrotCalculator : public QObject
{
    Q_OBJECT
public:
    explicit MandelbrotCalculator(QObject *parent = 0);
    void init(QSize imageSize);

private:
    QPointF mMoveOffset;
    double mScaleFactor;
    QSize mAreaSize;
    int mIterationMax;
    int mReceivedJobResults;
    QList<JobResult> mJobResults;
    QElapsedTimer mTimer;
};
```

We have already discussed mMoveOffset, mScaleFactor, mAreaSize, and mIterationMax in the previous section. We also have some new variables:

- The mReceivedJobResults variable is the count of the JobResult received, which was sent by the jobs
- The mJobResults variable is a list that contains received JobResult
- The mTimer variable calculates the elapsed time to run all jobs for a requested picture

Now that you get a better picture of all member variables, we can add the signals, slots, and private methods. Update your MandelbrotCalculator.h file:

```
...
class MandelbrotCalculator : public QObject
{
    Q_OBJECT
public:
    explicit MandelbrotCalculator(QObject *parent = 0);
    void init(QSize imageSize);

signals:
    void pictureLinesGenerated(QList<JobResult> jobResults);
    void abortAllJobs();

public slots:
    void generatePicture(QSize areaSize, QPointF moveOffset,
                         double scaleFactor, int iterationMax);
    void process(JobResult jobResult);

private:
    Job* createJob(int pixelPositionY);
    void clearJobs();

private:
    ...
};
```

Here are the roles of these:

- generatePicture(): This slot is used by the caller to request a new Mandelbrot picture. This function prepares and starts jobs.
- process(): This slot handles results generated by the jobs.
- pictureLinesGenerated(): This signal is regularly triggered to dispatch results.

- abortAllJobs(): This signal is used to abort all active jobs.
- createJob(): This is a helper function to create and configure a new job.
- clearJobs(): This slot removes queued jobs and aborts active jobs.

The header file is completed and we can now perform the implementation. Here is the beginning of the MandelbrotCalculator.cpp implementation:

```
#include <QDebug>
#include <QThreadPool>

#include "Job.h"

const int JOB_RESULT_THRESHOLD = 10;

MandelbrotCalculator::MandelbrotCalculator(QObject *parent)
    : QObject(parent),
      mMoveOffset(0.0, 0.0),
      mScaleFactor(0.005),
      mAreaSize(0, 0),
      mIterationMax(10),
      mReceivedJobResults(0),
      mJobResults(),
      mTimer()
{
}
```

As always, we are using the initializer list with default values for our member variables. The role of JOB_RESULT_THRESHOLD will be covered soon. Here is the generatePicture() slot:

```
void MandelbrotCalculator::generatePicture(QSize areaSize, QPointF
moveOffset, double scaleFactor, int iterationMax)
{
    if (areaSize.isEmpty()) {
        return;
    }

    mTimer.start();
    clearJobs();

    mAreaSize = areaSize;
    mMoveOffset = moveOffset;
    mScaleFactor = scaleFactor;
    mIterationMax = iterationMax;

    for(int pixelPositionY = 0;
```

```
            pixelPositionY < mAreaSize.height(); pixelPositionY++) {
            QThreadPool::globalInstance()->
                start(createJob(pixelPositionY));
        }
    }
```

If the `areaSize` dimension is 0x0, we have nothing to do. If the request is valid, we can start `mTimer` to track the whole generation duration. Each new picture generation will first cancel existing jobs by calling `clearJobs()`. Then we set our member variables with the ones provided. Finally, we create a new `Job` class for each vertical picture line. The `createJob()` function that returns a `Job*` value will be covered soon.

The `QThreadPool::globalInstance()` is a static function that gives us the optimal global thread pool depending on the core count of our CPU. Even if we call `start()` for all the `Job` classes, only the firsts starts immediately. Others are added to the pool queue waiting for an available thread.

Let's see now how a `Job` class is created with the `createJob()` function:

```
    Job* MandelbrotCalculator::createJob(int pixelPositionY)
    {
        Job* job = new Job();

        job->setPixelPositionY(pixelPositionY);
        job->setMoveOffset(mMoveOffset);
        job->setScaleFactor(mScaleFactor);
        job->setAreaSize(mAreaSize);
        job->setIterationMax(mIterationMax);

        connect(this, &MandelbrotCalculator::abortAllJobs,
                job, &Job::abort);

        connect(job, &Job::jobCompleted,
                this, &MandelbrotCalculator::process);

        return job;
    }
```

As you can see, the jobs are allocated on the heap. This operation takes some time in the `MandelbrotCalculator` thread. But the results are worth it; the overhead is being compensated by the multi-threading system. Notice that when we call `QThreadPool::start()`, the thread pool takes ownership of the `job`. As a consequence, it will be deleted by the thread pool when `Job::run()` ends. We set the input data of the `Job` class required by the Mandelbrot algorithm.

Then two connections are performed:

- Emitting our `abortAllJobs()` signal will call the `abort()` slot of all jobs
- Our `process()` slot is executed each time a `Job` completes its task

Finally, the `Job` pointer is returned to the caller, in our case, the `generatePicture()` slot.

The last helper function is `clearJobs()`. Add it to your `MandelbrotCalculator.cpp`:

```
void MandelbrotCalculator::clearJobs()
{
    mReceivedJobResults = 0;
    emit abortAllJobs();
    QThreadPool::globalInstance()->clear();
}
```

The counter of received job results is reset. We emit our signal to abort all active jobs. Finally, we remove queued jobs waiting for an available thread in the thread pool.

The last function of this class is `process()`, and is maybe the most important function. Update your code with the following snippet:

```
void MandelbrotCalculator::process(JobResult jobResult)
{
    if (jobResult.areaSize != mAreaSize ||
            jobResult.moveOffset != mMoveOffset ||
            jobResult.scaleFactor != mScaleFactor) {
        return;
    }

    mReceivedJobResults++;
    mJobResults.append(jobResult);

    if (mJobResults.size() >= JOB_RESULT_THRESHOLD ||
            mReceivedJobResults == mAreaSize.height()) {
        emit pictureLinesGenerated(mJobResults);
        mJobResults.clear();
    }

    if (mReceivedJobResults == mAreaSize.height()) {
        qDebug() << "Generated in " << mTimer.elapsed() << " ms";
    }
}
```

This slot will be called each time a job completes its task. The first thing to check is that the current `JobResult` is still valid with the current input data. When a new picture is requested, we clear the jobs queue and abort the active jobs. However, if an old `JobResult` is still sent to this `process()` slot, we must ignore it.

After that, we can increment the `mReceivedJobResults` counter and append this `JobResult` to our member queue, `mJobResults`. The calculator waits to get `JOB_RESULT_THRESHOLD` (that is, 10) results before dispatching them by emitting the `pictureLinesGenerated()` signal. You can try to tweak this value with caution:

- A lower value, for example 1, will dispatch each line of data to the widget as soon as the calculator gets it. But the widget will be slower than the calculator to handle each line. Moreover, you will flood the widget event loop.
- A higher value relieves the widget event loop. But the user will wait longer before seeing something happening. A continuous partial frame update gives a better user experience.

Also notice that when the event is dispatched, the `QList` class with the job result is sent by copy. But Qt performs implicit sharing with `QList`, so we only send a shallow copy not a costly deep copy. Then we clear the current `QList` of the calculator.

Finally, if the processed `JobResult` is the last one in the area, we display a debug message with the elapsed time since the user call, `generatePicture()`.

**Qt tip**
You can set the thread count used by the `QThreadPool` class with `setMaxThreadCount(x)` where x is the thread count.

# Displaying the fractal with MandelbrotWidget

Here we are, the Mandelbrot algorithm is done and the multi-threading system is ready to compute complex fractals over all your CPU cores. We can now create the widget that will convert all `JobResult` to display a pretty picture. Create a new C++ class called `MandelbrotWidget`. For this widget, we will handle the painting ourselves. Thus, we do not need any `.ui` Qt Designer Form file. Let's begin with the `MandelbrotWidget.h` file:

```
#include <memory>

#include <QWidget>
```

```
#include <QPoint>
#include <QThread>
#include <QList>

#include "MandelbrotCalculator.h"

class QResizeEvent;

class MandelbrotWidget : public QWidget
{
    Q_OBJECT

public:
    explicit MandelbrotWidget(QWidget *parent = 0);
    ~MandelbrotWidget();

private:
    MandelbrotCalculator mMandelbrotCalculator;
    QThread mThreadCalculator;
    double mScaleFactor;
    QPoint mLastMouseMovePosition;
    QPointF mMoveOffset;
    QSize mAreaSize;
    int mIterationMax;
    std::unique_ptr<QImage> mImage;
};
```

You should recognize some known variable names such as
`mScaleFactor`, `mMoveOffset`, `mAreaSize`, or `mIterationMax`. We have already covered
them in the `JobResult` and `Job` implementation. Here are the real new ones:

- The `mMandelbrotCalculator` variable is our multi-threaded `Job` manager. The
  widget will do requests to it and wait for results.
- The `mThreadCalculator` variable allows the Mandelbrot calculator to run in its
  own thread.
- The `mLastMouseMovePosition` variable is used by the widget to handle user
  events for the pan feature.
- The `mImage` variable is the current picture displayed by the widget. It is
  a `unique_ptr` pointer, so `MandelbrotWidget` is the owner of `mImage`.

We can now add the functions. Update your code like this:

```
class MandelbrotWidget : public QWidget
{
...
```

```
public slots:
    void processJobResults(QList<JobResult> jobResults);

signals:
    void requestPicture(QSize areaSize, QPointF moveOffset, double
scaleFactor, int iterationMax);

protected:
    void paintEvent(QPaintEvent*) override;
    void resizeEvent(QResizeEvent* event) override;
    void wheelEvent(QWheelEvent* event) override;
    void mousePressEvent(QMouseEvent* event) override;
    void mouseMoveEvent(QMouseEvent* event) override;

private:
    QRgb generateColorFromIteration(int iteration);

private:
    ...
};
```

Before we dive into the implementation, let's talk about these functions:

- The `processJobResults()` function will handle the `JobResult` list dispatched by `MandelbrotCalculator`.
- The `requestPicture()` signal is emitted each time the user changes the input data (offset, scale, or area size).
- The `paintEvent()` function draws the widget with the current `mImage`.
- The `resizeEvent()` function resizes the Mandelbrot area size when the user resizes the window.
- The `wheelEvent()` function handles the user mouse wheel event to apply a scale factor.
- The `mousePressEvent()` function and `mouseMoveEvent()` retrieve user mouse events to move the Mandelbrot picture.
- The `generateColorFromIteration()` is a helper function to colorize the Mandelbrot picture. The iteration value by pixel is converted into a color value.

We can now implement the `MandelbrotWidget` class. Here is the beginning of the `MandelbrotWidget.cpp` file:

```
#include "MandelbrotWidget.h"

#include <QResizeEvent>
#include <QImage>
```

```
#include <QPainter>
#include <QtMath>

const int ITERATION_MAX = 4000;
const double DEFAULT_SCALE = 0.005;
const double DEFAULT_OFFSET_X = -0.74364390249094747;
const double DEFAULT_OFFSET_Y = 0.13182589977450967;

MandelbrotWidget::MandelbrotWidget(QWidget *parent) :
    QWidget(parent),
    mMandelbrotCalculator(),
    mThreadCalculator(this),
    mScaleFactor(DEFAULT_SCALE),
    mLastMouseMovePosition(),
    mMoveOffset(DEFAULT_OFFSET_X, DEFAULT_OFFSET_Y),
    mAreaSize(),
    mIterationMax(ITERATION_MAX)
{
    mMandelbrotCalculator.moveToThread(&mThreadCalculator);

    connect(this, &MandelbrotWidget::requestPicture,
        &mMandelbrotCalculator,
        &MandelbrotCalculator::generatePicture);

    connect(&mMandelbrotCalculator,
        &MandelbrotCalculator::pictureLinesGenerated,
        this, &MandelbrotWidget::processJobResults);

    mThreadCalculator.start();
}
```

At the top of the snippet, we set some constant default values. Feel free to tweak these values if you want a different view when you start the application. The first thing the constructor does is to change the thread affinity of the mMandelbrotCalculator class. In this way, processing performed by the calculator (creating and starting jobs, aggregating job results, and clearing jobs) does not disturb the UI thread. Then we perform connections with the signal and slot of MandelbrotCalculator. Because the widget and the calculator have a different thread affinity, the connection will be automatically a Qt::QueuedConnection slot. Finally, we can start the thread of mThreadCalculator. We can now add the destructor:

```
MandelbrotWidget::~MandelbrotWidget()
{
    mThreadCalculator.quit();
    mThreadCalculator.wait(1000);
    if (!mThreadCalculator.isFinished()) {
        mThreadCalculator.terminate();
```

```
    }
}
```

We need to request the calculator thread to quit. When the calculator thread event loop handles our request, the thread will return a code 0. We wait 1,000 ms for the thread to end. We can continue this implementation with all the cases that request a new picture. Here is the `resizeEvent()` slot:

```
void MandelbrotWidget::resizeEvent(QResizeEvent* event)
{
    mAreaSize = event->size();

    mImage = std::make_unique<QImage>(mAreaSize,
        QImage::Format_RGB32);
    mImage->fill(Qt::black);

    emit requestPicture(mAreaSize, mMoveOffset, mScaleFactor,
        mIterationMax);
}
```

We update `mAreaSize` with the new widget size. Then, a new black `QImage` is created with the correct dimensions. Finally, we request a picture computation to `MandelbrotCalculator`. Let's see how the mouse wheel is handled:

```
void MandelbrotWidget::wheelEvent(QWheelEvent* event)
{
    int delta = event->delta();
    mScaleFactor *= qPow(0.75, delta / 120.0);
    emit requestPicture(mAreaSize, mMoveOffset, mScaleFactor,
        mIterationMax);
}
```

The mouse wheel value can be retrieved from `QWheelEvent::delta()`. We use a power function to apply a coherent value on `mScaleFactor` and we request an updated picture. We can now implement the pan feature:

```
void MandelbrotWidget::mousePressEvent(QMouseEvent* event)
{
    if (event->buttons() & Qt::LeftButton) {
        mLastMouseMovePosition = event->pos();
    }
}
```

The first function stores the mouse position where the user begins the move gesture. Then the next function will use mLastMouseMovePosition to create an offset:

```
void MandelbrotWidget::mouseMoveEvent(QMouseEvent* event)
{
    if (event->buttons() & Qt::LeftButton) {
        QPointF offset = event->pos() - mLastMouseMovePosition;
        mLastMouseMovePosition = event->pos();
        offset.setY(-offset.y());
        mMoveOffset += offset * mScaleFactor;
        emit requestPicture(mAreaSize, mMoveOffset, mScaleFactor,
            mIterationMax);
    }
}
```

The difference between the new and the old mouse position gives us the pan offset. Notice that we invert a y-axis value because the mouse event is in a top-left referential, whereas the Mandelbrot algorithm relies on a bottom-left referential. Finally, we request a picture with updated input values. We covered all the user events that emit a requestPicture() signal. Let's see now how we handle JobResult dispatched by MandelbrotCalculator:

```
void MandelbrotWidget::processJobResults(QList<JobResult> jobResults)
{
    int yMin = height();
    int yMax = 0;

    for(JobResult& jobResult : jobResults) {

        if (mImage->size() != jobResult.areaSize) {
            continue;
        }

        int y = jobResult.pixelPositionY;
        QRgb* scanLine =
            reinterpret_cast<QRgb*>(mImage->scanLine(y));

        for (int x = 0; x < mAreaSize.width(); ++x) {
            scanLine[x] =
                generateColorFromIteration(jobResult.values[x]);
        }

        if (y < yMin) {
            yMin = y;
        }

        if (y > yMax) {
            yMax = y;
```

```
            }
        }

        repaint(0, yMin,
                width(), yMax);
    }
```

The calculator sends us a `QList` of `JobResult`. For each one, we need to check if the
concerned area size is still valid. We directly update the pixel colors of `mImage`.
The `scanLine()` function returns a pointer on the pixel data. It is a fast way to update
a `QImage` pixel color. The `JobResult` function contains the iteration count, and our helper
function, `generateColorFromIteration()`, returns a RGB value depending on the
iteration value. A complete repaint of the widget is not necessary, because we only update
several lines of the `QImage`. Thus, we repaint only the updated region.

Here is how we convert an iteration value in an RGB value:

```
QRgb MandelbrotWidget::generateColorFromIteration(int iteration)
{
    if (iteration == mIterationMax) {
        return qRgb(50, 50, 255);
    }

    return qRgb(0, 0, (255.0 * iteration / mIterationMax));
}
```

Colorizing a Mandelbrot is an art on its own. We implement here a simple linear
interpolation on the blue channel. A nice Mandelbrot picture depends on the maximum
iteration per pixel and its color technique. Feel free to enhance it like you want!

Here we are, the last but not least function, `paintEvent()`:

```
void MandelbrotWidget::paintEvent(QPaintEvent* event)
{
    QPainter painter(this);
    painter.save();

    QRect imageRect = event->region().boundingRect();
    painter.drawImage(imageRect, *mImage, imageRect);

    painter.setPen(Qt::white);

    painter.drawText(10, 20, QString("Size: %1 x %2")
        .arg(mImage->width())
        .arg(mImage->height()));

    painter.drawText(10, 35, QString("Offset: %1 x %2")
```

```
        .arg(mMoveOffset.x())
        .arg(mMoveOffset.y())));

    painter.drawText(10, 50, QString("Scale: %1")
        .arg(mScaleFactor));

    painter.drawText(10, 65, QString("Max iteration: %1")
        .arg(ITERATION_MAX));

    painter.restore();
}
```

We must override this function because we handle the widget drawing by ourselves. The first thing to do is to draw the updated region of the image. The QPaintEvent object contains the region that needs to be updated. The QPainter class makes the drawing easy. Finally, we draw some information texts of the current input data in white. You now have a complete overview of the progressive picture display line by line. Let's sum up the workflow of this feature:

1. Each Job::run() generates a JobResult object.
2. The MandelbrotCalculator::process() signal aggregates the JobResult object and dispatches them by groups (by default, 10).
3. The MandelbrotWidget::processJobResults() signal updates only concerned lines of the picture and requests a partial repaint of the widget.
4. The MandelbrotWidget::paintEvent() signal only redraws the picture with the new values.

This feature causes a little overhead, but the user experience is smoother. Indeed, the application reacts quickly to the user events: the first lines are updated almost immediately. The user does not have to wait for the full picture generation to see something happening.

The widget is ready; do not forget to add it to MainWindow. Promoting a custom widget should be an easy task for you now. If you have any doubt, check Chapter 4, *Conquering the Desktop UI*, or the complete source code of this chapter. You should now be able to display and navigate into your multi-threaded Mandelbrot set!

If you start the application, you should see something like this:

Try to zoom now and pan into the Mandelbrot set. You should find some funny places like this one:

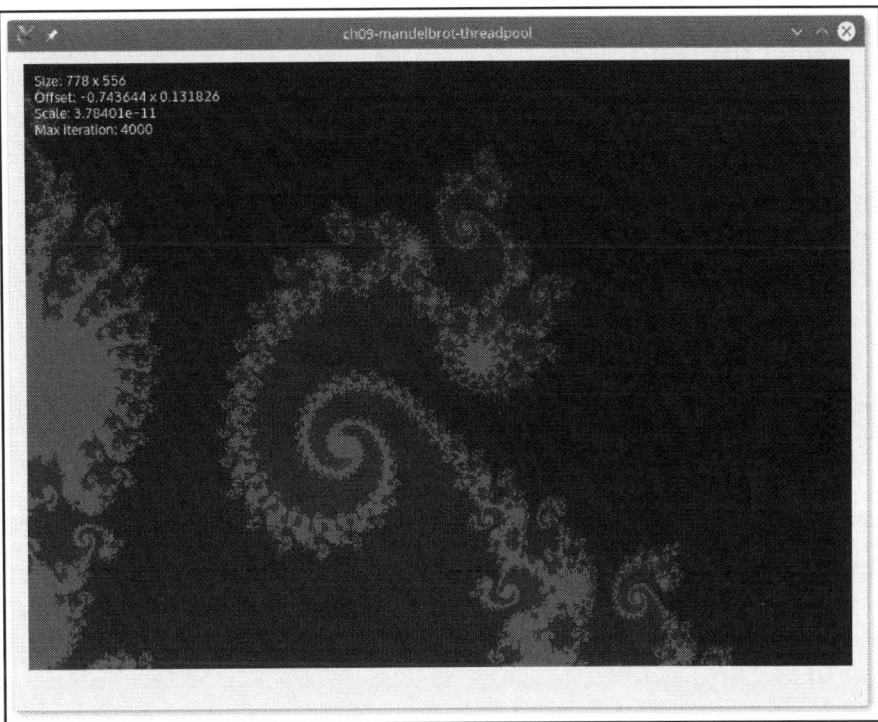

# Summary

You discovered how a `QThread` class works and learned how to efficiently use tools provided by Qt to create a powerful multi-threaded application. Your Mandelbrot application is able to use all cores of your CPU to compute a picture quickly.

Creating a multi-threaded application presents a lot of pitfalls (deadlock, event loop flood, orphan threads, overhead, and so on). The application architecture is important. If you are able to isolate the heavy code that you want to parallelize, everything should go well. Nevertheless, the user experience is of primary importance; you will sometimes have to accept a little overhead if your application gives the user a smoother feeling.

In the next chapter, we will see several ways to implement an IPC (Inter-Process Communication) between applications. The project example will enhance your current Mandelbrot application with a TCP/IP socket system. So the Mandelbrot generator will compute pictures over several CPU cores from multiple computers!

# 10
# Need IPC? Get Your Minions to Work

In the previous chapter, you learned how to send information across threads of the same process. In this chapter, you will discover how to share data between threads of different processes. We will even share information between applications running on different physical computers. We will enhance the Mandelbrot generator application from Chapter 9, *Keeping Your Sanity with Multithreading*. The Mandelbrot application will now only display results processed by the worker programs. These minions have only one mission: compute the tasks as fast as possible and return a result to your main application.

Here are the topics covered in this chapter:

- How two applications can communicate together
- Creating a multithreaded TCP server
- Reading and writing on a TCP socket
- Other IPC techniques like QSharedMemory, QProcess, and Qt D-Bus
- Network serialization using QDataStream
- Computer clustering
- Inter-process communication techniques

An **IPC (inter-process communication)** is a communication between two or more processes. They can be instances of the same or a different application. The Qt framework provides multiple modules to help you implement a communication between your applications. Most of these modules are cross-platform. Let's talk about the IPC tools provided by Qt.

The first tools are the TCP/IP sockets. They provide a bidirectional data exchange over a network. Therefore, you can use them to talk with processes on different computers. Moreover, the `loopback` interface allows you to communicate with processes running on the same computer. All the required classes are inside the `QtNetwork` module. This technique relies on a client-server architecture. Here is an example of the server part:

```
QTcpServer* tcpServer = new QTcpServer(this);
tcpServer->listen(QHostAddress::Any, 5000);

connect(tcpServer, &QTcpServer::newConnection, [tcpServer] {
    QTcpSocket *tcpSocket = tcpServer->nextPendingConnection();
    QByteArray response = QString("Hello").toLatin1();
    tcpSocket->write(response);
    tcpSocket->disconnectFromHost();
    qDebug() << "Send response and close the socket";
});
```

The first step is to instantiate a `QTcpServer` class. It deals with the new incoming TCP connections. Then, we call the `listen()` function. You can provide a network interface and specify the port on which the server must listen for incoming connections. In this example, we listen on all network addresses (for example, `127.0.0.1`, `192.168.1.4`, and so on) on the port `5000`. When a client establishes a connection with this server, the `QTcpServer::newConnection()` signal is triggered. Let's break together this lambda slot:

1. We retrieve the `QTcpSocket` class related to this new connection with a client.
2. A `QByteArray` response is prepared with the ASCII message "Hello". Forget the lack of originality.
3. The message is sent to the client through the socket.
4. Finally, we close the socket. So the client, on this side, will be disconnected.

You can test a `QTcpServer` class with a telnet tool like Putty on Windows or the `telnet` command on Linux and Mac OS.

The following snippet is the client part:

```
QTcpSocket *tcpSocket = new QTcpSocket(this);
tcpSocket->connectToHost("127.0.0.1", 5000);

connect(tcpSocket, &QTcpSocket::connected, [tcpSocket] {
    qDebug() << "connected";
});
```

```
connect(tcpSocket, &QTcpSocket::readyRead, [tcpSocket] {
    qDebug() << QString::fromLatin1(tcpSocket->readAll());
});
connect(tcpSocket, &QTcpSocket::disconnected, [tcpSocket] {
    qDebug() << "disconnected";
});
```

The client also uses a `QTcpSocket` class to communicate. It turns out that the connection is initiated by the client, therefore we need to call the `connectToHost()` function with the server address and port. This class provides a lot of useful signals such as `connected()` and `disconnected()` that indicate the connection status. The `readyRead()` signal is emitted when new data is available for reading. The `readAll()` function returns `QByteArray` with all the available data. In our case, we know that the server sends an ASCII message to its client. Thus, we can convert this byte array in a `QString` and display it.

For this example, the server writes in the TCP socket and the client reads in it. But this communication is bidirectional, so the client can also write data and the server can read it. Try to send data from the client and display it in the server. Notice that you need to keep the communication alive by removing the `disconnectFromHost()` call in the server part.

The Qt framework provides a helper class, `QDataStream`, to easily send a complex object and handle the package fragmentation. This notion will be covered later with the project example of this chapter.

Let's talk about the second IPC technique: **shared memory**. By default, different processes do not use the same memory space. The `QSharedMemory` class provides a cross-platform method to create and use a shared memory across multiple processes. Nevertheless, the processes must run on the same computer. A shared memory is identified by a key. All the processes must use the same key to share the same shared memory segment. The first process will create the shared memory segment and put data in it:

```
QString sharedMessage("Hello");
QByteArray sharedData = sharedMessage.toLatin1();

QSharedMemory* sharedMemory = new QSharedMemory(
    "sharedMemoryKey", this);
sharedMemory->create(sharedMessage.size());

sharedMemory->lock();

memcpy(sharedMemory->data(),
       sharedData.data(),
       sharedData.size());
```

```
sharedMemory->unlock();
```

Let's analyze all the steps together:

1. Once again, we want to share the `QString` "Hello" converted in a `QByteArray` class.

2. A `QSharedMemory` class is initialized with the key, `sharedMemoryKey`. This same key should be used by the second process.

3. The first process creates the shared memory segment with a specific size in bytes. The creation also attaches the process to the shared memory segment.

4. You should now be confident with the lock/unlock system. The `QSharedMemory` class uses semaphore to protect the shared access. You must lock it before manipulating the shared memory.

5. A classical `memcpy()` function is used to copy data from the `QByteArray` class to the `QSharedMemory` class.

6. Finally, we can unlock the shared memory.

Destroying a `QShareMemory` class will call the `detach()` function that detaches the process from the shared memory segment. If this process was the last one attached, `detach()` also destroys the shared memory segment. While an attached `QShareMemory` is alive, the shared memory segment is available for other processes. The next snippet describes how a second segment can access the shared memory:

```
QSharedMemory* sharedMemory = new QSharedMemory(
    "sharedMemoryKey", this);
sharedMemory->attach();

sharedMemory->lock();

QByteArray sharedData(sharedMemory->size(), '\0');

memcpy(sharedData.data(),
        sharedMemory->data(),
        sharedMemory->size());
sharedMemory->unlock();

QString sharedMessage = QString::fromLatin1(sharedData);
qDebug() << sharedMessage;

sharedMemory->detach();
```

Here are the key steps:

1. As with the first process, this second process initializes a QShareMemory class with the key, sharedMemoryKey.
2. Then we attach the process to the shared memory segment with the attach() function.
3. We must lock the QShareMemory class before accessing it.
4. We initialize a QByteArray with the null character, \0, with the size of the shared memory.
5. The memcpy() function copies the data from the QShareMemory to the QByteArray.
6. We can convert the QByteArray in a QString and display our message.
7. The last step is to call the detach() function to detach the process from the shared memory segment.

Please notice that create() and attach() functions specify by default a QShareMemory::ReadWrite access. You can also use the QShareMemory::ReadOnly access.

You can use the classes, QBuffer and QDataStream to serialize a complex object in or from a bytes array.

Another IPC way is to use the QProcess class. The main process starts an external application as a child process. The communication is done using the standard input and output devices. Let's create a hello console application relying on the standard input and output channels:

```
QTextStream out(stdout);
QTextStream in(stdin);

out << QString("Please enter your name:\n");
out.flush();

QString name = in.readLine();

out << "Hello " << name << "\n";
return 0;
```

We use the QTextStream class to easily work with the standards streams, stdout and stdin. The application prints the message Please enter your name:. Then we wait while the user types his name by calling the readLine() function. Finally, the program displays the message Hello and the user name. If you start yourself this console application, you must type your name on the keyboard to see the final hello message with your name.

The following snippet runs and communicates with the hello application. Furthermore, we can programmatically control the child hello application:

```
QProcess* childProcess = new QProcess(this);

connect(childProcess,
    &QProcess::readReadStandardOutput, [childProcess] {
        qDebug().noquote() << "[*]" << childProcess->readAll();
});

connect(childProcess, &QProcess::started, [childProcess] {
    childProcess->write("Sophie\n");
});

childProcess->start("/path/to/hello");
```

Here are all the steps performed by this main application:

1. We initialize a QProcess object that can start an external application.
2. The child process displays messages on the console and so writes in the standard output. Then, the readReadStandardOutput() signal is sent. In this case, we print the message as debug text with the prefix [*] to identify that it comes from the child process.
3. As soon as the child process is started, the started() signal is sent. In our case, we write in the child standard input the name Sophie (Lenna will be jealous!).
4. All is ready, we can start the QProcess class with the path to the hello console application.

If you start the main application you should get this result in its console:

```
[*] Please enter your name:
[*] Hello Sophie
```

Mission completed! The main application is a wrapper for the hello application. We receive all messages from the child process and we can send it some information like a specific name.

The `QProcess::start()` function also accepts a second variable: the command line arguments for the child process.

The last IPC mechanism that we will cover together is the **D-Bus protocol**. Currently, the Qt D-Bus module is officially supported only on Linux. If you need to use it on Windows, you will have to compile it from Qt sources. It can be seen as a unified protocol for IPC and **RPC (remote procedure calling)**. Many forms of communication are possible, such as:

- One-to-one
- One-to-many
- Many-to-many

The best thing about Qt D-Bus is that you can even use the signal/slot mechanism across the bus. A signal emitted from one application can be connected to a slot from another application. Linux desktop environments like KDE and GNOME use the D-Bus. That implies that you can (also) control your desktop with D-Bus.

Here are the main concepts of D-Bus:

- `Bus`: This is used in many-to-many communication. D-Bus defines two buses: the **system bus** and the **session bus**.
- `Service name`: This is the identifier of a service on a bus.
- `Message`: This is a message sent by one application. If a bus is used, the message contains the destination.

A Qt D-Bus Viewer tool can be found in your Qt installation folder (for example, `/Qt/5.7/gcc_64/bin/qdbusviewer`). All objects and messages from all services of the system and the session bus are displayed. Try to invoke exposed methods and retrieve a result.

Now that you have messed about with your Linux D-Bus services, it is time to create your own! At first, we will create a simple `HelloService` object:

```cpp
//HelloService.h
class HelloService : public QObject
{
    Q_OBJECT

public slots:
    QString sayHello(const QString &name);
};
```

```
//HelloService.cpp
QString HelloService::sayHello(const QString& name)
{
    qDebug().noquote() << name << " is here!";
    return QString("Hello %1!").arg(name);;
}
```

No big deal here, the only function is a public slot that requires a `name`, displays who is here, and returns a hello message. In the following snippet, the main application registers a new D-Bus service and the `HelloService` object:

```
HelloService helloService;
QString serviceName("org.masteringqt.QtDBus.HelloService");

QDBusConnection::sessionBus().registerService(serviceName);
QDBusConnection::sessionBus().registerObject("/",
    &helloService, QDBusConnection::ExportAllSlots);
```

The main application initializes an `HelloService` object. Then, we register a new service named `org.masteringqt.QtDBus.HelloService` on the session bus. Finally, we register the `HelloService` object, exposing all its slots. Notice the simple object path / used for this example. The service application part is finished. Here is the client application calling the `HelloService` object:

```
QString serviceName("org.masteringqt.QtDBus.HelloService");
QDBusInterface serviceInterface(serviceName, "/");
QDBusReply<QString> response = serviceInterface.call(
    "sayHello", "Lenna");
qDebug().noquote() << response;
```

Let's analyze the client part step by step:

1. We initialize a `QDBusInterface` object with the same service name and path as the service application.
2. We call the remote method, `sayHello()` on `HelloService`, with the parameter `Lenna` (Wait, where is Sophie!?).
3. The response is stored in a `QDBusReply` object. In our case, type `QString`.
4. Finally, we display the message generated by the `HelloService` object.

If you start the service application and then the client application, you should get this console output:

```
//service application output
Lenna is here!
```

```
//client application output
Hello Lenna!
```

Use the `QDBusViewer` tool to find your D-Bus service. Select the **Session Bus** tab. Choose your service in the list. Then you can select the method `sayHello`. A right-click on it allows you to call the method. An input popup will ask you to fill the method parameter that is a name in our example. The following screenshot shows you what it looks like (it seems that Sophie is here):

# Architecturing an IPC project

The Mandelbrot picture generator from `Chapter 9`, *Keeping Your Sanity with Multithreading*, uses all cores of your computer to speed up the computing. This time, we want to use all the cores of all your computers! The first thing to do is to choose an appropriated IPC technique. For this project example, we want to establish communication between several clients acting as workers to a server running the main application. The TCP/IP sockets allows a one-to-many communication. Moreover, this IPC method is not bounded to a single computer and can operate through a network on multiple computers. This project example uses sockets by implementing a multi-threaded TCP server.

The next diagram describes the architecture:

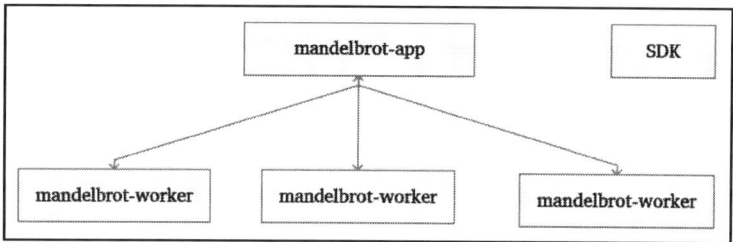

Let's talk about the global role of each actor:

- `mandelbrot-app`: This is the main application displaying the Mandelbrot picture and handling user mouse events. However, in this chapter, the application does not compute the algorithm itself but rather generates requests to connected workers. Then, it aggregates results provided by workers.
- `mandelbrot-worker`: Here is our minion! A worker is a standalone program. It is connecting to the `mandelbrot-app` through a TCP socket. A worker receives a request, computes a job, and sends back a result.
- `SDK`: This regroups common stuff used by both applications. If the SDK changes, all the dependent applications must be updated.

As you can see, this architecture fits well with the one-to-many communication required by this project. The `mandelbrot-app` application can use one or many workers to generate the same Mandelbrot picture.

Now that you get the big picture, let's look in detail at each module. You can see all of the classes in the SDK in the following diagram:

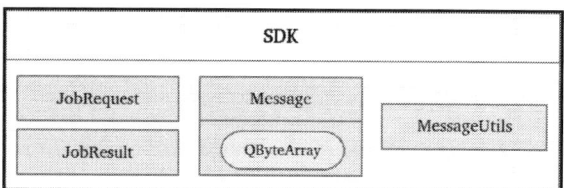

An SDK is essential when you have several modules (applications, libraries, and so on) that communicate together or need to perform the same actions. You can give the SDK to a third-party developer without compromising your main source code. In our project, mandelbrot-app and mandelbrot-worker communicate together by exchanging Message. The message structure must be known by both entities. A Message class contains a type and a raw data of the type, QByteArray. Depending on the message type, the raw data can be empty or can contain an object. In this project, a message data can be a JobRequest or a JobResult. The mandelbrot-app sends a JobRequest to mandelbrot-worker. Then, the worker returns JobResult to the main application. Finally, MessageUtils contains functions used by the main application and the workers to send and retrieve a Message.

We can now talk about the mandelbrot-worker in more detail. The next diagram describes it:

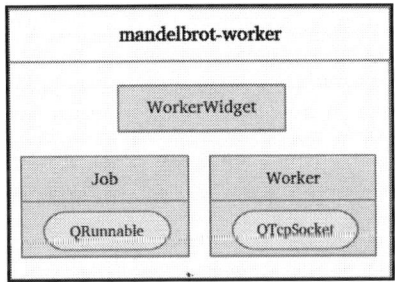

The mandelbrot-worker program is able to use all the CPU cores of a machine. The socket mechanism allows us to run it on multiple physical machines at the same time. The WorkerWidget class displays the status of the Worker object. The Worker object handles the communication with mandelbrot-app using a QTcpSocket. A Job is a QRunnable class that computes a task. Here is the workflow of this software:

1. Send a register Message to mandelbrot-app application.
2. Receive some JobRequest from mandelbrot-app and create several Job instances to complete all tasks.
3. Each Job is running in a dedicated thread and will generate a JobResult.
4. Send JobResult to mandelbrot-app.
5. On exit, send an unregister Message to mandelbrot-app.

It is now time to talk about the `mandelbrot-app` architecture. Look at the next diagram:

This is the main application. You can launch it on a computer with a weak CPU and the real heavy work is done by workers running the `mandelbrot-worker` software. The GUI `MainWindow` and `MandelbrotWidget` objects are the same as those in `Chapter 9`, *Keeping Your Sanity with Multithreading*. The `MandelbrotCalculator` class is a little different in this project, because it does not run any `QRunnable` itself. It is a TCP server that handles all registered workers and dispatches tasks to those tasks. Each `mandelbrot-worker` is managed by a `WorkerClient` object instance with a dedicated `QTcpSocket`. Here is the workflow for `mandelbrot-app`:

1. Run a TCP server on a specific port.
2. Receive a register `Message` and create a `WorkerClient` object for each registered worker.
3. When `MandelbrotWidget` requests a picture generation, `MandelbrotCalculator` creates the `JobRequest` object required to compute the full Mandelbrot picture.
4. The `JobRequest` objects are sent to the workers.
5. Receive and aggregate `JobResult` from the `mandelbrot-worker`.
6. Transmit `JobResult` to the `MandelbrotWidget` object that displays the picture.
7. If an unregister `Message` is received from a worker, the `WorkerClient` object is released and this worker will not be used for picture generation anymore.

You should now get a complete overview of this project architecture. We can begin the implementation of this project. Create a **Subdirs** project called `ch10-mandelbrot-ipc`. As you might guess, we now create two sub-projects: `mandelbrot-app` and `mandelbrot-worker`.

The implementation in the subsequent sections follows the architecture presentation order:

1. SDK.
2. `mandelbrot-worker`.
3. `mandelbrot-app`.

The implementation is a step up in complexity. Do not hesitate to take a break and come back to this section to keep the overall architecture clear.

# Laying down the foundations with an SDK

The first step is to implement the classes that will be shared between our application and the workers. To do so, we are going to rely on a custom SDK. If you need to refresh your memory about this technique, take a look at `Chapter 8`, *Animations– It's Alive, Alive!*.

As a reminder, here is the diagram describing the SDK:

Let's describe the job of each of these components:

- The `Message` component encapsulates a piece of information that is exchanged between the application and the worker
- The `JobRequest` component contains the necessary information to dispatch a proper job to a worker
- The `JobResult` component contains the result of the Mandelbrot set calculation for a given line
- The `MessageUtils` component contains helper functions to serialize/deserialize data across the TCP socket

All these files have to be accessible from each side of our IPC mechanism (application and worker). Note that the SDK will contain only header files. We did it on purpose to simplify the SDK usage.

Let's start with `Message` implementation in the `sdk` directory. Create a `Message.h` file with the following content:

```cpp
#include <QByteArray>

struct Message {

    enum class Type {
        WORKER_REGISTER,
        WORKER_UNREGISTER,
        ALL_JOBS_ABORT,
        JOB_REQUEST,
        JOB_RESULT,
    };

    Message(const Type type = Type::WORKER_REGISTER,
            const QByteArray& data = QByteArray()) :
        type(type),
        data(data)
    {
    }

    ~Message() {}

    Type type;
    QByteArray data;
};
```

The first thing to note is the `enum class Type` which details all the possible message types:

- `WORKER_REGISTER`: This is the message sent by the worker when it first connects to the application. The content of the message is only the number of cores of the worker's CPU. We will see soon why this is useful.
- `WORKER_UNREGISTER`: This is the message sent by the worker when it is disconnected. This lets the application know that it should remove this worker from its list and stop sending any messages to it.
- `ALL_JOBS_ABORT`: This is the message sent by the application each time a picture generation is canceled. The worker is then responsible for canceling all its current local threads.
- `JOB_REQUEST`: This is the message sent by the application to calculate a specific line of the desired picture.
- `JOB_RESULT`: This is the message sent by the worker with the calculated result from the `JOB_REQUEST` inputs.

A quick word about the `enum` class type, which is a C++11 addition. It is a safer version of enum (some might say that it is enum as it should have been from the beginning):

- The scope of the values is local. In this example, you can only reference an `enum` value with the syntax `Message::Type::WORKER_REGISTER`; no more `Message::WORKER_REGISTER` shortcuts. The good thing about this restriction is that you do not need to prefix `enum` values with a `MESSAGE_TYPE_` to be sure that the name does not conflict with anything else.
- There is no implicit conversion to `int`. The `enum` class acts like a real type, to cast an `enum` class to `int`, you have to write `static_cast<int>(Message::Type::WORKER_REGISTER)`.
- There is no forward declaration. You can specify that an `enum class` is a char type (with the syntax `enum class Test : char { ... }`), but the compiler will not be able to deduce the `enum` class size with a forward declaration. Therefore, it has been simply forbidden.

We tend to use the `enum` class whenever possible, meaning when it does not clash with Qt `enum` usage.

As you can see, a message has only two members:

- `type`: This is the message type we just described
- `data`: This is an opaque type that contains the piece of information to be transmitted

We chose to make `data` very generic to place the responsibility of serializing/deserializing on the `Message` callers. Based on the message `type`, they should know how to read or write the message content.

By using this approach, we avoid a tangled class hierarchy with `MessageRegister`, `MessageUnregister`, and so on. Adding a new `Message type` is simply adding a value in the `Type enum class` and doing the proper serialization/deserialization in `data` (which you have to do anyway).

To see the file in Qt Creator, do not forget to add the `Message.h` in `ch10-mandelbrot-ipc.pro` file:

```
OTHER_FILES += \
sdk/Message.h
```

The next header we will look at is `JobRequest.h`:

```
#include <QSize>
#include <QPointF>

struct JobRequest
{
    int pixelPositionY;
    QPointF moveOffset;
    double scaleFactor;
    QSize areaSize;
    int iterationMax;
};

Q_DECLARE_METATYPE(JobRequest)

// In ch10-mandelbrot-ipc
OTHER_FILES += \
    sdk/Message.h \
    sdk/JobRequest.h
```

This `struct` element contains all the necessary data for the worker to calculate a line of the target Mandelbrot picture. Because the application and the worker(s) will live in different memory spaces (or even different physical machines), the parameters to calculate the Mandelbrot set have to be transmitted somehow. This is the purpose of `JobRequest`. The meaning of each field is the same as `JobResult` from Chapter 9, *Keeping Your Sanity with Multithreading*.

Note the presence of the `Q_DECLARE_METATYPE(JobRequest)` macro. This macro is used to let the Qt meta-object system know about `JobRequest`. This is needed to be able to use the class in conjunction with `QVariant`. We will not use `QVariant` directly, but rather through the use of `QDataStream` which relies on `QVariant`.

Speaking of `JobResult`, here is the new `JobResult.h`:

```
#include <QSize>
#include <QVector>
#include <QPointF>

struct JobResult
{
    JobResult(int valueCount = 1) :
        areaSize(0, 0),
        pixelPositionY(0),
        moveOffset(0, 0),
        scaleFactor(0.0),
```

```
        values(valueCount)
    {
    }

    QSize areaSize;
    int pixelPositionY;
    QPointF moveOffset;
    double scaleFactor;

    QVector<int> values;
};

Q_DECLARE_METATYPE(JobResult)

// In ch10-mandelbrot-ipc
OTHER_FILES += \
    sdk/Message.h \
    sdk/JobRequest.h \
    sdk/JobResult.h
```

The new version is a shameless copy-paste (with the small Q_DECLARE_METATYPE addition) of the project example of Chapter 9, *Keeping Your Sanity with Multithreading*.

# Working with QDataStream and QTcpSocket

The missing piece of the SDK is MesssageUtils. It deserves a dedicated section because it covers two major topics: serialization and QDataStream transactions.

We will start with the serialization. We already know that Message stores only an opaque QByteArray data member. As a consequence, the desired data has to be serialized as a QByteArray before being passed to Message.

If we take the example of a JobRequest object, it is not directly sent. We first put in in a generic Message object with the appropriate Message type. The following diagram summarizes the sequence of actions to be done:

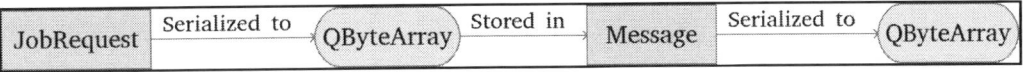

The JobRequest object is first serialized to a QByteArray class; it is then passed to a Message instance which is in turn serialized to a final QByteArray. The deserialization process is the exact mirror of this sequence (from right to left).

Serializing data brings a lot of questions. How can we do it in a generic fashion? How do we handle the possible endianness of the CPU architecture? How do we specify the length of the data to be able to deserialize it properly?

Once again, the Qt folks did a great job and provided us a great tool to deal with these issues: QDataStream.

The QDataStream class enables you to serialize binary data to any QIODevice (QAbstractSocket, QProcess, QFileDevice, QSerialPort, and so on). The great advantage of QDataStream is that it encodes the information in a platform-agnostic format. You do not have to worry about the byte order, the operating system, or the CPU.

The QDataStream class implements the serialization of C++ primitive types and several Qt type (QBrush, QColor, QString, and so on). Here is an example of a basic write:

```
QFile file("myfile");
file.open(QIODevice::WriteOnly);
QDataStream out(&file);
out << QString("QDataStream saved my day");
out << (qint32)42;
```

As you can see, QDataStream relies on the overload of the << operator to write data. To read information, open the file with the correct mode and read with the >> operator.

Back to our case; we want to serialize custom classes, like JobRequest. To do so, we have to overload the << operator for JobRequest. The signature of the function will be like so:

```
QDataStream& operator<<(QDataStream& out,
                        const JobRequest& jobRequest)
```

What we write have here is that we want to overload the out << jobRequest operator call with our custom version. By doing so, we intend to fill the out object with the content of jobRequest. Because QDataStream already supports the serialization of primitive types, all we have to do is serialize them.

Here is the updated version of JobRequest.h:

```
#include <QSize>
#include <QPointF>
#include <QDataStream>

struct JobRequest
{
    ...
};
```

```
inline QDataStream& operator<<(QDataStream& out,
                               const JobRequest& jobRequest)
{
    out << jobRequest.pixelPositionY
        << jobRequest.moveOffset
        << jobRequest.scaleFactor
        << jobRequest.areaSize
        << jobRequest.iterationMax;
    return out;
}

inline QDataStream& operator>>(QDataStream& in,
                               JobRequest& jobRequest)
{
    in >> jobRequest.pixelPositionY;
    in >> jobRequest.moveOffset;
    in >> jobRequest.scaleFactor;
    in >> jobRequest.areaSize;
    in >> jobRequest.iterationMax;
    return in;
}
```

We include `QDataStream` and overload the `<<` very easily. The returned `out` will be updated with the platform-agnostic content of the passed `jobRequest`. The `>>` operator overload follows the same pattern: we fill the `jobRequest` parameter with the content of the `in` variable. Behind the scenes, `QDataStream` stores the variable size in the serialized data to be able to read it afterwards.

Be careful to serialize and deserialize the members in the same order. If you do not pay attention to this, you might encounter very peculiar values in `JobRequest`.

The `JobResult` operators overload follows the same pattern, and it does not deserve to be included in the chapter. Look at the source code of the project if you have any doubt about its implementation.

On the other hand, `Message` operator overload needs to be covered:

```
#include <QByteArray>
#include <QDataStream>

#include <QByteArray>
#include <QDataStream>

struct Message {
    ...
};
```

```
inline QDataStream &operator<<(QDataStream &out, const Message &message)
{
    out <<  static_cast<qint8>(message.type)
        << message.data;
    return out;
}

inline QDataStream &operator>>(QDataStream &in, Message &message)
{
    qint8 type;
    in >> type;
    in >> message.data;

    message.type = static_cast<Message::Type>(type);
    return in;
}
```

Because the Message::Type enum class signal does not have an implicit conversion to int, we need to explicitly convert it to be able to serialize it. We know that there will not be more than 255 message types, therefore we can safely cast it to a qint8 type.

The same story applies to the reading part. We start by declaring a qint8 type variable that will be filled with in >> type, and then, the type variable is casted to a Message::Type in message.

Our SDK classes are ready to be serialized and deserialized. Let's see it in action in MessageUtils with the serialization of a message and its writing to a QTcpSocket class.

Always in the sdk directory, create a MessageUtils.h header with the following content:

```
#include <QByteArray>
#include <QTcpSocket>
#include <QDataStream>

#include "Message.h"

namespace MessageUtils {

inline void sendMessage(QTcpSocket& socket,
                        Message::Type messageType,
                        QByteArray& data,
                        bool forceFlush = false)
{
    Message message(messageType, data);

    QByteArray byteArray;
    QDataStream stream(&byteArray, QIODevice::WriteOnly);
```

```
        stream << message;
        socket.write(byteArray);
        if (forceFlush) {
            socket.flush();
        }
    }
```

There is no need to instantiate a `MessageUtils` class, as it does not hold any state. Here we used a `MessageUtils` namespace to simply protect our function against any name collision.

The meat of the snippet lies in `sendMessage()`. Let's look at the parameters:

- `socket`: This is the `QTcpSocket` class in which the message will be sent. It is the responsibility of the caller to ensure that it is properly opened.
- `messageType`: This is the type of the message to be sent.
- `data`: This is the serialized data to be included in the message. It is a `QByteArray` class, meaning that the caller already serialized its custom class or data.
- `forceFlush`: This is a flag to force the socket to flush upon the message shipment. The OS keeps socket buffers that wait to be filled before being sent across the wire. Some messages need to be delivered immediately, like an abort all jobs message.

In the function itself, we start by creating a message with the passed parameters. Then, a `QByteArray` class is created. This `byteArray` will be the receptacle of the serialized data.

As a matter of fact, `byteArray` is passed in the constructor of the `QDataStream` stream, which is opened in the `QIODevice::WriteOnly` mode. It means that the stream will output its data to the `byteArray`.

After that, the message is elegantly serialized to stream with `stream << message` and the modified `byteArray` is written to the socket with `socket.write(byteArray)`.

Finally, if the `forceFlush` flag is set to `true`, the socket is flushed with `socket.flush()`.

Some messages will not have any payload associated. For this reason, we add a small helper function for this purpose:

```
    inline void sendMessage(QTcpSocket& socket,
                            Message::Type messageType,
                            bool forceFlush = false) {
        QByteArray data;
        sendMessage(socket, messageType, data, forceFlush);
    }
```

Now that the `sendMessage()` is done, let's turn to the `readMessages()`. Because we are working in IPC and more specifically with sockets, interesting issues arise when we want to read and parse messages.

When something is ready to be read in the socket, a signal will notify us. But how do we know how much to read? In the case of a `WORKER_DISCONNECT` message, there is no payload. On the other hand, a `JOB_RESULT` message can be very heavy. Even worse, several `JOB_RESULT` messages can line up in the socket, waiting to be read.

To make things more difficult, we have to acknowledge the fact that we are working with the network. Packets can be lost, retransmitted, incomplete or whatever. Sure, TCP ensures that we eventually get all of the information, but it can be delayed.

If we had to do it ourselves, it would have implied a custom message header, with a payload size and a footer for each message.

A feature introduced in Qt 5.7 comes to the rescue: `QDataStream` transaction. The idea is the following: when you start reading on a `QIODevice` class, you already know how much you have to read (based on the size of the object you want to fill). However, you might not get all the data in a single read.

If the read is not complete, `QDataStream` stores what was already read in a temporary buffer and restores it upon the next read. The next read will contain what was already loaded plus the content of the new read. You can see it as a checkpoint in the read stream that can be loaded later.

This process can be repeated until data is read. The official documentation provides a simple enough example:

```
in.startTransaction();
qint8 messageType;
QByteArray messageData;
in >> messageType >> messageData;

if (!in.commitTransaction())
    return;
```

In the `QDataStream` class in which we want to read, `in.startTransaction()` marks the checkpoint in the stream. It will then try to read `messageType` and `messageData` atomically. If it cannot do it, `in.commitTransaction()` returns `false` and the read data is copied in an internal buffer.

Upon the next call to this code (more data to read), `in.startTransaction()` will restore the preceding buffer and try to finish the atomic read.

In our `readMessages()` situation, we can receive several messages at once. This is why the code is a bit more complex. Here is the updated version of `MessageUtils`:

```
#include <memory>
#include <vector>
#include <QByteArray>
#include <QTcpSocket>
#include <QDataStream>

#include "Message.h"

...

inline std::unique_ptr<std::vector<std::unique_ptr<Message>>>
readMessages(QDataStream& stream)
{
    auto messages =
std::make_unique<std::vector<std::unique_ptr<Message>>>();
    bool commitTransaction = true;
    while (commitTransaction
                    && stream.device()->bytesAvailable() > 0) {
        stream.startTransaction();
        auto message = std::make_unique<Message>();
        stream >> *message;
        commitTransaction = stream.commitTransaction();
        if (commitTransaction) {
            messages->push_back(std::move(message));
        }
    }
    return messages;
}

}
```

In the function, the parameter is only a `QDataStream`. We assume that the caller linked the stream with the socket with `stream.setDevice(socket)`.

Because we do not know the length of the content to be read, we prepare ourselves to read several messages. To explicitly indicate ownership and avoid any memory leaks, we return a `vector<unique_ptr<Message>>`. This `vector` has to be a `unique_ptr` pointer to be able to allocate it on the heap and avoid any copy during the return of the function.

In the function itself, we start by declaring the `vector`. After that, a `while` loop is executed. The two conditions to stay in the loop are:

- `commitTransaction == true`: This an atomic read in the stream that has been performed; a complete `message` has been read
- `stream.device().bytesAvailable() > 0`: This states that there is still data to read in the stream

In the `while` loop, we start by marking the stream with `stream.startTransaction()`. After that, we try to perform an atomic read of a `*message` signal and see the result with `stream.commitTransaction()`. If it succeeded, the new `message` is added to the `messages` vector. This is repeated until we read all the content of the stream with the `bytesAvailable() > 0` test.

Let's study a use case to understand what will happen. Consider that we receive multiple messages in `readMessages()`:

- The `stream` object will try to read it into `message`.
- The `commitTransaction` variable will be set to `true` and the first message will be added to `messages`.
- If there are still bytes to read in the `stream`, repeat from step one. Otherwise, exit the loop.

To sum up, working with sockets raises its own set of questions. On one hand, it is a very powerful IPC mechanism with a lot of flexibility. On the other hand, it brings a lot of complexity due the nature of the network itself. Luckily, Qt (and moreover Qt 5.7) brings great classes to help us.

Keep in mind that we tolerate the `QDataStream` serialization and transactions overhead because it fits well to our need. If you are working on a constrained embedded platform, you might not have so much liberty about serializing overhead and buffer copies. However, you will still have to rebuild messages by hand for incoming bytes.

# Interacting with sockets in the worker

Now that the SDK is completed, we can turn to the worker. The project is complex enough; we can refresh our memory with the `mandelbrot-worker` architecture:

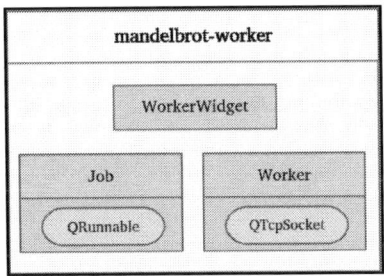

We will start by implementing the `Job` class. Inside the `mandelbrot-worker` project, create a new C++ class named `Job`. Here is the `Job.h` content:

```cpp
#include <QObject>
#include <QRunnable>
#include <QAtomicInteger>

#include "JobRequest.h"
#include "JobResult.h"

class Job : public QObject, public QRunnable
{
    Q_OBJECT
public:
    explicit Job(const JobRequest& jobRequest,
                 QObject *parent = 0);
    void run() override;

signals:
    void jobCompleted(JobResult jobResult);

public slots:
    void abort();

private:
    QAtomicInteger<bool> mAbort;
    JobRequest mJobRequest;
};
```

If you remember the `Job` class from Chapter 9, *Keeping Your Sanity with Multithreading*, this header should ring a bell. The only difference is that the parameters of the job (area size, scale factor, and so on) are extracted from the `JobRequest` object rather than stored directly as member variables.

As you can see, the JobRequest object is provided in the constructor of Job. We will not cover Job.cpp, as it is very much like the version of it in Chapter 9, *Keeping Your Sanity with Multithreading*.

We now proceed to the Worker class. This class has the following roles:

- It interacts with the mandelbrot-app using a QTcpSocket class
- It dispatches JobRequests to a QThreadPool class, aggregates the results, and sends them back to mandelbrot-app application through the QTcpSocket class

We will start by studying the interaction with the QTcpSocket class. Create a new class named Worker with the following header:

```
#include <QObject>
#include <QTcpSocket>
#include <QDataStream>

#include "Message.h"
#include "JobResult.h"

class Worker : public QObject
{
    Q_OBJECT
public:
    Worker(QObject* parent = 0);
    ~Worker();

private:
    void sendRegister();

private:
    QTcpSocket mSocket;
};
```

The Worker class is the owner of mSocket. The first thing we will implement is the connection with mandelbrot-app. Here is the constructor of Worker in Worker.cpp:

```
#include "Worker.h"

#include <QThread>
#include <QDebug>
#include <QHostAddress>

#include "JobRequest.h"
#include "MessageUtils.h"
```

```
Worker::Worker(QObject* parent) :
    QObject(parent),
    mSocket(this)
{
    connect(&mSocket, &QTcpSocket::connected, [this] {
        qDebug() << "Connected";
        sendRegister();
    });
    connect(&mSocket, &QTcpSocket::disconnected, [] {
        qDebug() << "Disconnected";
    });

    mSocket.connectToHost(QHostAddress::LocalHost, 5000);
}
```

The constructor initializes mSocket with this as the parent and it then proceeds to connecting the relevant mSocket signals to lambdas:

- QTcpSocket::connected: When the socket is connected, it will send its register message. We will soon cover this function
- QTcpSocket::disconnected: When the socket is disconnected, it simply prints a message in the console

Finally, mSocket tries to connect on the localhost on the port 5000. In the code example, we assume that you execute the worker and the application on the same machine. Feel free to change this value if you run the worker and the application on different machines.

The body of sendRegister() function looks like this:

```
void Worker::sendRegister()
{
    QByteArray data;
    QDataStream out(&data, QIODevice::WriteOnly);
    out << QThread::idealThreadCount();
    MessageUtils::sendMessage(mSocket,
                              Message::Type::WORKER_REGISTER,
                              data);
}
```

A QByteArray class is filled with the idealThreadCount function of the worker's machine. After that, we call MessageUtils::sendMessage to serialize the message and send it through our mSocket.

Once the worker is registered, it will start to receive job requests, process them, and send job results back. Here is the updated `Worker.h`:

```
class Worker : public QObject
{
    ...
signals:
    void abortAllJobs();

private slots:
    void readMessages();

private:
    void handleJobRequest(Message& message);
    void handleAllJobsAbort(Message& message);
    void sendRegister();
    void sendJobResult(JobResult jobResult);
    void sendUnregister();
    Job* createJob(const JobRequest& jobRequest);

private:
    QTcpSocket mSocket;
    QDataStream mSocketReader;
    int mReceivedJobsCounter;
    int mSentJobsCounter;
};
```

Let's review the role of each one of these new members:

- `mSocketReader`: This is the `QDataStream` class through which we will read `mSocket` content. It will be passed as a parameter to our `MessageUtils::readMessages()` function.
- `mReceivedJobsCounter`: This is incremented each time a new `JobRequest` is received from `mandelbrot-app`.
- `mSentJobsCounter`: This is incremented each time a new `JobResult` is sent to `mandelbrot-app`.

Now for the new functions:

- `abortAllJobs()`: This is a signal emitted when the `Worker` class receives the appropriate message.
- `readMessages()`: This is the slot called each time there is something to read in `mTcpSocket`. It parses the messages and, for each message type, it will call the corresponding function.

- `handleJobRequest()`: This function creates and dispatches a `Job` class according to the `JobRequest` object contained in the message parameter.
- `handleAllJobsAbort()`: This function cancels all the current jobs and clear the thread queue.
- `sendJobResult()`: This function sends the `JobResult` object to `mandelbrot-app`.
- `sendUnregister()`: This function sends the unregister message to `mandelbrot-app`.
- `createJob()`: This is a helper function to create and properly connect the signals of a new `Job`.

The header is now complete. We can proceed to the updated constructor in `Worker.cpp`:

```
Worker::Worker(QObject* parent) :
    QObject(parent),
    mSocket(this),
    mSocketReader(&mSocket),
    mReceivedJobsCounter(0),
    mSentJobsCounter(0)
{
    ...
    connect(&mSocket, &QTcpSocket::readRead,
            this, &Worker::readMessages);

    mSocket.connectToHost(QHostAddress::LocalHost, 5000);
}
```

The `QDataStream mSocketReader` variable is initialized with the address of `mSocket`. This means that it will read its content from the `QIODevice` class. After that, we add the new connect to the `QTcpSocket` signal, `readyRead()`. Each time that data is available to read on the socket, our slot, `readMessages()`, will be called.

Here is the implementation of `readMessages()`:

```
void Worker::readMessages()
{
    auto messages = MessageUtils::readMessages(mSocketReader);
    for(auto& message : *messages) {
        switch (message->type) {
            case Message::Type::JOB_REQUEST:
                handleJobRequest(*message);
                break;
            case Message::Type::ALL_JOBS_ABORT:
                handleAllJobsAbort(*message);
```

```
                    break;
            default:
                break;
        }
    }
}
```

The messages are parsed with the `MessageUtils::readMessages()` function. Note the use of C++11 semantics with `auto`, which elegantly hides the smart pointers syntax and still handles the memory for us.

For each parsed `message`, it is handled in the `switch` case. Let's review `handleJobRequest()`:

```
void Worker::handleJobRequest(Message& message)
{
    QDataStream in(&message.data, QIODevice::ReadOnly);
    QList<JobRequest> requests;
    in >> requests;

    mReceivedJobsCounter += requests.size();
    for(const JobRequest& jobRequest : requests) {
        QThreadPool::globalInstance()
                ->start(createJob(jobRequest));
    }
}
```

In this function, the `message` object is already deserialized. However, `message.data` still needs to be deserialized. To achieve this, we create a `QDataStream` in a variable that will read from `message.data`.

From here, we parse the requests `QList`. Because `QList` already overrides the `>>` operator, it works in cascade and calls our `JobRequest` `>>` operator overload. Deserializing data has never been so easy!

After that, we increment `mReceivedJobsCounter` and start processing these `JobRequests`. For each one, we create a `Job` class and dispatch it to the global `QThreadPool` class. If you have a doubt about `QThreadPool`, get back to `Chapter 9`, *Keeping Your Sanity with Multithreading*.

The `createJob()` function is straightforward to implement:

```
Job* Worker::createJob(const JobRequest& jobRequest)
{
    Job* job = new Job(jobRequest);
    connect(this, &Worker::abortAllJobs,
```

```
                    job, &Job::abort);
        connect(job, &Job::jobCompleted,
                this, &Worker::sendJobResult);
        return job;
    }
```

A new `Job` class is created and its signals are properly connected.
When `Worker::abortAllJobs` is emitted, every running `Job` should be canceled with
the `Job::abort` slot.

The second signal, `Job::jobCompleted` is emitted when the `Job` class has finished
calculating its values. Let's see the connected slot, `sendJobResult()`:

```
    void Worker::sendJobResult(JobResult jobResult)
    {
        mSentJobsCounter++;
        QByteArray data;
        QDataStream out(&data, QIODevice::WriteOnly);
        out << jobResult;
        MessageUtils::sendMessage(mSocket,
                                  Message::Type::JOB_RESULT,
                                  data);
    }
```

We first increment the `mSentJobsCounter` and then serialize the `JobResult` to
a `QByteArray` data which is passed to `MessageUtils::sendMessage()`.

We completed the tour of the `JobRequest` handling and the following `JobResult`
shipment. We still have to cover `handleAllJobsAbort()`, which is called
from `readMessages()`:

```
    void Worker::handleAllJobsAbort(Message& /*message*/)
    {
        emit abortAllJobs();
        QThreadPool::globalInstance()->clear();
        mReceivedJobsCounter = 0;
        mSentJobsCounter = 0;
    }
```

The `abortAllJobs()` signal is emitted first to tell all the running jobs to cancel their
process. After that, the `QThreadPool` class is cleared and the counters are reset.

The last piece of `Worker` is the `sendUnregister()`, which is called in the `Worker` destructor:

```
Worker::~Worker()
{
    sendUnregister();
}

void Worker::sendUnregister()
{
    MessageUtils::sendMessage(mSocket,
                              Message::Type::WORKER_UNREGISTER,
                              true);
}
```

The `sendUnregister()` function just calls `sendMessage` without any data to serialize. Note that it passes the `forceFlush` flag to `true` to make sure that the socket is flushed and that `mandelbrot-app` application will receive the message as fast as possible.

The `Worker` instance will be managed by a widget which will display the progress of the current calculation. Create a new class named `WorkerWidget` and update `WorkerWidget.h`, like so:

```
#include <QWidget>
#include <QThread>
#include <QProgressBar>
#include <QTimer>

#include "Worker.h"

class WorkerWidget : public QWidget
{
    Q_OBJECT
public:
    explicit WorkerWidget(QWidget *parent = 0);
    ~WorkerWidget();

private:
    QProgressBar mStatus;
    Worker mWorker;
    QThread mWorkerThread;
    QTimer mRefreshTimer;
};
```

The members of `WorkerWidget` are:

- `mStatus`: The `QProgressBar` that will display the percentage of processed `JobRequests`
- `mWorker`: The `Worker` instance owned and started by `WorkerWidget`
- `mWorkerThread`: The `QThread` class in which `mWorker` will be executed
- `mRefreshTimer`: The `QTimer` class that will periodically poll `mWorker` to know the process advancement

We can proceed to `WorkerWidget.cpp`:

```
#include "WorkerWidget.h"

#include <QVBoxLayout>

WorkerWidget::WorkerWidget(QWidget *parent) :
    QWidget(parent),
    mStatus(this),
    mWorker(),
    mWorkerThread(this),
    mRefreshTimer()
{
    QVBoxLayout* layout = new QVBoxLayout(this);
    layout->addWidget(&mStatus);

    mWorker.moveToThread(&mWorkerThread);

    connect(&mRefreshTimer, &QTimer::timeout, [this] {
        mStatus.setMaximum(mWorker.receivedJobsCounter());
        mStatus.setValue(mWorker.sentJobCounter());
    });

    mWorkerThread.start();
    mRefreshTimer.start(100);
}

WorkerWidget::~WorkerWidget()
{
    mWorkerThread.quit();
    mWorkerThread.wait(1000);
}
```

First, the `mStatus` variable is added to the `WorkerWidget` layout. Then the `mWorker` thread affinity is moved to `mWorkerThread` and `mRefreshTimer` is configured to poll `mWorker` and update `mStatus` data.

Finally, `mWorkerThread` is started, triggering the `mWorker` process. The `mRefreshTimer` object is also started with an interval of 100 milliseconds between each timeout.

The last thing to cover in `mandelbrot-worker` is the `main.cpp`:

```
#include <QApplication>

#include "JobResult.h"

#include "WorkerWidget.h"

int main(int argc, char *argv[])
{
    qRegisterMetaType<JobResult>();

    QApplication a(argc, argv);
    WorkerWidget workerWidget;

    workerWidget.show();
    return a.exec();
}
```

We start by registering `JobResult` with `qRegisterMetaType` because it is used in the signal/slot mechanism. After that, we instantiate a `WorkerWidget` layout and display it.

# Interacting with sockets from the application

The next project to complete is `mandelbrot-app`. It will contain the `QTcpServer` that will interact with the workers and the picture drawing of the Mandelbrot set. As a reminder, the diagram of the `mandelbrot-app` architecture is shown here:

We will build this application from the ground up. Let's start with the class responsible for maintaining the connection with a specific `Worker`: `WorkerClient`. This class will live in its specific `QThread` and will interact with a `Worker` class using the same `QTcpSocket`/`QDataStream` mechanism we covered in the last section.

In `mandelbrot-app`, create a new C++ class named `WorkerClient` and update `WorkerClient.h` like so:

```
#include <QTcpSocket>
#include <QList>
#include <QDataStream>

#include "JobRequest.h"
#include "JobResult.h"
#include "Message.h"

class WorkerClient : public QObject
{
    Q_OBJECT
public:
    WorkerClient(int socketDescriptor);

private:
    int mSocketDescriptor;
    int mCpuCoreCount;
    QTcpSocket mSocket;
    QDataStream mSocketReader;
};

Q_DECLARE_METATYPE(WorkerClient*)
```

It looks very similar to `Worker`. Yet it may behave differently from a life cycle point of view. Each time a new `Worker` connects to our `QTcpServer`, a new `WorkerClient` will be spawned with an associated `QThread`. The `WorkerClient` object will take the responsibility of interacting with the `Worker` class through the `mSocket`.

If the `Worker` disconnects, the `WorkerClient` object will be deleted and removed from the `QTcpServer` class.

Let's review the content of this header, starting with the members:

- `mSocketDescriptor`: This is the unique integer assigned by the system to interact with the socket. `stdin`, `stdout`, and `stderr` are also descriptors that point to specific streams in your application. For a given socket, the value will be retrieved in `QTcpServer`. More on this later on.

- mCpuCoreCount: This is the CPU core count for the connected Worker. This field will be initialized when the Worker sends the WORKER_REGISTER message.
- mSocket: This is the QTcpSocket used to interact with the Worker class.
- mSocketReader: This has the same role it had in Worker – it reads mSocket content.

Now we can add the functions to WorkerClient.h:

```cpp
class WorkerClient : public QObject
{
    Q_OBJECT
public:
    WorkerClient(int socketDescriptor);
    int cpuCoreCount() const;

signals:
    void unregistered(WorkerClient* workerClient);
    void jobCompleted(WorkerClient* workerClient,
                      JobResult jobResult);
    void sendJobRequests(QList<JobRequest> requests);

public slots:
    void start();
    void abortJob();

private slots:
    void readMessages();
    void doSendJobRequests(QList<JobRequest> requests);

private:
    void handleWorkerRegistered(Message& message);
    void handleWorkerUnregistered(Message& message);
    void handleJobResult(Message& message);

    ...
};
```

Let's see what each function does:

- WorkerClient(): This function expects a socketDescriptor as a parameter. As a consequence, a WorkerClient function cannot be initialized without a valid socket.
- cpuCoreCount(): This function is a simple getter to let the owner of WorkerClient know how many cores the Worker has.

The class has three signals:

- unregister(): This is the signal sent by WorkerClient when it has received the WORKER_UNREGISTER message.
- jobCompleted(): This is the signal sent by WorkerClient when it has received the JOB_RESULT message. It will pass by copying the deserialized JobResult.
- sendJobRequests(): This is emitted from the owner of WorkerClient to pass JobRequests in a queued connection to the proper slot: doSendJobRequests().

Here are the details of the slots:

- start(): This slot is called when WorkerClient can start its process. Typically, it will be connected to the start signal of the QThread associated with the WorkerClient.
- abortJob(): This slot triggers the shipment of the ALL_JOBS_ABORT message to the Worker.
- readMessages(): This slot is called each time there is something to read in the socket.
- doSendJobRequests(): This slot is the real slot that triggers the shipment of the JobRequests to the Worker.

And finally, here are the details of the private functions:

- handleWorkerRegistered(): This function processes the WORKER_REGISTER message and initializes mCpuCoreCount
- handleWorkerUnregistered(): This function processes the WORKER_UNREGISTER message and emits the unregistered() signal
- handleJobResult(): This function processes the JOB_RESULT message and dispatches the content through the jobCompleted() signal

The implementation in WorkerClient.cpp should be quite familiar. Here is the constructor:

```
#include "MessageUtils.h"

WorkerClient::WorkerClient(int socketDescriptor) :
    QObject(),
    mSocketDescriptor(socketDescriptor),
    mSocket(this),
    mSocketReader(&mSocket)
```

```
{
    connect(this, &WorkerClient::sendJobRequests,
            this, &WorkerClient::doSendJobRequests);
}
```

The fields are initialized in the initialization list and the `sendJobRequests` signal is connected to the private slot, `doSendJobRequests`. This trick is used to still have a queued connection across threads while avoiding multiple functions declarations.

We will proceed with the `start()` function:

```
void WorkerClient::start()
{
    connect(&mSocket, &QTcpSocket::readyRead,
            this, &WorkerClient::readMessages);
    mSocket.setSocketDescriptor(mSocketDescriptor);
}
```

This is very short indeed. It first connects the `readyRead()` signal from the socket to our `readMessages()` slot. After that, `mSocket` is properly configured with `mSocketDescriptor`.

The connect has to be done in `start()` because it should be executed in the `QThread` class associated with our `WorkerClient`. By doing so, we know that the connect will be a direct connection and that `mSocket` will not have to queue signals to interact with `WorkerClient`.

Note that at the end of the function, the associated `QThread` is not terminated. On the contrary, it is executing its event loop with `QThread::exec()`. The `QThread` class will continue to run its event loop until someone calls `QThread::exit()`.

The only purpose of the `start()` function is to do the `mSocket` connect work in the right thread affinity. After that, we rely solely on the Qt signal/slot mechanism to process data. There is no need for a busy `while` loop.

The `readMessages()` class is waiting for us; let's see it:

```
void WorkerClient::readMessages()
{
    auto messages = MessageUtils::readMessages(mSocketReader);
    for(auto& message : *messages) {
        switch (message->type) {
            case Message::Type::WORKER_REGISTER:
                handleWorkerRegistered(*message);
                break;
            case Message::Type::WORKER_UNREGISTER:
```

```
                    handleWorkerUnregistered(*message);
                    break;
                case Message::Type::JOB_RESULT:
                    handleJobResult(*message);
                    break;
                default:
                    break;
            }
        }
    }
```

No surprises here. It's exactly like we did for `Worker`. The `Messages` are deserialized using `MessageUtils::readMessages()` and, for each message type, the appropriate function is called.

Here is the content of each of these functions, starting with `handleWorkerRegistered()`:

```
    void WorkerClient::handleWorkerRegistered(Message& message)
    {
        QDataStream in(&message.data, QIODevice::ReadOnly);
        in >> mCpuCoreCount;
    }
```

For the `WORKER_REGISTER` message, `Worker` only serialized an `int` in `message.data`, so we can initialize `mCpuCoreCount` on the spot with `in >> mCpuCoreCount`.

Now the body of `handleWorkerUnregistered()`:

```
    void WorkerClient::handleWorkerUnregistered(Message& /*message*/)
    {
        emit unregistered(this);
    }
```

It is a relay to send the `unregistered()` signal, which will be picked up by the owner of `WorkerClient`.

The last "read" function is `handleJobResult()`:

```
    void WorkerClient::handleJobResult(Message& message)
    {
        QDataStream in(&message.data, QIODevice::ReadOnly);
        JobResult jobResult;
        in >> jobResult;
        emit jobCompleted(this, jobResult);
    }
```

This is deceptively short. It only deserializes the `jobResult` component from `message.data` and emits the `jobCompleted()` signal.

The "write-to-socket" functions are `abortJob()` and `doSendJobRequest()`:

```
void WorkerClient::abortJob()
{
    MessageUtils::sendMessage(mSocket,
                              Message::Type::ALL_JOBS_ABORT,
                              true);
}

void WorkerClient::doSendJobRequests(QList<JobRequest> requests)
{
    QByteArray data;
    QDataStream stream(&data, QIODevice::WriteOnly);
    stream << requests;

    MessageUtils::sendMessage(mSocket,
                              Message::Type::JOB_REQUEST,
                              data);
}
```

The `abortJob()` function sends the `ALL_JOBS_ABORT` message with the `forceFlush` flag set to `true` and `doSendJobRequests()` serializes the `requests` to stream before sending them using `MessageUtils::sendMessage()`.

# Building your own QTcpServer

Everything is ready to read and write in our sockets. We still need a server to orchestrate all these instances. To do so, we will develop a modified version of the `MandelbrotCalculator` class, which was covered in Chapter 9, *Keeping Your Sanity with Multithreading*.

The idea is to respect the same interface, in order to have `MandelbrotWidget` oblivious to the fact that the Mandelbrot picture generation is deported on different processes/machines.

The main difference between the old `MandelbrotCalculator` and the new one is that we replaced the `QThreadPool` class by a `QTcpServer`. The `MandelbrotCalculator` class now only has the responsibility to dispatch `JobRequests` to Workers and aggregate the result, but it never interacts anymore with a `QThreadPool` class.

Create a new C++ class named `MandelbrotCalculator.cpp` and update
`MandelbrotCalculator.h` to match this:

```cpp
#include <memory>
#include <vector>

#include <QTcpServer>
#include <QList>
#include <QThread>
#include <QMap>
#include <QElapsedTimer>

#include "WorkerClient.h"
#include "JobResult.h"
#include "JobRequest.h"

class MandelbrotCalculator : public QTcpServer
{
    Q_OBJECT
public:
    MandelbrotCalculator(QObject* parent = 0);
    ~MandelbrotCalculator();

signals:
    void pictureLinesGenerated(QList<JobResult> jobResults);
    void abortAllJobs();

public slots:
    void generatePicture(QSize areaSize, QPointF moveOffset,
                         double scaleFactor, int iterationMax);

private slots:
    void process(WorkerClient* workerClient, JobResult jobResult);
    void removeWorkerClient(WorkerClient* workerClient);

protected:
    void incomingConnection(qintptr socketDescriptor) override;

private:
    std::unique_ptr<JobRequest> createJobRequest(
                                        int pixelPositionY);
    void sendJobRequests(WorkerClient& client,
                         int jobRequestCount = 1);
    void clearJobs();

private:
    QPointF mMoveOffset;
    double mScaleFactor;
```

```
        QSize mAreaSize;
        int mIterationMax;
        int mReceivedJobResults;
        QList<JobResult> mJobResults;
        QMap<WorkerClient*, QThread*> mWorkerClients;
        std::vector<std::unique_ptr<JobRequest>> mJobRequests;
        QElapsedTimer mTimer;
};
```

The modified (or new) data is highlighted. First, note that the class now inherits from QTcpServer rather than QObject. The MandelbrotCalculator class is now a QTcpServer and is able to accept and manage connections. Before digging into this topic, we can review the new members:

- mWorkerClients: This is a QMap that stores the pair WorkerClient and QThread. Each time a WorkerClient is created, an associated QThread is also spawned and both of them are stored in mWorkerClients.
- mJobRequests: This is the list of JobRequests for the current picture. Each time a picture generation is requested, the full list of JobRequest is generated, ready to be dispatched to WorkerClients (that is, to the Worker on the other side of the socket).

And the functions are:

- process(): This function is a slightly modified version of the one seen in Chapter 9, *Keeping Your Sanity with Multithreading*. It not only aggregates JobResults before sending them with the pictureLinesGenerated() signal, but also dispatches JobRequest to the passed WorkerClient to keep them busy.
- removeWorkerClient(): This function removes and deletes the given WorkerClient from mWorkerClients.
- incomingConnection(): This function is an overloaded function from QTcpServer. It is called each time a new client tries to connect to MandelbrotCalculator.
- createJobRequest(): This is a helper function that creates a JobRequest that is added to mJobRequests.
- sendJobRequests(): This function is responsible for sending a list of JobRequests to the specified WorkerClient.

Let's turn to `MandelbrotCalculator.cpp` with the constructor:

```
#include <QDebug>
#include <QThread>

using namespace std;

const int JOB_RESULT_THRESHOLD = 10;

MandelbrotCalculator::MandelbrotCalculator(QObject* parent) :
    QTcpServer(parent),
     mMoveOffset(),
    mScaleFactor(),
    mAreaSize(),
    mIterationMax(),
    mReceivedJobResults(0),
    mWorkerClients(),
    mJobRequests(),
    mTimer()
{
    listen(QHostAddress::Any, 5000);
}
```

This is the common initialization list with the `listen()` instruction in the body. Because we are subclassing `QTcpServer`, we can call listen on ourselves. Note that `QHostAddress::Any` works either for IPv4 and IPv6.

Let's see the overloaded function, `incomingConnection()`:

```
void MandelbrotCalculator::incomingConnection(
                                    qintptr socketDescriptor)
{
    qDebug() << "Connected workerClient";
    QThread* thread = new QThread(this);
    WorkerClient* client = new WorkerClient(socketDescriptor);
    int workerClientsCount = mWorkerClients.keys().size();
    mWorkerClients.insert(client, thread);
    client->moveToThread(thread);

    connect(this, &MandelbrotCalculator::abortAllJobs,
            client, &WorkerClient::abortJob);

    connect(client, &WorkerClient::unregistered,
            this, &MandelbrotCalculator::removeWorkerClient);
    connect(client, &WorkerClient::jobCompleted,
            this, &MandelbrotCalculator::process);

    connect(thread, &QThread::started,
```

```
            client, &WorkerClient::start);
    thread->start();

    if(workerClientsCount == 0 &&
        mWorkerClients.size() == 1) {
        generatePicture(mAreaSize, mMoveOffset,
                        mScaleFactor, mIterationMax);
    }
}
```

Once `listen()` has been called, each time someone connects to our ip/port pair, `incomingConnection()` will be triggered with `socketDescriptor` passed as a parameter.

> You can test this on your machine connection with a simple `telnet 127.0.0.1 5000` command. You should see the `Connected workerClient` log in `mandelbrot-app`.

We start by creating a `QThread` class and a `WorkerClient`. This pair is immediately inserted in the `mWorkerClients` map and `client` thread affinity is changed to `thread`.

After that, we do all the connects to manage the `client` (`abortJob`, `unregister`, and `jobCompleted`). We continue with the `QThread::started()` signal, which is connected to the `WorkerClient::start()` slot and finally, `thread` is started.

The last part of the function is used to trigger a picture generation upon the first `client` connection. If we did not do this, the screen would have remained black until we panned or zoomed.

We have covered the `WorkerClient` creation; let's finish its life cycle with its destruction with `removeWorkerClient()`:

```
void MandelbrotCalculator::removeWorkerClient(WorkerClient* workerClient)
{
    qDebug() << "Removing workerClient";
    QThread* thread = mWorkerClients.take(workerClient);
    thread->quit();
    thread->wait(1000);
    delete thread;
    delete workerClient;
}
```

The `workerClient`/`thread` pair is removed from `mWorkerClients` and cleanly deleted. Note that this function can be called from the `WorkerClient::unregistered` signal or in the `MandelbrotCalculator` destructor:

```
MandelbrotCalculator::~MandelbrotCalculator()
{
    while (!mWorkerClients.empty()) {
        removeWorkerClient(mWorkerClients.firstKey());
    }
}
```

When `MandelbrotCalculator` is deleted, `mWorkerClients` has to be properly emptied. The iterator style `while` loop does a good job of calling `removeWorkerClient()`.

In this new version of `MandelbrotCalculator`, `generatePicture()` does not have exactly the same behavior:

```
void MandelbrotCalculator::generatePicture(
                    QSize areaSize, QPointF moveOffset,
                    double scaleFactor, int iterationMax)
{
    // sanity check & members initization
    ...

    for(int pixelPositionY = mAreaSize.height() - 1;
        pixelPositionY >= 0; pixelPositionY--) {
        mJobRequests.push_back(move(
                        createJobRequest(pixelPositionY)));
    }

    for(WorkerClient* client : mWorkerClients.keys()) {
        sendJobRequests(*client, client->cpuCoreCount() * 2);
    }
}
```

The beginning is the same. However, the end is quite different. Rather than creating `Jobs` and giving them to a `QThreadPool`, `MandelbrotCalculator` now:

- Creates `JobRequests` to generate the whole picture. Note that they are created in reverse order. We will soon see why.
- Dispatches a number of `JobRequests` to each `WorkerClient` it owns.

The second point deserves a strong emphasis. If we want to maximize the speed of our system, we have to use multiple workers, each one having multiple cores to process multiple jobs at the same time.

Even though a `Worker` class can process multiple jobs at the same time, it can only send us `JobResults` one by one (through `WorkerClient::jobCompleted`). Each time we process a `JobResult` object from a `WorkerClient`, we will dispatch a single `JobRequest` to it.

Assume that the `Worker` class has eight cores. If we send `JobRequests` one by one, the `Worker` will always have seven cores idle. We are here to heat up your CPUs, not to let them drink mojitos on the beach!

To mitigate this, the first batch of `JobResults` we send to a worker has to be higher than its `coreCount()`. By doing so, we ensure that is always has a queue of `JobRequests` to process until we generate the whole picture. This is why we send `client->cpuCoreCount() * two` initial `JobRequests`. If you play with this value, you will see that:

- If `jobCount < cpuCoreCount()`, some cores of your `Worker` will be idle and you will not leverage the full power of its CPU
- If `jobCount > cpuCoreCount()` by too much, you might overload the queue of one your `Workers`

Remember that this system is flexible enough to have multiple workers. If you have a RaspberryPI and an x86 with 16 cores, the RaspberryPI will lag behind the x86 CPU. By giving too much initial `JobRequests`, the RaspberryPI will hinder the whole picture generation while the x86 CPU has already finished all its jobs.

Let's cover the remaining functions of `MandelbrotCalculator`, starting with `createJobRequest()`:

```
std::unique_ptr<JobRequest> MandelbrotCalculator::createJobRequest(int
pixelPositionY)
{
    auto jobRequest = make_unique<JobRequest>();
    jobRequest->pixelPositionY = pixelPositionY;
    jobRequest->moveOffset = mMoveOffset;
    jobRequest->scaleFactor = mScaleFactor;
    jobRequest->areaSize = mAreaSize;
    jobRequest->iterationMax = mIterationMax;
    return jobRequest;
}
```

This is a simple creation of a `jobRequest` with the member fields of
`MandelbrotCalculator`. Again, we use `unique_ptr` to explicitly indicate the ownership
of `jobRequest` and avoid any memory leaks.

Next, with `sendJobRequests()`:

```
void MandelbrotCalculator::sendJobRequests(WorkerClient& client, int
jobRequestCount)
{
    QList<JobRequest> listJobRequest;
    for (int i = 0; i < jobRequestCount; ++i) {
        if (mJobRequests.empty()) {
            break;
        }

        auto jobRequest = move(mJobRequests.back());
        mJobRequests.pop_back();
        listJobRequest.append(*jobRequest);
    }

    if (!listJobRequest.empty()) {
        emit client.sendJobRequests(listJobRequest);
    }
}
```

Because we can send multiple `JobRequests` at the same time, we loop on
`jobRequestCount` by taking the last `jobRequest` of `mJobRequests` and adding it
to `listJobRequest`. This is the reason for which we had to fill `mJobRequests` in the
reverse order.

Finally, the `client.sendJobRequests()` signal is emitted, which in turns triggers
the `WorkerClient::doSendJobRequests()` slot.

We are now going to see the modified version of `process()`:

```
void MandelbrotCalculator::process(WorkerClient* workerClient,
                                    JobResult jobResult)
{
    // Sanity check and JobResult aggregation

    if (mReceivedJobResults < mAreaSize.height()) {
        sendJobRequests(*workerClient);
    } else {
        qDebug() << "Generated in" << mTimer.elapsed() << "ms";
    }
}
```

In this version, we pass `workerClient` as a parameter. This is used at the end of the function, to be able to dispatch a new `JobRequest` to the given `workerClient`.

Finally, the updated version of `abortAllJobs()`:

```
void MandelbrotCalculator::clearJobs()
{
    mReceivedJobResults = 0;
    mJobRequests.clear();
    emit abortAllJobs();
}
```

This simply cleared `mJobRequests` instead of emptying `QThreadPool`.

The `MandelbrotCalculator` class is completed! You can copy and paste `MandelBrotWidget` and `MainWindow` (`.ui` file included) from Chapter 9, *Keeping Your Sanity with Multithreading*. We designed it to be plug and play, without knowing who generates the picture: a local `QThreadPool` with `QRunnable` or minions through an IPC mechanism.

There is only a tiny difference in `main.cpp`:

```
#include <QApplication>
#include <QList>

#include "JobRequest.h"
#include "JobResult.h"
#include "WorkerClient.h"

int main(int argc, char *argv[])
{
    qRegisterMetaType<QList<JobRequest>>();
    qRegisterMetaType<QList<JobResult>>();
    qRegisterMetaType<WorkerClient*>();

    QApplication a(argc, argv);
    MainWindow w;
    w.show();

    return a.exec();
}
```

You can now launch `mandelbrot-app` and after that, the one or many `mandelbrot-worker` programs that will connect to the application. It should automatically trigger a picture generation. The Mandelbrot picture generation is now working across multiple processes! Because we chose to use sockets, you can start the application and the workers on different physical machines.

 Using IPv6, you may very easily test the app/worker connection in different locations. If you do not have a high-speed Internet connection, you will see how the network hinders the picture generation.

You may want to take some time to deploy the application on multiple machines and see how this cluster works together. During our tests, we ramped up our cluster up to 18 cores with very heterogeneous machines (PC, laptop, Macbook, and so on).

# Summary

IPC is a fundamental mechanism in computer science. In this chapter, you learned the various techniques offered by Qt to do IPC and how to create an application that uses sockets to interact, send, and receive commands. You took the original `mandelbrot-threadpool` application to the next level by enabling it to generate pictures on a cluster of machines.

Adding IPC on top of a multi-threaded application brings some issues. You have many more possible bottlenecks, chances of leaking memory, and have an inefficient calculation. Qt provides multiple mechanisms to do IPC. In Qt 5.7, the addition of transactions makes the serialization/deserialization part much easier.

In the next chapter, you will discover the Qt Multimedia framework and how to save and load an C++ object from a file. The project example will be a virtual drum machine. You will be able to save and load your tracks.

# 11
# Having Fun with Serialization

The previous chapter was a firework of threads, sockets, and workers. We hope that your minions have been working hard. In this chapter, we will turn our attention to the serialization with Qt. You will learn how to serialize data in multiple formats with a flexible system. The example project will be a virtual drum machine, in which you can compose you own drum beat, record it, play it, save it, and load it back. Your drum beat will be probably so awesome that you will want to share it: you will now be able to do it in various formats.

This chapter will cover the following topics:

- How to architecture an application that plays and records sounds
- The QVariant class and its inner mechanics
- A flexible serialization system
- JSON serialization
- XML serialization
- Binary serialization
- The Qt Multimedia framework
- Drag and drop handling with Qt
- Triggering a button from your keyboard

# Architecting the drum machine project

As usual, before diving into the code, let's study the structure of the project. The aim of the project is to be able to:

- Play and record a sound track from a drum machine
- Save this track to a file and load it to play it back

To play a sound, we will lay out four big buttons that will play a specific drum sound upon click (or a keyboard event): a kick, a snare, a hi-hat, and a cymbal crash. These sounds will be `.wav` files loaded by the application. The user will be able to record his sequence of sounds and replay it.

For the serialization part, we do not only want to save the track to a single file format, we would rather do three:

- **JSON (JavaScript Object Notation)**
- **XML (eXtensible Markup Language)**
- **Binary**

Not only is it more fun to cover three formats, but it also gives us the opportunity to understand the advantages and limitations of each one, and how it fits within the Qt framework. The architecture we are going to implement will try to be flexible to handle future evolutions. You never know how a project can evolve!

The classes' organization looks like this:

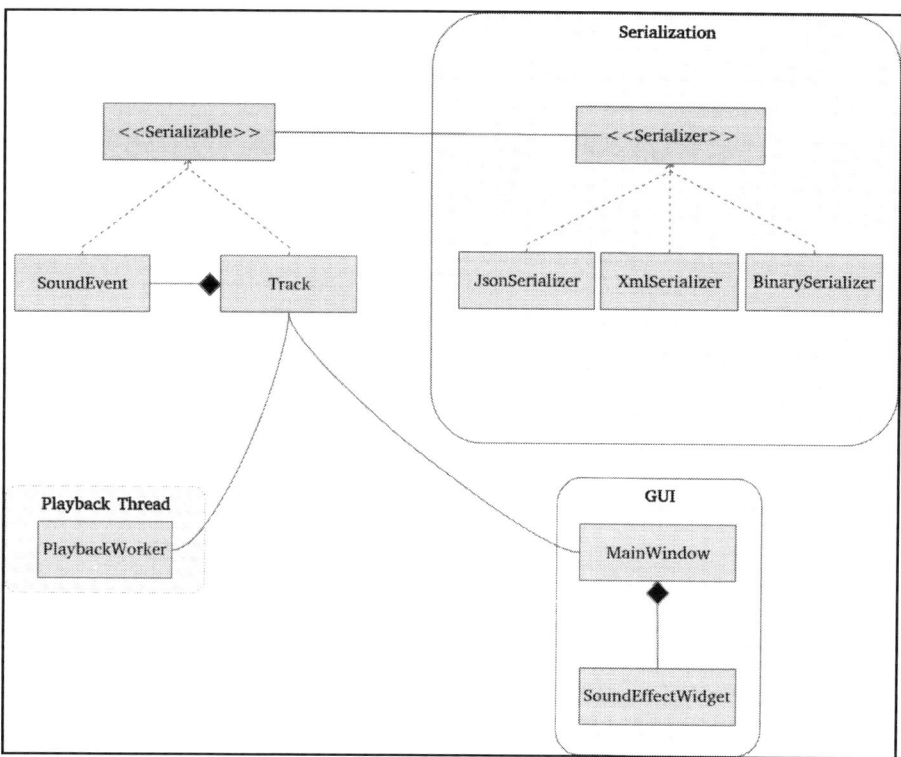

Let's review the role of these classes:

- The SoundEvent class is the basic building block of a track. It is a simple class containing timestamp (when the sound has been played) and soundId variables (what sound has been played).
- The Track class contains a list of SoundEvents, a duration and a state (playing, recording, stopped). Each time the user plays a sound, a SoundEvent class is created and added to the Track class.
- The PlaybackWorker class is a worker class that runs in a different thread. It is responsible of looping through the Track class's soundEvents and triggering the proper sound when its timestamp has been reached.
- The Serializable class is an interface that must be implemented by each class that wants to be serialized (in our case: SoundEvent and Track).
- The Serializer class is an interface that must be implemented by each format-specific implementation class.
- The JsonSerializer, XmlSerializer, and BinarySerializer are the sub-classes of Serializer class that do the format-specific job to serialize/deserialize a Serializable instance.
- The SoundEffectWidget class is the widget that holds the information to play a single sound. It displays the button for one of our four sounds. It also owns a QSoundEffect class that sends the sound to the audio card.
- The MainWindow class holds everything together. It owns the Track class, spawns the PlaybackWorker thread, and triggers the serialization/deserialization.

The output format should be easily swapped. To achieve this, we will rely on a modified version of the bridge design pattern that will allow Serializable and Serializer classes to evolve independently.

The whole project revolves around this notion of independence between modules. It goes to the extent that a sound can be replaced on the spot during a playback. Let's say that you listen to your incredible beat, and you want to try another snare sound. You will be able to replace it with a simple drag and drop of a .wav file on the SoundEffectWidget class holding the snare sound.

# Creating a drum track

Let's buckle up and do this project! Create a new **Qt Widgets Application** project named `ch11-drum-machine`. As usual, add the `CONFIG += c++14` in `ch11-drum-machine.pro`.

Now create a new C++ class named `SoundEvent`. Here is `SoundEvent.h` stripped from its functions:

```cpp
#include <QtGlobal>

class SoundEvent
{

public:
    SoundEvent(qint64 timestamp = 0, int soundId = 0);
    ~SoundEvent();

    qint64 timestamp;
    int soundId;
};
```

This class contains only two public members:

- `timestamp`: A `qint64` (`long long` type) that contains the current time of the `SoundEvent` in milliseconds since the beginning of the track
- `soundId`: The ID of the sound that has been played

In recording mode, each time the user plays a sound, a `SoundEvent` is created with the appropriate data. The `SoundEvent.cpp` file is so boring that we will not inflict it on you.

The next class to build is `Track`. Again, create the new C++ class. Let's review `Track.h` with its members only:

```cpp
#include <QObject>
#include <QVector>
#include <QElapsedTimer>

#include "SoundEvent.h"

class Track : public QObject
{
    Q_OBJECT
public:
    enum class State {
        STOPPED,
```

```
        PLAYING,
        RECORDING,
    };

    explicit Track(QObject *parent = 0);
    ~Track();

private:
    qint64 mDuration;
        std::vector<std::unique_ptr<SoundEvent>> mSoundEvents;
    QElapsedTimer mTimer;
    State mState;
    State mPreviousState;
};
```

We can now go into detail about them:

- mDuration: This variable holds the duration of the Track class. This member is reset to 0 when a recording is started and updated when the recording is stopped.
- mSoundEvents: This variable is the list of SoundEvents for the given Track. As the unique_ptr semantic states it, Track is the owner of the sound events.
- mTimer: This variable is started each time Track is played or recorded.
- mState: This variable is the current State of Track class, which can have three possible values: STOPPED, PLAYING, RECORDING.
- mPreviousState: This variable is the previous State of Track. This is useful when you want to know which action to do on a new STOPPEDState. We will have to stop the playback if mPreviousState is in the PLAYING state.

The Track class is the pivot of the business logic of the project. It holds mState, which is the state of the whole application. Its content will be read during a playback of your awesome musical performance and also be serialized to a file.

Let's enrich Track.h with functions:

```
class Track : public QObject
{
    Q_OBJECT
public:
    ...
    qint64 duration() const;
    State state() const;
    State previousState() const;
    qint64 elapsedTime() const;
    const std::vector<std::unique_ptr<SoundEvent>>& soundEvents() const;
```

```
signals:
    void stateChanged(State state);

public slots:
    void play();
    void record();
    void stop();
    void addSoundEvent(int soundEventId);

private:
    void clear();
    void setState(State state);

private:
    ...
};
```

We will skip the simple getters and concentrate on the important functions:

- elapsedTime(): This function returns the value of the mTimer.elapsed().
- soundEvents(): This function is a little more complicated getter. The Track class is the owner of mSoundEvents content and we really want to enforce it. For this, the getter returns a const & to mSoundEvents.
- stateChanged(): This function is emitted when the mState value is updated. The new State is passed as a parameter.
- play(): This function is a slot that starts to play the Track. This play is purely logical, the real playback will be triggered by PlaybackWorker.
- record(): This function is a slot that starts the recording state of Track.
- stop(): This function is a slot that stops the current start or record state.
- addSoundEvent(): This function creates a new SoundEvent with the given soundId and adds it to mSoundEvents.
- clear(): This function resets the content of Track: it clears mSoundEvents and sets mDuration to 0.
- setState(): This function is a private helper function that updates mState, mPreviousState and emits the stateChanged() signal.

Now that the header has been covered, we can study the interesting parts of Track.cpp:

```
void Track::play()
{
    setState(State::PLAYING);
    mTimer.start();
}
```

Calling `Track.play()` simply updates the state to `PLAYING` and starts `mTimer`. The `Track` class does not hold anything related to the Qt Multimedia API; it is limited to an evolved data holder (as it also manages a state).

Now for `record()`, which brings a lot of surprises:

```
void Track::record()
{
    clearSoundEvents();
    setState(State::RECORDING);
    mTimer.start();
}
```

It starts by clearing the data, sets the state to `RECORDING`, and also starts `mTimer`. Now consider `stop()`, which is a slight variation:

```
void Track::stop()
{
    if (mState == State::RECORDING) {
        mDuration = mTimer.elapsed();
    }
    setState(State::STOPPED);
}
```

If we are stopping in the `RECORDING` state, `mDuration` is updated. Nothing very fancy here. We saw three times the `setState()` call without seeing its body:

```
void Track::setState(Track::State state)
{
    mPreviousState = mState;
    mState = state;
    emit stateChanged(mState);
}
```

The current value of `mState` is stored in `mPreviousState` before being updated. Finally, `stateChanged()` is emitted with the new value.

The state system of `Track` is completely covered. The last missing part is the `SoundEvents` interactions. We can start with the `addSoundEvent()` snippet:

```
void Track::addSoundEvent(int soundEventId)
{
    if (mState != State::RECORDING) {
        return;
    }
    mSoundEvents.push_back(make_unique<SoundEvent>(
                           mTimer.elapsed(),
```

```
                            soundEventId));
    }
```

A soundEvent is created only if we are in the RECORDING state. After that, a SoundEvent is
added to mSoundEvents with the current elapsed time of mTimer and the
passed soundEventId.

Now for the clear() function:

```
void Track::clear()
{
    mSoundEvents.clear();
    mDuration = 0;
}
```

Because we use unique_ptr<SoundEvent> in mSoundEvents,
the mSoundEvents.clear() function is enough to empty the vector and also delete
each SoundEvent. This is one less thing you have to worry with smart pointers.

The SoundEvent and Track are the base classes that hold the information about your
future beat. We are going to see the class responsible for reading this data to play
it: PlaybackWorker.

Create a new C++ class and update PlaybackWorker.h like so:

```
#include <QObject>
#include <QAtomicInteger>

class Track;

class PlaybackWorker : public QObject
{
    Q_OBJECT
public:
    explicit PlaybackWorker(const Track& track, QObject *parent = 0);

signals:
    void playSound(int soundId);
    void trackFinished();

public slots:
    void play();
    void stop();

private:
    const Track& mTrack;
    QAtomicInteger<bool> mIsPlaying;
```

```
};
```

The `PlaybackWorker` class will be running in a different thread. If your memory needs to be refreshed, go back to `Chapter 9`, *Keeping Your Sanity with Multithreading*. Its role is to iterate through the `Track` class's content to trigger the sounds. Let's break down this header:

- `mTrack`: This function is the reference to the `Track` class on which `PlaybackWorker` is working. It is passed in the constructor as a `const` reference. With this information, you already know that `PlaybackWorker` cannot modify `mTrack` in any way.
- `mIsPlaying`: This function is a flag used to be able to stop the worker from another thread. It is a `QAtomicInteger` to guarantee an atomic access to the variable.
- `playSound()`: This function is emitted by `PlaybackWorker` each time a sound needs to be played.
- `trackFinished()`: This function is emitted when the playback has been played until the end. If it has been stopped along the way, this signal will not be emitted.
- `play()`: This function is the main function of `PlaybackWorker`. In it, `mTrack` content will be queried to trigger sounds.
- `stop()`: This function is the function that updates the `mIsPlaying` flag and causes `play()` to exit its loop.

The meat of the class lies in the `play()` function:

```
void PlaybackWorker::play()
{
    mIsPlaying.store(true);
    QElapsedTimer timer;
    size_t soundEventIndex = 0;
    const auto& soundEvents = mTrack.soundEvents();

    timer.start();
    while(timer.elapsed() <= mTrack.duration()
            && mIsPlaying.load()) {
        if (soundEventIndex < soundEvents.size()) {
            const auto& soundEvent =
                            soundEvents.at(soundEventIndex);

            if (timer.elapsed() >= soundEvent->timestamp) {
                emit playSound(soundEvent->soundId);
                soundEventIndex++;
            }
```

```
        }
        QThread::msleep(1);
    }

    if (soundEventIndex >= soundEvents.size()) {
        emit trackFinished();
    }
}
```

The first thing that `play()` function does is to prepare its reading: `mIsPlaying` is set to `true`, a `QElapsedTimer` class is declared, and a `soundEventIndex` is initialized. Each time `timer.elapsed()` is called, we will know if a sound should be played.

To know which sound should be played, `soundEventIndex` will be used to know where we are in the `soundEvents` vector.

Right after that, the `timer` object is started and we enter in the `while` loop. This `while` loop has two conditions to continue:

- `timer.elapsed() <= mTrack.duration()`: This condition states that we did not finish playing the track
- `mIsPlaying.load()`: This condition returns **true**: nobody asked `PlaybackWorker` to stop

Intuitively, you might have added the `soundEventIndex < soundEvents.size()` condition in the `while` condition. By doing so, you would have exited `PlaybackWorker` as soon as the last sound has been played. Technically, it works, but that would not have respected what the user recorded.

Consider a user that created a complex beat (do not underestimate what you can do with four sounds!) and decided on a long pause of 5 seconds at the end of the song. When he clicks on the stop button, the time display indicates 00:55 (for 55 seconds). However, when he plays back his performance, the last sound finishes at 00:50. The playback stops at 00:50 and the program does not respect what he recorded.

For this reason, the `soundEventIndex < size()` test is moved inside the `while` loop and is used only as a fuse for the `soundEvents` read through.

Inside this condition, we retrieve the reference to the current `soundEvent`. We then compare the elapsed time against the `timestamp` of the `soundEvent`. If `timer.elapsed()` is greater or equal to `soundEvent->timestamp`, the signal `playSound()` is emitted with the `soundId`.

This is only a request to play a sound. The `PlaybackWorker` class limits itself to read through `soundEvents` and trigger a `playSound()` at the proper moment. The real sound will be handled later on, with the `SoundEffectWidget` class.

At each iteration in the `while` loop, a `QThread::msleep(1)` is done to avoid a busy loop. We minimize the sleep because we want the playback to be as faithful as possible to the original score. The longer the sleep, the more discrepancy we may encounter in the playback timing.

Finally, if the whole `soundEvents` has been processed, the `trackFinished` signal is emitted.

# Making your objects serializable with QVariant

Now that we implemented the logic in our business classes, we have to think about what we are going to serialize and how we are going to do it. The user interacts with a `Track` class that contains all the data to be recorded and played back.

Starting from here, we can assume that the object to be serialized is `Track`, which in turn should somehow bring along its `mSoundEvents` containing a list of `SoundEvent` instances. To achieve this, we will rely heavily on the `QVariant` class.

You might have worked with `QVariant` before. It is a generic placeholder for any primitive type (`char`, `int`, `double`, and so on) but also complex types (`QString`, `QDate`, `QPoint`, and many more).

The complete list of QVariant supported types is available at `http://doc.qt.io/qt-5/qmetatype.html#Type-enum`.

A simple example of `QVariant` is:

```
QVariant variant(21);

int answer = variant.toInt() * 2;

qDebug() << "what is the meaning of the universe,
          life and everything?"
       << answer;
```

We store `21` in `variant`. From here, we can ask for `variant` to have a copy of the value casted to our desired type. Here we want an `int` value, so we call `variant.toInt()`. There are a lot of conversions already available with the `variant.toX()` syntax.

We can take a very quick peek at what happens behind the curtain in `QVariant`. How does it store all we feed it? The answer lies in the C++ type `union`. The `QVariant` class is a kind of super `union`.

A `union` is a special class type that can hold only one of its non-static data members at a time. A short snippet should illustrate this:

```
union Sound
{
    int duration;
    char code;
};

Sound s = 10;
qDebug() << "Sound duration:" << s.duration;
// output= Sound duration: 10

s.code = 'K';
qDebug() << "Sound code:" << s.code;
// output= Sound code: K
```

First, a `union` class is declared like a `struct`. By default, all the members are `public`. The specificity of the `union` is that it takes only the largest member size in memory. Here, `Sound` will take only as much as the `int duration` space in memory.

Because `union` takes only this specific space, every member variable shares the same memory space. Therefore, only one member is available at a time, unless you want to have undefined behaviors.

When using the `Sound` snippet, we start by initializing with the value `10` (by default the first member is initialized). From here, `s.duration` is accessible but `s.code` is considered undefined.

Once we assign a value to `s.code`, `s.duration` becomes undefined and `s.code` is now accessible.

The `union` class makes the memory usage very efficient. In `QVariant`, when you store a value, it is stored in a private `union`:

```
union Data
{
    char c;
    uchar uc;
    short s;
    signed char sc;
    ushort us;
    ...
    qulonglong ull;
    QObject *o;
    void *ptr;
    PrivateShared *shared;
} data;
```

Note the list of primitive types and at the end the complex types, `QObject *` and `void*`.

Besides `Data`, a `QMetaType` object is initialized to know the type of the stored object. The combination of `union` and `QMetaType` lets `QVariant` know which `Data` member it should use to cast the value and give it back to the caller.

Now that you know what a `union` is and how `QVariant` uses it, you might ask: why make a `QVariant` class at all? A simple `union` would not have been enough?

The answer is no. It is not enough because a `union` class cannot have members that do not have a default constructor. It drastically reduces the number of classes you can put in a `union`. Qt folks wanted to include many classes that did not have a default constructor in `union`. To mitigate this, `QVariant` was born.

What makes `QVariant` very interesting is that it is possible to store custom types. If we wanted to convert `SoundEvent` class to a `QVariant` class, we would have added the following in `SoundEvent.h`:

```
class SoundEvent
{
    ...
};
Q_DECLARE_METATYPE(SoundEvent);
```

We already used Q_DECLARE_METATYPE macro in Chapter 10, *Need IPC? Get Your Minions to Work*. This macro effectively registers SoundEvent to the QMetaType register, making it available for QVariant. Because QDataStream relies on QVariant, we had to use this macro in the last chapter.

Now to convert back and forth with a QVariant:

```
SoundEvent soundEvent(4365, 0);
QVariant stored;
stored.setValue(soundEvent);

SoundEvent newEvent = stored.value<SoundEvent>();
qDebug() << newEvent.timestamp;
```

As you can guess, the output of this snippet is 4365, the original timestamp stored in soundEvent.

This approach would have been perfect if we wanted to do only binary serialization. Data can be easily written and read from. However, we want to output our Track and SoundEvents to standard formats: JSON and XML.

There is a major issue with the Q_DECLARE_METATYPE/QVariant combo: it does not store any key for the fields of the serialized class. We can already foresee that the JSON object of a SoundEvent class will look like this:

```
{
    "timestamp": 4365,
    "soundId": 0
}
```

There is no way the QVariant class could know that we want a timestamp key. It will only store the raw binary data. The same principle applies for the XML counterpart.

For this reason, we are going to use a variation of a QVariant with a QVariantMap. The QVariantMap class is only a typedef on QMap<QString, QVariant>. This map will be used to store the key names of the fields and the value in the QVariant class. In turn, these keys will be used by the JSON and XML serialization system to output a pretty file.

Because we aim to have a flexible serialization system, we have to be able to serialize and deserialize this QVariantMap in multiple formats. To achieve this, we will define an interface that gives the ability for a class to serialize/deserialize its content in a QVariantMap.

This `QVariantMap` will be used as an intermediate format, agnostic of the final JSON, XML, or binary.

Create a C++ header named `Serializer.h`. Here is the content:

```
#include <QVariant>

class Serializable {
public:
    virtual ~Serializable() {}
    virtual QVariant toVariant() const = 0;
    virtual void fromVariant(const QVariant& variant) = 0;
};
```

By implementing this abstract base class, a class will be `Serializable`. There are only two virtual pure functions:

- The `toVariant()` function, in which the class must return a `QVariant` (or, more precisely a `QVariantMap`, which can be casted to a `QVariant` thanks to the `QMetaType` system)
- The `fromVariant()` function, in which the class must initialize its members from the variant passed as a parameter

By doing so, we give the responsibility to the final class to load and save its content. After all, who knows better `SoundEvent` than `SoundEvent` itself?

Let's see `Serializable` in action with `SoundEvent`. Update `SoundEvent.h` like this:

```
#include "Serializable.h"

class SoundEvent : public Serializable
{
    SoundEvent(qint64 timestamp = 0, int soundId = 0);
    ~SoundEvent();

    QVariant toVariant() const override;
    void fromVariant(const QVariant& variant) override;

    ...
};
```

The `SoundEvent` class is now `Serializable`. Let's do the real work in `SoundEvent.cpp`:

```
QVariant SoundEvent::toVariant() const
{
    QVariantMap map;
    map.insert("timestamp", timestamp);
    map.insert("soundId", soundId);
    return map;
}

void SoundEvent::fromVariant(const QVariant& variant)
{
    QVariantMap map = variant.toMap();
    timestamp = map.value("timestamp").toLongLong();
    soundId = map.value("soundId").toInt();
}
```

In `toVariant()`, we simply declare a `QVariantMap` that gets filled with `timestamp` and `soundId`.

On the other side, in `fromVariant()`, we convert `variant` to a `QVariantMap` and retrieve its content with the same keys we used in `toVariant()`. It is as simple as that!

The next class that have to be `Serializable` is `Track`. After making `Track` inherit from `Serializable`, update `Track.cpp`:

```
QVariant Track::toVariant() const
{
    QVariantMap map;
    map.insert("duration", mDuration);

    QVariantList list;
    for (const auto& soundEvent : mSoundEvents) {
        list.append(soundEvent->toVariant());
    }
    map.insert("soundEvents", list);

    return map;
}
```

The principle is the same, although a bit more complex. The `mDuration` variable is stored in `map` object as we have seen for `SoundEvent`. For `mSoundEvents`, we have to generate a list of `QVariant` (a `QVariantList`) where each item is the converted `QVariant` version of a `soundEvent` key.

To do so, we simply loop over `mSoundEvents` and fill `list` with
the `soundEvent->toVariant()` result we covered a few paragraphs before.

Now for `fromVariant()`:

```
void Track::fromVariant(const QVariant& variant)
{
    QVariantMap map = variant.toMap();
    mDuration = map.value("duration").toLongLong();

    QVariantList list = map.value("soundEvents").toList();
    for(const QVariant& data : list) {
        auto soundEvent = make_unique<SoundEvent>();
        soundEvent->fromVariant(data);
        mSoundEvents.push_back(move(soundEvent));
    }
}
```

Here, for each element of the key `soundEvents`, we create a new `SoundEvent`, load it with
the content of `data`, and finally add it to the vector `mSoundEvents`.

# Serializing objects in JSON format

The `Track` and `SoundEvent` classes can now be converted to a common Qt
format `QVariant`. We now need to write a `Track` (and its `SoundEvent` objects) class in a
file with a text or a binary format. This example project allows you to handle all the formats.
It will allow you to switch the saved file format in one line. So where to put the specific
format code? That is the million dollar question! Here is a primary approach:

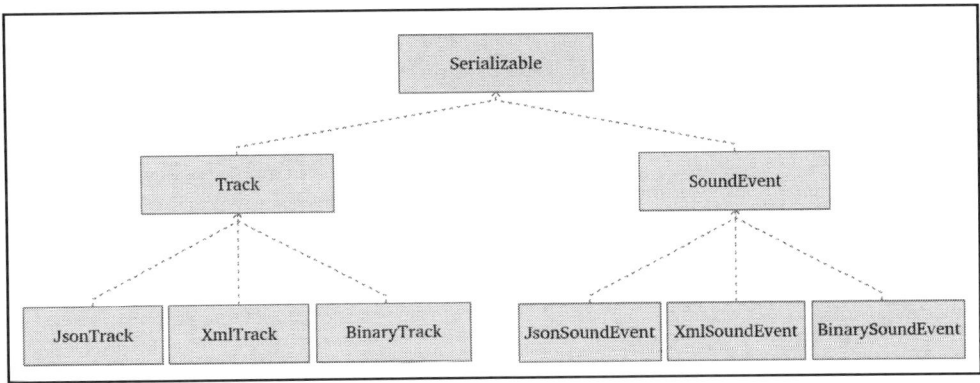

In this proposition, the specific file format serialization code is inside a dedicated child class. Well, it works but what would the hierarchy look like if we add two new file formats? Moreover, each time we add a new object to serialize, we have to create all these children classes to handle the different serialization file formats. This massive inheritance tree can quickly become a sticky mess. The code will be unmaintainable. You do not want to do that. So, here is where the bridge pattern can be a good solution:

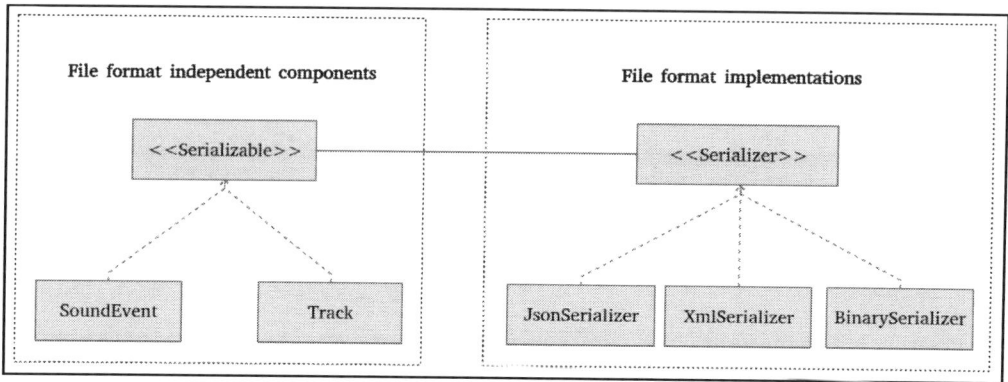

In a bridge pattern, we decouple the classes in two inheritance hierarchies:

- The components independent from the file format. The SoundEvent and Track objects do not care about JSON, XML, or a binary format.
- The file format implementations. The JsonSerializer, XmlSerializer and BinarySerializer handle a generic format, Serializable, not a specific component such as SoundEvent or Track.

Notice that in a classic bridge pattern, an abstraction (Serializable) should contains an implementor (Serializer) variable. The caller only deals with the abstraction. However in this project example, MainWindow has the ownership of Serializable and also of Serializer. This is a personal choice to use the power of design pattern while keeping uncoupled functional classes.

The architecture of Serializable and Serializer is clear. The Serializable class is already implemented so you can now create a new C++ header file called Serializer.h:

```
#include <QString>

#include "Serializable.h"

class Serializer
{
```

```
public:
    virtual ~Serializer() {}

    virtual void save(const Serializable& serializable,
        const QString& filepath,
        const QString& rootName = "") = 0;
    virtual void load(Serializable& serializable,
        const QString& filepath) = 0;
};
```

The `Serializer` class is an interface, an abstract class with only pure virtual functions and no data. Let's talk about the `save()` function:

- This function saves `Serializable` to a file on the hard disk drive.
- The `Serializable` class is `const` and cannot be modified by this function.
- The `filepath` function indicates the destination file to create.
- Some `Serializer` implementations can use the `rootName` variable. For example, if we request to save a `Track` object, the `rootName` variable could be the string `track`. This is the label used to write the root element. The XML implementation requires this information.

The `load()` function is also easy to understand:

- This function loads data from a file to fill a `Serializable` class
- The `Serializable` class will be updated by this function
- The `filepath` function indicates which file to read

The interface `Serializer` is ready and waits for some implementations! Let's start with JSON. Create a C++ class, `JsonSerializer`. Here is the header for `JsonSerializer.h`:

```
#include "Serializer.h"

class JsonSerializer : public Serializer
{
public:
    JsonSerializer();

    void save(const Serializable& serializable,
        const QString& filepath,
        const QString& rootName) override;
    void load(Serializable& serializable,
        const QString& filepath) override;
};
```

No difficulties here; we have to provide an implementation of `save()` and `load()`. Here is the `save()` implementation:

```
void JsonSerializer::save(const Serializable& serializable,
    const QString& filepath, const QString& /*rootName*/)
{
    QJsonDocument doc =
        QJsonDocument::fromVariant(serializable.toVariant());
    QFile file(filepath);
    file.open(QFile::WriteOnly);
    file.write(doc.toJson());
    file.close();
}
```

The Qt framework provides a nice way to read and write a JSON file with the `QJsonDocument` class. We can create a `QJsonDocument` class from a `QVariant` class. Notice that the `QVariant` accepted by `QJsonDocument` must be a `QVariantMap`, `QVariantList`, or `QStringList`. No worries, the `toVariant()` function of `Track` class and `SoundEvent` generates a `QVariantMap`. Then, we can create a `QFile` file with the destination `filepath`. The `QJsonDocument::toJson()` function converts it to a UTF-8 encoded text representation. We write this result to the `QFile` file and close the file.

> The `QJsonDocument::toJson()` function can produce an `Indented` or a `Compact` JSON format. By default, the format is `QJsonDocument::Indented`.

The `load()` implementation is also short:

```
void JsonSerializer::load(Serializable& serializable,
    const QString& filepath)
{
    QFile file(filepath);
    file.open(QFile::ReadOnly);
    QJsonDocument doc = QJsonDocument::fromJson(file.readAll());
    file.close();
    serializable.fromVariant(doc.toVariant());
}
```

We open a `QFile` with the source `filepath`. We read all the data with `QFile::readAll()`. Then we can create a `QJsonDocument` class with the `QJsonDocument::fromJson()` function. Finally, we can fill our destination `Serializable` with the `QJsonDocument` converted to a `QVariant` class. Notice that the `QJsonDocument::toVariant()` function can return `QVariantList` or a `QVariantMap` depending the nature of the JSON document.

Here is an example of a `Track` class saved with this `JsonSerializer`:

```
{
    "duration": 6205,
    "soundEvents": [
        {
            "soundId": 0,
            "timestamp": 2689
        },
        {
            "soundId": 2,
            "timestamp": 2690
        },
        {
            "soundId": 2,
            "timestamp": 3067
        }
    ]
}
```

The root element is a JSON object, represented by a map with two keys:

- `Duration`: This is a simple integer value
- `soundEvents`: This is an array of objects. Each object is a map with the following keys:

- `soundId`: This is an integer
- `timestamp`: This is also an integer

# Serializing objects in XML format

The JSON serialization was a direct representation of the C++ objects and Qt already provides all we need. However, the serialization of a C++ object can be done with various representations in an XML format. So we have to write the XML <-> `QVariant` conversion ourselves. We have decided to use the following XML representation:

```
<[name]> type="[type]">[data]</[name]>
```

For example, the `soundId` type gives this XML representation:

```
<soundId type="int">2</soundId>
```

Create a C++ class XmlSerializer that also inherits from Serializer. Let's begin with the save() function, here is XmlSerializer.h:

```
#include <QXmlStreamWriter>
#include <QXmlStreamReader>

#include "Serializer.h"

class XmlSerializer : public Serializer
{
public:
    XmlSerializer();

    void save(const Serializable& serializable,
        const QString& filepath,
        const QString& rootName) override;
};
```

Now we can see the save() implementation in XmlSerializer.cpp:

```
void XmlSerializer::save(const Serializable& serializable, const QString&
filepath, const QString& rootName)
{
    QFile file(filepath);
    file.open(QFile::WriteOnly);
    QXmlStreamWriter stream(&file);
    stream.setAutoFormatting(true);
    stream.writeStartDocument();
    writeVariantToStream(rootName, serializable.toVariant(),
        stream);
    stream.writeEndDocument();
    file.close();
}
```

We create a QFile file with the filepath destination. We construct a QXmlStreamWriter object that writes in the QFile. By default, the writer will produce a compact XML; you can generate a pretty XML with the QXmlStreamWriter::setAutoFormatting() function. The QXmlStreamWriter::writeStartDocument() function writes the XML version and the encoding. We write our QVariant in the XML stream with our writeVariantToStream() function. Finally, we end the document and close the QFile. As already explained, writing a QVariant to an XML stream depends on how you want to represent the data. So we have to write the conversion function. Please update your class with writeVariantToStream() like this:

```
//XmlSerializer.h
private:
```

```
        void writeVariantToStream(const QString& nodeName,
            const QVariant& variant, QXmlStreamWriter& stream);

//XmlSerializer.cpp
void XmlSerializer::writeVariantToStream(const QString& nodeName,
    const QVariant& variant, QXmlStreamWriter& stream)
{
    stream.writeStartElement(nodeName);
    stream.writeAttribute("type", variant.typeName());

    switch (variant.type()) {
        case QMetaType::QVariantList:
            writeVariantListToStream(variant, stream);
            break;
        case QMetaType::QVariantMap:
            writeVariantMapToStream(variant, stream);
            break;
        default:
            writeVariantValueToStream(variant, stream);
            break;
    }

    stream.writeEndElement();
}
```

This `writeVariantToStream()` function is a generic entry point. It will be called each time we want to put a `QVariant` in the XML stream. The `QVariant` class could be a list, a map, or data. So we apply a specific treatment if the `QVariant` is a container (`QVariantList` or `QVariantMap`). All the other cases are considered to be a data value. Here are the steps of this function:

1. Start a new XML element with the `writeStartElement()` function. The `nodeName` will be used to create the XML tag. For example, `<soundId`.

2. Write an XML attribute called `type` in the current element. We use the name of the type stored in the `QVariant`. For example, `<soundId type="int"`.

3. Depending on the `QVariant` data type, we call one of our XML serialization functions. For example, `<soundId type="int">2`.

4.  Finally, we end the current XML element with `writeEndElement()`:

    - The final result is: `<soundId type="int">2</soundId>`
    - In this function, we call three helper functions that we will create now. The easiest one is `writeVariantValueToStream()`. Please update your `XmlSerializer` class with:

```
//XmlSerializer.h
void writeVariantValueToStream(const QVariant& variant,
    QXmlStreamWriter& stream);

//XmlSerializer.cpp
void XmlSerializer::writeVariantValueToStream(
    const QVariant& variant, QXmlStreamWriter& stream)
{
    stream.writeCharacters(variant.toString());
}
```

If the `QVariant` is a simple type, we retrieve its `QString` representation. Then we use `QXmlStreamWriter::writeCharacters()` to write this `QString` in the XML stream.

The second helper function is `writeVariantListToStream()`. Here is its implementation:

```
//XmlSerializer.h
private:
    void writeVariantListToStream(const QVariant& variant,
        QXmlStreamWriter& stream);

//XmlSerializer.cpp
void XmlSerializer::writeVariantListToStream(
    const QVariant& variant, QXmlStreamWriter& stream)
{
    QVariantList list = variant.toList();

    for(const QVariant& element : list) {
        writeVariantToStream("item", element, stream);
    }
}
```

At this step, we already know that the `QVariant` is a `QVariantList`. We call `QVariant::toList()` to retrieve the list. Then we iterate over all elements of the list and call our generic entry point, `writeVariantToStream()`. Notice that we retrieve the elements from a list so we do not have an element name. But the tag name does not matter for a list item serialization, so insert the arbitrary label `item`.

The last write helper function is `writeVariantMapToStream()`:

```
//XmlSerializer.h
private:
    void writeVariantMapToStream(const QVariant& variant,
        QXmlStreamWriter& stream);

//XmlSerializer.cpp
void XmlSerializer::writeVariantMapToStream(
    const QVariant& variant, QXmlStreamWriter& stream)
{
    QVariantMap map = variant.toMap();
    QMapIterator<QString, QVariant> i(map);

    while (i.hasNext()) {
        i.next();
        writeVariantToStream(i.key(), i.value(), stream);
    }
}
```

The `QVariant` is a container but a `QVariantMap` this time. We
call `writeVariantToStream()` for each element found. The tag name is important because
this is a map. We use the map key from `QMapIterator::key()` as the node name.

The saving part is over. We can now implement the loading part. Its architecture follows the
same spirit as the saving functions. Let's begin with the `load()` function:

```
//XmlSerializer.h
public:
    void load(Serializable& serializable,
        const QString& filepath) override;

//XmlSerializer.cpp
void XmlSerializer::load(Serializable& serializable,
    const QString& filepath)
{
    QFile file(filepath);
    file.open(QFile::ReadOnly);
    QXmlStreamReader stream(&file);
    stream.readNextStartElement();
    serializable.fromVariant(readVariantFromStream(stream));
}
```

The first thing to do is to create a QFile with the source filepath. We construct a QXmlStreamReader with the QFile. The QXmlStreamReader ::readNextStartElement() function reads until the next start element in the XML stream. Then we can use our read helper function, readVariantFromStream(), to create a QVariant class from an XML stream. Finally, we can use our Serializable::fromVariant() to fill the destination serializable. Let's implement the helper function, readVariantFromStream():

```
//XmlSerializer.h
private:
    QVariant readVariantFromStream(QXmlStreamReader& stream);

//XmlSerializer.cpp
QVariant XmlSerializer::readVariantFromStream(QXmlStreamReader& stream)
{
    QXmlStreamAttributes attributes = stream.attributes();
    QString typeString = attributes.value("type").toString();

    QVariant variant;
    switch (QVariant::nameToType(
            typeString.toStdString().c_str())) {
        case QMetaType::QVariantList:
            variant = readVariantListFromStream(stream);
            break;
        case QMetaType::QVariantMap:
            variant = readVariantMapFromStream(stream);
            break;
        default:
            variant = readVariantValueFromStream(stream);
            break;
    }

    return variant;
}
```

The role of this function is to create a QVariant. Firstly, we retrieve the "type" from the XML attributes. In our case, we have only one attribute to handle. Then, depending on the type, we will call one of our three read helper functions. Let's implement the readVariantValueFromStream() function:

```
//XmlSerializer.h
private:
    QVariant readVariantValueFromStream(QXmlStreamReader& stream);

//XmlSerializer.cpp
QVariant XmlSerializer::readVariantValueFromStream(
```

```
    QXmlStreamReader& stream)
{
    QXmlStreamAttributes attributes = stream.attributes();
    QString typeString = attributes.value("type").toString();
    QString dataString = stream.readElementText();

    QVariant variant(dataString);
    variant.convert(QVariant::nameToType(
        typeString.toStdString().c_str()));
    return variant;
}
```

This function create a QVariant with its data depending on the type. Like the previous function, we retrieve the type from the XML attribute. We also read the data as a text with the QXmlStreamReader::readElementText() function. A QVariant class is created with this QString data. At this step, the QVariant type is a QString. So we use the QVariant::convert() function to convert the QVariant to the real type (int, qlonglong, and so on).

The second read helper function is readVariantListFromStream():

```
//XmlSerializer.h
private:
    QVariant readVariantListFromStream(QXmlStreamReader& stream);

//XmlSerializer.cpp
QVariant XmlSerializer::readVariantListFromStream(QXmlStreamReader& stream)
{
    QVariantList list;
    while(stream.readNextStartElement()) {
        list.append(readVariantFromStream(stream));
    }
    return list;
}
```

We know that the stream element contains an array. So, this function creates and returns a QVariantList. The QXmlStreamReader::readNextStartElement() function reads until the next start element and returns true if a start element is found within the current element. We call the entry-point function, readVariantFromStream(), for each element. Finally, we return the QVariantList.

The last helper function to cover is `readVariantMapFromStream()`. Update your file with the following snippet:

```
//XmlSerializer.h
private:
    QVariant readVariantMapFromStream(QXmlStreamReader& stream);

//XmlSerializer.cpp
QVariant XmlSerializer::readVariantMapFromStream(
    QXmlStreamReader& stream)
{
    QVariantMap map;
    while(stream.readNextStartElement()) {
        map.insert(stream.name().toString(),
                    readVariantFromStream(stream));
    }
    return map;
}
```

This function sounds like the `readVariantListFromStream()`. This time we have to create a `QVariantMap`. The key used for inserting a new item is the element name. We retrieve the name with the `QXmlStreamReader::name()` function.

A `Track` class serialized with the `XmlSerializer` looks like this:

```
<?xml version="1.0" encoding="UTF-8"?>
<track type="QVariantMap">
    <duration type="qlonglong">6205</duration>
    <soundEvents type="QVariantList">
        <item type="QVariantMap">
            <soundId type="int">0</soundId>
            <timestamp type="qlonglong">2689</timestamp>
        </item>
        <item type="QVariantMap">
            <soundId type="int">2</soundId>
            <timestamp type="qlonglong">2690</timestamp>
        </item>
        <item type="QVariantMap">
            <soundId type="int">2</soundId>
            <timestamp type="qlonglong">3067</timestamp>
        </item>
    </soundEvents>
</track>
```

# Serializing objects in binary format

The XML serialization is fully functional! We can now switch to the last type of serialization covered in this chapter.

The binary serialization is easier because Qt provides a direct way to do it. Please create a `BinarySerializer` class that inherits from `Serializer`. The header is common, we have only the override functions, `save()` and `load()`. Here is the implementation of the `save()` function:

```
void BinarySerializer::save(const Serializable& serializable,
    const QString& filepath, const QString& /*rootName*/)
{
    QFile file(filepath);
    file.open(QFile::WriteOnly);
    QDataStream dataStream(&file);
    dataStream << serializable.toVariant();
    file.close();
}
```

We hope you recognized the `QDataStream` class used in *Chapter 10, Need IPC? Get Your Minions to Work*. This time we use this class to serialize binary data in a destination `QFile`. A `QDataStream` class accepts a `QVariant` class with the << operator. Notice that the `rootName` variable is not used in the binary serializer.

Here is the `load()` function:

```
void BinarySerializer::load(Serializable& serializable, const QString&
filepath)
{
    QFile file(filepath);
    file.open(QFile::ReadOnly);
    QDataStream dataStream(&file);
    QVariant variant;
    dataStream >> variant;
    serializable.fromVariant(variant);
    file.close();
}
```

Thanks to the `QVariant` and the `QDataStream` mechanism, the task is easy. We open the `QFile` with the source `filepath`. We construct a `QDatastream` class with this `QFile`. Then, we use the >> operator to read the root `QVariant`. Finally, we fill the source `Serializable` with our `Serializable::fromVariant()` function.

Do not worry, we will not include an example of a `Track` class serialized with the `BinarySerializer` class.

The serialization part is completed. The GUI part of this example project has been covered many times during the previous chapters of this book. The following sections will only cover specific features used in our `MainWindow` and `SoundEffectWidget` classes. Check the source code if you need the complete C++ classes.

# Playing low latency sounds with QSoundEffect

The project application `ch11-drum-machine` displays four `SoundEffectWidget` widgets: `kickWidget`, `snareWidget`, `hihatWidget`, and `crashWidget`.

Each `SoundEffectWidget` widget displays a `QLabel` and a `QPushButton`. The label displays the sound name. If the button is clicked, a sound is played.

The Qt Multimedia module provides two main ways to play an audio file:

- `QMediaPlayer`: This file can play songs, movies, and Internet radio with various input formats
- `QSoundEffect`: This file can play low-latency `.wav` files

This project example is a virtual drum machine, so we are using a `QSoundEffect` object. The first step to use a `QSoundEffect` is to update your `.pro` file like this:

```
QT       += core gui multimedia
```

Then you can initialize the sound. Here is an example:

```
QUrl urlKick("qrc:/sounds/kick.wav");
QUrl urlBetterKick = QUrl::fromLocalFile("/home/better-kick.wav");

QSoundEffect soundEffect;
QSoundEffect.setSource(urlBetterKick);
```

The first step is to create a valid QUrl for your sound file. The urlKick is initialized from a .qrc resources file path, while urlBetterKick is created from a local file path. Then we can create QSoundEffect and set the URL sound to play with the QSoundEffect::setSource() function.

Now that we have a QSoundEffect object initialized, we can play the sound with the following code snippet:

```
soundEffect.setVolume(1.0f);
soundEffect.play();
```

# Triggering a QButton with your keyboard

Let's explore the public slot, triggerPlayButton(), in the SoundEffectWidget class:

```
//SoundEffectWidget.h
class SoundEffectWidget : public QWidget
{
...
public slots:
    void triggerPlayButton();
    ...

private:
    QPushButton* mPlayButton;
    ...
};

//SoundEffectWidget.cpp
void SoundEffectWidget::triggerPlayButton()
{
    mPlayButton->animateClick();
}
```

This widget has a QPushButton called mPlayButton. The triggerPlayButton() slot calls the QPushButton::animateClick() function, which simulates a click on the button over 100 ms by default. All signals will be sent as a real click does. The button really appears to be down. If you do not want the animation you can call QPushButton::click().

Let's see now how to trigger this slot with a key. Each `SoundEffectWidget` has a `Qt:Key`:

```
//SoundEffectWidget.h
class SoundEffectWidget : public QWidget
{
...
public:
    Qt::Key triggerKey() const;
    void setTriggerKey(const Qt::Key& triggerKey);
};

//SoundEffectWidget.cpp
Qt::Key SoundEffectWidget::triggerKey() const
{
    return mTriggerKey;
}

void SoundEffectWidget::setTriggerKey(const Qt::Key& triggerKey)
{
    mTriggerKey = triggerKey;
}
```

The `SoundEffectWidget` class provides a getter and a setter to get and set the member variable, `mTriggerKey`.

The `MainWindow` class initializes the keys of its four `SoundEffectWidget` like this:

```
ui->kickWidget->setTriggerKey(Qt::Key_H);
ui->snareWidget->setTriggerKey(Qt::Key_J);
ui->hihatWidget->setTriggerKey(Qt::Key_K);
ui->crashWidget->setTriggerKey(Qt::Key_L);
```

By default, the `QObject::eventFilter()` function is not called. To enable it and intercept these events, we need to install an event filter on the `MainWindow`:

```
installEventFilter(this);
```

So each time the `MainWindow` receives an event, the `MainWindow::eventFilter()` function is called.

Here is the `MainWindow.h` header:

```
class MainWindow : public QMainWindow
{
    Q_OBJECT
public:
    ...
    bool eventFilter(QObject* watched, QEvent* event) override;
```

```
    private:
        QVector<SoundEffectWidget*> mSoundEffectWidgets;
        ...
    };
```

The `MainWindow` class has a `QVector` with the four `SoundEffectWidgets`
(`kickWidget`, `snareWidget`, `hihatWidget`, and `crashWidget`). Let's see the
implementation in `MainWindow.cpp`:

```
bool MainWindow::eventFilter(QObject* watched, QEvent* event)
{
    if (event->type() == QEvent::KeyPress) {
        QKeyEvent* keyEvent = static_cast<QKeyEvent*>(event);
        for(SoundEffectWidget* widget : mSoundEffectWidgets) {
            if (keyEvent->key() == widget->triggerKey()) {
                widget->triggerPlayButton();
                return true;
            }
        }
    }
    return QObject::eventFilter(watched, event);
}
```

The first thing to do is to check that the `QEvent` class is a `KeyPress` type. We do not care
about other event types. If the event type is correct, we proceed to the following steps:

1. Cast the `QEvent` class to `QKeyEvent`.
2. Then we search if the pressed key belongs to the `SoundEffectWidget` class.
3. If a `SoundEffectWidget` class corresponds to the key, we call
   our `SoundEffectWidget::triggerPlayButton()` function and we
   return `true` to indicate that we consumed the event and it must not be
   propagated to others classes.
4. Otherwise, we call the `QObject` class implementation of `eventFilter()`.

# Bringing PlaybackWorker to life

The user can play a sound live with a mouse click or a keyboard key. But when he records
an awesome beat, the application must be able to play it again with the `PlaybackWorker`
class. Let's see how `MainWindow` uses this worker. Here is the `MainWindow.h` related to
the `PlaybackWorker` class:

```
class MainWindow : public QMainWindow
{
```

```
    ...
private slots:
    void playSoundEffect(int soundId);
    void clearPlayback();
    void stopPlayback();
    ...

private:
    void startPlayback();
    ...

private:
    PlaybackWorker* mPlaybackWorker;
    QThread* mPlaybackThread;
    ...
};
```

As you can see, MainWindow has PlaybackWorker and a QThread member variables. Let's see the implementation of startPlayback():

```
void MainWindow::startPlayback()
{
    clearPlayback();

    mPlaybackThread = new QThread();

    mPlaybackWorker = new PlaybackWorker(mTrack);
    mPlaybackWorker->moveToThread(mPlaybackThread);

    connect(mPlaybackThread, &QThread::started,
            mPlaybackWorker, &PlaybackWorker::play);
    connect(mPlaybackThread, &QThread::finished,
            mPlaybackWorker, &QObject::deleteLater);

    connect(mPlaybackWorker, &PlaybackWorker::playSound,
            this, &MainWindow::playSoundEffect);

    connect(mPlaybackWorker, &PlaybackWorker::trackFinished,
            &mTrack, &Track::stop);

    mPlaybackThread->start(QThread::HighPriority);
}
```

Let's analyze all the steps:

1. We clear the current playback with the `clearPlayback()` function, which will be covered soon.
2. The new `QThread` and `PlaybackWorker` are constructed. The current track is given to the worker at this moment. As usual, the worker is then moved to its dedicated thread.
3. We want to play the track as soon as possible. So, when the `QThread` emits the `started()` signal, the `PlaybackWorker::play()` slot is called.
4. We do not want to worry about the `PlaybackWorker` memory. So when the `QThread` is over and it has sent the `finished()` signal, we call the `QObject::deleteLater()` slot, which schedules the worker for deletion.
5. When the `PlaybackWorker` class needs to play a sound, the `playSound()` signal is emitted and our `MainWindow:playSoundEffect()` slot is called.
6. The last connect covers when the `PlaybackWorker` class finishes playing the whole track. A `trackFinished()` signal is emitted and we call the `Track::Stop()` slot.
7. Finally, the thread is started with a high priority. Notice that some operating systems (for example, Linux) do not support thread priorities.

We can now see the `stopPlayback()` body:

```
void MainWindow::stopPlayback()
{
    mPlaybackWorker->stop();
    clearPlayback();
}
```

We call the `stop()` function of the `PlaybackWorker` from our thread. Because we use a `QAtomicInteger` in `stop()`, the function is thread-safe and can be directly called. Finally, we call our helper function, `clearPlayback()`. This is the second time that we use `clearPlayback()`, so let's implement it:

```
void MainWindow::clearPlayback()
{
    if (mPlaybackThread) {
        mPlaybackThread->quit();
        mPlaybackThread->wait(1000);
        mPlaybackThread = nullptr;
        mPlaybackWorker = nullptr;
    }
}
```

No surprises here. If the thread is valid, we ask the thread to exit and wait 1 second. Then, we set the thread and the worker to `nullptr`.

The `PlaybackWorker::PlaySound` signal is connected to `MainWindow::playSoundEffect()`. Here is the implementation:

```
void MainWindow::playSoundEffect(int soundId)
{
    mSoundEffectWidgets[soundId]->triggerPlayButton();
}
```

This slot retrieves the `SoundEffectWidget` class corresponding to the `soundId`. Then, we call the `triggerPlayButton()`, the same method that is called when you press the trigger key on your keyboard.

So, when you click on the button, press a key, or when the `PlaybackWorker` class requests to play a sound, the `QPushButton` of `SoundEffectWidget` emits the signal, `clicked()`. This signal is connected to our `SoundEffectWidget::play()` slot. The next snippet describes this slot:

```
void SoundEffectWidget::play()
{
    mSoundEffect.play();
    emit soundPlayed(mId);
}
```

Nothing fancy here. We call the `play()` function on the `QSoundEffect` already covered. Finally, we emit the `soundPlayed()` signal that is used by `Track` to add a new `SoundEvent` if we are in the `RECORDING` state.

# Accepting mouse drag and drop events

In this project example, if you drag and drop a `.wav` file on a `SoundEffectWidget`, you can change the sound played. The constructor of `SoundEffectWidget` performs a specific task to allow drag and drop:

```
setAcceptDrops(true);
```

We can now override the drag and drop callbacks. Let's start with the `dragEnterEvent()` function:

```
//SoundEffectWidget.h
class SoundEffectWidget : public QWidget
{
```

```
...
protected:
    void dragEnterEvent(QDragEnterEvent* event) override;
...
};

//SoundEffectWidget.cpp
void SoundEffectWidget::dragEnterEvent(QDragEnterEvent* event)
{
    if (event->mimeData()->hasFormat("text/uri-list")) {
        event->acceptProposedAction();
    }
}
```

The dragEnterEvent() function is called each time the user drags an object on the widget. In our case, we only want to allow drag and drop on files that are of the MIME type: "text/uri-list" (a list of URIs, which can be file://, http://, and so on). In this case, though we can call the QDragEnterEvent::acceptProposedAction() function to notify that we accept this object for a drag and drop.

We can now add a second function, dropEvent():

```
//SoundEffectWidget.h
class SoundEffectWidget : public QWidget
{
...
protected:
    void dropEvent(QDropEvent* event) override;
...
};

//SoundEffectWidget.cpp
void SoundEffectWidget::dropEvent(QDropEvent* event)
{
    const QMimeData* mimeData = event->mimeData();
    if (!mimeData->hasUrls()) {
        return;
    }
    const QUrl url = mimeData->urls().first();
    QMimeType mime = QMimeDatabase().mimeTypeForUrl(url);
    if (mime.inherits("audio/wav")) {
        loadSound(url);
    }
}
```

The first step is a sanity check. If the event does not have a URL, we do nothing. The QMimeData::hasUrls() function returns true only with the MIME type: "text/uri-text". Notice that a user can drag and drop multiple files at once. In our case, we only handle the first URL. You can check that the file is a .wav file with its MIME type. If the MIME type is "audio/wav", we call the loadSound() function, which updates the sound assigned to this SoundEffectWidget.

The following screenshot show the complete application for ch11-drum-machine:

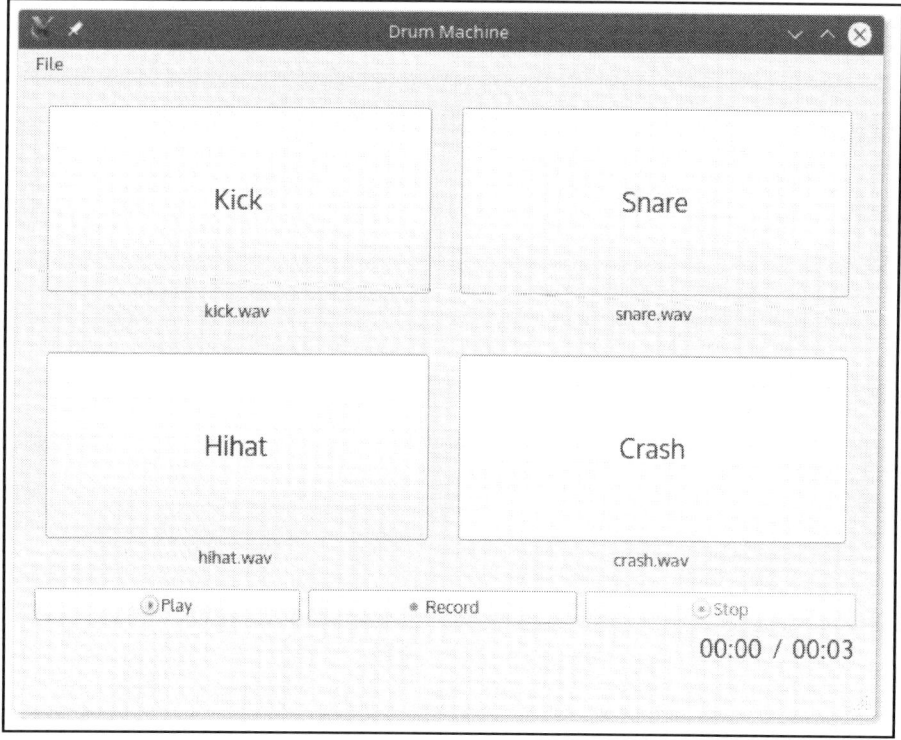

# Summary

Serialization is a good way to make your data persistent when you close your application. In this chapter, you learned to make your C++ objects serializable with `QVariant`. You created a flexible serialization structure with the Bridge pattern. You saved an object in a different text format such as JSON or XML and also in a binary format.

You also learned to use the Qt Multimedia module to play some sound effects. These sounds can be triggered by a mouse click or by a keyboard key. You implemented a friendly user interaction, allowing you to load a new sound with a file drag and drop.

In the next chapter, we will discover the `QTest` framework and how you can organize your project so it has a clean application/test separation.

# 12

# You Shall (Not) Pass with QTest

In the previous chapter, we created a drum machine software with some serialization feature. In this chapter, we will write the unit tests for this application. To achieve this goal, we will use Qt Test, a dedicated test module for Qt applications.

The example project is a test application using CLI commands to execute and generate a test report. We will cover different types of tests including datasets, GUI, signals, and benchmarking.

This chapter will cover the following topics:

- Qt Test framework
- Project layout for unit tests
- Personalize your test execution
- Write tests with datasets
- Benchmark your code
- Simulating GUI events
- Perform signal introspection with the `QSignalSpy` class

# Discovering Qt Test

The Qt framework provides Qt Test, a complete API to create your unit tests in C++. A test executes the code of your application and performs verification on it. Usually, a test compares a variable with an expected value. If the variable does not match the specific value, the test fails. If you wish to go further, you can benchmark your code and get the time/CPU tick/events required by your code. Clicking over and over on a GUI to test it can quickly become boring. Qt Test offers you the possibility to simulate keyboard entries and mouse events on your widgets to completely check your software.

In our case, we want to create a unit test program named `drum-machine-test`. This console application will check the code of our famous drum machine from the previous chapter. Create a `subdirs` project called `ch12-drum-machine-test` with the following topology:

- `drum-machine`:
    - `drum-machine.pro`
- `drum-machine-test`:
    - `drum-machine-test.pro`
- `ch12-drum-machine-test.pro`
- `drum-machine-src.pri`

The `drum-machine` and `drum-machine-test` projects share the same source code. So all common files are put in a project include file: `drum-machine-src.pri`. Here is the updated `drum-machine.pro`:

```
QT += core gui multimedia widgets
CONFIG += c++14

TARGET = drum-machine
TEMPLATE = app

include(../drum-machine-src.pri)

SOURCES += main.cpp
```

As you can see, we only perform a refactoring task; the project drum-machine is not affected by the drum-machine-test application. You can now create the `drum-machine-test.pro` file like this:

```
QT += core gui multimedia widgets testlib
CONFIG += c++14 console
```

```
TARGET = drum-machine-test
TEMPLATE = app

include(../drum-machine-src.pri)

DRUM_MACHINE_PATH = ../drum-machine
INCLUDEPATH += $$DRUM_MACHINE_PATH
DEPENDPATH += $$DRUM_MACHINE_PATH

SOURCES += main.cpp
```

The first thing to notice is that we need to enable the `testlib` module. Then even if we are creating a console application, we want to perform a test on the GUI so the modules (`gui`, `multimedia`, and `widgets`) used by the primary application are also required here. Finally, we include the project include file with all application files (sources, headers, forms, and resources). The `drum-machine-test` application will also contain new source files, so we must correctly set the `INCLUDEPATH` and `DEPENDPATH` variables to the source files folder.

Qt Test is easy to use and relies on some simple assumptions:

- A test case is a `QObject` class
- A private slot is a test function
- A test case can contain several test functions

Notice that the private slots with the following names are not test functions, but special functions automatically called to initialize and clean up your test:

- `initTestCase()`: This function is called before the first test function
- `init()`: This function is called before each test function
- `cleanup()`: This function is called after each test function
- `cleanupTestCase()`: This function is called after the last test function

Alright, we are ready to write our first test case in the `drum-machine-test` application. The serialization of the `drum-machine` object is an important part. A bad modification on the save feature can easily break the load feature. It can produce no errors at compile time, but it can lead to an unusable application. That is why tests are important. The first thing is to validate the serialization/deserialization process. Create a new C++ class, `DummySerializable`. Here is the header file:

```
#include "Serializable.h"

class DummySerializable : public Serializable
```

```
{
public:
    DummySerializable();

    QVariant toVariant() const override;
    void fromVariant(const QVariant& variant) override;

    int myInt = 0;
    double myDouble = 0.0;
    QString myString = "";
    bool myBool = false;
};
```

It is a simple class implementing our Serializable interface created in Chapter
11, *Having Fun with Serialization*. This class will be helpful to validate the lower layer in our
serialization process. As you can see, the class contains some variables with various types to
ensure a complete functioning serialization. Let's see the file,
DummySerializable.cpp:

```
#include "DummySerializable.h"

DummySerializable::DummySerializable() :
    Serializable()
{
}

QVariant DummySerializable::toVariant() const
{
    QVariantMap map;
    map.insert("myInt", myInt);
    map.insert("myDouble", myDouble);
    map.insert("myString", myString);
    map.insert("myBool", myBool);
    return map;
}

void DummySerializable::fromVariant(const QVariant& variant)
{
    QVariantMap map = variant.toMap();
    myInt = map.value("myInt").toInt();
    myDouble = map.value("myDouble").toDouble();
    myString = map.value("myString").toString();
    myBool = map.value("myBool").toBool();
}
```

No surprise here; we perform our operation with a QVariantMap, as already performed in the previous chapter. Our dummy class is ready; create a new C++ class, TestJsonSerializer, with the following header:

```
#include <QtTest/QTest>

#include "JsonSerializer.h"

class TestJsonSerializer : public QObject
{
    Q_OBJECT

public:
    TestJsonSerializer(QObject* parent = nullptr);

private slots:
    void cleanup();
    void saveDummy();
    void loadDummy();

private:
    QString loadFileContent();

private:
    JsonSerializer mSerializer;
};
```

Here we are, our first test case! This test case performs verifications on our class, JsonSerializer. You can see two test functions, saveDummy() and loadDummy(). The cleanup() slot is the special Qt Test slot that we covered earlier, which is executed after each test function. We can now write the implementation in TestJsonSerializer.cpp:

```
#include "DummySerializable.h"

const QString FILENAME = "test.json";
const QString DUMMY_FILE_CONTENT = "{\n    "myBool": true,\n    "myDouble":
5.2,\n    "myInt": 1,\n    "myString": "hello"\n}\n";

TestJsonSerializer::TestJsonSerializer(QObject* parent) :
    QObject(parent),
    mSerializer()
{
}
```

Two constants are created here:

- FILENAME: This is the filename used to test the save and load the data
- DUMMY_FILE_CONTENT: This is the referential file content used by the test functions, saveDummy() and loadDummy()

Let's implement the test function, saveDummy():

```
void TestJsonSerializer::saveDummy()
{
    DummySerializable dummy;
    dummy.myInt = 1;
    dummy.myDouble = 5.2;
    dummy.myString = "hello";
    dummy.myBool = true;

    mSerializer.save(dummy, FILENAME);

    QString data = loadFileContent();
    QVERIFY(data == DUMMY_FILE_CONTENT);
}
```

The first step is to instantiate a DummySerializable class with some fixed values. So, we call the function to test, JsonSerializer::save(), that will serialize our dummy object in the test.json file. Then, we call a helper function, loadFileContent(), to get the text contained in the test.json file. Finally, we use a Qt Test macro, QVERIFY(), to perform the verification that the text saved by the JSON serializer is the same as the expected value in DUMMY_FILE_CONTENT. If data equals the correct value, the test function succeeds. Here is the log output:

```
PASS   : TestJsonSerializer::saveDummy()
```

If the data is different than the expected value, the test fails and an error is displayed in the console log:

```
FAIL!  : TestJsonSerializer::saveDummy()
'data == DUMMY_FILE_CONTENT' returned FALSE. ()
Loc: [../../ch12-drum-machine-test/drum-machine-
test/TestJsonSerializer.cpp(31)]
```

Let's briefly see the helper function, loadFileContent():

```
QString TestJsonSerializer::loadFileContent()
{
    QFile file(FILENAME);
    file.open(QFile::ReadOnly);
```

```
    QString content = file.readAll();
    file.close();
    return content;
}
```

No big deal here. We open the file, `test.json`, read all the text content, and return the corresponding `QString`.

The macro, `QVERIFY()`, is great to check a Boolean value, but Qt Test provides a better macro when you want to compare data to an expected value. Let's discover `QCOMPARE()` with the test function, `loadDummy()`:

```
void TestJsonSerializer::loadDummy()
{
    QFile file(FILENAME);
    file.open(QFile::WriteOnly | QIODevice::Text);
    QTextStream out(&file);
    out << DUMMY_FILE_CONTENT;
    file.close();

    DummySerializable dummy;
    mSerializer.load(dummy, FILENAME);

    QCOMPARE(dummy.myInt, 1);
    QCOMPARE(dummy.myDouble, 5.2);
    QCOMPARE(dummy.myString, QString("hello"));
    QCOMPARE(dummy.myBool; true);
}
```

The first part creates a `test.json` file, with a referential content. Then we create an empty `DummySerializable` and call the function to test `Serializable::load()`. Finally, we use the Qt Test macro, `QCOMPARE()`. The syntax is simple:

```
QCOMPARE(actual_value, expected_value);
```

We can now test each field of the dummy loaded from JSON. The test function, `loadDummmy()`, will only succeed if all `QCOMPARE()` calls succeed. An error with a `QCOMPARE()` is much more detailed:

```
FAIL!  : TestJsonSerializer::loadDummy() Compared values are not the same
   Actual   (dummy.myInt): 0
   Expected (1)          : 1
Loc: [../../ch12-drum-machine-test/drum-machine-
test/TestJsonSerializer.cpp(45)]
```

Each time a test function is executed, the special `cleanup()` slot is called. Let's update your file, `TestJsonSerializable.cpp`, like this:

```
void TestJsonSerializer::cleanup()
{
    QFile(FILENAME).remove();
}
```

This is a simple security that will remove the `test.json` file after each test function and prevent the save and load tests from colliding.

# Executing your tests

We wrote a test case, `TestJsonSerializer`, with some test functions. We need a `main()` function in our `drum-machine-test` application. We will explore three possibilities:

- The `QTEST_MAIN()` function
- Write our own simple `main()` function
- Write our own enhanced `main()` supporting multiple test classes

The `QTest` module provides an interesting macro, `QTEST_MAIN()`. This macro generates a complete `main()` function for your application. This generated method runs all the test functions of your test case. To use it, add the following snippet at the end of the `TestJsonSerializer.cpp` file:

```
QTEST_MAIN(TestJsonSerializer)
```

Moreover, if you declare and implement your test class only in the `.cpp` file (without a header file), you need to include the generated moc file after the `QTEST_MAIN` macro:

```
QTEST_MAIN(TestJsonSerializer)
#include "testjsonserializer"
```

If you use the `QTEST_MAIN()` macro, do not forget to remove the existing `main.cpp`. Otherwise, you will have two `main()` functions and a compilation error will happen.

You can now try to run your drum-machine-test application and look at the application output. You should see something similar to this:

```
$ ./drum-machine-test
********* Start testing of TestJsonSerializer *********
Config: Using QtTest library 5.7.0, Qt 5.7.0 (x86_64-little_endian-lp64
shared (dynamic) release build; by GCC 4.9.1 20140922 (Red Hat 4.9.1-10))
```

```
PASS    : TestJsonSerializer::initTestCase()
PASS    : TestJsonSerializer::saveDummy()
PASS    : TestJsonSerializer::loadDummy()
PASS    : TestJsonSerializer::cleanupTestCase()
Totals: 4 passed, 0 failed, 0 skipped, 0 blacklisted, 1ms
********* Finished testing of TestJsonSerializer *********
```

Our test functions, saveDummy() and loadDummy(), are executed in the declaration order. Both succeed with the PASS status. The generated test application handles some options. Commonly, you can display the help menu executing this command:

```
$ ./drum-machine-test -help
```

Let's see some cool features. We can execute only one function with the name. The following command only executes the saveDummy test function:

```
$ ./drum-machine-test saveDummy
```

You can also execute several test functions separating their names with a space.

The QTest application provides log detail options:

- -silent for silent. Only displays fatal errors and summary messages.
- -v1 for verbose. Shows the test function entered information.
- -v2 for extended verbose. Shows each QCOMPARE() and QVERIFY().
- -vs for verbose signal. Shows the emitted signal and the connected slot.

For example, we can display details of the execution of loadDummy with the following command:

```
$ ./drum-machine-test -v2 loadDummy
********* Start testing of TestJsonSerializer *********
Config: Using QtTest library 5.7.0, Qt 5.7.0 (x86_64-little_endian-lp64
shared (dynamic) release build; by GCC 4.9.1 20140922 (Red Hat 4.9.1-10))
    INFO    : TestJsonSerializer::initTestCase() entering
    PASS    : TestJsonSerializer::initTestCase()
    INFO    : TestJsonSerializer::loadDummy() entering
    INFO    : TestJsonSerializer::loadDummy() QCOMPARE(dummy.myInt, 1)
        Loc: [../../ch12-drum-machine-test/drum-machine-
test/TestJsonSerializer.cpp(45)]
    INFO    : TestJsonSerializer::loadDummy() QCOMPARE(dummy.myDouble, 5.2)
        Loc: [../../ch12-drum-machine-test/drum-machine-
test/TestJsonSerializer.cpp(46)]
    INFO    : TestJsonSerializer::loadDummy() QCOMPARE(dummy.myString,
QString("hello"))
        Loc: [../../ch12-drum-machine-test/drum-machine-
```

```
test/TestJsonSerializer.cpp(47)]
    INFO   : TestJsonSerializer::loadDummy() QCOMPARE(dummy.myBool, true)
       Loc: [../../ch12-drum-machine-test/drum-machine-
test/TestJsonSerializer.cpp(48)]
    PASS   : TestJsonSerializer::loadDummy()
    INFO   : TestJsonSerializer::cleanupTestCase() entering
    PASS   : TestJsonSerializer::cleanupTestCase()
    Totals: 3 passed, 0 failed, 0 skipped, 0 blacklisted, 1ms
    ********* Finished testing of TestJsonSerializer *********
```

Another great feature is the logging output format. You can create a test report file with various formats (.txt, .xml, .csv, and so on). The syntax requires a filename and a file format separated by a comma:

```
$ ./drum-machine-test -o <filename>,<format>
```

In the following example, we create an XML report named test-report.xml:

```
$ ./drum-machine-test -o test-report.xml,xml
```

Notice that some log level affects only the plain text output. Moreover, the CSV format can be used only with the test macro QBENCHMARK, which is covered later in this chapter.

If you want to customize the generated test application, you can write the main() function. Remove the QTEST_MAIN macro in TestJsonSerializer.cpp. Then create a main.cpp like this:

```
#include "TestJsonSerializer.h"

int main(int argc, char *argv[])
{
    TestJsonSerializer test;
    QStringList arguments = QCoreApplication::arguments();
    return QTest::qExec(&test, arguments);
}
```

In this case, we are using the static function, QTest::qExec(), to start a TestJsonSerializer test. Do not forget to provide the command-line arguments to enjoy the QTest CLI options.

If you wrote your test functions in different test classes, you would have created one application by a test class. If you keep one test class by test application you can even use the QTEST_MAIN macro to generate the main functions.

Sometimes you want to create only one test application to handle all your test classes. In this case, you have multiple test classes in the same application, so you cannot use the QTEST_MAIN macro because you do not want to generate several main functions for each test class.

Let's see a simple way to call all your test classes in a unique application:

```
int main(int argc, char *argv[])
{
    int status = 0;
    TestFoo testFoo;
    TestBar testBar;
    status |= QTest::qExec(&testFoo);
    status |= QTest::qExec(&testBar);
    return status;
}
```

In this simple custom main() function, we are executing the TestFoo and TestBar tests. But we are losing the CLI options. Indeed, executing the QTest::qExec() function with command-line arguments more than once will lead to errors and bad behaviors. For example, if you want to execute only one specific test function from TestBar. The execution of TestFoo will not find the test function, display an error message, and stop the application.

Here is a workaround to handle several test classes in a unique application. We will create a new CLI option, -select, to our test application. This option allows you to select a specific test class to execute. Here is a syntax example:

```
$ ./drum-machine-test -select foo fooTestFunction
```

The -select option, if used, must be at the beginning of the command followed by the test class name (foo in this example). Then, we can optionally add Qt Test options. To achieve this goal, we will create an enhanced main() function that parses the new select option and execute the corresponding test class.

We will create our enhanced main() function together:

```
QApplication app(argc, argv);
QStringList arguments = QCoreApplication::arguments();

map<QString, unique_ptr<QObject>> tests;
tests.emplace("jsonserializer",
    make_unique<TestJsonSerializer>());
tests.emplace("foo", make_unique<TestFoo>());
tests.emplace("bar", make_unique<TestBar>());
```

The `QApplication` will be required later by our other GUI test cases. We retrieve the command line arguments for later use. The `std::map` template named `tests` contains the smart pointers of the test classes and a `QString` label is used as a key. Notice that we are using the `map::emplace()` function that does not copy the source to the map, but creates it in place. Using the `map::insert()` function leads to an error due to the illegal copy of a smart pointer. Another syntax that could be used with a `std::map` template and a `make_unique` is:

```
tests["bar"] = make_unique<TestBar>();
```

We can now parse the command line arguments:

```
if (arguments.size() >= 3 && arguments[1] == "-select") {
    QString testName = arguments[2];
    auto iter = tests.begin();
    while(iter != tests.end()) {
        if (iter->first != testName) {
            iter = tests.erase(iter);
        } else {
            ++iter;
        }
    }
    arguments.removeOne("-select");
    arguments.removeOne(testName);
}
```

If the `-select` option is used, this snippet performs two important tasks:

- Removes from the map `tests`, the test classes that do not match the test name
- Removes the arguments from the `-select` option and the `testName` variable to provide cleaned arguments to the `QTest::qExec()` function

We can now add the final step to execute the test classes:

```
int status = 0;
for(auto& test : tests) {
    status |= QTest::qExec(test.second.get(), arguments);
}

return status;
```

Without the `-select` option, all the test classes will be performed. If we use the `-select` option with a test class name, only this one will be executed.

# Writing factorized tests with datasets

We will now turn our attention to testing the `Track` class. We will focus specifically on the different states a `Track` class can have: STOPPED, PLAYING, and RECORDING. For each one of these states, we want to make sure that adding `SoundEvents` works only if we are in the proper state (RECORDING).

To do so, we could write the following test functions:

- `testAddSoundEvent()`: This function puts the `Track` in the STOPPED state, calls `track.addSoundEvent(0)`, and checks `track.soundEvents().size == 0`
- `testAddSoundEvent()`: This function puts the `Track` in the PLAYING state, calls `track.addSoundEvent(0)`, and checks `track.soundEvents().size == 0`
- `testAddSoundEvent()`: This function puts the `Track` in the RECORDING state, calls `track.addSoundEvent(0)`, and checks `track.soundEvents().size == 1`

As you can see, the logic is the same, we simply change the inputs and the desired outputs. To factorize this, Qt Test provides another module: datasets.

A dataset can be seen as a two-dimensional table where each row is a test, and the columns are the inputs and expected outputs. For our `Track` state test, it would look like this:

| index | name | input (Track::State) | result (soundEvents count) |
|-------|------|----------------------|----------------------------|
| 0 | STOPPED | State::STOPPED | 0 |
| 1 | PLAYING | State::PLAYING | 0 |
| 2 | RECORDING | State::RECORDING | 1 |

With this approach, you write a single `addSoundEvent()` test function and Qt Test takes care of iterating over this table and comparing the result. Right now, it seems like magic. Let's implement it!

Create a new C++ class named `TestTrack`, following the same pattern used for the `TestJsonSerializer` class (inherits `QObject`, includes `QTest`). Update `TestTrack.h` like so:

```
class TestTrack : public QObject
{
    Q_OBJECT
public:
    explicit TestTrack(QObject *parent = 0);

private slots:
    void addSoundEvent_data();
    void addSoundEvent();
};
```

Here we added two functions:

- `addSoundEvent_data()`: This is the function that fills the dataset for the real test
- `addSoundEvent()`: This is the function that executes the test

As you can see, the function that fills the dataset for a given `xxx()` function must be named `xxx_data()`. Let's see the implementation of `addSoundEvent_data()`:

```
void TestTrack::addSoundEvent_data()
{
    QTest::addColumn<int>("trackState");
    QTest::addColumn<int>("soundEventCount");

    QTest::newRow("STOPPED")
                << static_cast<int>(Track::State::STOPPED)
                << 0;
    QTest::newRow("PLAYING")
                << static_cast<int>(Track::State::PLAYING)
                << 0;
    QTest::newRow("RECORDING")
                << static_cast<int>(Track::State::RECORDING)
                << 1;
}
```

As you can see, a dataset is constructed like a table. We start by defining the structure of the table with the `trackState` and `soundEventCount` columns. Note that `QTest::addColumn` relies on templating to know the type of the variable (`int` in both cases).

After that, a row is appended to the table with the `QTest::newRow()` function, with the name of the test passed as a parameter. The `QTest::newRow` syntax supports the `<<` operator, making it very easy to pack all the data for a given row.

Note that each row added to the dataset corresponds to an execution of the `addSoundEvent()` function in which the data of the row will be available.

We can now turn our attention to `addSoundEvent()`:

```
void TestTrack::addSoundEvent()
{
    QFETCH(int, trackState);
    QFETCH(int, soundEventCount);

    Track track;
    switch (static_cast<Track::State>(trackState)) {
        case Track::State::STOPPED:
            track.stop();
            break;
        case Track::State::PLAYING:
            track.play();
            break;
        case Track::State::RECORDING:
            track.record();
            break;
        default:
            break;
    }

    track.addSoundEvent(0);
    track.stop();

    QCOMPARE(track.soundEvents().size(),
             static_cast<size_t>(soundEventCount));
}
```

Because `addSoundEvent()` is executed by QTest and is fed with the dataset data, we can safely access the current row of the dataset like we would do with a cursor on a database. The `QFETCH(int, trackState)` is a helpful macro that does two things:

- Declares an `int` variable named `trackState`
- Fetches the current column index data of the dataset and stores its content in `trackState`

The same principle is applied to `soundEventCount`. Now that we have our desired track state and the expected sound events count, we can proceed to the real test:

1. Put the track in the proper state according to `trackState`. Remember that the `Track::setState()` function is private, because the `Track` keyword handles the `trackState` variable alone, based on the caller instruction (`stop()`, `play()`, `record()`).
2. Try to add a `SoundEvent` to track.
3. Stop the track.
4. Compare the number of `SoundEvents` in track to what is expected in `soundEventCount`.

Do not forget to add the `TestTrack` class in `main.cpp`:

```cpp
#include "TestJsonSerializer.h"
#include "TestTrack.h"

...

int main(int argc, char *argv[])
{
    ...
    map<QString, unique_ptr<QObject>> tests;
    tests.emplace("jsonserializer",
                  make_unique<TestJsonSerializer>());
    tests.emplace("track",
                  make_unique<TestTrack>());
    ...
}
```

You can now run the tests and see the three tests of `addSoundEvent()` output their result in the console:

```
PASS   : TestTrack::addSoundEvent(STOPPED)
PASS   : TestTrack::addSoundEvent(PLAYING)
PASS   : TestTrack::addSoundEvent(RECORDING)
```

Datasets make the writing of tests less dull, by factorizing variations of data for a single test.

You can also run a single test for a specific entry of a dataset using the command line:

```
$ ./drum-machine-test <testfunction>:<dataset entry>
```

Let's say we want to execute the test function addSoundEvent() from TestTrack with only the RECORDING state. Here is the command line to run:

```
$ ./drum-machine-test -select track addSoundEvent:RECORDING
```

# Benchmarking your code

Qt Test also provides a very easy to use semantic to benchmark the execution speed of your code. To see it in action, we will benchmark the time it takes to save a Track in the JSON format. Depending on the track length (the number of SoundEvents), the serialization should take more or less time.

Of course, it is more interesting to benchmark this feature with different track lengths and see if the time saving is linear. Datasets come to the rescue! It is not only useful to run the same function with expected inputs and outputs, but also to run the same function with different parameters.

We will start by creating the dataset function in TestJsonSerializer:

```
class TestJsonSerializer : public QObject
{
    ...

private slots:
    void cleanup();
    void saveDummy();
    void loadDummy();

    void saveTrack_data();
    ...
};

void TestJsonSerializer::saveTrack_data()
{
    QTest::addColumn<int>("soundEventCount");

    QTest::newRow("1") << 1;
    QTest::newRow("100") << 100;
    QTest::newRow("1000") << 1000;
}
```

The saveTrack_data() function simply stores the number of SoundEvent to be added to a Track class before it is saved. The "1", "100", and "1000" strings are here to have a clear label in the test execution output. These strings will be displayed in each execution of saveTrack(). Feel free to tweak these numbers!

Now for the real test with the benchmark call:

```
class TestJsonSerializer : public QObject
{
    ...
    void saveTrack_data();
    void saveTrack();
    ...
};

void TestJsonSerializer::saveTrack()
{
    QFETCH(int, soundEventCount);
    Track track;
    track.record();
    for (int i = 0; i < soundEventCount; ++i) {
        track.addSoundEvent(i % 4);
    }
    track.stop();

    QBENCHMARK {
        mSerializer.save(track, FILENAME);
    }
}
```

The saveTrack() function starts by fetching the soundEventCount column from its dataset. After that, it adds the correct number of soundEvent (with the proper record() state!) and finally benchmarks the serialization in the JSON format.

You can see that the benchmark itself is simply a macro that looks like this:

```
QBENCHMARK {
    // instructions to benchmark
}
```

The instructions enclosed in the QBENCHMARK macro will be measured automatically. If you execute the test with the updated TestJsonSerializer class, you should see an output similar to this:

```
PASS   : TestJsonSerializer::saveTrack(1)
RESULT : TestJsonSerializer::saveTrack():"1":
     0.041 msecs per iteration (total: 84, iterations: 2048)
```

```
PASS   : TestJsonSerializer::saveTrack(100)
RESULT : TestJsonSerializer::saveTrack():"100":
    0.23 msecs per iteration (total: 59, iterations: 256)
PASS   : TestJsonSerializer::saveTrack(1000)
RESULT : TestJsonSerializer::saveTrack():"1000":
    2.0 msecs per iteration (total: 66, iterations: 32)
```

As you can see, the QBENCHMARK macro makes Qt Test output very interesting data. To save a Track class with a single SoundEvent, it took 0.041 milliseconds. Qt Test repeated this test 2048 times and it took a total of 84 milliseconds.

The power of the QBENCHMARK macro starts to be visible in the following test. Here, the saveTrack() function tried to save a Track class with 100 SoundEvents. It took 0.23 milliseconds to do it and it repeated the instruction 256 times. This shows you that the Qt Test benchmark automatically adjusts the number of iterations based on the average time a single iteration takes.

The QBENCHMARK macro has this behavior because a metric tends to be more accurate if it is repeated multiple times (to avoid possible external noise).

 If you want your test to be benchmarked without multiple iterations, use QBENCHMARK_ONCE.

If you execute the test using the command line, you can provide additional metrics to QBENCHMARK. Here is the table recapitulating the available options:

| Name | Command-line argument | Availability |
| --- | --- | --- |
| Walltime | (default) | All platforms |
| CPU tick counter | -tickcounter | Windows, OS X, Linux, many UNIX-like systems. |
| Event Counter | -eventcounter | All platforms |
| Valgrind Callgrind | -callgrind | Linux (if installed) |
| Linux Perf | -perf | Linux |

Each one of these options will replace the selected backend used to measure the execution time of the benchmarked code. For example, if you run `drum-machine-test` with the `-tickcounter` argument:

```
$ ./drum-machine-test -tickcounter
...
RESULT : TestJsonSerializer::saveTrack():"1":
     88,062 CPU cycles per iteration (total: 88,062, iterations: 1)
PASS   : TestJsonSerializer::saveTrack(100)
RESULT : TestJsonSerializer::saveTrack():"100":
     868,706 CPU cycles per iteration (total: 868,706, iterations: 1)
PASS   : TestJsonSerializer::saveTrack(1000)
RESULT : TestJsonSerializer::saveTrack():"1000":
     7,839,871 CPU cycles per iteration (total: 7,839,871, iterations:
1)
...
```

You can see that the wall time, measured in milliseconds, has been replaced by the number of CPU cycles completed for each iteration.

Another interesting option is `-eventcounter`, which measures the numbers that were received by the event loop before they are sent to their corresponding target. This could be an interesting way of checking that your code emits the proper number of signals.

# Testing your GUI

It is now time to see how you can test your GUI using the Qt Test API. The `QTest` class offers several functions to simulate keys and mouse events.

To demonstrate it, we will stay with the notion of testing a `Track` state, but on an upper level. Rather than testing the `Track` state itself, we will check that the UI state of the `drum-machine` application is properly updated when the `Track` state is changed. Namely, the control buttons (play, stop, record) should be in a specific state when a recording is started.

Start by creating a `TestGui` class in the `drum-machine-test` project. Do not forget to add the `TestGui` class in the `tests` map of `main.cpp`. As usual, make it inherit `QObject` and update `TestGui.h` like so:

```
#include <QTest>

#include "MainWindow.h"

class TestGui : public QObject
{
```

```
    Q_OBJECT
public:
    TestGui(QObject* parent = 0);

private:
    MainWindow mMainWindow;
};
```

In this header, we have a member, mMainWindow, which is an instance of the MainWindow keyword from the drum-machine project. Throughout the tests of TestGui, a single MainWindow will be used, in which we will inject events and check how it reacts.

Let's switch to the TestGui constructor:

```
#include <QtTest/QtTest>

TestGui::TestGui(QObject* parent) :
    QObject(parent),
    mMainWindow()
{
    QTestEventLoop::instance().enterLoop(1);
}
```

The constructor initializes the mMainWindow variable. Notice that mMainWindow is never shown (using mMainWindow.show()). We do not need to display it, we solely want to test its states.

Here, we use a rather obscure function call (QTestEventLoop is not documented at all) to force the event loop to be started after 1 second.

The reason why we have to do this lies in the QSoundEffect class. The QSoundEffect class is initialized when the QSoundEffect::setSource() function is called (in MainWindow, this is done at the initialization of the SoundEffectWidgets). If we omit the explicit enterLoop() call, the drum-machine-test execution will crash with a segmentation fault.

It seems that the event loop has to be explicitly entered to let the QSoundEffect class properly complete its initialization. We found this undocumented workaround by studying the Qt unit tests of the QSoundEffect class.

Now for the real GUI test! To test the control buttons, update `TestGui`:

```cpp
// In TestGui.h
class TestGui : public QObject
{
    ...
private slots:
    void controlButtonState();
    ...
};

// In TestGui.cpp
#include <QtTest/QtTest>
#include <QPushButton>
...
void TestGui::controlButtonState()
{
    QPushButton* stopButton =
        mMainWindow.findChild<QPushButton*>("stopButton");
    QPushButton* playButton =
        mMainWindow.findChild<QPushButton*>("playButton");
    QPushButton* recordButton =
        mMainWindow.findChild<QPushButton*>("recordButton");

    QTest::mouseClick(recordButton, Qt::LeftButton);

    QCOMPARE(stopButton->isEnabled(), true);
    QCOMPARE(playButton->isEnabled(), false);
    QCOMPARE(recordButton->isEnabled(), false);
}
```

In the `controlButtonState()` function, we start by retrieving our buttons by using the handy `mMainWindow.findChild()` function. This function is available in `QObject`, and the passed name corresponds to the `objectName` variable we used for each button in Qt Designer when we created `MainWindow.ui`.

Once we retrieve all the buttons, we inject a mouse click event using the `QTest::mouseClick()` function. It takes a `QWidget*` parameter as a target and the button that should be clicked. You can even pass keyboard modifiers (control, shift, and so on) and a possible click delay in milliseconds.

Once the `recordButton` has been clicked, we test the states of all the control buttons to make sure that they are in the desired enabled state.

This function can be easily extended to test all the states (PLAYING, STOPPED, RECORDING) with a dataset where the input is the desired state and the outputs are the expected buttons states.

The QTest class offers many useful functions to inject events, including:

- keyEvent(): This function is used to simulate a key event
- keyPress(): This function is used to simulate a key press event
- keyRelease(): This function is used to simulate a key release event
- mouseClick(): This function is used to simulate a key click event
- mouseDClick(): This function is used to simulate a mouse double click event
- mouseMove(): This function is used to simulate a mouse move event

# Spying on your application with QSignalSpy

The last part we will cover in the Qt Test framework is the ability to spy on signals with QSignalSpy. This class allows you to do introspection of the emitted signal of any QObject.

Let's see it in action with SoundEffectWidget. We will test that when the SoundEffectWidget::play() function is called, the soundPlayed signal is emitted with the correct soundId parameter.

Here is the playSound() function of TestGui:

```
#include <QTest>

#include "MainWindow.h"

// In TestGui.h
class TestGui : public QObject
{
    ...
    void controlButtonState();
    void playSound();
    ...
};

// In TestGui.cpp
#include <QPushButton>
#include <QtTest/QtTest>
```

```
#include "SoundEffectWidget.h"
...
void TestGui::playSound()
{
    SoundEffectWidget widget;
    QSignalSpy spy(&widget, &SoundEffectWidget::soundPlayed);
    widget.setId(2);
    widget.play();

    QCOMPARE(spy.count(), 1);
    QList<QVariant> arguments = spy.takeFirst();
    QCOMPARE(arguments.at(0).toInt(), 2);
}
```

We start by initializing a `SoundEffectWidget` widget and a `QSignalSpy` class. The `spy` class's constructor takes the pointer to the object to spy and the pointer to the member function of the signal to be watched. Here, we want to check the `SoundEffectWidget::soundPlayed()` signal.

Right after, `widget` is configured with an arbitrary `soundId` (2) and `widget.play()` is called. This is where it gets interesting: `spy` stores the signal's emitted parameters in a `QVariantList`. Each time `soundPlayed()` is emitted, a new `QVariantList` is created in `spy`, which contains the emitted parameters.

The first step is to check that the signal is emitted only once, by comparing `spy.count()` to 1. Just after that, we store the parameters of this signal in `arguments` and check that it has the value 2, the initial `soundId` that `widget` was configured with.

As you can see, `QSignalSpy` is simple to use; you can create as many as you need for each signal you want to spy on.

# Summary

The Qt Test module gracefully helps us to easily create a test application. You learned to organize your project with a standalone test application. You are able to compare and verify a specific value in your simple tests. For your complex tests, you could use the datasets. You implemented a simple benchmark, recording the time or the CPU ticks required to execute a function. You have simulated GUI events and spy Qt signals to ensure that your application works well.

Your application is created and your unit tests indicates a PASS status. In the next chapter, we will learn how to deploy your application.

# 13

# All Packed and Ready to Deploy

In the previous chapter, you learned to create a robust application with unit tests. The final step for an application is packaging. The Qt framework enables you to develop cross-platform applications but packaging is really a platform-specific task. Moreover, when your application is ready to be shipped, you need a one-step procedure to generate and pack your application.

In this chapter, we will reuse the gallery application (both on desktop and mobile platforms) to learn the steps required to package a Qt application. There are many ways to prepare the packaging of an application. In this chapter, we want to package the gallery application, from Chapters 4, *Conquering the Desktop UI*, and Chapter 5, *Dominating the Mobile UI*, on the supported platforms (Windows, Linux, Mac, Android, and iOS).

Here are the topics covered in this chapter:

- Packaging a Qt application on Windows
- Packaging a Qt application on Linux
- Packaging a Qt application on Mac
- Packaging a Qt application on Android
- Packaging a Qt application on iOS

# Packaging your application

You will create, for each platform, a dedicated script to perform all the tasks required to build a standalone application. Depending on the OS type, the packaged application will be `gallery-desktop` or `gallery-mobile`. Because the whole gallery project has to be compiled, it also has to include `gallery-core`. Therefore, we will create a parent project with `gallery-core`, `gallery-desktop`, and `gallery-mobile`.

For each platform, we will prepare the project to be packaged and create a specific script. All the scripts follow the same workflow:

1. Set the input and output directories.
2. Create Makefiles with `qmake`.
3. Build the project.
4. Regroup only the necessary files in the output directory.
5. Package the application with platform-specific tasks.
6. Store the packed application in the output directory.

These scripts could run on a developer computer or on a continuous integration server running software such as Jenkins as long as the packaging computer OS matches the script target OS (except for the mobile platforms). In other words, you need to run the Windows script on a computer that runs Windows to be able to package a Qt application for Windows.

Technically, you can perform cross-compilation (given the appropriate toolchain and libraries), but this is beyond the scope of this book. It is easy to cross-compile for a RaspberryPI when you are on Linux, but the same cannot be said when you want to compile for MacOS and you are on Windows.

 From Linux, you can cross-compile Qt for Windows with tools such as MXE at `http://mxe.cc/`.

Create a new subdir project named `ch13-gallery-packaging` with the following hierarchy:

- `ch13-gallery-packaging`:
    - `gallery-core`
    - `gallery-desktop`

- `gallery-mobile`

Even if you are now an expert on Qt subdirs projects, here is the `ch13-gallery-packaging.pro` file:

```
TEMPLATE = subdirs

SUBDIRS += \
    gallery-core \
    gallery-desktop \
    gallery-mobile

gallery-desktop.depends = gallery-core
gallery-mobile.depends = gallery-core
```

You are now ready to work through any of the following sections, depending on the platform you are targeting.

# Packaging for Windows

To package a standalone application on Windows, you need to provide all the dependencies of your executable. The `gallery-core.dll` file, the Qt libraries (for example, `Qt5Core.dll`), and compiler-specific libraries (for example, `libstdc++-6.dll`) are some examples of dependencies required by our executable. If you forget to provide a library, an error will be displayed when you run the `gallery-desktop.exe` program.

 On Windows, you can use the utility Dependency Walker (`depends`). It will give you a list of all libraries required by your application. You can download it here: `www.dependencywalker.com`.

For this section, we will create a script to build the project via the command line interface. Then we will use the Qt tool `windeployqt` to gather all dependencies required by our application. This example is for a MinGW compiler but you can easily adapt it for a MSVC compiler.

Here is a list of required files and folders gathered by `winqtdeploy`, to properly run `gallery-desktop` on Windows:

- `iconengines`:
    - `qsvgicon.dll`
- `imageformats`:
    - `qjpeg.dll`
    - `qwbmp.dll`
    - `...`
- `Platforms`:
    - `qwindows.dll`
- `translations`:
    - `qt_en.qm`
    - `qt_fr.qm`
    - `...`
- `D3Dcompiler_47.dll`
- `gallery-core.dll`
- `gallery-desktop.exe`
- `libEGL.dll`
- `libgcc_s_dw2-1.dll`
- `libGLESV2.dll`
- `libstdc++-6.dll`
- `libwinpthread-1.dll`
- `opengl32sw.dll`
- `Qt5Core.dll`
- `Qt5Gui.dll`
- `Qt5Svg.dll`
- `Qt5Widgets.dll`

Check that your environment variables are correctly set:

| Name | Example |
|---|---|
| QTDIR | C:\Qt\5.7\mingw49_32 |
| MINGWROOT | C:\Qt\Tools\mingw492_32 |

Create a file, `package-windows.bat`, in the `scripts` directory:

```
@ECHO off

set DIST_DIR=dist\desktop-windows
set BUILD_DIR=build
set OUT_DIR=gallery

mkdir %DIST_DIR% && pushd %DIST_DIR%
mkdir %BUILD_DIR% %OUT_DIR%

pushd %BUILD_DIR%
%QTDIR%\bin\qmake.exe ^
  -spec win32-g++ ^
  "CONFIG += release" ^
  ..\..\..\ch13-gallery-packaging.pro

%MINGWROOT%\bin\mingw32-make.exe qmake_all

pushd gallery-core
%MINGWROOT%\bin\mingw32-make.exe && popd

pushd gallery-desktop
%MINGWROOT%\bin\mingw32-make.exe && popd

popd
copy %BUILD_DIR%\gallery-core\release\gallery-core.dll %OUT_DIR%
copy %BUILD_DIR%\gallery-desktop\release\gallery-desktop.exe %OUT_DIR%
%QTDIR%\bin\windeployqt %OUT_DIR%\gallery-desktop.exe %OUT_DIR%\gallery-
core.dll

popd
```

Let's talk about the steps performed:

1. Set the main path variables. The output directory is `DIST_DIR`. All files are generated in the `dist/desktop-windows/build` directory.
2. Create all directories and launch `dist/desktop-windows/build`.
3. Execute `qmake` in release mode for the Win32 platform to generate the parent project `Makefile`. The spec `win32-g++` is for the MinGW compiler. You should use the spec `win32-msvc` if you want to use the MSVC compiler.
4. Run the `mingw32-make qmake_all` command to generate the sub-project Makefiles. With an MSVC compiler you must replace `mingw32-make` with `nmake` or `jom`.
5. Perform the `mingw32-make` commands to build each required sub-project.

6. Copy the generated files, `gallery-desktop.exe` and `gallery-core.dll`, into the `gallery` directory.

7. Call the Qt tool, `windeployqt`, on both files and copy all required dependencies (for example, `Qt5Core.dll`, `Qt5Sql.dll`, `libstdc++-6.dll`, `qwindows.dll`, and so on).

# Packaging for Linux with a distribution package

Packaging an application for a Linux distribution is a bumpy road. Because each distribution can have its own packaging format (`.deb`, `.rpm`, and so on), the first question to answer is: which distribution do you wish to target? Covering every major packaging format would take several chapters. Even detailing a single distribution could be unfair (you wanted to package for RHEL? Too bad, we only covered Arch Linux!). After all, from a Qt application developer perspective, what you want is to ship your product to your users, you do not (yet) aim to become an official Debian repository maintainer.

Having all this in mind, we decided to focus on a tool that packages the application for you for each distribution. That is right, you do not need to learn the internals of Debian or Red Hat! We will still explain the common principles in the packaging systems without excessive detail.

For our purpose, we will demonstrate how a packaging can be done using the `.deb` format on an Ubuntu machine, but as you will see it can be easily updated to generate a `.rpm`.

The tool we are going to use is named `fpm` (**eFfing Package Management**).

The `fpm` tool is available at `https://github.com/jordansissel/fpm`.

The `fpm` tool is a Ruby application that aims to do exactly what we need: take care of the distribution-specific details and generate the final package. First, take the time to install `fpm` on your machine and make sure that it is working.

In a nutshell, a Linux package is a file format that contains all the files you want to deploy with a lot of metadata. It can contain description of the content, a changelog, a license file, the list of dependencies, checksums, pre- and post-installation triggers, and much, much more.

 If you want to learn how to package a Debian binary by hand, go to `http` `://tldp.org/HOWTO/html_single/Debian-Binary-Package-Building-H` `OWTO/`.

In our case, we still have to do some project preparation to let `fpm` do its job. The files we want to deploy have to match the target filesystem. Here is how the deployment should look:

- `gallery-desktop`: This binary should be deployed in `/usr/bin`
- `libgallery-core.so`: This should be deployed in `/usr/lib`

To achieve this, we are going to organize our outputs in `dist/desktop-linux` like so:

- The `build` directory will contain the compiled project (it is our release shadow build)
- The `root` directory will contain the to-be-packaged files, meaning the binary and library files in the proper hierarchy (`usr/bin` and `usr/lib`)

To generate the root directories, we will rely on Qt and the power of the `.pro` files. When compiling a Qt project, the target files are already tracked. All we have to do is to add an additional install target for `gallery-core` and `gallery-desktop`.

Add the following scope in `gallery-core/gallery-core.pro`:

```
linux {
    target.path = $$_PRO_FILE_PWD_/../dist/desktop-linux/root/usr/lib/
    INSTALLS += target
}
```

Here we define a new `target.path` that is going to deploy the `DISTFILES` (the `.so` files) to our desired root tree. Note the use of `$$_PRO_FILE_PWD_`, which points to the directory where the current `.pro` file is stored.

Almost the same procedure is carried out in `gallery-desktop/gallery-desktop.pro`:

```
linux {
    target.path = $$_PRO_FILE_PWD_/../dist/desktop-linux/root/usr/bin/
    INSTALLS += target
}
```

With these lines, when we call make install, the files are going to be deployed in `dist/desktop-linux/root/....`

Now that the project configuration is completed, we can switch to the packaging script. We will cover the script in two parts:

- Project compilation and `root` preparation
- The `.deb` package generation with `fpm`

First, check that your environment variables are correctly set:

| Name | Example |
|------|---------|
| QTDIR | $HOME/qt/5.7/gcc_64 |

Create `scripts/package-linux-deb.sh` with the following content:

```
#!/bin/bash

DIST_DIR=dist/desktop-linux
BUILD_DIR=build
ROOT_DIR=root

BIN_DIR=$ROOT_DIR/usr/bin
LIB_DIR=$ROOT_DIR/usr/lib

mkdir -p $DIST_DIR && cd $DIST_DIR
mkdir -p $BIN_DIR $LIB_DIR $BUILD_DIR

pushd $BUILD_DIR
$QTDIR/bin/qmake \
    -spec linux-g++ \
    "CONFIG += release" \
    ../../../ch13-gallery-packaging.pro

make qmake_all
pushd gallery-core && make && make install ; popd
pushd gallery-desktop && make && make install ; popd
popd
```

Let's break this down:

1. Set the main path variables. The output directory is DIST_DIR. All files are generated in the dist/desktop-linux/build folder.

2. Create all the directories and launch dist/desktop-linux/build.

3. Execute qmake in release mode for the Linux platform to generate the parent project Makefile.

4. Run the make qmake_all command to generate the sub-projects Makefiles.

5. Perform the make commands to build each required sub-project.

6. Use the make install command to deploy the binary and the libraries to the dist/desktop-linux/root directory.

If you execute scripts/package-linux-deb.sh, the final file tree in dist/desktop-linux looks like this:

- build/
    - gallery-core/*.o
    - gallery-desktop/*.p
    - Makefile

- root/
    - usr/bin/gallery-desktop
    - usr/lib/libgallery-core.so

Everything is now ready for fpm to work. The final part of scripts/package-linux-deb.sh contains this:

```
fpm --input-type dir \
    --output-type deb \
    --force \
    --name gallery-desktop \
    --version 1.0.0 \
    --vendor "Mastering Qt 5" \
    --description "A Qt gallery application to organize and manage your
pictures in albums" \
    --depends qt5-default \
    --depends libsqlite3-dev \
    --chdir $ROOT_DIR \
    --package gallery-desktop_VERSION_ARCH.deb
```

Most of the arguments are explicit enough. We will focus on the most important ones:

- `--input-type`: This argument refers to what `fpm` will work with. It can take `deb`, `rpm`, `gem`, `dir` and so on and repackage it to another format. Here we use the `dir` option to tell `fpm` to use a directory tree as the input source.
- `--output-type`: This argument refers to the desired output type. Take a look at the official documentation to see how many platforms are supported.
- `--name`: This is the name given to the package (if you want to uninstall it, you write `apt-get remove gallery-desktop`).
- `--depends`: This argument refers to a library package dependency of the project. You can add as many dependencies as you want. In our case, we only depend on `qt5 -default` and `sqlite3-dev`. This option is very important so be sure that the application will be able to run on the target platform. You can specify the version of the dependency with `--depends library >= 1.2.3`.
- `--chdir`: This argument refers to the base directory from which `fpm` will run. We set it to `dist/desktop-linux/root`, where our file tree is ready to be loaded!
- `--package`: This argument is the name of the final package. The `VERSION` and `ARCH` are placeholders that are automatically filled based on your system.

The rest of the options are purely informative; you can specify a changelog, a license file, and much more. Just by changing the `--output-typedeb` to `rpm`, the package format is properly updated. The `fpm` tool also provides specific package format options, letting you have fine control over what is generated.

If you now execute `scripts/package-linux-deb.sh`, you should get a new `dist/desktop-linux/gallery-desktop_1.0.0_amd64.deb` file. Try to install it with the commands:

```
sudo dpkg -i  dist/desktop-linux/gallery-desktop_1.0.0_amd64.deb
sudo apt-get install -f
```

The first command deploys the package in your system. You should now have the files `/usr/bin/gallery-desktop` and `/usr/lib/libgallery-core.so`.

However, because we installed the package using the `dpkg` command, the dependencies are not automatically installed. This would be done if the package was provided by a Debian repository (thus, installing the package with `apt-get install gallery-desktop`). The missing dependencies are still "marked" and `apt-get install -f` does their installation.

You can now start `gallery-desktop` from anywhere in your system with the command, `gallery-desktop`. When we wrote this chapter in 2016, if you execute it on a "fresh" Ubuntu, you might run into the following issue:

```
$ gallery-desktop
gallery-desktop: /usr/lib/x86_64-linux-gnu/libQt5Core.so.5: version
`Qt_5.7' not found (required by gallery-desktop)
gallery-desktop: /usr/lib/x86_64-linux-gnu/libQt5Core.so.5: version
`Qt_5' not found (required by gallery-desktop)
...
gallery-desktop: /usr/lib/x86_64-linux-gnu/libQt5Core.so.5: version
`Qt_5' not found (required by /usr/lib/libgallery-core.so.1)
```

What happened? We installed the dependencies with `apt-get install -f`! We encounter here a major pain point in Linux package management. The dependencies we specify in our `.deb` could refer to a specific version of Qt, but the reality is that we depend on the package version maintained by the upstream. In other words, each time a new version of Qt is released, the distribution maintainers (Ubuntu, Fedora, and so on) have to repackage it to make it available in the official repository. This can be a long process and the maintainers have a huge number of packages to port!

To be confident about what we are stating, let's view the library dependencies of `gallery-desktop` with an `ldd` command:

```
$ ldd /usr/bin/gallery-desktop
    libgallery-core.so.1 => /usr/lib/libgallery-core.so.1
(0x00007f8110775000)
    libQt5Widgets.so.5 => /usr/lib/x86_64-linux-gnu/libQt5Widgets.so.5
(0x00007f81100e8000)
    libQt5Gui.so.5 => /usr/lib/x86_64-linux-gnu/libQt5Gui.so.5
(0x00007f810fb9f000)
    libQt5Core.so.5 => /usr/lib/x86_64-linux-gnu/libQt5Core.so.5
(0x00007f810f6c9000)
    ...
    libXext.so.6 => /usr/lib/x86_64-linux-gnu/libXext.so.6
(0x00007f810966e000)
```

As you can see, `libgallery-core.so` is correctly resolved in `/usr/lib` and the Qt dependencies too in `/usr/lib/x86_64-linux-gnu`. But what version of Qt is used? The answer lies in the details of the libraries:

```
$ ll /usr/lib/x86_64-linux-gnu/libQt5Core.*
-rw-r--r-- 1 root root    1014 may    2 15:37 libQt5Core.prl
lrwxrwxrwx 1 root root      19 may    2 15:39 libQt5Core.so ->
libQt5Core.so.5.5.1
lrwxrwxrwx 1 root root      19 may    2 15:39 libQt5Core.so.5 ->
```

```
libQt5Core.so.5.5.1
    lrwxrwxrwx 1 root root      19 may    2 15:39 libQt5Core.so.5.5 ->
libQt5Core.so.5.5.1
    -rw-r--r-- 1 root root 5052920 may    2 15:41 libQt5Core.so.5.5.1
```

The `libQt5Core.so` file is a soft link to `libQt5Core.so.5.5.1`, meaning that the system version of Qt is 5.5.1, whereas `gallery-desktop` relies on Qt 5.7. You can configure your system to have the system Qt pointing to your Qt installation (done with the Qt installer). However, it is highly improbable that your customer will install Qt by hand just to have `gallery-desktop` running.

Even worse, for an older version of your distribution, the packages are usually not updated at all after some time. Just try to install a Qt 5.7 Debian package on Ubuntu 14.04 to understand how complicated things become. We did not even mention incompatible dependencies. If we rely on a specific version of `libsqlite3-dev` and another application needs another one, things will get ugly, and only one can survive.

A Linux package has many advantages if you want it to be available on an official repository or if you have specific needs. Using official repositories is a common way of installing an application on Linux and your users will not be disoriented. If you can restrict your Qt version to the one deployed on the Linux distribution that may be a fine solution.

Unfortunately, it also brings major headaches: you need to support multiple distributions, handle the dependencies without breaking the system, and make sure that your application has old enough dependencies, and so on.

Do not worry, everything is not lost; smart people are already resolving this issue on Linux with self-contained packages. As a matter of fact, we are going to cover a self-contained package.

# Packaging for Linux with AppImage

On Windows or Mac, an application is self-sufficient: it contains all the dependencies it needs to be executed. On the one hand, this creates more file duplication, and on the other hand it simplifies packaging for the developer.

Based on this premise, efforts have been made to have the same pattern on Linux (as opposed to a repository/distribution-specific package). Today, several solutions offer a self-contained package on Linux. We suggest you study one of these solutions: AppImage. This particular tool is gaining traction in the Linux community. There is a growing number of developers relying on AppImage to package and deploy their application.

AppImage is a file format that contains an application with all its libraries included. You download a single AppImage file, execute it, and you are done: the application is running. Behind the scenes, an AppImage is an ISO file on steroids, mounted on-the-fly when you execute it. The AppImage file itself is read-only and can also run in a sandbox such as Firejail (a SUID sandbox program that reduces the risk of security breaches by restricting the running environment of applications).

> More information on AppImage is available at http://appimage.org/.

To package gallery-desktop into an AppImage, there are two major steps:

1. Gather all the dependencies of gallery-desktop.
2. Package gallery-desktop and its dependencies in the AppImage format.

Fortunately, this whole process can be done by using a nifty tool: linuxdeployqt. It started as a hobby project and became the official way to package a Qt application in the AppImage documentation.

> Get linuxdeployqt from https://github.com/probonopd/linuxdeploy qt/.

The script we are going to write now assumes that the binary linuxdeployqt is available in your $PATH variable. Check that your environment variables are correctly set:

| Name | Example |
|---|---|
| QTDIR | $HOME/qt/5.7/gcc_64 |

Create scripts/package-linux-appimage.sh and update it like so:

```
#!/bin/bash

DIST_DIR=dist/desktop-linux
BUILD_DIR=build

mkdir -p $DIST_DIR && cd $DIST_DIR
mkdir -p $BUILD_DIR

pushd $BUILD_DIR
```

```
$QTDIR/bin/qmake \
    -spec linux-g++ \
    "CONFIG += release" \
    ../../../ch13-gallery-packaging.pro
make qmake_all
pushd gallery-core && make ; popd
pushd gallery-desktop && make ; popd
popd

export QT_PLUGIN_PATH=$QTDIR/plugins/
export LD_LIBRARY_PATH=$QTDIR/lib:$(pwd)/build/gallery-core

linuxdeployqt \
    build/gallery-desktop/gallery-desktop \
    -appimage

mv build/gallery-desktop.AppImage .
```

The first part is the compilation of the project:

1. Set the main path variables. The output directory is DIST_DIR. All files are generated in the dist/desktop-linux/build folder.
2. Create all the directories and go in dist/desktop-linux/build.
3. Execute qmake in release mode for the Linux platform to generate the parent project Makefile.
4. Run the make qmake_all command to generate the sub-project Makefiles.
5. Perform the make commands to build each required sub-project.

The second part of the script concerns linuxdeployqt. We first have to export some paths to let linuxdeployqt properly find all the dependencies of gallery-desktop (Qt libraries and the gallery-core library).

After that, we execute linuxdeployqt by specifying the source binary to work with and the target file type (AppImage). The resulting file is a single gallery-desktop.AppImage ready to be launched on the user's computer without any Qt package installed!

# Packaging for Mac OS X

On OS X, applications are built and run from a bundle: a single directory that contains the application binary and all its dependencies. In the Finder, these bundles are viewed as .app special directories.

When running `gallery-desktop` from Qt Creator, the application is already bundled in a `.app` file. Because we are using a custom library, `gallery-core`, this `gallery-desktop.app` does not contain all the dependencies and Qt Creator handles it for us.

What we aim to create is a script that completely packages `gallery-desktop` (`gallery-core` included) in a `.dmg` file, a Mac OS X disk image file that is mounted upon execution and lets the user install the application with ease.

To achieve this, Qt provides the `macdeployqt` tool, which gathers the dependencies and creates the `.dmg` file.

First, check that your environment variables are correctly set:

| Name | Example |
|------|---------|
| QTDIR | $HOME/Qt/5.7/clang_64 |

Create the `scripts/package-macosx.sh` file with the following content:

```bash
#!/bin/bash

DIST_DIR=dist/desktop-macosx
BUILD_DIR=build

mkdir -p $DIST_DIR && cd $DIST_DIR
mkdir -p $BUILD_DIR

pushd $BUILD_DIR
$QTDIR/bin/qmake \
  -spec macx-clang \
  "CONFIG += release x86_64" \
  ../../../ch13-gallery-packaging.pro
make qmake_all
pushd gallery-core && make ; popd
pushd gallery-desktop && make ; popd

cp gallery-core/*.dylib \
    gallery-desktop/gallery-desktop.app/Contents/Frameworks/

install_name_tool -change \
  libgallery-core.1.dylib \
  @rpath/libgallery-core.1.dylib \
  gallery-desktop/gallery-desktop.app/Contents/MacOS/gallery-desktop
popd

$QTDIR/bin/macdeployqt \
```

```
    build/gallery-desktop/gallery-desktop.app \
    -dmg

  mv build/gallery-desktop/gallery-desktop.dmg .
```

We can split the script in two. The first part prepares the application for `macdeployqt`:

1. Set the main path variables. The output directory is `DIST_DIR`. All files are generated in the `dist/desktop-macosx/build` folder.
2. Create all the directories and go in `dist/desktop-macosx/build`.
3. Execute `qmake` in release mode for the Mac OS X platform to generate the parent project `Makefile`.
4. Run the `make qmake_all` command to generate the sub-projects Makefiles.
5. Perform the `make` commands to build each required sub-project.

The following part includes the `gallery-core` library in the generated `gallery-desktop.app`. If we do not execute the `cp` command stated in the script and everything that comes after it, we might be quite surprised by the `gallery-desktop` binary content. Let's take a look at it by executing the following command:

```
$ otool -L dist/desktop-macosx/build/gallery-desktop/gallery-
desktop.app/Contents/MacOS/gallery-desktop
    dist/desktop-macosx/build/gallery-desktop/gallery-
desktop.app/Contents/MacOS/gallery-desktop:
      libgallery-core.1.dylib (compatibility version 1.0.0, current version
1.0.0)
      @rpath/QtWidgets.framework/Versions/5/QtWidgets (compatibility
version 5.7.0, current version 5.7.0)
    ...
      /usr/lib/libSystem.B.dylib (compatibility version 1.0.0, current
version 1226.10.1)
```

As you can see, `libgallery-core.1.dylib` is resolved in the local path but not in the special dependencies path as is done for `QtWidget` with `@rpath` (namely `Contents/Frameworks/`). To mitigate this, `package-macosx.sh` copies the `.dylib` file in `gallery-desktop.app/Contents/Frameworks/` and regenerates the dependencies index of the binary with `install_name_tool`.

Finally, in `package-macosx.sh`, `macdeployqt` is called with the updated `gallery-deskop.app` and the target `dmg` format. The resulting `gallery-desktop.dmg` can be deployed on your user computer.

# Packaging for Android

The aim of this section is to generate a standalone APK file for the `gallery-mobile` application. Packaging and deploying an application for Android require multiple steps:

1. Configure the Android build details.
2. Generate a keystore and a certificate.
3. Customize the Android manifest from a template.
4. Create a script to automate the packaging.

You can do most of the tasks directly from Qt Creator. Under the hood, the Qt tool, `androiddeployqt`, is called to generate the APK file. Go to **Projects | Android for armeabi-v7a | Build Steps**. You should see a special build step: **Build Android APK**. The details look like the following screenshot:

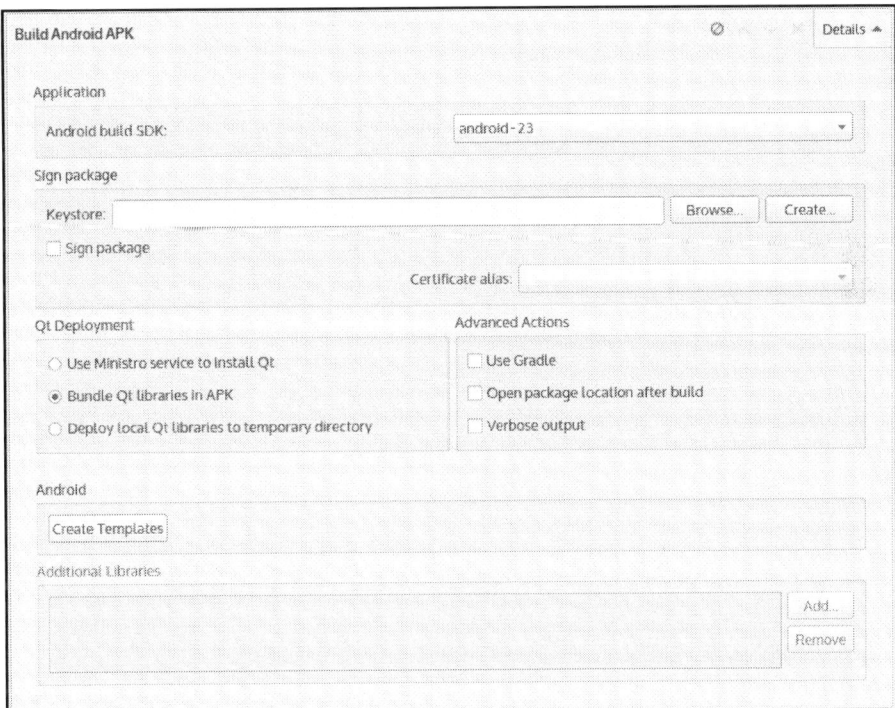

The first thing to do is to select which Android API level you want to use to generate the **Application**. In our case, we selected **android-23** for the Android API Level 23. Try to always build your application with the latest SDK version available.

To publish your application on the Play Store, you must sign the package. To be able to update an application, the signature of the current version and the new version must be the same. This procedure is a protection to make sure that any future versions of the application were really created by you. The first time you should create a keystore, the next time you can reuse it with the **Browse...** button. For now, click on the **Create...** button on the **Sign package** |**Keystore** line. You will get the following popup:

Follow these steps to generate a new keystore:

1. The keystore must be protected by a password. Do not forget it or you will not be able to use this keystore for a future release.

2. Specify an **Alias name** for the certificate. The default values for **Keysize** and **Validity(days)** are fine. You can specify a different password for the certificate or use the keystore one.

3. In the **Certificate Distinguished Names** group, enter information about you and your company.

4. Save the keystore file in a safe place.

5. Enter the keystore password to validate its selection for the deployment.

The next part concerns **Qt deployment**. Indeed, your application needs some Qt libraries. Qt supports three kinds of deployment:

* Create a minimal APK relying on **Ministro** for the Qt dependencies. Ministro is an Android application that can be downloaded from the Play Store. It acts as a Qt shared libraries installer/provider for all Qt applications on Android.
* Create a standalone **bundle** APK that embeds Qt libraries.
* Create an APK that relies on the fact that the Qt libraries are in a specific directory. The libraries are copied into a **temporary directory** during the first deployment.

During the developing and debugging phase, you should select the **temporary directory** way to reduce the packaging time. For a deployment, you can use the **Ministro** or the **bundle** option. In our case, we chose the standalone bundle to generate a complete APK.

The **Advanced actions** pane offers three options:

* **Use Gradle**: This option generates Gradle wrappers and a script, useful if you plan to customize the Java part in an IDE such as Android Studio
* **Open package location after build**: This option opens the directory with the packages generated by `androiddeployqt`
* **Verbose Output**: This option displays additional information about the `androiddeployqt` processing

The Android build details and signing options are finished. We can now customize the Android manifest. Click on **Create Templates**, select the `gallery-mobile.pro` file, and click on **Finish**. The wizard creates for you an `android` sub-directory with several files; for example, `AndroidManifest.xml`. The `gallery-mobile.pro` file has to be updated automatically with these files. However, do not forget to add the `android` scope like the following snippet:

```
TEMPLATE = app
...
android {
    contains(ANDROID_TARGET_ARCH,x86) {
        ANDROID_EXTRA_LIBS = \
            $$[QT_INSTALL_LIBS]/libQt5Sql.so
    }

    DISTFILES += \
        android/AndroidManifest.xml \
        android/gradle/wrapper/gradle-wrapper.jar \
```

```
            android/gradlew \
            android/res/values/libs.xml \
            android/build.gradle \
            android/gradle/wrapper/gradle-wrapper.properties \
            android/gradlew.bat

    ANDROID_PACKAGE_SOURCE_DIR = $$PWD/android
}
```

You can now edit the `AndroidManifest.xml` file. Qt Creator provides a dedicated editor. You can also edit it with a plain text editor with caution. You can open it from the hierarchical project view: **gallery-mobile** | **Other files** | **android**.

Here is our Android manifest in Qt Creator:

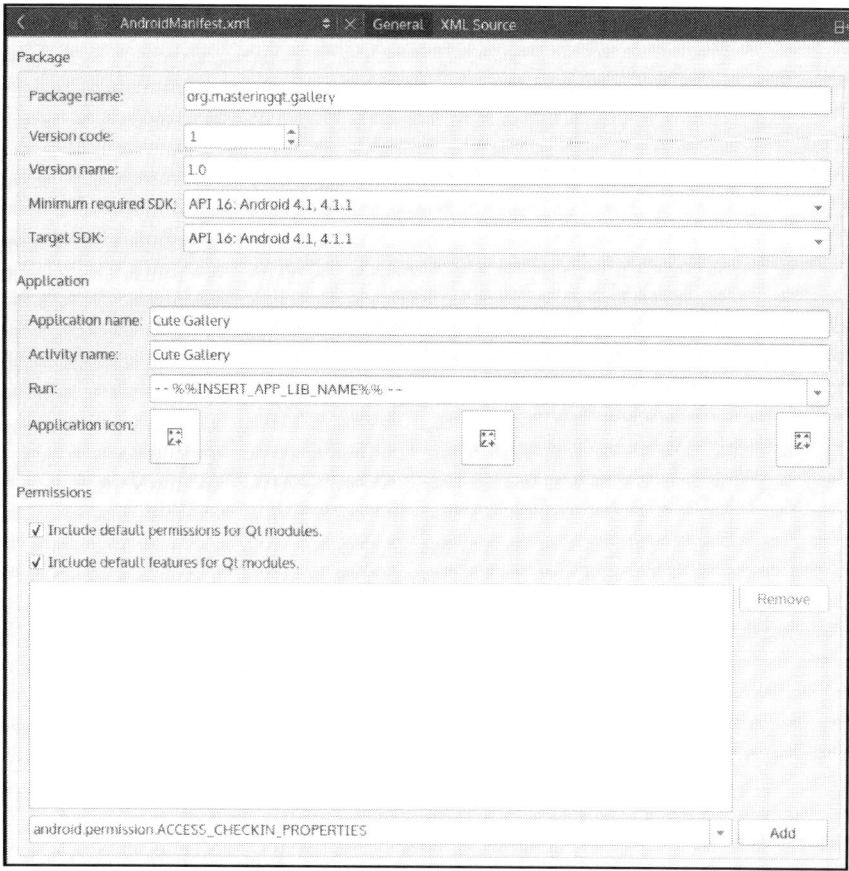

Here are the most important steps:

1. Replace the default **Package name** with yours.
2. The **Version code** is an integer that must be increased for each official release.
3. The **Version name** is the displayed version for users.
4. Select the **Minimum required SDK**. Users with an older version will not be able to install your application.
5. Select the SDK that will be used to compile your application with the **Target SDK**.
6. Change the application and activity name.
7. Select an **Application icon** depending on the screen DPI (Dots per Inch). From left to right: the low, medium, and high DPI icon.
8. Finally, if required by your application, you can add some Android permissions.

You can already build and deploy your signed application from Qt Creator. You should see the new application name and icon on your Android phone or emulator. However, we will now create a script to easily generate and package the signed APK from the command line.

Several environment variables are required by the Android and Qt tools but also for the script itself. Here is a summary with an example:

| Name | Example |
|---|---|
| QTROOT | $HOME/qt/5.7 |
| QTDIR_ANDROID | $QTROOT/android_armv7 |
| JAVA_HOME | /usr/lib/jvm/java-8-openjdk-amd64 |
| ANT_ROOT | /opt/apache-ant |
| ANDROID_SDK_ROOT | $HOME/android-sdk |
| ANDROID_NDK_ROOT | $HOME/android-ndk |

This example is a bash script but feel free to adapt it to a .bat file if you are on Windows. Create a `package-android.sh` file in the `scripts` directory:

```
#!/bin/bash

DIST_DIR=dist/mobile-android
BUILD_DIR=build
APK_DIR=apk
KEYSTORE_PATH="$(pwd)/scripts/android-data"
ANDROID_BUILD_PATH="$(pwd)/$DIST_DIR/$BUILD_DIR/android-build"

mkdir -p $DIST_DIR && cd $DIST_DIR
mkdir -p $APK_DIR $BUILD_DIR
```

```
pushd $BUILD_DIR
$QTDIR_ANDROID/bin/qmake \
    -spec android-g++ \
    "CONFIG += release" \
    ../../../ch13-gallery-packaging.pro
make qmake_all
pushd gallery-core && make ; popd
pushd gallery-mobile && make ; popd
pushd gallery-mobile && make INSTALL_ROOT=$ANDROID_BUILD_PATH install ;
popd

$QTDIR_ANDROID/bin/androiddeployqt
    --input ./gallery-mobile/android-libgallery-mobile.so-deployment-
settings.json \
    --output $ANDROID_BUILD_PATH \
    --deployment bundled \
    --android-platform android-23 \
    --jdk $JAVA_HOME \
    --ant $ANT_ROOT/ant \
    --sign $KEYSTORE_PATH/android.keystore myandroidkey \
    --storepass 'masteringqt'
cp $ANDROID_BUILD_PATH/bin/QtApp-release-signed.apk ../apk/cute-gallery.apk
popd
```

Let's analyze this script together:

1. Set the main path variables. The output directory is `DIST_DIR`. All files are generated in the `dist/mobile-android/build` directory. The final signed APK is copied in the `dist/mobile-android/apk` directory.
2. Create all the directories and go in `dist/mobile-android/build`.
3. Execute `qmake` in release mode for the Android platform to generate the parent project Makefile.
4. Run the `make qmake_all` command to generate the sub-project Makefiles.
5. Perform the `make` commands to build each required sub-project.
6. Run the `make install` command on the `gallery-mobile` directory specifying the `INSTALL_ROOT` to copy all binaries and files required by the APK generation.

The final part of the script calls the `androiddeployqt` binary, a Qt tool to generate the APK. Take a look at the following options:

- The `--deployment` option used here is `bundled` like the mode we used in Qt Creator.
- The `--sign` option requires two parameters: the URL to the keystore file and the alias to the key for the certificate.

- The `--storepass` option is used to specify the keystore password. In our case the password is "masteringqt".

Finally, the generated signed APK is copied to the `dist/mobile-android/apk` directory with the name `cute-gallery.apk`.

# Packaging for iOS

Packaging a Qt application for iOS relies on XCode. When you build and run gallery-mobile from Qt Creator, XCode will be called under the hood. In the end, an `.xcodeproj` file is generated and passed to XCode.

Knowing this, the packaging part will be fairly limited: the only thing than can be automated is the generation of the `.xcodeproj`.

First, check that your environment variables are correctly set:

| Name | Example |
|------|---------|
| QTDIR_IOS | $HOME/Qt/5.7/ios |

Create `scripts/package-ios.sh` and add this snippet to it:

```bash
#!/bin/bash

DIST_DIR=dist/mobile-ios
BUILD_DIR=build

mkdir -p $DIST_DIR && cd $DIST_DIR
mkdir -p $BIN_DIR $LIB_DIR $BUILD_DIR

pushd $BUILD_DIR
$QTDIR_IOS/bin/qmake \
  -spec macx-ios-clang \
  "CONFIG += release iphoneos device" \
  ../../../ch13-gallery-packaging.pro
make qmake_all
pushd gallery-core && make ; popd
pushd gallery-mobile && make ; popd

popd
```

The script performs the following steps:

1. Set the main path variables. The output directory is `DIST_DIR`. All files are generated in the `dist/mobile-ios/build` folder.
2. Create all the directories and go in `dist/mobile-ios/build`.
3. Execute `qmake` in release mode for the iPhone device (as opposed to the iPhone simulator) platform to generate the parent project `Makefile`.
4. Run the `make qmake_all` command to generate the sub-project Makefiles.
5. Perform the `make` command to build each required sub-projects.

Once this script has been executed, `dist/mobile-ios/build/gallery-mobile/gallery-mobile.xcodeproj` is ready to be opened in XCode. The remaining steps are entirely done in XCode:

1. Open `gallery-mobile.xcodeproj` in XCode.
2. Compile the application for an iOS device.
3. Follow the Apple procedure to distribute your application (through the App Store or as a standalone file).

After that, `gallery-mobile` will be ready for your users!

# Summary

Even if your application runs well on your computer, your development environment can affect this behavior. Its packaging must be correct to run your application on the user's hardware. You learned the steps required to package an application before deploying it. Some platforms required specific tasks that must be followed carefully. You can now bake a standalone package if your application is running a unique script.

The next chapter describes some tricks that can be useful for developing applications with Qt. You will learn some tips concerning Qt Creator.

# 14
# Qt Hat Tips and Tricks

The previous chapter taught you how to package a Qt application on all the major desktop and mobile platforms. This was the final step before shipping your application to your users. This chapter gathers some tips and tricks that will help you to develop your Qt applications with more ease.

This chapter covers the following topics:

- Qt Creator tips – Useful keyboard shortcuts, session management, and more
- Examining the memory with Qt Creator
- Generating random numbers
- Silencing unused variables and compiler warnings
- How to easily log an object's content to QDebug
- Customizing QDebug formatting
- Saving logs to a file
- Creating a friendly command-line interface
- Sending HTTPGET and POST requests

# Managing your workspace with sessions

It is common for a commercial product to be composed of several Qt projects. We regularly encountered this practice in this book-for example, an application composed of a core project and a GUI project. The Qt subdirs project is a nice way of handling inter-dependent projects within the same application.

However, when your product grows up, you'll want to open some unrelated projects in Qt Creator. In this case, you should use a **session**. A session is a complete snapshot of your workspace in Qt Creator. You can easily create a new session from **File | Session Manager | New**. Do not forget to switch to the new session. For example, you can create a session "Mastering Qt5" and load all project examples in a common workspace.

The sessions are useful when you need to quickly switch between two different workspaces. The following items in Qt Creator will be automatically saved in the session:

- Opened projects of the hierarchical view
- Editor's windows (including the splits)
- Debug breakpoints and expressions views
- Bookmarks

You can change to a different session with **File | Session Manager** or by using the **Welcome** tab. A session can be destroyed without any impact on your projects.

# Searching with the Locator

Another way to improve your productivity with Qt Creator is to use keyboard shortcuts. Qt Creator provides a lot of great keyboard shortcuts. Here is our selection:

| Action | Shortcut |
|---|---|
| Comment / uncomment | Ctrl + / |
| Autocomplete | Ctrl + Space |
| View help of symbol under cursor | F1 |
| Follow symbol under cursor | F2 |
| Switch between header / source file | F4 |
| Switch between function declaration and definition | Shift + F2 |
| Switch between form / source file | Shift + F4 |
| Rename symbol under cursor | Ctrl + Shift + R |
| Find usages of symbol under cursor | Ctrl + Shift + U |
| Select the kit | Ctrl + T |
| Build current project | Ctrl + B |
| Start / continue debugging | F5 |
| Debugging : step over | F10 |
| Debugging : step into | F11 |
| Debugging : step out | Shift + F11 |
| Run | Ctrl + R |
| Open next file from Open Documents | Ctrl + Tab |
| Open previous file from Open Documents | Ctrl + Shift + Tab |
| Toggle the left sidebar | Alt + 0 |
| Toggle Issues pane | Alt + 1 |
| Activate Locator | Ctrl + K |
| Auto indent the selection | Ctrl + I |
| Go to the line | Ctrl + L |
| Toggle fullscreen | Ctrl + Shift + F11 |
| Remove current split editor | Ctrl + E, 0 |
| Split editor horizontally | Ctrl + E, 2 |
| Split editor vertically | Ctrl + E, 3 |

One of our favorites is the Locator. Press *Ctrl + K* to activate it. Then you can enjoy several features:

- Enter a filename (you can even use a partial entry) and press *Enter* to open this file. If the Locator suggests multiple files, you can use the arrows up and down to navigate.
- Prefix your search by `.` (a dot followed by a space) to search C++ symbols in the current document. For example, on the `Task.cpp` file of the first chapter, try to use the Locator with `. set` and press *Enter* to go to the `Task::setName()` function.
- Enter `l` (*L* followed by a space) to go to a specific line. For example, "l 37" will bring us to line 37 of the current file

The Locator provides plenty of features; take a look when you press *Ctrl + K* the next time!

# Increasing the compilation speed

You can speed up the compilation on a multicore computer. By default, when you build your project with Qt Creator, you only use one job (and, therefore, one core). But `make` supports the compilation with multiple jobs. You can use the `make -j N` option to allow N jobs at once. Do not forget to update your packaging scripts!

If you build your project from Qt Creator, you can set this option from **Projects | Build Steps | Make**. Click on **Details**, then, in the **Make arguments** field, put the value `-j 8` to allow eight jobs during the compilation, as shown in the following screenshot:

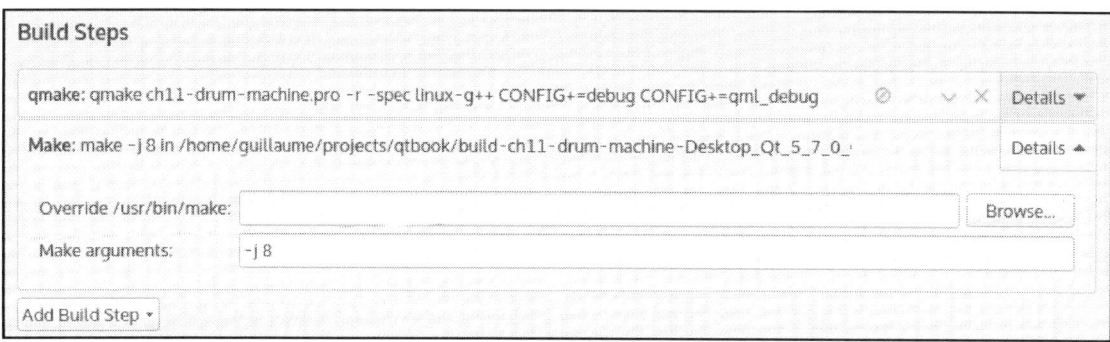

# Examining the memory with Qt Creator

For this section, we will use the following code snippet:

```
bool boolean = true;
int integer = 5;
char character = 'A';
int* integerPointer = &integer;

qDebug() << "boolean is:" << boolean;
qDebug() << "integer is:" << integer;
qDebug() << "character is:" << character;
qDebug() << "integerPointer is:" << integerPointer;
qDebug() << "*integerPointer is:" << *integerPointer;
qDebug() << "done!";
```

We declared three primitive types: `boolean`, `integer`, and `character`. We also added a `integerPointer` pointer that refers to the `integer` variable. Put a breakpoint at the last line and start the debugging. On the Debug pane, you should have the **Locals and Expressions** view. You can easily add/remove it from **Window | Views | Locals and Expressions**. Here is a screenshot of it:

| Locals and Expressions | | | | |
|---|---|---|---|---|
| Name | Value | | | Type |
| boolean | true | | | bool |
| character | 'A' | 65 | 0x41 | char |
| integer | 5 | | | int |
| integerPointer | 5 | | | int |

You can see that all our local variables are displayed with their values. The `character` line even displays three formats (ASCII, integer, and hexadecimal) of the letter '**A**'. You may also notice that the `integerPointer` line displays the automatically dereferenced value, not the pointer address. You can disable it with a right-click on the background of the **Locals and Expressions** window and then select **Dereference Pointers automatically**. You can see the pointer address and the dereferenced value appearing as shown in the following screenshot:

| Locals and Expressions | | | | |
|---|---|---|---|---|
| Name | Value | | | Type |
| boolean | true | | | bool |
| character | 'A' | 65 | 0x41 | char |
| integer | 5 | | | int |
| ▼ integerPointer | 0x7ffe601153ac | | | int * |
| *integerPointer | 5 | | | int |

The console output displays the following information:

```
boolean is: true
integer is: 5
character is: A
integerPointer is: 0x7ffe601153ac
*integerPointer is: 5
```

You can see that we retrieve the same information in the console output. The **Locals and Expressions** view helps you to save time. You can display a lot of information without logging it with a `qDebug()` function.

Qt Creator provides a useful memory editor. You can open it with a right-click on a variable name in the **Locals and Expressions** window, and then select **Open Memory Editor | Open Memory Editor at Object's Address**.

Within the memory editor, look at the value of the `boolean` variable:

```
0000:7ffe:6011:5390 30 55 11 60 fe 7f 00 00 58 4d 40 00 00 00 00 00   0U·`····XM@·····
0000:7ffe:6011:53a0 20 54 11 60 fe 7f 00 00 20 54 01 41 05 00 00 00    T·`····  T·A····
0000:7ffe:6011:53b0 30 3a 18 02 00 00 00 00 ac 53 11 60 fe 7f 00 00   0:·······S·`····
```

A hexadecimal editor appears with three parts (from the left to the right):

- The memory address of the data
- The hexadecimal representation of the data
- The ASCII representation of the data

The selection in the hexadecimal representation corresponds to the variable. We can confirm that the `boolean` variable is represented in memory by 1 byte. Because the value is `true`, the memory representation is **0x01**.

Let's examine the `character` memory with the **Memory Editor** tool:

```
0000:7ffe:6011:5390 30 55 11 60 fe 7f 00 00 58 4d 40 00 00 00 00 00   0U·`····XM@·····
0000:7ffe:6011:53a0 20 54 11 60 fe 7f 00 00 20 54 01 41 05 00 00 00    T·`····  T·A····
0000:7ffe:6011:53b0 30 3a 18 02 00 00 00 00 ac 53 11 60 fe 7f 00 00   0:·······S·`····
```

The character is also stored in memory with 1 byte. The hexadecimal representation is **0x41**. The character is encoded with the well-known ASCII format. Note that, on the right-hand side, the ASCII representation displays the **'A'**.

Here is the **Memory Editor** location of the `integer` variable:

```
0000:7ffe:6011:5390 30 55 11 60 fe 7f 00 00 58 4d 40 00 00 00 00 00   0U·`····XM@·····
0000:7ffe:6011:53a0 20 54 11 60 fe 7f 00 00 20 54 01 41 05 00 00 00    T·`····  T·A····
0000:7ffe:6011:53b0 30 3a 18 02 00 00 00 00 ac 53 11 60 fe 7f 00 00   0:·······S·`····
```

There are two interesting facts to note. The integer is stored on 4 bytes. The value **05** is stored in hexadecimal as **05 00 00 00**. The byte order depends on the endianness of your processor. We are using an Intel CPU that is Little-Endian. Another CPU architecture with a Big-Endian memory storage will display the variable as **00 00 00 05**.

Before we continue to dive into the memory of our application, look at the last three screenshots closely. You might notice that, in this case, the three variables are contiguous in the stack memory. This behavior is not guaranteed depending on the implementation of your OS.

Try to open the memory editor on the `integerPointer` variable. The context menu offers you two different ways:

- The **Open Memory Editor at Object's Address** option dereferences the pointer and brings you directly to the pointed value. You get the same result as the integer memory view.
- The **Open Memory Editor at Pointer's Address** option displays the raw pointer data, which is a memory address to where it is pointing.

Here is the **Memory Editor** tool showing the pointer's address of `integerPointer`:

```
0000:7ffe:6011:53a0 20 54 11 60 fe 7f 00 00 20 54 01 41 05 00 00 00    T·`···· T·A····
0000:7ffe:6011:53b0 30 3a 18 02 00 00 00 00 ac 53 11 60 fe 7f 00 00    0:······ ·S·····
0000:7ffe:6011:53c0 02 00 00 00 66 00 00 00 10 9e 40 00 00 00 00 00    ····f····@·····
```

We are on a 64-bit OS, so our pointer is stored on 8 bytes. The data of this pointer is the hexadecimal value `ac 53 11 60 fe 7f 00 00`. This is the Little-Endian representation of the memory address `0x7ffe601153ac` displayed by the **Locals and Expressions** and by our console output.

We display the memory, but we can also change it. Follow these steps:

1. Remove the current breakpoint and add a new one on the first `qDebug()` line.
2. Restart the debugging and look at the **Locals and Expressions**. If you double-click a variable's value, you can edit it. Note that the **Memory Editor** window immediately updates its representation.
3. In our case, we set `boolean` value to false, `character` to 68 (that is 'D') and `integer` to 9. When you are confident with your changes, continue the debugging.

Here is the final console output reflecting our modifications:

```
boolean is: false
integer is: 9
character is: D
integerPointer is: 0x7fff849203dc
*integerPointer is: 9
done!
```

The **Memory Editor** is a powerful tool: You can display and change your variable's value, at runtime, without changing your source code and recompiling your application.

# Generating random numbers

Generating real random numbers is quite a difficult task for a computer. Commonly, we are using only a **pseudo-random number generation (PRNG)**. The Qt framework provides the function qrand(), a thread-safe version of std::rand(). This function returns an integer between 0 and RAND_MAX (defined in stdlib.h). The following code shows two pseudo-random numbers:

```
qDebug() << "first number is" << qrand() % 10;
qDebug() << "second number is" << qrand() % 10;
```

We are using a modulo operator to get a value between 0 and 9. Try to run your application several times. The numbers are always the same, in our case, 3 then 7. That is because each time we call qrand(), we retrieve the next number of the pseudo-random sequence, but the sequence is always the same! Fortunately, we can use qsrand() to initialize the PRNG with a seed. A seed is an unsigned integer that is used to generate a sequence. Try the next snippet:

```
qsrand(3);
qDebug() << "first number is" << qrand() % 10;
qDebug() << "second number is" << qrand() % 10;
```

In this example, we are using the seed 3, and we get a different value from qrand()—on our computer it is 5 and 4. Great, but if you run this application several times, you will always have this sequence. One way of generating a different sequence each time you run your application is to use a different seed on each run. Run the following code snippet:

```
qsrand(QDateTime::currentDateTime().toTime_t());
qDebug() << "first number is" << qrand() % 10;
qDebug() << "second number is" << qrand() % 10;
```

As you can see, we are now initializing the PRNG with the epoch time from QDateTime. You can try to run your application multiple times to see that we get different numbers each time! However, this solution is not recommended for cryptography. In this case, you should use a stronger random number engine.

# Silencing unused variable warnings

If your compiler is configured to output its warnings, you will probably sometimes see this kind of log:

```
warning: unused parameter 'myVariable' [-Wunused-parameter]
```

This is a safety warning to tell the developer to keep their code clean and avoid dead variables. It is a good practice to try to minimize this kind of warning. However, sometimes you have no choice: You override an existing function and you do not use all the parameters. You now face a conundrum: On the one hand you can silence the warning for your whole application, and on the other hand, you can let these safety warnings pile up in your compile output. There must be a better option.

Indeed, you can silence the warning for your function only. There are two ways of doing this:

- Using the C/C++ syntax
- Using a Qt macro

Let's say you override `myFunction(QString name, QString myVariable)` and you do not use `myVariable`. Using the C/C++ syntax, you just have to implement `myFunction()` like so:

```
void myFunction(QString name, QString /*myVariable*/)
```

By commenting the variable's name, `myVariable`, in the function signature, you ensure that you will not (that is, cannot) use the variable in the function body. The compiler will also interpret it like this and will not output any warning.

Qt also provides a way of marking unused variables with the Q_UNUSED macro. Let's see it in action:

```
void myFunction(QString name, QString myVariable)
{
    Q_UNUSED(myVariable)
    ...
}
```

Simply pass `myVariable` to `Q_UNUSED` and it will remove the warning from the compiler output. Behind the curtain, `Q_UNUSED` does not do anything magical with the variable:

```
#define Q_UNUSED(x) (void)x;
```

It is a simple trick to fool the compiler; it sees `myVariable` "used", but nothing is done with it.

# Logging custom objects to QDebug

When you are debugging complex objects, it is nice to output their current members' value to qDebug(). In other languages (such as Java), you may have encountered the toString() method or equivalent, which is very convenient.

Sure, you could add a function void toString() to each object you want to log in order to write code with the following syntax:

```
qDebug() << "Object content:" << myObject.toString()
```

There must be a more natural way of doing this in C++. Moreover, Qt already provides this kind of feature:

```
QDate today = QDate::currentDate();
qDebug() << today;
// Output: QDate("2016-10-03")
```

To achieve this, we will rely on a C++ operator overload. This will look very similar to what we did with QDataStream operators in Chapter 10, *Need IPC? Get Your Minions to Work.*

Consider a struct Person:

```
struct Person {
    QString name;
    int age;
};
```

To add the ability to properly output to QDebug, you just have to override the << operator between QDebug and Person like so:

```
#include <QDebug>

struct Person {
    ...
};

QDebug operator<<(QDebug debug, const Person& person)
{
    QDebugStateSaver saver(debug);
    debug.nospace() << "("
                    << "name: " << person.name << ", "
                    << "age: " << person.age
                    << ")";
    return debug;
}
```

The `QDebugStateSaver` is a convenience class to save the settings of `QDebug` and restore them automatically upon destruction. It is good practice to always use it to be sure that you do not break `QDebug` in an << operator overload.

The rest of the function is the usual way of using `QDebug` and finally returning the modified `debug` variable. You can now use `Person` like this:

```
Person person = { "Lenna", 64 };
qDebug() << "Person info" << person;
```

No need for a `toString()` function; simply use the person object. For those of you who wondered, yes, `Lenna` is really 64 at the time of wrting (2016).

# Improving log messages

Qt offers multiple ways of doing this. A good compromise between the result and its complexity is to combine the Qt log type with a custom message pattern.

Qt defines five log types, from the least to the most critical level:

- `qDebug()`: This is used to write custom debug messages
- `qInfo()`: This is used to write informational messages
- `qWarning()`: This is used to write warnings and recoverable errors in your applications
- `qCrtitical()`: This is used to write critical error messages and report system errors
- `qFatal()`: This is used to write a last message before automatically existing

Try to always use the most appropriate one!

By default, the message pattern is configured to only display your message without any extra data, but you can customize the pattern to display more information. This pattern can be changed at runtime by setting the `QT_MESSAGE_PATTERN` environment variable. You can also call the `qSetMessagePattern` function from your software to change the pattern. The pattern is just a string with some placeholders.

These are the most common placeholders you can use:

- %{appname}: This is your application name
- %{file}: This is the path to the source file
- %{function}: This is the function name
- %{line}: This is a line in the source file
- %{message}: This is an original message
- %{type}: This is the Qt log type ("debug", "info", "warning", "critical" or "fatal")
- %{time [format]}: This is the system time when the message occurred

An easy way to use it is to edit your main.cpp file like this:

```
#include <QApplication>
#include <QDebug>
...
int main(int argc, char *argv[])
{
    qSetMessagePattern("[%{Lime yyyy-MM-dd hh:mm:ss}] [%{type}]
        %{function} %{message}");
    qInfo() << "Application starting...";

    QApplication a(argc, argv);
    ...
    return a.exec();
}
```

You should get something like this in your application output:

```
[2016-10-03 10:22:40] [info] qMain Application starting...
```

Try to play around with the Qt log types and the custom message pattern until you find a useful pattern for you.

For more complex applications, you can use the QLoggingCategory class to define categories of logging. Visit http://doc.qt.io/qt-5/qloggingca tegory.html for more information on this.

# Saving your logs to a file

A common need for a developer is to have logs. In some situations, you cannot have access to the console output, or you have to study the application state afterwards. In both cases, the log has to be outputted to a file.

Qt provides a practical way of redirecting your logs (qDebug, qInfo, qWarning, and so on) to any device that is convenient for you: QtMessageHandler. To use it, you have to register a function that will save the logs to the desired output.

For example, in your main.cpp, add the following function:

```
#include <QFile>
#include <QTextStream>

void messageHander(QtMsgType type,
                   const QMessageLogContext& context,
                   const QString& message) {
    QString levelText;
    switch (type) {
        case QtDebugMsg:
            levelText = "Debug";
            break;
        case QtInfoMsg:
            levelText = "Info";
            break;
        case QtWarningMsg:
            levelText = "Warning";
            break;
        case QtCriticalMsg:
            levelText = "Critical";
            break;
        case QtFatalMsg:
            levelText = "Fatal";
            break;
    }
    QString text = QString("[%1] %2")
                        .arg(levelText)
                        .arg(message);
    QFile file("app.log");
    file.open(QIODevice::WriteOnly | QIODevice::Append);
    QTextStream textStream(&file);
    textStream << text << endl;
}
```

The signature of the function must be respected to be properly called by Qt. Let's review the parameters:

- `QtMsgType type`: This is an `enum` that describes the function that generated the message (`qDebug()`, `qInfo()`, `qWarning()`, and so on)
- `QMessageLogContext& context`: This contains additional information about the log message (source file where the log was produced, name of the function, line number, and so on)
- `const QString& message`: This is the actual message that was logged

The body of the function formats the log message before appending it to a file named `app.log`. You can easily add features in this function by adding a rotating log file, sending the logs through the network, or anything else.

The last missing part is the registration of `messageHandler()`, which is done in the `main()` function:

```
int main(int argc, char *argv[])
{
    QCoreApplication a(argc, argv);
    qInstallMessageHandler(messageHander);
    ...
}
```

The call to the `qInstallMessageHander()` function is enough to reroute all the log messages to `app.log`. Once this is done, the logs will no longer be displayed in the console output and will be appended to `app.log` only.

 If you need to unregister your custom message handler function, call `qInstallMessageHandler(0)`.

# Generating a command-line interface

The command-line interface can be a wonderful way to start your application with some specific options. The Qt framework provides an easy way to define your options with the `QCommandLineParser` class. You can provide a short (for example, `-t`) or a long (for example, `--test`) option name. The application version and help menu is automatically generated. You can easily retrieve in your code if an option is set or not. An option can take a value and you can define a default value.

For example, we can create a CLI to configure the log files. We want to define three options:

- The -debug command, if set, enables the log file writing
- The -f or --file command to define where to write the logs
- The -l or --level <level> command to specify the minimum log level

Look at the following snippet:

```
QCoreApplication app(argc, argv);

QCoreApplication::setApplicationName("ch14-hat-tips");
QCoreApplication::setApplicationVersion("1.0.0");

QCommandLineParser parser;
parser.setApplicationDescription("CLI helper");
parser.addHelpOption();
parser.addVersionOption();

parser.addOptions({
    {"debug",
        "Enable the debug mode."},

    {{"f", "file"},
        "Write the logs into <file>.",
        "logfile"},

    {{"l", "level"},
        "Restrict the logs to level <level>. Default is 'fatal'.",
        "level",
        "fatal"},
});

parser.process(app);

qDebug() << "debug mode:" << parser.isSet("debug");
qDebug() << "file:" << parser.value("file");
qDebug() << "level:" << parser.value("level");
```

Let's talk about each step:

1. The first part uses the functions from QCoreApplication to set the application name and version. This information will be used by the --version option.
2. Instantiate a QCommandLineParser class. Then we instruct it to automatically add the help (-h or --help) and version (-v or --version) options.
3. Add our options with the QCommandLineParser::addOptions() function.

4. Request the `QCommandLineParser` class to process the command-line arguments.
5. Retrieve and use the options.

Here are the parameters to create an option:

- `optionName`: By using this parameter, you can use a single or multiple names
- `description`: In this parameter, the description of the option is displayed in the help menu
- `valueName` (Optional): This shows the value name if your option expects one
- `defaultValue` (Optional): This shows the default value of the option

You can retrieve and use the option using `QCommandLineParser::isSet()`, which returns true if the option was set by the user. If your option requires a value, you can retrieve it with `QCommandLineParser::value()`.

Here is the display of the generated help menu:

```
$ ./ch14-hat-tips --help
Usage: ./ch14-hat-tips [options]
Helper of the command-line interface

Options:
  -h, --help              Displays this help.
  -v, --version           Displays version information.
  --debug                 Enable the debug mode.
  -f, --file <logfile>    Write the logs into <file>.
  -l, --level <level>     Restrict the logs to level <level>. Default is
'fatal'.
```

Finally, the following snippet displays the CLI in use:

```
$ ./ch14-hat-tips --debug -f log.txt --level info
debug mode:  true
file:  "log.txt"
level:  "info"
```

# Sending and receiving HTTP data

Requesting information to an HTTP server is a common task. Here again, the Qt folks prepared some useful classes to make it easy. To achieve this, we will rely on three classes:

- `QNetworkAccessManager`: This class allows your application to send requests

and receive replies
* QNetworkRequest: This class holds the request to be sent with all the information (headers, URL, data, and so on)
* QNetworkReply: This class contains the result of a QNetworkRequest class with the headers and the data

The QNetworkAccessManager class is the pivot point of the whole Qt HTTP API. It is built around a single QNetworkAccessManager object that holds the configuration of the client, proxy settings, cache information, and much more. This class is designed to be asynchronous, so you do not need to worry about blocking your current thread.

Let's see it in action in a custom HttpRequest class. First, the header:

```cpp
#include <QObject>
#include <QNetworkAccessManager>
#include <QNetworkReply>

class HttpRequest : public QObject
{
    Q_OBJECT
public:
    HttpRequest(QObject* parent = 0);

    void executeGet();

private slots:
    void replyFinished(QNetworkReply* reply);

private:
    QNetworkAccessManager mAccessManager;
};
```

The QNetworkAccessManager class works with the signal/slot mechanism, so HttpRequest inherits from QObject and uses the Q_OBJECT macro. We declare the following functions and member:

* executeGet(): This is used to trigger an HTTP GET request
* replyFinished(): This is the slot called when the GET request has completed
* mAccessManager: This is the object that will be used for all our asynchronous requests

Let's turn our attention to the constructor of the `HttpRequest` class in the `HttpRequest.cpp`:

```
HttpRequest::HttpRequest(QObject* parent)  :
    QObject(parent),
    mAccessManager()
{
    connect(&mAccessManager, &QNetworkAccessManager::finished,
            this, &HttpRequest::replyFinished);
}
```

In the body of the constructor, we connect the `finished()` signal from `mAccessManager` to our `replyFinished()` slot. This implies that every request sent through `mAccessManager` will trigger this slot.

Enough with the preparation; let's see the request and reply in action:

```
// Request
void HttpRequest::executeGet()
{
    QNetworkRequest request(QUrl("http://httpbin.org/ip"));
    mAccessManager.get(QNetworkRequest(request));
}

// Response
void HttpRequest::replyFinished(QNetworkReply* reply)
{
    int statusCode =
reply->attribute(QNetworkRequest::HttpStatusCodeAttribute).toInt();
    qDebug() << "Reponse network error" << reply->error();
    qDebug() << "Reponse HTTP status code" << statusCode;
    qDebug() << "Reply content:" << reply->readAll();
    reply->deleteLater();
}
```

The `HTTP GET` request is processed using `mAccessManager.get()`. The `QNetworkAccessManager` class provides the function for other HTTP verbs (`head()`, `post()`, `put()`, `delete()`, and so on. It expects a `QNetworkRequest` access, which takes a URL in its constructor. This is the simplest form of an HTTP request.

Note that we did our request using the URL `http://httpbin.org/ip`, which will respond to the emitter's IP address in the JSON format:

```
{
  "origin": "1.2.3.4"
}
```

This website is a practical developer resource, where you can send your test requests and have useful information sent back to you. It avoids having to launch a custom web server to only test a few requests. This website is an open-source project freely hosted by Runscope. Of course, you can replace the request URL with anything you wish.

 Take a look at `http://httpbin.org/` to see all the supported request types.

After the `executeGet()` function is completed, the `mAccessManager` object executes the request in a separate thread and calls our slot, `replyFinished()`, with the resulting `QNetworkReply*` object. In this code snippet, you can see how to retrieve the HTTP status code and check if any network error happened, as well as how to get the body of the response with `reply->readAll()`.

The `QNetworkReply` class inherits from `QIODevice`, and therefore, you can read it all at once with `readAll()`, or by chunks with a loop on `read()`. This lets you adapt the reading to your needs using a familiar `QIODevice` API.

Note that you are the owner of the `QNetworkReply*` object. You should not delete it by hand (your application might crash if you do so); instead, it's better to use the `reply->deleteLater()` function, which will let the Qt event loop pick the appropriate moment to delete this object.

Now let's see a more complex example of `QNetworkReply` with an HTTP POST method. There are times where you will need to keep track of the `QNetworkReply` class and have a more fine-grained control over its life cycle.

Here is the implementation of an HTTP POST method that also relies on `HttpRequest::mAccessManager`:

```
void HttpRequest::executePost()
{
    QNetworkRequest request(QUrl("http://httpbin.org/post"));
    request.setHeader(QNetworkRequest::ContentTypeHeader,
                      "application/x-www-form-urlencoded");
    QUrlQuery urlQuery;
    urlQuery.addQueryItem("book", "Mastering Qt 5");

    QUrl params;
    params.setQuery(urlQuery);

    QNetworkReply* reply = mAccessManager.post(
```

```
                                    request, params.toEncoded());
        connect(reply, &QNetworkReply::readyRead,
            [reply] () {
            qDebug() << "Ready to read from reply";
        });
        connect(reply, &QNetworkReply::sslErrors,
                [this] (QList<QSslError> errors) {
            qWarning() << "SSL errors" << errors;
        });
    }
```

We start by creating a QNetworkRequest class with a custom header: Content-Type is now application/x-www-form-urlencoded to respect the HTTP RFC. After that, a URL form is built, ready to be sent with the request. You can add as many items as you wish to the urlQuery object.

The next part gets interesting. When executing mAccessManager.post() with the request and the URL encoded form, the QNetworkReply* object is immediately returned to us. From here, we use some lambdas slots connected directly to reply rather than using mAccessManage slots. This lets you have precise control over what happens for each reply.

Note that the QNetworkReploy::readyRead signal comes from the QIODevice API and that it does not pass the QNetworkReply* object in the parameter. It is your job to store the reply in a member field somewhere or retrieve the emitter of the signal.

Finally, this code snippet does not undo our preceding slot, replyFinished(), which is connected to mAccessManager. If you execute this code, you will have the following output sequence:

```
Ready to read from reply
Reponse network error QNetworkReply::NetworkError(NoError)
Reponse HTTP status code 200
```

The lambda connected to the QNetworkReply::readyRead signal is first called, and after that, the HttpRequest::replyFinished signal is called.

The last feature we will cover on the Qt HTTP stack is synchronous requests. If you happen to need to manage the request threading yourself, the default asynchronous work mode of QNetworkAccessManager can get in your way. To circumvent this, you can use a custom QEventLoop:

```
void HttpRequest::executeBlockingGet()
{
    QNetworkAccessManager localManager;
```

```
QEventLoop eventLoop;
QObject::connect(
    &localManager, &QNetworkAccessManager::finished,
    &eventLoop, &QEventLoop::quit);

QNetworkRequest request(
            QUrl("http://httpbin.org/user-agent"));
request.setHeader(QNetworkRequest::UserAgentHeader,
                "MasteringQt5Browser 1.0");

QNetworkReply* reply = localManager.get(request);
eventLoop.exec();

qDebug() << "Blocking GET result:" << reply->readAll();
reply->deleteLater();
}
```

In this function, we declare another QNetworkAccessManager that will not interfere with the one declared in HttpRequest. Right after, a QEventLoop object is declared and connected to localManager. When QNetworkAccessManager emits the finished() signal, eventLoop will quit and the calling function will resume.

The request is built as usual, the reply object is retrieved, and the function becomes blocked with the call to eventLoop.exec(). The function is blocked until localManager has emitted its finished signal. In other words, the request is still done asynchronously; the sole difference is that the function is blocked until the request is completed.

Finally, the reply object can be safely read and deleted at the end of the function. This QEventLoop trick can be used any time a synchronous wait for a Qt signal is needed; use it wisely to avoid blocking the UI thread!

# Summary

In this chapter, you learned some tips that complete your Qt knowledge. You should now have the ability to use Qt Creator with ease and efficiency. The QDebug format should not hold any secrets now, and you can now save your logs to a file without even blinking. You can create a good-looking CLI interface, debug the memory of any program without shaking, and execute an HTTP request with confidence.

We sincerely hope that you had as much fun reading this book as we did writing it. In our opinion, Qt is a great framework, and it covers many areas that deserve to be deepened with a book (or several books!). We hope you keep coding C++ Qt code with fun and pleasure by building efficient and beautifully crafted applications.

# Index

Printed in Great Britain
by Amazon